Praise for **THE GIRL EXPLORERS**

"In riveting detail that builds to insightful crescendo, *The Girl Explorers* reveals feats and firsts of remarkable achievers who we'd already know if they weren't women. It's about time."

—**DR. MARGARET WILLSON**, cultural anthropologist and author of *Seawomen of Iceland*

"Jayne Zanglein's *The Girl Explorers* is both a celebration and a reminder that not only can women hike, climb, fly, and swim with the best of them, but they've been doing it all along... This well-researched and enjoyable book restores women to their proper place in history, which is: anywhere they want to go."

—**MELISSA L. SEVIGNY**, author of *Mythical River* and *Under Desert Skies*

"*The Girl Explorers* profiles intrepid women who dared to leave their skirts under rocks to boldly occupy space their male counterparts did. A compelling collection of intrepid women—pilots, scientists, mountain climbers, social reformers, and more—it uniquely celebrates the work of lesser-known explorers. Highly recommended!"

—**KATHRYN AALTO**, author of *Writing Wild: Women Poets, Ramblers, and Mavericks Who Shape How We See the Natural World*

THE GIRL EXPLORERS

The Untold Story of the Globetrotting Women Who Trekked, Flew, and Fought Their Way Around the World

JAYNE ZANGLEIN

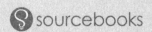

sourcebooks

Cover design by Sarah Brody
Cover images © Miss Annie S. Peck full-length portrait, photograph by Chickering Photo, from New York Herald Syndicate, New York World-Telegram and the Sun Newspaper Photograph Collection, Prints and Photographs Division, Library of Congress, LC-USZ62-118273;
© Bettmann/Getty Images; © Wildlife Conservation Society, reproduced by permission of the WCS Archives, Gloria Hollister 1006; © Anna Heyward Taylor (1879-1956), 1903, by William Merritt Chase (American, 1849-1916), 1937.003.0001, image courtesy of the Gibbes Museum of Art/Carolina Art Association

Published by Sourcebooks
P.O. Box 4410, Naperville, Illinois 60567-4410
(630) 961-3900
sourcebooks.com

The Library of Congress has catalogued the hardcover edition as follows:

Names: Zanglein, Jayne E., author.
Title: The girl explorers : the untold story of the globetrotting women who trekked, flew, and fought their way around the world / Jayne Zanglein.
Description: Naperville : Sourcebooks, 2021. | Includes bibliographical references.
Identifiers: LCCN 2020053533 (print) | LCCN 2020053534 (ebook) | (hardback) | ISBN 9781728215259 (epub) | (pdf)
Subjects: LCSH: Women explorers. | Society of Woman Geographers. | Niles, Blair. | Earhart, Amelia, 1897-1937.
Classification: LCC G200 . Z27 2021 (print) | LCC G200 (ebook) | DDC 910.92/52 [B]--dc23
LC record available at https://lccn.loc.gov/2020053533
LC ebook record available at https://lccn.loc.gov/2020053534

Printed and bound in Canada.
MBP 10 9 8 7 6 5 4 3 2 1

To my mom and my husband, Steve:
for your steadfast belief that I could bring the
stories of these unsung heroes to life

From the days of the mythical Argonauts until relatively recent times, the business of discovery and exploration, whether legendary or real, inevitably featured an all-male cast. Women stayed at home, awaiting the adventurers' return, presumably stitching away on some interminable tapestry, in the tradition of that stoic image of patient resignation, Penelope. But in the twentieth century, the situation began to change. Women freed themselves from their Victorian upbringing to organize and lead expeditions of their own, asserting themselves as serious experts. While almost forgotten today, they were far from ignored in their time. With the passage of time, however, the names and contributions tended to sink from sight, their achievements questioned or minimized. The essence of this era found a voice in 1925 in the creation of the International Society of Woman Geographers by many of these brilliant women. They sought intellectual companionship in a period when their global assaults were still regarded as decided aberrations from the norm. The trailblazing adventures of these women remain unique, and their contributions deserve reinstatement in the history of American explorers.

—ELIZABETH FAGG OLDS

My shock lies in the fact that there's so much inspiration to be drawn from real-life history that I don't understand how, after so many years, there's still a lack of tales about daring, gutsy, even reckless women. Yes, reckless! Why not? Show them being reckless! I'm not suggesting that they're perfect. I'm suggesting that they're interesting and that cinemas and libraries everywhere are missing out on spellbinding characters and, more importantly, on their ability as characters to inspire in young girls the realisation that life is for living, risks, mistakes and adrenalin-inducing bravery included.

—KAYA PURCHASE

Illustration 1. Map from the New York Section of the Society of Woman Geographers, ca. 1932

Arctic Ocean
Indian Ocean
Pacific Ocean
OF
HERS

CONTENTS

List of Illustrations xiii
Cast of Characters xvii
Author's Note xxii
Prologue: Banned xxvii

PART 1: MERE WOMEN 1
Reckless 3
A Place of Their Own 21
Go Home Where You Belong! 39
A Mere Woman 63
Reno-vation 89

PART 2: EARLY ADVOCATES FOR HUMAN RIGHTS 101
The Prison Special 103
The Backwash of War 123
Birth of a Nation 135

PART 3: THE "GIRLS" OF THE TROPICAL RESEARCH STATION 145
Wanted: A Chaperone 147
Too Many Girl Pictures 163

PART 4: ADVOCATING FOR BLACK PEOPLE, GAY MEN, AND FRENCH PRISONERS 189
Imprisoned by Whiteness 191
Condemned to Devil's Island 203
Gay Harlem 221
Races of Mankind 231

PART 5: NETWORKING WOMEN 247
Only a Passenger 249
Friction 265
Networking 279

PART 6: PAVING THE WAY FOR WOMEN TODAY 289
The Matilda Effect 291
Seeing with Both Eyes 305

Epilogue: The Loss Will Be Ours 317
Members of the Society of Woman Geographers 321
Selected Bibliography 323
Abbreviations 328
Illustration Credits 329
Notes 333
Acknowledgments 375
About the Author 378

LIST OF ILLUSTRATIONS

Illustr. 1 Map from the New York Section of the Society of Women Geographers (ca. 1932)

Illustr. 2.1 Marguerite Harrison (ca. 1921)

Illustr. 2.2 Blair [Beebe] Niles (1910)

Illustr. 2.3 Gertrude Emerson [Sen] (1921)

Illustr. 2.4 Gertrude Mathews [Shelby] (1922)

Illustr. 2.5 Harriet Chalmers Adams (1918)

Illustr. 2.6 Te Ata (1920)

Illustr. 2.7 Mary Ritter Beard (1915)

Illustr. 2.8 Amelia Earhart (1928)

Illustr. 2.9 Malvina Hoffman (1928)

Illustr. 2.10 Gloria Hollister (ca. 1930)

Illustr. 2.11 Osa Johnson (1970)

Illustr. 2.12 Ellen La Motte (1902)

Illustr. 2.13 Margaret Mead (ca. 1930)

Illustr. 2.14 Annie Smith Peck (1893)

Illustr. 2.15 Ella Riegel (ca. 1918)

Illustr. 2.16 Grace Thompson Seton (ca. 1901)

Illustr. 2.17 Anna Heyward Taylor (1918)

Illustr. 3 Don't Take a Woman—When You Go Exploring, *Public Ledger* (1932)

Illustr. 4 Osa Johnson with Crocodile in Borneo (1917)

Illustr. 5 Osa Johnson and Nagapate (1916)

Illustr. 6 Marguerite Harrison with Bakhtiari Men (ca. 1924)

Illustr. 7 Annie Peck (Press Photo, 1911)

Illustr. 8 Blair and Tandook (1910)

Illustr. 9 The Shooter of the Poisoned Arrows (1910)

Illustr. 10 Ella Riegel and Picketing Suffragists from Pennsylvania (1917)

Illustr. 11 The Horror of War; Possibly Ellen La Motte Attending Belgian Wounded (1915)

Illustr. 12 NAACP Picket Outside Theater Protesting Movie "Birth of a Nation" (1947)

Illustr. 13 Roosevelts at Kalacoon (1916)

Illustr. 14 Gloria Hollister and Diving Helmet (ca. 1926)

Illustr. 15 Gloria Hollister, William Beebe, John Tee-Van with Bathysphere (1932)

Illustr. 16 Zonia Barber's Class in Mathematical Geography Studying Earth's Rotation around the Sun, Hampton Institute, Hampton, Virginia (n.d.)

Illustr. 17 Part of Detention House on Devil's Island (1934)

Illustr. 18 A Night-Club Map of Harlem (1932)

Illustr. 19 Malvina Hoffman Sketching a Man Named Mare for a Bronze Sculpture for the Races of Man Exhibit (ca. 1929)

Illustr. 20 Races of Mankind Exhibit (n.d.)

Illustr. 21 Amelia Earhart (n.d.)

Illustr. 22 Society Members On Their Way to Washington to Meet Amelia Earhart (1932)

Illustr. 23 New York Members of the Society of Woman Geographers, 1930–1931 Season
Illustr. 24 Members in Exploring Costumes at the Tenth Anniversary Dinner of the Society of Woman Geographers (1935)
Illustr. 25 Margaret Mead with Manus Mother and Child (1953)
Illustr. 26 Gloria Hollister, Will Beebe, and Jocelyn Crane Looking at Eclipse (1937)
Illustr. 27 Kathryn Sullivan on Space Walk (1984)

CAST OF CHARACTERS

Society of Woman Geographers Founders and First President

Illustration 2.1. Marguerite Harrison, ca. 1921

Illustration 2.2. Blair [Beebe] Niles, 1910

Illustration 2.3. Gertrude Emerson [Sen], 1921

Illustration 2.4. Gertrude Mathews [Shelby], 1922

Illustration 2.5. Harriet Chalmers Adams, 1918

Featured Early Members of the Society

Illustration 2.6. Te Ata, 1920

Illustration 2.7. Mary Ritter Beard, 1915

Illustration 2.8. Amelia Earhart, 1928

Illustration 2.9. Malvina Hoffman, 1928

Illustration 2.10. Gloria Hollister, ca. 1930

Illustration 2.11. Osa Johnson, 1917

Illustration 2.12. Ellen La Motte, 1902

Illustration 2.13. Margaret Mead, ca. 1930

Illustration 2.14. Annie Smith Peck, 1893

Illustration 2.15. Ella Riegel, ca. 1918

Illustration 2.16. Grace Thompson Seton, ca. 1901

Illustration 2.17. Anna Heyward Taylor, 1918

AUTHOR'S NOTE

In 2016, after a ten-week trip traveling throughout China, relaxing in Thailand, and studying Balinese gamelan (the traditional music of Indonesia), I returned home, inspired to write a book about explorers. My research turned up Blair Niles, a forward-thinking woman explorer. I was immediately taken aback by this woman. Blair was born on a Virginia plantation in 1880, surrounded by freed slaves. Nearly two decades earlier, her maternal grandfather, a Virginia congressman* had provoked the Confederacy into launching the Civil War against the Union. When Blair was a child, her mother started a mixed-race night school to educate Blair, her brothers, and the children of the household's former slaves. She did this to expose her children to diverse viewpoints at a time when the family could not afford to send them off to school. Because of her mother's influence, and in spite of her grandfather's reputation, Blair became an advocate for marginalized and oppressed people.

---

* Roger Atkinson Pryor (D. Va.).

Although Blair is remembered as the author of the first compassionate book about gay people in Harlem (*Strange Brother*), her books on the brutal treatment of prisoners in French Guiana (*Condemned to Devil's Island*), the uprising of slaves during the Haitian Revolution (*Black Haiti: A Biography of Africa's Eldest Daughter*), and the mutiny of the *Amistad* slave ship (*East by Day*) have been forgotten. Also overlooked is Blair's role in founding the Society of Woman Geographers, an organization with more than five hundred members worldwide that will soon celebrate its one hundredth anniversary. When I learned about the diverse group of women who were early members of the Society, I expanded my writing project to tell the story of the founding of the Society. I was not disappointed: the early members of the Society are every bit as interesting as Blair Niles.

These women were not diverse in the restrictive sense that we sometimes use the word today to denote inclusion of people of color. Most of the early members were white. But they were diverse in other ways: socio-economic status, educational attainment, occupation, sexual orientation, marital status, ethnicity, and nationality.

This eclectic group of woman geographers—explorers, artists, scientists, musicians, writers, and storytellers—shared common interests, all of which originated from their love of travel and exploration. During World War I, they sailed to Europe to assist the Allies, long before the United States entered the war. They also shared horizons broadened by travel experiences that altered their perspectives. Blair Niles viewed travel as a spiritual journey with the object of studying the national soul. She wrote, "One of the results of much wandering is undoubtedly to develop in the wanderer as many standards of beauty as there are races." Travel inspired these women to celebrate differences and encourage homebodies to see the world through a different lens.

Many of the early members of the New York branch of the Society found a common cause in celebrating the rich cultural heritage of indigenous people. In the 1920s and 1930s—a time when social scientists feared that the way of life of indigenous people would soon disappear—Society members rushed to visit other countries so they could portray these civilizations before they vanished. Blair Niles focused on the Mayans and Incans, Te Ata introduced the public to her Chickasaw heritage, and Margaret Mead concentrated on Oceanic people. Perhaps most emblematic of this desire to preserve cultures was Malvina Hoffman, who sculpted images of more than one hundred people of different races for a 1933 exhibit at the Chicago Field Museum. Like many members of the Society, Malvina portrayed marginalized people with respect and understanding, modeling an attitude of tolerance that she hoped others would adopt.

Although readers might assume the Society fought for women's rights, this was not the case. The Society itself did not tackle issues of discrimination as its mission. Many members, however, marched for equal rights during the suffrage movement and were leaders in that struggle. Some members, such as aviator Amelia Earhart and mountaineer Annie Peck, claimed their victories on behalf of women. Other members, such as the Society's first president, Harriet Chalmers Adams, focused less on competition between the sexes. Harriet believed that women's perceptions of the world differed from men's and that "both were essential to offer a more complete idea of what has been seen and to present a more satisfying viewpoint than a purely masculine one can do alone." Like Harriet, Blair believed in the Baha'i* principle that "the world of humanity has two wings—one is woman and the other man. Not until both wings are equally developed can the bird fly." Later, geographer Margaret Edith Trussell would summarize the same thought: "How can a discipline realize its full potential while walking on only one leg?"

Society member Mary Ritter Beard devoted most of her career as a historian to reminding the public that women's contributions, although often ignored, had been central to the advancement of the human race. The problem was not that women had failed to develop their wings, but rather that women's achievements often went unrecorded or were overlooked. Her motto was, "No documents, no history." Mary dedicated much of her career to restoring woman's place in history. The Society's founders embraced this concept and required each prospective member to demonstrate not only that she had contributed to the world's store of knowledge about a specific geographical region, but that she had recorded this knowledge in writing, on phonographs or film, or through art, music, or dance.

The Girl Explorers resurrects the history of many of the early Society members, women whose contributions to humanity have been forgotten. The story of this group of women gives us hope in an era when Americans have become more divisive and less tolerant. It reminds us that if we are to soar to great heights as a nation, we must find strength in our differences.

---

* The Baha'i Faith, founded in Persia (Iran) in the mid-1800s, includes spiritual teachings about the oneness of humanity and gender equality.

Illustration 3. Don't Take a Woman—When You Go Exploring, *Public Ledger* (1932)

PROLOGUE
BANNED

> *In exploration, more, I think, than in any other career, a woman's success is dependent upon her determination not to be discouraged or deflected from the path of her chosen ambition.*
>
> —BLAIR NILES, AUTHOR AND SOCIETY MEMBER

FEBRUARY 6, 1932

American Museum of Natural History, Manhattan

On a brisk winter evening in 1932, Blair Niles stood in the American Museum of Natural History, where the New York City branch of the Society of Woman Geographers was holding its first formal dinner. Blair and her friends had founded the Society seven years earlier as a sanctuary for women explorers after the Explorers Club refused to lift its ban on women members. Blair was now fifty-two. Although she grew up on an isolated plantation in Virginia, she had become a world traveler. She had hiked through the Himalayas and journeyed down the Yangtze River as Chinese citizens rioted on the shore. With her Southern drawl, she had negotiated with the chief of a Bornean tribe of head-hunters and, with the limited knowledge she had gained in an emergency medicine class, she had nursed the expedition's cook through "Moon Madness." She had traveled through Malaysia by houseboat, ridden a camel through an Egyptian sandstorm, lived among convicts on Devil's Island off the coast of French Guiana, and witnessed voodoo ceremonies in Haiti. But thanks to Roy Chapman Andrews, she still couldn't get through the front door of the prestigious all-male Explorers Club.

Roy Chapman Andrews was the president of the Explorers Club. He had cultivated an image as a rugged adventurer who traveled across the desert in vintage automobiles or caravans of camels. He claimed that, during his fifteen years of exploration, he had escaped near death ten times. Blair was always suspicious of near-death claims; they made good headlines, but they tended to be tall tales. She believed that "to a Munchausen,* a foreign itinerary offers limitless temptations to exaggerate."

Blair knew that the evening's program would be nothing short of spectacular, and so she invited reporters to cover the event. The program featured women with remarkable experiences. It also showcased a letter from Andrews who, to no one's surprise, had declined the Society's invitation to explain his recent contentious remarks at Barnard College, Columbia University's college for women. Blair could not wait to hear the members' reactions when they heard that Andrews had told the assembled students, "Women are not adapted to exploration." Blair interpreted this to mean that it was acceptable for a woman to accompany her husband on an expedition or to organize a trek with other women as long as she did not upstage the men or challenge their masculinity.

---

* A teller of tall tales, named after Baron von Munchausen.

As one member of the Explorers Club explained, "The secret's out. One can live comfortably in the African jungle. We could formerly come back and tell our lady friends almost anything about our perilous adventures and fights with tigers and boa constrictors. Now we can't get away with it." Women explorers knew when men were stretching the truth.

Andrews believed that, in many ways, women were equal to men. But they were not as strong as men, he thought, and their nervous systems were more sensitive. "With them, it is the drops of water that wear away the stone. The trivialities which men manage to ignore completely disturb them and prevent them from settling down to hard and concentrated work." Without a trace of irony, Andrews continued: "Take, for instance, a man who gurgles his soup. I have seen a man fly into a rage over such a simple thing as this, clench his hands at mealtime, turn to the offender and cry out: 'Great Scott, man, can't you eat your soup quietly?'"

Blair must have wondered: Did Andrews honestly believe that a woman cannot deal with the minor annoyance of a soup-slurping man on journeys fraught with danger?

Newspapers throughout the country publicized Andrews's speech, and most editorials took the side of women. The *New York Sun* wrote, "When Roy Chapman Andrews told the Barnard girls recently that women had no place in exploration, he forgot to take into account the women who already had proved him wrong." The *Newark Advocate* in Ohio warned, "This is no time in the world's history to try to convince women that they cannot do anything a man can do." The *Albuquerque Journal* joked, "This should be evident to any man—if women want to go, they'll go." The *Gazette* of Cedar Rapids, Iowa, wrote, "Men excel women as explorers for the same reason that they excel in most other lines, simply because leaders of expeditions, like Mr. Andrews, have denied women the opportunities to prove themselves."

In its first seven years, the Society had admitted more than two hundred members in three branches. The largest group was in metropolitan New York, followed by the District of Columbia and Chicago. The remaining active members were scattered throughout the United States and Canada. Members held informal meetings almost monthly, usually at a member's home. The Society had also admitted thirty-seven corresponding members, from countries as remote as the Union of South Africa and Cambodia.

Blair watched as thirty members of the Society's New York branch roamed the museum's Hall of Birds of the World in their brilliantly colored silk, velvet, and crepe gowns. She was pleased with the turnout; nearly 70 percent of the New York branch had attended, a remarkable achievement for a group of women who spent much of their time abroad. The adventurers conversed in small groups, sharing knowledge, experiences, and contacts. Blair was honored to be among these strong, independent, and fierce women who climbed mountains, explored jungles, descended into the depths of the ocean, and studied aborigines. They opened doors to other worlds for their sister explorers. Although Blair did not know it, one of the evening's speakers would unwittingly find a sponsor for her upcoming trip to Peru.

She ushered a reporter over to interview the Society's oldest member, Annie Peck, who was sitting at a table, trying not to wince. Annie had recently broken three ribs in a streetcar accident, and her abdomen was bound tightly in bandages under her evening gown. Blair admired the spunk of the 81-year-old mountaineer, who was an expert in Latin America. Born into the Victorian Age in 1850, she flamboyantly defied expectations that "women be firmly harnessed to domesticity." New Jersey's *Monmouth Democrat* later reported that Annie had attended the Society's dinner two days after she got out of the hospital. The reporter noted, "The same spirit that took her to the tip of lofty peaks took her to that dinner. If I was awarding a medal for gameness, it would go to Miss Annie Smith Peck."

Afterward, Blair arranged for a photographer to take a picture of the prominent explorers at the dinner. She gathered the evening's three speakers: aviator Amelia Earhart, zoologist Gloria Hollister, and explorer Elizabeth Dickey. She located Grace Barstow Murphy, the Society's rare example of an explorer who brought her three young children on her naturalist husband's expeditions. Grace firmly believed that her sons would become better men because she answered the call of adventure, even though she was deaf. Blair also rounded up Osa Johnson, who was famous for her wildlife adventure films. Osa was a stormy, temperamental woman who had captivated the hearts of Americans when at age twenty—she looked like a cute fifteen-year-old—she starred in her husband's silent movies. The moving pictures, which featured adorable, pale Osa with the indigenous dark-skinned people of Oceania, were, in part, stellar ethnographic films and, in part, racist vaudeville shows. Blair may have wondered whether Osa was a shining example of a woman geographer.

The dinner bell rang, and Blair sat at the head table. The program was about to begin.

The Society's youngest member, Gloria Hollister, age thirty-one, rose to speak. She had a master's degree in zoology from Columbia and was an expert on fish coloration. Gloria had adopted a revolutionary technique that made fish transparent so that she could observe their bone structure without the need for dissection. She described the process: "Like the fading of one cinema picture and the gradual appearance of another, the skin and flesh of the fish become less and less opaque before our eyes, while the skeleton, stained a brilliant scarlet, crystallizes into plain view." The Bermudans she worked with called it "Fish Magic."

Blair could feel the excitement in the room as Gloria described her dive 410 feet below the ocean in a bathysphere, a metal diving globe lowered into the water by a cable. During the descent, she was connected to land by a telephone line. "But for the telephone communication, I might have been an isolated planet swinging in mid-ether!" She told the audience how the fish bumped against the bathysphere's small porthole. "This has opened up a whole new world for scientific investigation." She was proud to be the "only girl who has adventured into the ocean." The audience applauded.

Despite this remarkable presentation, a *Minneapolis Star* journalist who covered the formal event reported later that Gloria looked "more like one of Ziegfeld's glories than a scientist." Blair would not have been surprised—she knew that it was nearly impossible for men to see genius when beauty is staring them down.

But this was nothing new. Advertisements for Gloria's lecture series noted, "She looks like a musical comedy star, but she has one of the finest scientific minds ever found in a woman." *The Family Circle* published an article about Hollister under the banner "Gloria, the Beautiful Ichthyologist or Some Blondes Have Brains." This type of publicity was precisely what Blair tried to avoid. But Blair was a legend at working with the media and knew that copywriters liked to emphasize the sensational because it sold more papers.

Gloria was one of the many young women assisting Blair's

ex-husband, William Beebe, in his deep-sea explorations for the Department of Tropical Research at the New York Zoological Park (now the Bronx Zoo). Newspapers often pictured her wearing a bathing suit as she prepared to descend into the ocean. Will Beebe was known for giving incredible opportunities to young women scientists and artists. Those "opportunities" sometimes included sexual liaisons. Blair was pretty sure that Will, whose new wife had agreed on an open marriage, was having an affair with Gloria at his Bermuda research site. Blair, who had grown up in the Victorian era with its Puritanical morals, believed that her generation had simultaneously degraded sex and made a fetish out of it. She thought that the younger generation of flappers, like Gloria, who were trying to live life to the fullest, were bound to make mistakes and ruin their lives with this sexual freedom. But she also believed that Puritanical taboos had ruined many lives. As long as they were not injuring anyone, Blair believed that human beings should be as free as birds. Blair did not resent the women who worked with her ex-husband, but instead welcomed them into the Society.

Next, South American explorer Elizabeth Dickey rose to address the audience. She wore a pale blue evening gown. Dazzling earrings peeked from under her coiffed hair. She told the audience that during her honeymoon in Ecuador, she met headhunters who shrink the heads of their dead enemies so they can keep them as trophies.

"Here's one," she said, as she pulled it out of a box. "This is a particularly beautiful specimen."

As she held the head high, long black hair dangled from its sides—two ribbons made of iridescent beetle wings nestled against its hair. Absentmindedly, Elizabeth stroked the head as she explained why the man had been killed. "The Jivaro headhunters have a peculiar way of making love—if I may call it that. They do not marry their own women but steal their wives from neighboring tribes. When there is a shortage of wives, they go to war for their mates. But general warfare is uncommon since their chief concern in life is to learn to steal women with skill and precision."

Elizabeth spoke of the day that she and her husband, Herbert Spencer Dickey, arrived at the Jivaro Indian village. Anguashi, a member of another tribe, had just stolen the chief's wife. The clan was in an uproar. The leader dispatched the warriors to retrieve his wife and to kill the kidnapper. One of the Jivaro warriors, Chunga, killed Anguashi and returned with the abductor's head. But on the way back, a poisonous snake bit the hero.

Elizabeth's husband treated Chunga and watched over him as he slowly recovered. The villagers were astounded that Chunga did not die. As Elizabeth talked, her earrings shimmered in the light. She told the audience the rest of the story with relish.

"At once, they looked upon us as supernatural." As a result of Chunga's bravery, the chief ordered the head of Anguashi to be shrunken and given to Chunga to hang on his belt as a totem.

The villagers set to work embalming the head. Elizabeth described the process: "The body of the victim is allowed to remain untouched for several days. Then an incision is made across the chest and another across the back. They meet above the shoulders. The skin is then pulled over the neck and skull. The result of this process is to reverse it, but before further treatment, it is returned to its natural position." The skin was soaked in a tanbark solution, then filled with hot sand and clay. Ten days later, the head was removed from the solution and emptied of sand. Next, they combed its hair and adorned the head. "Gaudy feathers are hung from the ears; the nostrils are delicately stuffed, and the mouth is tightly sewn 'to keep the bad spirits inside.'"

After the chief presented the head to Chunga, the hero gave it to Herbert to thank him for saving his life. Elizabeth regarded it as their honeymoon present.

Amelia Earhart, a new member of the Society, spoke next. She was preparing for a solo transatlantic flight, which she planned to coincide with the fifth anniversary of Charles Lindbergh's transatlantic flight. She glanced over at Annie Peck. At Blair's request, Amelia had recently endorsed Annie's book *Flying over South America*, which chronicled her twenty thousand miles of flights over South America at age eighty. Earhart wrote, "When I plan my trip southward, I shall use *Flying over South America* as a reference. Perhaps I shall even take a copy with me in the cockpit to remind me that I am only following in the footsteps of one who pioneered when it was brave enough just to put on the bloomers necessary for mountain climbing." Amelia told the audience that, unlike Annie, who climbed mountains, she simply buzzed over them in her plane.

The crowd stirred as Ruth Crosby Noble, the chair of the Society's New York branch, stood to read Roy Chapman Andrews's letter. She reminded the audience that Andrews recently told Barnard College's all-female student body that they did not have the physique to be good explorers. Andrews complained that, after he announced his expedition to the Gobi Desert, he received a letter from a woman who desired to become the expedition's field secretary. She wanted to create a welcoming environment for the explorers. Andrews sneered, "I am skeptical about the possibilities for a 'home atmosphere' in a desert where sandstorms continue for weeks. I am equally unimpressed with ladies who put on riding breeches and plunge into jungles and deserts hunting live savages and dead fossils." Then he bragged about his accomplishments finding fossilized dinosaur eggs in the Gobi Desert.

Noble read his letter aloud.

"What I said was this: That on a big expedition where the staff includes a half dozen or so men I consider women to be a great detriment; they cannot do a technical job in most cases any better than a man, and their sex alone makes for complications. A leader has enough difficulties in running a big expedition without saddling himself with any that can be avoided.

"I also said that if a man and his wife wish to explore alone, or a woman wants to organize her own expedition, there is no reason why such arrangements should not give excellent results." But he would not mix women and men on an expedition. It was asking for trouble.

The audience erupted in an incredulous buzz.

Andrews concluded: "I know of no more effective way to wreck an expedition than to put in one woman, or worse still, two." In support, he cited the Chinese character for trouble, which is a roof with two women under it.* "One woman in an expedition is bad enough," he said, "two are impossible."

It would not take long for members of the Society to prove him wrong. Members would set records as they climbed higher, flew faster, and dove deeper than men. But these women were not motivated by a desire to beat men's records, for they knew that they were capable explorers. Nor did they find a need to confine their travels to expeditions approved by men or to seek male approval. As deep-sea diver Sylvia Earle, one of the more famous members of the Society alive today, explained, "Sometimes people find it hard to take us seriously. But most of the problems are in the minds of the men." Several members of the Society

---

* Andrews was alluding to the first half of the Chinese character for woman 麻. This character alone means *hemp*. 麻烦 is Chinese for trouble.

would struggle to reorient the focus of history to include women by establishing archives so that women would not be ignored, for as Society member Mary Ritter Beard cautioned, "Without documents; no history. Without history; no memory."

PART 1
MERE WOMEN

Illustration 4. Osa Johnson with Crocodile in Borneo (1917)

CHAPTER 1
RECKLESS

Is it reckless? Maybe. But what do dreams know of boundaries?

—AMELIA EARHART, AVIATOR AND SOCIETY MEMBER

1932
Manhattan

Blair was fond of referring to egotistical, domineering male explorers as the "we-white-men, red-blood-in-your-veins variety" of explorers—male explorers who exploited opportunities in colonized lands by leading scientific expeditions, thus proving their courage, strength, and superiority by recounting their hairbreadth escapes. These men had egos that compelled them to explore and "seek expression in heroics." Blair knew that men loved "to swap the usual soiled and time-frayed stories inherited from generations of smoking-rooms, and to strike attitudes of importance, boasting of achievements and prowess. Power, in its many forms, was their obsession." That is the reason that members of the Explorers Club so jealously enforced its ban on women. Blair preferred explorers who were not "the heroes of their own volumes," who could poke fun at themselves.

She also faulted editors who pushed travel writers to "come forward with narrow escapes and hair-whitening experiences, with the curious result that in the twentieth century, when exploration has been simplified by automobile and airplane, when radio and wireless summon aid in emergencies, we find many of the modern chronicles of travel bristling with dangers and hardships as a porcupine bristles with quills." Blair thought these journeys paled in comparison with "the exploits of the old *Conquistadors*, of the first white women who made the arduous journey of 1,000 miles up the Magdalena River, through jungle and over Andes." She mused, "Those women *even* bore children *en route*! But that was in the days before the pot of gold had been found at the end of the publicity rainbow."

Blair wondered if women were falling into the same trap as men when they announced that they were "'the first white woman' to do this or that." She wondered how explorers avoided stepping on each other's toes as the first. It reminded her of the cartoon that showed male explorers flying to the North Pole in a plane with a bumper sticker that read, "If you are near enough to read this, you are too damn close."

She thought of her exploring friends. They were courageous, no doubt, but did they recklessly pursue their explorations? Blair knew there was a fine line between showing strength when danger loomed ahead and completely disregarding that danger. She considered her friend Mickie Akeley.

During her first African safari with her husband, Carl Akeley, Mickie had quickly become a crack markswoman out of necessity. She recognized that a woman who could not take care of herself was a handicap to the safari. Mickie frequently told her friends the story of why she learned to shoot.

"We were going quietly along the bush-covered banks of a stream looking for birds when a lion growled at us, and I became petrified with fright."

Her young guide gently put his hand on her shoulder and whispered, "Very bad, memsahib! Very bad!"

"I am fully aware that it is 'very bad,'" Mickie thought.

She collected her wits and backed up, clutching her shotgun, which she knew would not be lethal enough to save her from the lion. Soon she was a safe distance from the predator. But he did not attack. She recalled, "I don't know what happened to the lion. His growl had been merely a warning. He may have been as badly frightened as I was. But I did some heavy thinking as I walked back to camp." She quickly learned how to shoot a .256 Mannlicher-Schoenauer rifle. "With only three birds to her credit as a marksman, she shot a charging bull elephant and dropped him six feet from where she stood." As Mickie wryly noted, "It is not necessary to be a man to fire a rifle."

Mickie admitted, "In a country where anything may happen and where even at night one must wake from a sound sleep and be ready for instant action, it would be folly to say there is no fear. But it is the sort of fear that stimulates, and perhaps it is that element that I have learned to love."* She continued, "I do not feel especially

---

* Mickie was not afraid to show her weaknesses, even in front of Theodore Roosevelt. The former president liked to tell an incident about Mickie that occurred when they were hunting elephants on Mount Kenya. They had to cut a path through the steep, dense jungle to get to the elephants. They would climb two steps and slide back a step. After days of trudging up the mountainside, Mickie was exhausted. She was dirty, her muscles were sore, and tears were streaming down her face. Suddenly, her husband, Carl, saw elephant footprints. He was amazed that the elephants had climbed so high. He shouted to Mickie, "My dear, the elephants have been here!" Mickie was silent.

"I say!" he exclaimed, this time louder, "The elephants have been here!"

Mickie sniffled and choked back a sob.

"The damn fools," she said, wishing that the elephants had been smart enough to remain on the plains.

brave. My work calls me to Africa, and I go gladly. It is hard to say what constitutes bravery. It may be a tautening of nerves in the face of danger; it may be the thrill of overcoming that stimulates and strengthens, in proportion to the thing to be overcome."

Mickie admitted that she had come close to death a few times, once with a fever. "I was delirious half of the time. When I wasn't, I could hear the cook and my personal boy sitting outside the tent, discussing how they would prepare my body and arguing over how they would divide up my clothes. Each morning one of them would come in and ask politely if I was going to die that day. I always responded that I didn't think so."

But Blair knew that sometimes, when Mickie was confronted by injustice, she acted rashly. Once, on an expedition in the Belgian Congo, she screamed at a sultan who shoved his wife onto the floor because a piece of pork fell off the spit and into the fire. The men sitting around, waiting for dinner, encouraged the sultan to hit his wife again. The sultan leaped over his cowering wife.

"*Toka, toka!*" Mickie roared. *Get out!*

The sultan charged at Mickie. Menace filled his eyes. Towering over her, he beat his chest. He could hardly contain his fury. Mickie stood silently, quaking with fear, and drenched in sweat.

After a few moments, Mickie laughed—not from condescension, but because he looked funny. He stared at her in disbelief and then calmed down. Mickie was thankful because, as she later wrote, "I knew he could blot me and my little caravan off the map."

Certainly, Mickie was not being reckless: she was just doing what needed to be done to defuse a dangerous situation.

During the expedition, Mickie collected specimens for the Brooklyn Museum of Arts and Sciences, including hyenas, a lion, gazelles, antelopes, and a rare rodent. She also collected memories of the cruelty of the Congo, which she tried to prevent along the way: prostitution in the camps, abuse of prisoners, and domestic violence by the sultan. When the sultan sent Mickie's porters a boiled human arm for dinner, she did not intervene or judge, as she knew cannibalism was a dietary custom. But she did lament: "No wonder the sky sheds tears at night and the thunder booms and the lightning threatens. The Congo is cruel."

Wildlife filmmaker Armand Georges Denis would have labeled Mickie as reckless. He met many women explorers during the filming of his feature-length films. Later, he would tell a reporter, "I welcome the opportunity to tell what is wrong with them, as explorers. And I hope that what I have to say may be discouraging enough to stop their wanderlust." He thought that women were much more reckless than men. "A man makes a cold calculation, and if the danger is too great, he will not take it. The average woman doesn't think. She takes unnecessary chances or forces man to. Either he has to appear cowardly or follow after. It's embarrassing." For instance, Denis cites a woman who sees lion cubs. She says, "Oh, aren't they cute" and walks up to them. "Trouble begins. And then the timid man has to rescue fearless woman again." Another man claimed, "One woman can cause more trouble on an exploring expedition than a whole horde of wild elephants, a tribe of wild and bloodthirsty savages, or a dozen lions and tigers ready for food."

Next, Blair considered Osa Johnson. Osa was an anomaly. She was an independent, feisty, quick-tempered, brusque woman. But she was also tiny, adorable, and exuberant. Her "energy of purpose could brush aside obstacles entailing physical danger or hardship." She was able to "disarm antagonism, and through adaptability, allay any spirit of distrust. Her eagerness was saved from recklessness by caution and intuition." But Blair may have wondered how much of her stories were true. After all, her book about her adventures had been ghostwritten.

Osa liked to tell of her South Seas expedition in 1916. By then, Osa and her husband, Martin, had saved enough money to buy a Universal motion picture camera and several thousand feet of film. They headed to the Solomon Islands, where, nine years earlier, Martin had filmed cannibals while he was a passenger on a round-the-world voyage on writer Jack London's ship, the *Snark*.

When they reached the Solomon Islands, they cruised around for months, hopping from one boat to the next, looking for indigenous people who were "completely untouched by civilization." Rumor had it that some parts of Malekula Island had never been visited by white people. When they told the captain where they wanted to go, there was an uproar.

"Now listen to me, young fellow. I don't want to scare the little lady, but it says right here in the *Pacific Island Pilot* that the natives of Malekula are a wild and savage race, that they're treacherous and it's a known fact that they still practice cannibalism!" He told them that forty thousand natives lived on Malekula, and they were rumored to be cannibals. The chief, Nagapate, was a "holy terror."

The captain shook his head. He threw back his head and took a long swig of liquor. As he spoke, his voice rose.

"And I'll not go off my course to set you down on Malekula, understand? Not with a woman along. It would be murder, that's what, woman-murder, and I'll not be guilty of it!"

After he calmed down, the captain agreed to take them to Vao, an island one mile from Malekula.

On Vao, they met a missionary who lent them a whaleboat and five men. Soon they were off to Malekula, camera in hand.

They landed on a small strip of beach.

Boldly, Osa stepped out of the boat and onto the sand. She gathered some tobacco and calico they had brought to trade and headed for the jungle.

"Wait, Osa!" Martin called. "I can't risk it! Not with you. I'll come back tomorrow."

Osa continued walking.

"All right, then, wait." He motioned for the porters to carry the photographic equipment.

When she reached the jungle, she was plunged into darkness. Osa groped around to orient herself as her eyes adjusted to the darkness. The jungle floor hid murky streams and vines, and the stink of rotting vegetation overwhelmed her. The trail led to the base of a hill, and she climbed back into the brilliant sunlight. Osa recollected, "We climbed for what seemed hours. A pulse beat hard in the roof of my mouth, my breath was like a knife in my chest, and perspiration dripped from my hands."

She scrambled up to a plateau. Far below, Osa saw a sliver of beach. Their boat looked like a speck in the water.

As she caught her breath, she heard a rustling in the bushes around them. She turned.

Twenty Malekulans stood behind them.

"Don't let them see you're afraid, Osa," instructed Martin. "Leave the trade stuff on the ground and ease down the trail. I'll attract their attention with the camera, and that'll give you a good head start."

Osa turned to the trail, but the Malekulans blocked her. She heard the sound of drums in the distance. Close by, she heard a twig crack. She turned and glanced at the porters, who had terror etched on their faces as Chief Nagapate parted the bushes.

As he walked toward Osa, she heard the whir of the motion picture camera.

Osa smiled at the chief.

"Hello, Mr. Nagapate." She handed him some tobacco.

The chief ignored the offering.

Osa froze as she noticed four rings on the chief's fingers, each with a different crest. She wondered whether they were souvenirs from the victims the cannibal had allegedly cooked.

In a loud voice, Osa said, "This is a very nice piece of calico. You would be very handsome in it."

The chief reached out. Osa thought he would take the fabric, but instead, he grabbed her arm.

The chief began to rub her skin. He was puzzled by her white skin. When he could not rub off the white with his fingers, he picked up a piece of cane and used it to scrape her skin. It turned pink. The chief shook his head, astonished. As he poked and prodded her, Osa felt as though she was "in a world gone grotesquely wrong."

The drumbeats got louder and closer.

Martin said, "Get on down that trail with the carriers, Osa. I'll follow."

Malekulans intercepted Osa as she ran toward the trail. They dragged her to a clearing overlooking the water. Suddenly, the drums stilled, and the Malekulans went silent. Osa noticed that Nagapate was looking down the hill toward the ocean, where a British patrol boat was approaching the island.

"Man-o-war—Man-o-war—Man-o-war!" Martin yelled and pointed to the boat, implying that the British had come to rescue them.

Nagapate glowered at Martin. He ordered the Malekulans to release Osa and Martin. The tribe withdrew into the jungle.

Osa ran toward the trail, but Martin caught her and slowed her. They walked to the trailhead. When the tribe was out of sight, they raced down the steep ridge and into the jungle.

Illustration 5. Osa Johnson and Nagapate (1916)

Osa later recalled, "Cane grass slapped at our faces. We fell and scrambled up again more times than I could count. In places, there were sheer drops to the jungle below of hundreds of feet, but we never slackened for an instant. We both knew that should the gunboat leave the bay, our recapture was certain."

When they got to the clearing above the bay, they saw the gunboat retreating.

The drums started again, and Osa knew that Nagapate's men had seen the gunboat leave.

Osa recalled, "We plunged on, the increasingly rapid beat of the boo-boo drums driving us recklessly over the slimy, treacherous trail." She raced through the jungle, pushing away the vines that clutched at them like "enemy hands."

On the beach, the reflection of the sun off the sand and water almost blinded her. The deep sand slowed her pace to a slow-motion walk.

When she reached the hard-packed sand, she dashed into the water toward the boat, where the porters reached down and hauled her across onto the deck.

Osa lay panting. Slowly she raised her head and looked over the gunwale. The tribe had just reached the beach.

They had barely escaped.

Blair thought that Osa Johnson was brave, although perhaps her story did not ring completely true. Blair had never encountered cannibals, although she had dined with headhunters. Although at first they seemed frightening, Blair knew that they were just like her in most respects but had different cultural values.

Blair considered Grace Thompson Seton, who traveled to Egypt in 1922 to report on the Egyptian women's fight for equality. After interviewing women in Cairo, she set off for the desert, leaving her valuables with a hotel manager. She recalled, "The manager looked astonished and disapproving when I told him that if we are not back in a month, it would be wise to ask the American Counsel to investigate." Blair considered this to be a prudent precaution rather than a reckless endeavor.

When Grace set out with her male guide, Shehata, to witness a Bedouin feast, she discovered firsthand the difficulties Egyptian women faced in their struggle against male oppression. Grace noted, "I was absolutely dependent on this man to guide me. An expression upon the Bedouin's face told me that his thoughts were far from peaceful, that he was not concerning himself with the beauty of the night. But I was not alarmed. I had already established supremacy over the Captain of our Caravan."

Before they reached the Bedouin camp, Grace heard shouts. In the distance, she saw a veiled woman dancing. Two hundred men surrounded the dancer, clapping in time to the music. Grace recalled, "She danced faster and faster. Her gestures and postures became more provocative until she threw her veil over a handsome youth in the violently pleading circle. He instantly seized her, swung her from the ground, and carried her away, out of the circle into the night." Another woman took her place, and "the love game went on." "Frankly, it is a sex dance," Grace thought. "No one could remain unconscious of the purpose of the suggestive movements."

Shehata introduced Grace to the *emdeh,* the most important sheik of the Utad Ali tribe.

He led her to the sheik. The crowd parted respectfully.

"This is the American Lady, who is a great Sheik among women in her country."

The sheik bowed.

Grace held out her right hand to shake his hand.

"My God, Madame, what are you doing?" Shehata whispered.

The *emdeh* stepped toward Grace. "Suddenly, he seemed to tower over me and around me. I stiffened with fear."

She sought out Gameel, the donkey keeper, and asked him to take her to the women's quarters in the Bedouin camp.

He led her toward the quarters. Before they reached them, he pulled her off the path and into a ravine.

"Gameel, stop. Let go of my hand," she protested. She thought, "His blood has been stirred by the weird moonlight revelries of his people."

Gameel refused to release her hand. Grace pulled him toward the path.

"You are in a dream. Wake up, Gameel."

No reaction.

"Gameel," she said in her movie queen voice, "Go and get the donkeys. I wish to return to camp."

Gameel hesitated, as though he was trying to make a decision. Then he released Grace's hand.

They headed back to their camp. After they had ridden for about forty minutes, Grace started to feel uneasy.

Gameel laughed.

"You are alone in the desert with me. No one will hear you cry. You are miles away from camp. Only I can take you there. You will be lost—die in the desert without me."

Grace felt her stomach lurch. "He is right. He speaks the brutal truth," she thought.

She tried to look casual.

"Oh, no," she said, "George Washington knows the way home." George Washington was her horse.

"Rubbish!"

Gameel leaped off his horse and grabbed George Washington's bridle.

As Grace looked down at Gameel, she thought of a panther: "He is lithe and powerful. His black eyes flash like lightning; his nostrils quiver like a thoroughbred. To match my puny muscles with his magnificent physique is futile. I must act quickly."

"For weeks, your glorious white face has filled my heart. I cannot sleep. I cannot eat because of you. Night and day I am mad for you." His arm encircled her waist, and he swept her off of the saddle.

"Gameel, wait." She felt his breath, hot on her cheek.

"I have one weapon, and I must use it," she thought, but she did not act. "Why should I hesitate? It is a weapon I have been taught never to use upon a human being save in a matter of life and death. But I am justified in using it now."

"Gameel! Look at me! Look into my eyes." She moved her head forward until it was six inches from him. She stared at him defiantly.

Grace had studied hypnotism for several years. She later told a reporter, "When I caught his eyes, I seemed to gather some powerful force into my gaze, as a lens focuses light—and Gameel, starting back, fell prone on the sand. I commanded him to take me back, and he did, after kissing the hem of my riding cloak, and calling out that I was a goddess." Grace later recalled, "It seemed most strange to see that maddened animal with his pride in physical strength beaten." The *Baltimore Sun* quipped, "You may search through the whole book of etiquette and not find out what is the correct thing to do when a sheik* makes violent love to you on a dark night in the middle of the Egyptian desert, but Mrs. Grace Thompson Seton, author and globetrotter, has the answer. It is to hypnotize him."

Although Blair thought this technique was unlikely to succeed, she knew that Grace believed in such mysterious powers. And anthropologist Margaret Mead took a similar approach in the early 1920s when she had to recover a book of matches stolen by men from another village. In New Guinea, Margaret Mead was responsible for two hundred male workers. She recalled, "I was alone in a village where there wasn't a single white person within two day's walk. All alone and nothing but women in the village." Some strangers came by and tried to sell her beans that

* It was actually the donkey keeper, but a sheik sounds more glamorous to news reporters.

had worms in them. She rejected the men's offer to buy the beans. They left, and Margaret noticed that a box of matches was missing. She recalled, "I had to get that box of matches back. If I didn't, I would have been as good as dead. White people who let a thief go used to be killed; they had shown themselves as weak. So I stormed up to the end of the village. This was a fine exercise of sheer white supremacy, nothing else. I didn't have a gun."

Margaret walked up to the men and said, "Give me those matches back."

One of the men reached into his bag and handed her the matches. "I didn't steal them; I just took them."

Margaret was pleased with herself; she had saved herself and the tribe that stole the matches. She recalled, "Now if I had made one misstep I'd have been dead, and then the administration would have sent in a punitive expedition, and the whole tribe would have been dead." She added, "I have never been in the position of believing that I had any rights because I was white." In order to save all of their lives, Margaret had taken advantage of the villagers' perception, implanted by the colonial government, that she was superior because she was white.

Blair knew that women explorers tended to downplay the dangers of the jungle in interviews with reporters. In this respect, Blair thought that women were no different than men. Blair's ex-husband often told reporters that the jungle was safe: "A babe in a hammock is as safe as a cradled baby in a northland home." Blair recalled that in 1921, Mickie's husband, Carl, went on an expedition to hunt gorillas in Africa. There were six members of the team; four were female, and one was his secretary. Writer Mary Hastings Bradley accompanied Akeley with her husband and their five-year-old daughter merely because she wanted to see gorillas. Mary's friend was incredulous: "You're going to Africa with a gun in one hand and a baby in the other?" It seemed reckless. Mary replied, "But it isn't as mad as it sounds. Mr. Akeley has been on three previous African expeditions and would not burden the safari with a child unless it is both safe and feasible." So Mary packed a gun and crayons, and they went off to Africa. That expedition helped qualify Mary Bradley for membership in the Society.

Blair also thought of Marguerite Harrison, who had spied on Russia for the United States. Some might label a woman spy as "reckless," but it was the only way that Marguerite could obtain the credentials she needed to visit the Eastern Front during World War I. In 1915, Marguerite Harrison's husband died, leaving the thirty-six-year-old with their thirteen-year-old son and $70,000 of debt. Desperate for money, she walked into the *Baltimore Sun* office with a letter of recommendation from her brother-in-law, recently nominated the attorney general of Maryland. The newspaper hired her as assistant society editor, perhaps to curry favor with the soon-to-be attorney general. They overlooked the fact that Marguerite did not have any writing experience and did not know how to type. On her first day on the job, she couldn't figure out how to flip the desktop to reveal the typewriter.

During World War I, the *Baltimore Sun* assigned Marguerite to report on women's contributions to the war. But Marguerite wanted to visit the front. She tried to convince the *Sun* to send her to Europe as a war correspondent. The newspaper refused because she was a widow with a teenage son. Determined to report on the war, Marguerite contacted General Marlborough Churchill, the head of the Army's Military Intelligence Division, about becoming a spy, armed with a letter of introduction from her father-in-law, Churchill's friend. She noted on the application form, "I have absolute command of French and German, am very fluent and have a good accent in Italian, and speak a little Spanish. Without any trouble, I could pass as a French woman, and after a little practice, as German-Swiss. I have been to Europe fourteen times." Her interviewer told his superiors, "I have no doubt that she could readily deceive the average person. She remarked that she is fearless, full of adventure, and has an intense desire to do something for her country. She impressed me most favorably." The Army hired her, but the war ended before she was deployed. Within hours after a truce was declared, however, the Military Intelligence Division notified her that they were sending her to Europe to spy undercover as a journalist for the *Sun*.

In Moscow, Marguerite integrated herself into the political scene. She attended a lecture by Lenin and interviewed Trotsky. She recalled, "So far as possible, I made myself absolutely sexless and impersonal, partly as a measure of self-protection in an atmosphere fraught with dangers of this description, and partly, because I had a contempt for such tactics." One night, she was walking home after midnight from the Foreign Office, where she telegraphed her articles to the United States. A Russian soldier detained her and asked her name.

"Margherita Bernardovna Garrison," she replied, announcing her name in Russian.

"You are under arrest." He took her to Lubyanka Prison No. 2, which held political prisoners and spies. She was searched, fingerprinted, photographed, and thrown into a cell, where she immediately fell asleep, confident that the matter would be promptly resolved. She did not know that the Russians had been gathering information on her for a long time. She later wrote, the Russians had been "collecting bits of damning evidence…playing with me like a cat with a mouse. I had been blissfully unconscious of the fact."

The Russians gave her a way out: they would release her if she became a double agent. Marguerite later recalled, "In that moment, I renounced everything that hitherto made up my existence. I felt as though I had already died and been born into a new nightmare world." She sent covert messages to relatives telling them that she had been "caught like a rat in a trap." Marguerite reluctantly agreed to become a counterspy, and the Russians relocated her to a guesthouse and ordered her to provide them with intelligence on the foreign boarders who lived there. When Marguerite's family informed the U.S. military that Marguerite was now a double agent, officials remained confident that Marguerite was smart enough to deceive the Russians in her new role. But the Bolsheviks soon caught on and arrested her and imprisoned her again in Lubyanka.

After ten months, the Soviets released her along with several other Americans in return for food aid from the United States. Marguerite sailed to the United States, where she wrote *Marooned in Moscow*.

Blair wondered what would happen if these courageous women got together and shared their stories. She decided to find out.

Illustration 6. Marguerite Harrison with Bakhtiari Men (ca. 1924)

CHAPTER 2
A PLACE OF THEIR OWN

> *Sometimes I feel very isolated in my position. So it's very nice to go to the Society of Woman Geographers, where I can feel just one of the crowd. Where else could I meet a geographer, a sculptor, and someone who trekked across Nepal?*
>
> —ALLISON BROOKS, ARCHAEOLOGIST AND SOCIETY MEMBER

WINTER 1924–SPRING 1925
Manhattan

On a winter afternoon in 1925, Blair had tea with Marguerite Harrison. They had much in common besides exploration. Both women were writers who were anxious to develop a new narrative style. Blair was refining a unique approach to travel writing that focused on people, rather than places, and Marguerite, who was no longer a Soviet spy, was developing the art of the ethnographic documentary.

Soon they would discuss several common concerns: the media's focus on women's appearances rather than their achievements, the

Explorers Club's exclusion of women, and the need for an organization to unite women explorers. But first, they caught each other up on their latest adventures.

Marguerite had recently returned to the United States. During World War I, she met Merian Cooper, an American aviator, at a Red Cross dance in Warsaw, where he was assisting the Polish in air combat against the Russians. As a former reporter for the *New York Times,* he had much in common with Marguerite, who was working undercover for the *Baltimore Sun.* But the day after the dance, he returned to his squadron. They kept in touch.

During an airstrike, the Germans captured Cooper and held him as a prisoner of war until the war ended. In 1920, he was captured by the Russians and imprisoned in Moscow. When released, he discovered that the Russians had imprisoned Marguerite for the second time and made plans to rescue her, but before he could carry out the project, the Russians freed her.

In 1923, they met in New York. Cooper told Marguerite that he and cameraman Shorty Schoedsack were thinking about directing a travel documentary. Cooper found most travel films boring—they were mere "sightseeing tours of one tourist mecca or another." Marguerite agreed and volunteered to finance the movie. She suggested that they "do something different—something imaginative, something with a new attack."

After much research, they decided that the migration of a nomadic Bakhtiari tribe in Persia* would make a compelling story. Cooper asked Marguerite to go on the trek with them, and she agreed. He knew that he had struck gold: the nomads would be fascinating characters, the trek would be dangerous and riveting, and the film had a better chance of becoming a box office hit because it

---

* Present-day Iran.

starred a beautiful woman such as Marguerite. (Seven years later, Cooper and Schoedsack would team up with another beautiful woman, Faye Wray, to film a box office hit, *King Kong*.)

For seven weeks, they accompanied fifty thousand Bakhtiari nomads as they guided their livestock—a half million cows, horses, goats, and sheep—from the hot Persian Gulf across six mountain ranges to their winter pastures in central Persia. The film crew almost froze to death while "they filmed the breathtaking, almost unbelievable, sight of an endless river of men, women, and children—their feet bare or wrapped in rags—winding up the side of the sheer, snow-covered rock face of the 15,000-foot-high Zardeh Kuh mountain." Marguerite described the crossing of the raging Karun River, where rafts bobbed in the whirling rapids: "I piled onto the raft with half a dozen saddlebags, my own belongings, three women and five goats. We shot out of the current, whirled round and round dizzily until I had to shut my eyes to keep from falling off into the water, and at last reached the opposite bank—then a steep rocky ascent, several miles of scrambling over a rough trail, and we came out on a grassy plateau." It took a week for the entire tribe to cross the river.

Grass: A Nation's Struggle for Life was the second ethnographic film ever produced. (*Nanook of the North* was the first.) Marguerite wished that *Grass* had been more authentic. It was an epic documentary of a massive migration, but in her opinion, the editors had ruined the silent film by adding superfluous subtitles. For example, when a male nomad entered into the glacial river waters, the subtitle read, "Br-r-. This water's cold." When a young girl came on screen carrying a lamb, the caption read, "Everywhere that Mary went…" Marguerite had fought to get rid of the inane captions, but the men overruled her. She explained, "I wanted to tell the story of the migration simply and straightforwardly without overstatement or exaggeration."

Blair was also experimenting with a new approach to documenting travel. Like Marguerite, Blair believed that travelogues had "become synonymous with the trivial, the dull and the cheap." She despised purely informational books. She thought that banks, not publishers, should issue travel guides that had lots of statistics and dates: "Such books will encourage people to stay at home and raise sweet peas for diversion." Instead, publishers should print books that will "compel a reader to buy a steamship ticket." Blair believed that the travel writer must use the same creativity and techniques as historians and biographers. "Travel, after all, is biography and history and drama, never the puerile narrative of a personal incident which has given the whole species a bad name." She thought, "I can't see any reason why a travel book should be called a 'mere travel book'; nobody talks about a mere novel or a mere biography."

Blair called this new creative approach the "human travel book." First, she would decide what human interest attracted her to a country and spend months reading everything she could about the country. Then she would travel to the country, live there for months, and investigate the issue that had intrigued her, trying to keep an open mind. Finally, she would write the book in a narrative nonfiction style.

For her most recently published book, *Colombia: Land of Miracles*, Blair had traveled to learn about San Pedro Claver, the patron saint of slaves, who baptized 300,000 Africans in the 1600s before they were sold into slavery, and vowed to be "the slave of the slaves forever." She wanted to learn why a priest would baptize Africans instead of intervening to prevent their sale as slaves. For forty years, Claver had rejoiced when slave ships entered the Cartagena harbor, but when there was a lull in the slave traffic, Claver would lament. Blair wondered, "Did he not realize that he was happy only when slave ships docked?" She concluded that

Claver brushed aside the horrors of slavery as a small price to pay for the salvation of the slaves' souls: "Claver may have brushed aside the horrors of slavery, but I cannot brush them aside. My mind is not clouded by the prospect of salvation."

When she had tea with Marguerite, Blair was still smarting from Harrison Smith's review of *Colombia: Land of Miracles* in the *New York Herald,* which called attention to the fact that she was a "woman explorer." Smith had written a favorable review, but Blair was miffed when Smith wrote that Blair carried with her the "impregnable armor of a woman who expects to be treated as she treats others and who does not take advantage of her sex for extraordinary favors." Blair thought it was as futile to generalize about women and men as it was to generalize about people of all races: "The assumption that women are thus, and men are so is completely fallacious."

She wrote a letter to the editor: "I am sorry to have had Mr. Smith lay so much stress in his review on my being a 'woman traveler' and—oh, horror of horrors!—to have him call me a 'lady.' For this reason, I regret emphasis upon the sex of the author, although even while I protest, I chuckle with delight over Mr. Smith's review of my book. I also am cocky, for it is much to be 'heartily recommended' by Harrison Smith."

She probably mentioned her frustration to Marguerite.

Both Blair and Marguerite were exasperated that reporters treated female explorers differently than male explorers. In particular, they were frustrated that reporters asked them about "feminine" topics like clothing, makeup, and marriage. When a reporter for the *Sioux City Journal* titled Marguerite's story about the filming of *Grass* as *My Adventures among the Wild Persian Nomads,* Marguerite, then a forty-six-year-old widow and mother of a twenty-two-year-old son, must have cringed for so many reasons.

The article was subtitled "Out-of-the-Way Places Are a Hobby with Miss Marguerite Harrison, the Girl Explorer Who Finds Joy in the Queer Corners of the Earth." Meanwhile, an article about film producer Merian Cooper—a male—in the *Minneapolis Star* was titled "*Twice Shot Down from Clouds, and Twice Sentenced to Death, Minneapolis Boy Lives to Astonish the World with New Exploit.*"

"I am annoyed," Marguerite said, "that when I return from wandering far afield in little known countries and among primitive people, I am interviewed by a reporter who is convinced that the public would be chiefly interested in finding out whether I had used lipstick during my Persian trek." (Marguerite did carry makeup with her on treks, especially when being filmed. She admitted, "Even in prison in Russia, I clung to my pocket mirror and my last grains of face powder, and I waved my hair on bits of rags or paper. These things have always helped me keep up my morale.")

Although Blair did not apply cosmetics during treks, the press also focused on her beauty rather than her brawn. After her round-the-world pheasant expedition ended in 1911, the *Richmond Enquirer* released an article about the trip under the heading "Her Beauty Saved Husband's Life." The story was fanciful enough, but as retold by the *Buffalo Sunday Morning News* it was even more dramatic: "The charms of face and figure which earned for Mrs. Blair Beebe the reputation of being one of the most beautiful girls in Virginia recently saved her husband from death at the hands of the 'head hunters.'"* The newspaper reported that when Bornean headhunters took Will and Blair to their longhouse, supposedly to cut off their heads, Blair whipped off the veil that covered her face. Her skin dazzled in the bright sunshine, and the chief rescinded his

* This is another example of copywriters exaggerating to engage readers. Blair was a handsome woman but not "one of the most beautiful girls in Virginia."

order of execution and gave Blair a baby bear. This was far from the truth, especially as Blair had made friends with the headhunters, she did not wear a veil, and an expedition member found the bear.

Blair probably confided in Marguerite about the comfort of a good bath on a long trek. Marguerite had brought along a collapsible bathtub, and Blair would have been jealous. Marguerite said, "This I insisted upon. Our motion picture outfit was very heavy, and we had a difficult journey to make. So we couldn't take any provisions along, but I wouldn't set foot on the trail without these baths. And they were necessary, I can assure you."

Marguerite spoke of the prejudice women faced when seeking funding for expeditions. "I am quite eager to go on another trek, just as soon as I can find somebody to send me." Blair agreed. All explorers faced the obstacle of financing expeditions, but it was a particular problem for women. Blair knew that organizations were sexist and refused to finance women's teams. She still struggled with raising money for her trips.

Not only did women have difficulty getting money for expeditions, often they did not get credit for the work they did. *Grass* was a perfect example. The film officially debuted during the January 1925 annual dinner of the all-male New York Explorers Club.[†] Marguerite was peeved because, although the Explorers Club had invited Cooper to join the organization, it had rejected her because she was a woman.

Blair, too, was frustrated with the Explorers Club's exclusion of women. She told Marguerite, "Men have organizations where explorers can meet and receive help and inspiration from each other. Women need such a society." An organization could give

---

† Cooper had already unofficially debuted the film for Blair's ex-husband Will Beebe and other friends.

comradeship and intellectual companionship to women, inevitably lonely because women's global explorations "were still regarded as decided aberrations from the norm."

Marguerite agreed that when women returned from an expedition, they needed a place to meet with other women explorers. It would be a momentary reprieve from one of the most pressing difficulties they faced: isolation.

Blair firmly set down her teacup. "Look up a man explorer, and you'll find that he belongs to the Boone and Crockett Club, the Camp-Fire Club of America, the Adventurers' Club, the Explorers Club. But a woman whose interests are similar is going it alone."

"I've often thought that women ought to have such a club of our own," said Harrison.

"Let's found one!" Blair exclaimed, raising her teacup.

"An Explorers Club for women!" they cried.

They decided that its purpose would be to provide a medium of contact between geographical women.

They telephoned Gertrude Mathews Shelby and Gertrude Emerson and invited them to help plan the organization. Gertrude Mathews had traveled on an expedition to British Guiana with Blair's ex-husband, William Beebe, and was a feminist economic geographer who studied land use, cooperatives, farm credit, and natural resources. She spent her first honeymoon traveling the Mississippi River on a houseboat, studying economic conditions. After World War I, she wrote *How to Face Peace*, a practical guide on how to convert organizations that were created during the war to aid in reconstruction. She won a 1922 Ford automobile in a writing contest sponsored by the New York *Evening World*.

Gertrude was quirky; she once wrote a letter to columnist Heywood Broun about asterisks. She alluded to the use of asterisks in novels to indicate the passage of time. She noted that the punctuation mark "might have saved all the ruined heroines in the fiction universe from outrage if its various members had only warned the police in time." She surmised that asterisks were sexless but then wryly wondered how "an unsexed piece of punctuation" could multiply. Gertrude was now studying the language of the Black people of Dutch Guiana (now Surinam) and the Gullah people of South Carolina.

Gertrude Emerson was an expert on Asia. Writer Lowell Thomas described her as "90 pounds of courage" and "five feet of sheer determination, softened by humor and charm." Blair agreed: Gertrude was unflappable, and dauntless, and filled with compassion for others.

In 1921, Gertrude Emerson, the editor of *Asia Magazine*, led an expedition to Asia for the publication. En route, she heard about "a little man in India that was making a terrible chaos of everything and he was a revolutionary." This was the first time Gertrude had heard of the pacifist, civil rights leader, Mahatma Gandhi. She wrote him and asked for an interview. When they met, she explained that she wanted to live in a small village in India for a year to study rural life. Gandhi said he would find her a town. "But, I didn't want anyone to dictate to me what I was to think or feel. So I refused that and went to Lucknow." The governor of Lucknow told her that he had selected a village for her and had delivered forty thousand bricks to her property. She recalled, "Well, I had thought I was going to select my own village." When she went to the village she was stunned: "It had only 17 houses and not a single thing that you could buy in the village. No salt, no grain—nothing at all—and there were my bricks, 40,000 of them, all neatly piled up ready for me to build my house. I thought that wouldn't do at all." Instead, she selected a village near the Nepal border with fifteen hundred residents, where the villagers spent nine weeks helping her construct a house out of mud and plaster. She lived in a tent until it was done.

The villagers did not understand why Gertrude was living there. "I said that I wanted to study village life, and that did not sound very reasonable to them. So then, I became a mystery, and they invented their own explanations." Blair was not surprised at what happened next—the villagers started to visit Gertrude in her little mud house to complain of their illnesses. They figured all Westerners must know about medicine. Within a short time, she was seeing one hundred patients a day.

Blair invited Marguerite and both of the Gertrudes for tea at her apartment on a snowy afternoon. She called it their indignation meeting because they spoke of their outrage at reporters who ignored their work while they praised men's work. The women agreed to form a club and came up with a list of potential members. Blair volunteered as the Society's first secretary, and Marguerite stepped up as the treasurer. No one wanted to be president. They were all too busy. Later, Gertrude Emerson said, "We were not organizers. We were inspirers."

Blair's first task as secretary was to send letters to their peers, asking for an indication of interest in the new organization. Immediately, they received responses from three women.

A few weeks later, they met to discuss the responses. Blair reported that, by far, the most enthusiastic responder was Harriet Chalmers Adams, who lived in Washington, DC. When she was fourteen, Harriet Chalmers and her father traveled the length of California by horseback along the Sierra Nevada mountain range. She later recalled, "This wonderful journey stirred powerfully my imagination and set a thousand gypsy spirits to dancing in my blood." She married Franklin Pierce Adams a few weeks before her twenty-fifth birthday. Harriet accompanied Franklin when he got a job surveying Mexican mines. She was enchanted by the culture. A few years later, when Franklin got a job inspecting Latin American mines owned by U.S. corporations, they eagerly set a goal: they would follow the trail of Spanish conquistadors. For almost three years, they traveled throughout Central and South America, clocking forty thousand miles. A newspaper reporter joked that Harriet had "solved the age-old problem of what to do with a husband after one procures one. She continues to travel and takes him with her to look after camp things and be generally useful as a choreman."

Harriet took a long, historical view of civilization and believed that white people did not have a monopoly on greatness. As a humanitarian, Harriet wanted to "dispel many of the myths that had led to prejudice against those of Spanish descent." Currently on a quest to visit every country that had flown the flag of Spain, she was disturbed by the collapse of indigenous empires of peoples and the destruction of their cultures when conquistadors claimed South American land and people for Spain.*

When they returned to the United States, Franklin got a job in Washington, DC, as the editor of the *Pan American Union.* Harriet wrote a letter to Gilbert Grosvenor, the president of the National Geographic Society describing her travels and offering to lecture. He was enthralled with her message and invited her to give talks and write for the magazine. *National Geographic* magazine's chief editor, John Oliver La Gorce, praised Harriet as the person "whom we regard as the foremost traveler and writer in the United States. She possesses a beautiful writing style and her facts we have found to be accurate and unusual; in fact, we place every confidence in her

---

* Several other members would echo these sentiments. For example, Society member Edith Ogden Harrison would state that the aim of the Spanish invaders, "as a conquering race, was to crush out the vanquished foe and to never absorb any useful feature the latter might possess."

work." Harriet gave her first speech for the National Geographic Society and published her first article in its magazine.

Harriet was a well-received lecturer. She illustrated her speeches with colored photographic slides and frequently spoke at the National Geographic Society before crowds as large as fifteen hundred people. Her brochure claimed, "There is no greater lecturer today, man or woman, who possesses a more magnetic hold over the audience nor a greater personal charm than she." She was a petite, adorable, charming, sparkling bundle of energy, well liked by all who met her.

When riding horseback on the South American trails, Harriet wore a shorter skirt, a khaki jacket, high boots, and a sombrero. One time, in the lobby of a hotel, a bystander asked Harriet if she was in the circus. But when she was onstage, she dressed in a feminine manner: "petite, dainty, dressed in a happy combination of smartness, becoming lines and colors, and commonsense." Frances Densmore, an ethnomusicologist who would soon join the Society, commented on Harriet's lectures, "It seemed incredible that the small, charming woman, gowned in deep red velvet with a long train, could have visited such strange places."* When Harriet told a reporter that she had climbed to 19,200 feet and had nestled close to llamas on a mountain ledge during a blizzard, the reporter gasped. "This pretty woman in her Paris gown, talking under the softly shaded lights of a New York apartment, seemed to think nothing of hardships that would appall the average man."

Harriet appreciated the *National Geographic Society*'s support of her work. In 1916, she told Gilbert Grosvenor, its president, "What I would like most on earth to do is to accomplish work which would

---

* This may have been a calculated strategy to emphasize that she was a woman first and an explorer second, thus making her less threatening to the male audience members. In contrast, a male explorer did not need to maintain separate identities.

reflect glory on the National Geographic Society, which has so befriended me." Harriet frequently sought expedition funds from the National Geographic Society but was always denied, although men received money.

When it came to electing a president for the Society of Woman Geographers, the choice was obvious: Harriet Chalmers Adams. Not only did Harriet have an excellent reputation as an explorer, but she was an outspoken feminist who attracted the attention of the press. She criticized men who skulked about in "their hide-bound, exclusive little explorers' and adventurers' clubs afraid that some mere women might penetrate their sanctums of discussion." She believed that a "woman's place is anywhere she jolly well pleases to go." When a reporter asked her why men dominate exploration, Harriet claimed to be at a loss to understand the phenomenon. "I've wondered why men have so absolutely monopolized the field of exploration. I've never found my sex a hinderment; never faced a difficulty, which a woman, as well as a man, could not surmount; never felt a fear of danger; never lacked the courage to protect myself." As a war correspondent for *Harper's Magazine* during World War I, Harriet had been "in tight places and had seen harrowing things." She scoffed at the idea that women are more prone to injury than men: "That sounds like rather a stupid notion."

She was just the right person to advocate for women geographers.

When Blair contacted her about the new explorers' club, Harriet volunteered to come to New York to plan its structure. They met at Gertrude Mathews Shelby's home. First, they agreed that they wanted to attract an eclectic group of women. They decided that the name should reflect the diverse nature of its members: The Society of Woman Geographers. They settled on the term "geographers" instead of explorers because it was flexible enough to encompass explorers, scientists, anthropologists, ethnographers, writers, mountain climbers, and even ethnographic artists and musicians. As Gertrude Emerson later stated, “We all had our different fields of work—exploration. I didn’t ever call us explorers. I don’t like the word. I don’t think it fitted us at any rate. Now at the beginning, our ideas were always one of interest in the countries where we were, and we tried to submerge our Americanism and to identify ourselves as far as possible sympathetically with the civilization, the history, and the present conditions of the people among whom we were living.”

Second, they discussed membership requirements. They would limit membership to women whose “distinctive work has added to the world’s store of knowledge concerning countries on which they specialized.” The Society would not invite women who traveled as a hobby. Blair reasoned, “Women cannot merely buy a ticket and travel to some distant place and write some pleasant little book about a surface journey over already known territory. Nor can women join if they simply accompany their husband on an expedition and write a book with him: the initiative, impetus, study, and report must be the woman traveler’s alone.” Later, at Harriet’s urging, they would relax this requirement and invite travel hobbyists, who tended to be wealthy, to join as sponsors with much higher dues and no voting rights. Marguerite summed up the exclusive nature of the Society: it would include “only women who have *really* done things.” As a reporter noted, “No matter how many times a woman has circled the globe, a mere desire to adventure will not win a passport to the Society.”

Third, the purpose of the Society would primarily be social. Initially, they had two social goals. First, the Society would hold an annual banquet and invite as a speaker the “woman who has done the most interesting piece of work accomplished during the year.”

Occasional meetings would give women returning from a remote frontier—usually as the only female on the expedition—a place to network. Women could exchange experiences, learn from one another, and make new connections. Blair thought they could swap yarns and "pool lore about baggage, hotels, servants, and trails." It would offer "a comradeship among women of world-interests; however, their individual pursuits might differ." Jane Eppinga, author of *They Made Their Mark: An Illustrated History of the Society of Woman Geographers,* who is a member of the Society today, noted that the Society differed from the Explorers Club in that it focused on "building personal relationships among members, archiving the work of its membership in the society's collections, and celebrating the achievements of women." Although the New York branch of the Society quickly adopted monthly meetings, it took them seven years to host an annual dinner. Second, they would "secure dignified and suitable publicity for the Society's members." They planned, when they had sufficient funds, to publish an annual bulletin of the members' accomplishments. But like Ida Pfeiffer, who wrote *A Lady's Voyage around the World* in 1852, initially, they only hoped to be spared condemnation from men, rather than seeking praise. Later, the Society would expand its purpose to include publicizing the accomplishments of women explorers, giving medals, and granting scholarships.

Blair and the other founders set to work inviting qualified women to apply to join the Society. In the first year, three women joined; in the second, fifteen. It was easy for the founders to nominate friends, and sometimes the nominations failed because the woman did not meet the requirements. Friends who did not have the appropriate credentials often pressured the members of the executive committee to nominate them for membership. Occasionally, a less-than-qualified person would slip in. Blair was determined to maintain rigorous membership requirements, so she convinced the executive board to strengthen the eligibility rules for membership. They added two requirements: first, an explorer should not only travel to the country but should specialize in the country, and second, the explorer must have "published or produced in permanent form, a record" of her work.

Blair thought the Society could benefit from attracting more high-profile explorers, such as Alexandra David-Néel. Born in France, Alexandra had wanderlust in spades. When she was fifteen, and on vacation in Belgium, she ran away to the Netherlands before returning to her parents. At seventeen, she boarded a train bound for Switzerland and trekked through the Swiss Alps. At eighteen, she took a bicycle trip through Spain. When her father urged her to go to college, she studied voice at the Royal Conservatory in Brussels. She became a touring opera singer and traveled to French Indochina, North Africa, and the Middle East. Upon returning to France, Alexandra audited religion courses at the Sorbonne. She converted to Buddhism and traveled to India on a spiritual journey, where she visited the Dalai Lama while he was in exile. Alexandra wrote three books on her adventures and Buddhism. She was also the first Western woman to enter Lhasa, Tibet, a feat she accomplished disguised as an elderly Chinese woman. The executive committee easily approved Alexandra as a corresponding member.

Another high-profile member was twenty-six-year-old anthropologist Margaret Mead, who shocked the world by publishing *Coming of Age in Samoa*. In the book, she concluded that, unlike American adolescents, Polynesian adolescents did not go through a period of "storm and stress." She surmised that the Samoans took a casual "attitude toward sex that avoids the neuroses that develop in a more complex civilization with such an intensely developed taboo system in sex matters as the United States." Margaret concluded that the Samoans accepted the "mercy of God without the doctrine of original sin." *Coming of Age* catapulted Margaret to fame, and she became a popularizer of cultural relativism.

The founders also approved poet Muna Lee de Muñoz Marín. When Muna Lee applied for a job as a translator of French, Portuguese, and Spanish for the U.S. Secret Service in New York City, she did not speak Spanish. She confined herself to her bed and studied Spanish nonstop for three weeks to pass the test. She was disappointed when the job turned out to be censoring letters during World War I. While working in Manhattan, she met Luis Muñoz Marín, a Puerto Rican poet who offered to publish her poetry in a new bilingual magazine. They married and moved to Puerto Rico, where Muna became involved in the struggle for equal rights. After her divorce, she published an anthology of poetry from fourteen Spanish-American countries. She described the book as a "cage full of birds from every climate." Her poetry was so admired in the United States that newspapers reported on her activities and described her as a person with "an extremely vigorous mind whose speed of thinking is amazing. She is unselfish, reserved, and has a great gift of irony which she can employ to advantage in argument or in snubbing a remark. She is a spirit shining forth with a body attached. Her earthly body seems to mean so little to her that she would sit up and talk to a queen with her hands and arms covered in ink spots." The New York members of the Society cherished Muna Lee.

The founders wanted more high-profile members. Blair considered whether Annie Smith Peck met the membership requirements. She was an expert on Latin America and an accomplished mountaineer who had written three books on South America. She was one of the first women members of the Royal Geographical Society. Blair thought the seventy-five-year-old mountaineer would be a good role model for younger members.

Illustration 7. Annie Peck (Press Photo, 1911)

CHAPTER 3
GO HOME WHERE YOU BELONG!

My home is where my trunk is.

—ANNIE SMITH PECK, MOUNTAINEER AND SOCIETY MEMBER

OCTOBER 13, 1934
Manhattan

Blair stood by mountaineer Annie Peck, ready to toast her friend's eighty-fourth birthday. She was wearing an elegant black dress with a white-trimmed scoop neck. A short bob framed her face. She glanced down at Annie, who was reclining on a chaise lounge surrounded by roses and orchids. Her black hair, lightly streaked with gray, was pulled back in a bun. Several women hunched over her birthday cake, trying to light all eighty-four candles. At the head of the table, a news photographer stood behind a camera, waiting to capture the moment.

A hush descended on the dining room of the Upper West Side apartment. The candle-lighting ceremony was almost done. *Eighty-two. Eighty-three.* The tiny candles began to slide, like an avalanche, down the slopes of the white frosted cake. A toppled candle sputtered, shooting embers onto Miss Peck's dress. Blair casually reached down and brushed off the embers.

Blair reminded the assembled women of Miss Peck's late start as a mountain climber. "Miss Peck, a former college professor, started climbing mountains at 45 when most men think they're too old."

"Two years ago," Blair continued, "she strolled up Mount Madison in New Hampshire just for fun." The women applauded.

As she watched the women eating cake, Blair recalled the stories Annie had told her.

"Idiots and women!"

Seventeen-year-old Annie Smith Peck wriggled to the edge of her chair to better hear Anna E. Dickinson speak about women's rights. Annie and her father had good seats. They knew that Dickinson was popular, and they had arrived early to get the best places at the Lyceum. It was 1867, and Dickinson was speaking on this hot topic in Providence, Rhode Island.

Annie listened to the petite Dickinson, whose voice was "as clear as the tone of metal and yet with a reed-like softness." Annie found it hard to believe that Dickinson had achieved such success by age twenty-five.

> Idiots and women! They might say that this phrase is not complimentary to my own sex, but it is the law. It prescribes that people twenty-one years of age can vote if they are not criminals, paupers, idiots, or women. It is, however, only as to the latter class that the law is strictly enforced. Why should a government professing

> freedom for all, deny it to about one-half of the citizens? Why should it be stated that taxation and representation always go together, and then have women's property taxed, while she is denied representation?
>
> They say woman is incapable of making laws. But they take it for granted that she understands them and punish her if she violates them. It is said that if women vote, they will also hold offices. Well, what then?

A male spectator spoke up, and Annie turned to find the heckler.

"Would it be fine to see a woman President, and to see her at a Cabinet meeting with a little baby in her arms?"

Dickinson responded without hesitation. "If such a thing should happen, and a pure-minded, bright-eyed, clear-brained woman was in the Presidential Chair, with a little child in her arms, she would command at least as much respect from the nation as the drunken, bad, traitorous person now occupying that position."

At the reference to Andrew Johnson, the audience burst into applause. A few months later, Congress would impeach Johnson because he attempted to remove the Secretary of War in violation of the Tenure of Office Act.

Decades later, Annie would remember Dickinson not only for her speech on women's rights but for the fact that when she earned $300 ($5,200 today) a year, she "had been considered a very nice lady," but when she made $300 a night, men strongly disapproved of her. Annie made up her mind to become an independent woman, despite what men might think. She wrote to her brother, "I wish I were smart enough to lecture."

After high school, Annie attended a local teacher's college for one year and got her teaching certificate. She was dismayed when a Michigan high school offered her $700 a year ($14,000 today) to teach. She assumed that her salary would be much more: after all, her older brother, William, was offered a job as a principal for $1,100 ($22,000 today) when he graduated from Brown University.

In 1873, Annie decided to apply to the University of Michigan's baccalaureate program. Even though Michigan had opened its doors to women in 1870, Annie had to fight against the myth that education was dangerous to women. In *Sex in Education or a Fair Chance for the Girls,* a popular book during Annie's first year at Michigan, Edward H. Clarke argued that American women who went to college were endangering their ability to bear children. Studying drew energy away from a woman's reproductive system, according to Clarke. "The regimen of our schools, colleges, and social life may shut the uterine portals of the blood up, and keep poison in." Clarke predicted that by 1929, American men who wanted to have children would be forced to marry foreign women because educated American women would be barren. Annie thought Clarke's assertions were rubbish since he "never worried about women scrubbing floors or working fourteen hours a day in the home or a factory."

Annie had to convince her father and brother John that it was more important for her to go to college than return to Providence to help her mother. Her father thought that Annie, now twenty-four, was too old to attend college. John wrote to Annie, "I do not esteem it to be at all a desirable thing for you to graduate at a college." Instead, he encouraged her to study privately in Providence: "In the end, you could lay claim to a far better education than if you become a graduate of Michigan University. You have too good talents to take them to a university."

Annie responded angrily:

> Years ago I made up my mind that I should never marry and consequently that it would be desirable for me to get my living in the best possible way and to set about it as any boy would do. I do not think it is my duty to sacrifice myself, my happiness, and all prospect of distinction, to say nothing of usefulness for the very doubtful pleasure of my parents. Should I remain at home, as some people would have me, I should then be utterly unfitted for active life and should only be a burden to my brothers, useless and unhappy. If you people had read many of the recent works on the woman question, I think you would have taken broader views. 'Too good talents to give them the benefit of a collegiate education.' Dare you say that aloud? What if you applied it to a young man? Are you crazy?

Annie was a member of a new generation of feisty Victorian women and was not content to sit at home by the hearth, waiting for "her man." Instead, she was determined to make her own way in the world. Although she had dated, she did not want to be stuck at home, raising a child and keeping house. In the 1870s, it was daring for a young woman to reject the call of domesticity and set off to see the world.

But Annie got her way.

In the fall of 1874, she enrolled in the University of Michigan, where the other students treated her as an equal. Within a month, her classmates elected her as the vice-president of the class. Annie's biographer, Hannah Kimberley, surmises that the first women at Michigan were equitably treated because there were not enough of them to pose a threat to men. Annie appreciated the fact that Michigan did not treat women as "mere appendages."

After she graduated, Annie taught high school for a few years but was disappointed in her teaching assignments. She returned to Michigan for her master's degree and then continued her studies in Greece. (Annie would agree with the assessment of Margaret Mead, who would become her colleague in the Society of Woman Geographers, that higher education was a "kind of disaster insurance" in case a woman did not marry.) When she applied for a job at the University of Michigan, her favorite professor predicted that the university would not hire her for the job, even though she was "undoubtedly better qualified for the position than any young man we shall be likely to get." The equality Annie had enjoyed at the University of Michigan did not extend to her after she graduated.

Always concerned about money—a refrain that would thread its way throughout her life—Annie soon realized that if she followed in Anna Dickinson's footsteps and lectured groups of wealthy women, she could work a fraction of the time and earn more than her meager teaching salary. Soon she was making $100 per lecture. In just seven lectures, she could make as much as she could teaching college for a year. Within a year, Annie was lecturing to large crowds at the National Geographic Society, museums, and colleges. Her "very charming personality and easy conversational style" made her a speaker who was in demand. She took her audiences on imaginary trips to other countries "without the discomfort of the ocean voyage."

Soon she was crisscrossing the country on a lecture circuit, just like Dickinson. To relieve the stress of her hectic schedule, Annie turned to mountain climbing. When she ran out of material for her lectures, she approached magazines to pay her to go abroad and write an article.

The first time Annie saw the Swiss Matterhorn in 1885, she knew that she had to climb it: "When I first saw this magnificent rock towering above me, I was seized with an irresistible longing to attain its summit. It does, indeed, look rather formidable; yet, to one who has a taste for rock climbing, no other mountain seems so inviting." But she knew it was an expensive and challenging climb. She returned to the United States and practiced climbing California and New Hampshire mountains for several years while she saved up for an expedition to the Swiss Alps. When a friend found out that Annie, who was not even five-feet tall, planned to climb the Matterhorn, she wrote, "If you are determined to commit suicide, why not come home and do it in a quiet, lady-like manner?" This comment only strengthened Annie's resolve.

In 1895, Annie became the third woman to ascend the Matterhorn. She hired two guides for $50 ($1,500 today). At 3 a.m., they started for the summit by starlight. Annie recalled, "We saw nothing in the least alarming, though some persons might think it uncomfortable to be able to look down upon either side for a distance of several thousand feet. The grade was rather steep, sometimes perpendicular. But the rocks were irregular, and there was usually a fair foot- and hand-hold in the so-called 'chimneys.'" When she reached the most dangerous part of the trek, Annie found that someone had left new ropes hanging over the two hundred-yard passage. "I found this the nicest part of the climb," she recalled. "The rocks were so smooth that they would have been almost impassable without the ropes." She recalled that during the first human ascent of the Matterhorn, thirty years earlier, four of the seven climbers fell to their death on this mountain passage. Annie arrived at the summit at 9:30 a.m.

After a half hour, they began the descent. Annie wrote, "The descent is, of course, much more dangerous than the ascent. Nothing eventful happened. I allowed myself once to slide down the rope without taking pains to secure a foothold, and suddenly lost my footing altogether and swung around with my back to the face of the cliff at a point where I might have dropped as far as 4,000 feet. A pull from my guide at the rope around my waist brought me back to where I belonged. Otherwise, I made no slip in any place that counted. But thirteen people have lost their life on the Matterhorn."

Although Annie was not the first woman to scale the Matterhorn, she was the first woman to climb the mountain in knickers and without a corset. One man became inexplicably enraged when he saw Annie's unorthodox climbing outfit. He yelled, "Go home where you belong!" She wore knickerbockers, a tunic, sturdy boots, and a sage green canvas hat that tied under her chin. Reporters thought that the outfit, which defied Victorian sensibilities, was reckless. Annie thought the aspersion was ridiculous: "I dare assert that knickerbockers are not only more comfortable, but more becoming, whether to the stout or slender figure." She rejected the notion that she was reckless in her apparel or actions: "I do not do foolhardy things and take risks although people think I do. The difficulties and dangers of mountaineering are greatly overestimated by those who have no practical acquaintance with this form of athletics. All it takes is a sure foot and steady head in high places, a sound heart, strong lungs, and good nerves." Annie liked to say that she thought bicycling was more dangerous than mountain climbing because she had never suffered an injury on a climb, but she broke her kneecap the first time she tried to ride a bike.

According to the *Harrisburg Daily Independent*, not only had Annie climbed the Matterhorn, but she had surmounted the "peaks of prejudice." She had broken so many barriers that in 1897, an overly optimistic *Harrisburg* reporter claimed, "Today, there is scarcely a strictly masculine enterprise which has not a petticoat counterpart." The reporter then tempered his or her exuberance and wrote, "Is a new world opening for women or is she simply reaching beyond her sphere in a vain effort to usurp the position held by man?" Annie would have likely replied, as she did on another occasion, "Climbing is unadulterated hard labor. The only real pleasure is the satisfaction of going where no man has been before and where few can follow."

After she climbed the Matterhorn, Annie felt that perhaps she was no longer an amateur climber. She established a routine: she would research the story, climb nearby mountains, and return to the United States to write the essay, lecture, and save up for the next trip.

She began to write about her climbs. The timing was right because Annie's mother, now a widow, wrote to tell Annie that she could no longer offer her financial support. She warned Annie, "Self-denial and labor will have to be the order of the future. I suppose your Matterhorn expedition is accomplished ere this. I hope it and all of the rest will prove more satisfactory to you than it does to us." The message was clear: stop this nonsense; I can't afford to give you any money. But, as usual, Annie defied her mother's edicts. A year later, her mother died, and Annie was free to pursue her dreams, hounded only by her brothers.

In 1897, Annie planned to climb Mexico's Mount Popocatépetl, an active volcano. In anticipation of the ascent, she visited the offices of the *Sunday World* to pitch a story. No woman had reached the summit, and Annie thought it "would be a brilliant feather in the *Sunday World*'s cap to have its banner planted on that terrific peak." The editor, Arthur Brisbane, was excited about the story. In ten minutes, she negotiated the deal, and Annie "went out triumphant, with her contract and a good advance payment in her pocket."

Elizabeth Jordan, who sat in on the meeting, later recalled, "It was plain to us, and we assumed it was to her, that the nerve-racking perils of the climb would be what most interested the public, and that these must be dramatically played up in her story—if she survived to write that story." Jordan said, "As we bade her good-bye, we wondered if we would ever see her again. We even wondered—and this thought is the last to lodge in the minds of newspaper editors, whether we were justified in letting a woman take such risks." The *World* advertised the upcoming expedition, which would be featured in a Sunday supplement. To meet the deadline, Annie had to wire the photos and copy to the *World*'s office on a Thursday.

On Thursday night, Jordan was waiting at her desk. She had the background information ready but was waiting for the lead story, which was "to be Miss Peck's vivid recital of her appalling difficulties, her hair-raising perils, her final triumphant climax." When the story came in, Jordan picked it up with anticipation. Her enthusiasm soon dissipated. Peck reported that the weather was perfect, some hotel guests accompanied her on the climb, they had a picnic on the way, and a boy came along but his mother sent him home. When Annie got to the summit, "the small boy was already there: having disobeyed his mother, he found a shorter route and firmly planted himself on the top of Popocatépetl as a human banner, waving a triumphant greeting to the latecomers."

Jordan gave the story to her boss.

"You're going to fix this thing, aren't you?" Brisbane snorted.

"Of course."

Later, Jordan recalled, "I took out the picnic party, the lunch baskets, the joyous stroll up the mountainside, the pleasant camaraderie. Last of all, and with the most poignant regret, I took out the little boy on the crater. I sent Annie Peck to the top of that fiery citadel dauntless and alone. I made the *Sunday World*'s banner of triumph wave in the evening breeze."

When Annie read the article, she said, "I thought you would want the facts."

But, as contemporary writer Alice Fahs put it, "Of course, the *World* did not want mere 'facts' in its adventure pieces: it wished to create a heightened reality for its audience."

Annie decided she would give publishers exciting all-true stories. She pushed herself to climb more difficult mountains.

Her expeditions were always on a shoestring budget, with a meager allotment to hire native Alpine guides. To save money, Annie often climbed with amateurs, and sometimes with men who had never climbed before. Although she was a militant feminist, her Victorian upbringing cautioned her against traveling without a man. She rationalized that it was safer to pay English-speaking male travelers to accompany her—even though she had just met them and they had little knowledge of the area—than it was to travel alone with native guides. Annie was still, at heart, a Victorian woman when it came to choosing her traveling partners.

She failed to see the fallacy of her assumption that an incompetent white man was better than no man, and she blamed her failures on the men who accompanied her. Sometimes the blame was warranted, as when her male expedition members refused to climb Mount Sorata in Bolivia because they were afraid of being attacked by indigenous Indians. She later wrote, "To manage three men seemed beyond my power. Perhaps some of my more experienced married sisters would have done better. Rage and mortification filled my soul!" When a rumor reached America that she had climbed Mount Sorata, she told the press, "If it hadn't been for a man I should have climbed to the top of the mountain." When the reporter asked for details, Annie reiterated, "I'll tell you why I failed. It was all on account of a man."

Annie would never forget when a man let her down because it "merely confirmed the opinion of those persons who had previously regarded me as insane." Hannah Kimberley, Peck's biographer, notes that Annie "often described her male climbing companions with stereotypical female traits. They were frequently meek and afraid. They talked too much. They worried and nagged instead of aiding and assisting. And above all, they lacked the courage to get the job done." Unlike Amelia Earhart, who toned down her accomplishments to appear less of a threat, Annie publicly attacked her male companions by pointing out their inferiority. It was not an endearing trait, and she "managed to alienate almost everyone she met."

Annie left behind Mount Sorata and the cowardly men and looked for another mountain to climb. She settled on Mount Huascarán in Peru and, again, hired inexperienced male escorts. When she first spied the mountain, she was frightened: "I was filled with dismay at my own temerity in dreaming, for a moment, of its conquest. The immense glacier below the peaks was so visibly and terribly cut by a multitude of crevasses that it seemed impossible for the most skillful, much less for men wholly inexperienced, to find their way through such a maze." To her knowledge, no one had ever reached the mountain's summit. She planned to be the first.

It would take Annie four years and five attempts to defeat the mountain. As usual, men and weather thwarted her early efforts. On a 1904 reconnaissance trek, the expedition team encountered a glacier that "was so seamed with crevasses that it appeared to be more holes than ice." Her climbing partner and the barefoot porters refused to cross it. Angry, she sent her trekking mate back to Lima. She explained, "He had proved to be of no real service, declaring everything to be impossible and groaning over his discomforts; he hadn't slept, he had a headache, he couldn't eat this, he didn't like that; he was in no respect amenable to my wishes, and tiresome with his voluble protestations. He was a strong, well-meaning fellow, but more accustomed to swearing at the members of a gang of workmen than to the society of ladies. So I sent him on his way back to Lima without hinting that I thought of making a second attempt." Later, the president of the Alpine Mountain Club in Boston took her to task for this decision, saying, "I cannot sympathize with your attitude toward your companion—a mere amateur of slight experience—in being unwilling to go beyond a certain point where the risks seemed to him excessive. The position you later found yourself in would seem to show that his caution was justifiable."

After she got rid of her climbing companion, Annie approached the mountain for the second time. The climbing was difficult: "We seemed to proceed from bad to worse, yet having passed so many ugly places we were disinclined to retrace our steps, every moment, expecting that a little farther on, our difficulties would cease. Several times our valiant little leader declared that there was no way farther. Then I would advance to his side, and after carefully scanning the field point out a possible route. He would promptly agree to try it, and on we would go." Unfortunately, a snowstorm ended the climb. Although Annie wanted to continue, she begrudgingly conceded that it would be "cruel to ask the Indians, thinly clad as they were, to proceed farther; probably they would not have gone if I had asked." She quit, declaring, "If I had not accomplished all I desired, I had at least done enough to show that I was not insane in believing that I was personally capable, with proper assistance, of making the ascent of a great mountain."

Annie returned to the United States to beg for funding and go on a lecture circuit. She was determined to be the first person to ascend the mountain, then believed to be the highest in the Western hemisphere. In a speech before the Alpine Mountain Club in Boston, she said of Mount Huascarán, "To reach a higher point than anywhere man had previously stood seemed worthy of a sportsman's efforts; in a small way, like Peary's getting a degree nearer to the North Pole."

Her third attempt was in 1906. Due to logistical difficulties beyond her control, she was two months late in getting to the mountain. She hired men so unskilled that she had to show them how to assemble the tents. After she fell into an ice gully during a climb, the native porters refused to go further, telling Annie's climbing partner, "E.," that if they continued, they would turn into stone. The porters gave no further explanation, and Annie was forced to return to town. The fourth attempt was a few days later, this time with porters who were not superstitious.

The situation did not improve. The porters repeatedly refused to follow her orders, preferring, instead, to sit around and drink alcohol. Annie threatened them: "I am the one paying for the expedition, and if in future you do not obey me, you can look to someone else for pay." A few days later, E. broke away from the rest of the climbers, carrying the barometer they needed to calculate altitude. Hours later, they found him in a fifty-foot gully. Annie asked E. if he had fallen, and he said he had climbed down. The porters could not reach E. and gave up and headed back to camp. When Annie's attempts to rescue E. were unsuccessful, she returned to the camp and asked the porters to meet E. and bring him back to camp, but they again declined. At 9 p.m., E. stumbled into the base. Annie asked him for the barometer, and E. said that he had left it behind to save his life. He offered to retrieve it the next day. Annie thought, "There was nothing to be said. Of course, E.'s life was more important than the barometer, and the latter could not have been saved without the former. But it was his own fault. With such people, the task was hopeless."

The next day, E. set off to look for the barometer. While he was gone, Annie decided to take a photograph of a large crevasse. Ramos, one of the men, asked if he could be in the picture. It was easier to agree than to argue, so Annie replied, "Very well."

Ramos took off his pack and set it on the slope. When Annie turned around, she saw the rucksack sliding down the mountain while Ramos watched. "Why Ramos did not at once run forward and stop it, I cannot see, except for the old reason that they never hurry. In a moment it disappeared over the brink." Annie suggested that the porters tie Ramos and lower him into the crevasse, but Ramos was unwilling. Instead, he tied his ice pick to a rope and tried to snag the pack. But he was unsuccessful. A pair of borrowed binoculars and the fuel for the stove was in the pack.

Just then, E. returned and said that he could not find the barometer. Annie suspected that he had not looked for it. Instead, she believed that on the previous day, E. had slid down the slope and broken it. Annie had no choice but to retreat. She had no fuel, no binoculars, and no barometer.

In 1908, Annie returned to Peru for her fifth attempt. This time she hired Swiss guides, Gabriel Zumtaugwald and Rudolf Taugwalder. She hired only two porters, which proved to be a problem, as the porters had to make two trips from each camp to carry all of the supplies. She also forgot the film for her camera and sent back for it, although the porter brought the wrong film, so there could be no photographic record from the mountaintop.

They set off, but after eight hours, they had not reached the summit; the ascent would take another two hours and so Annie agreed to turn back.

When they descended, the townsfolk, who were watching them by telescope, lost sight of the team and reported them missing. The media distorted the news beyond recognition. The *Topeka State Journal* reported that one of the Alpine guides was ill: "To have deserted him would have meant his death. To attempt to carry him seemed equally sure to mean death to the other two members of the party, but the chance was taken. Hour after hour, day after day, Annie and her one strong-limbed Alpine climber struggled on."

Back in town, Annie heard that officials had reported the expedition team missing. She thought, "I am sure that my peaceful death in my native city or elsewhere would occasion far less excitement than my brief disappearance."

The expedition team needed warmer clothing for their next attempt, and so Annie had shopped for a heavy flannel cloth to sew long underwear for herself and the men. She must have laughed when she discovered that the only heavy flannel cloth available was bright pink, imaging the men in vibrant pink long underwear. She refused to spend her meager funds to hire a seamstress and so she settled comfortably in her room and sewed the long johns. After two weeks, they set out for the mountain again.

On the last ascent, they climbed for two days. During the climb, Annie asked Taugwalder to hand over her mittens, and he realized one was lost. Annie later wrote, "I was angry and alarmed at his inexcusable carelessness, but it was useless to talk." They continued toward the summit. As the crest came into sight, Annie took off her only mitten and found that her hand was almost black with frostbite. She massaged it with snow and put on a poncho to shield her hand. When they were near the apex, they tried to calculate the altitude with a hypsometer,* but the flame would not stay lit. As Annie was deciding whether to give up on the hypsometer, she saw Taugwalder returning from the direction of the summit. He told her that he had been to the top of the mountain. Annie was furious: "Once more I resolved, if ever we got down again, to give that man a piece of my mind, a large one." She turned and walked to the northern summit, disappointed in the view and with Taugwalder. When they reached the base, she could not bear to scold him, for his frostbite was so severe that it would require several amputations. One finger on his right hand, all the fingers on his left hand, and half of his left foot had to be amputated. When Annie returned to the United States, she went on a lecture tour to help cover Taugwalder's hospital expenses.

In her honor, Peru named the peak she climbed Cumbre Aña Peck. Even more impressive was her tenacity in achieving this record. Fans described Annie as a "monster of persistence." But Annie scoffed, "Persistence is worthy of note?"

Annie told the media that if, as she estimated, Mount Huascarán was twenty-four thousand feet, then "I shall have the honor of breaking the world's record for men as well as women." That, she thought, was worthy of note, not the fact that it was not until the sixth trek up the mountain that they were finally successful. Her prediction that she broke the world record raised Fanny Bullock Workman's hackles. Workman currently held the record at 23,300 feet, and she did not believe that Annie had broken her record. To prove this point, Workman paid $13,000 ($368,000

* A hypsometer determines altitude by the length of time it takes the water inside a cylinder to boil.

today) to hire three engineers to triangulate Mount Huascarán. They found it to be 21,840 feet. Triumphant, Workman held a press conference to announce that she still held the world record.

In response, Annie said, "I am not concerned as to anyone's claim as a champion. I have made no such claims myself, nor have I employed a press agent." She was, however, annoyed with Workman's implication that she did not know how to measure altitude. Annie had attempted to light the hypsometer for thirty minutes before she gave up. It would have been impossible to continue to use it without further risking the team's exposure to the cold. She also criticized Workman's expenditure for calculating the mountain's height, saying, "$13,000 seems a large sum to spend for the triangulation of a single mountain which it cost but $3,000 to climb. With $1,000 more for my expedition, I should have been able with an assistant to triangulate the peak myself."

During the press conference, Workman bragged, "I suppose you expected to see a young woman. I am not young, for I have been climbing mountains for twenty years." At forty-nine, Workman was more than a decade younger than Annie. Next, she criticized Annie's decision to climb in pants, noting, "I have never found it necessary to dispense with the skirt."

Annie was pragmatic about wearing her climbing apparel: "Men, we all know, climb in knickerbockers. Women, on the contrary, will declare that a skirt is no hindrance to their locomotion. This is obviously absurd. For a woman in difficult mountaineering to waste her strength and endanger her life with a skirt is foolish in the extreme." She encouraged women to wear a skirt "until out of sight of the hotel or beyond the path of ordinary tourists, then leave the skirt under a rock or in a mountain hut."

Male explorers also tried to diminish Annie's accomplishment by jeering at Annie's climbing outfit. She wore layers of long underwear, sweaters, knickerbockers, long socks, boots, mittens, a fuzzy scarf, and an Eskimo suit borrowed from the American Museum of Natural History. But her mask attracted the most attention. It was a white woolen face mask with, as Annie put it, "a rather superfluous mustache painted on it."* Whenever reporters asked why she wore a mustachioed mask, Annie responded that it was the only mask she could find to protect her face from the cold. But Blair Niles, thirty years Annie's junior, who would later become Annie's friend and publicity mentor, suspected that Annie had deliberately attracted the media's attention with her mask. She would wonder whether a woman explorer could get as much attention for her accomplishments as for her clothing.

After she climbed Mount Huascarán, Annie Peck set her sights on Mount Coropuna in Peru. When she asked her brother William for funds, he refused: "I am sorry to have you at sixty years of age engage in mountain climbing. I wish you would give it up now and stay at home. I cannot lend or give you money to do what I entirely disapprove of. I hope no trouble will come to you. I dread to think of you making attempts on high mountains without Swiss guides."

Annie chose Mount Coropuna because she had read in the newspaper that Hiram Bingham (age thirty-five), an assistant professor of Latin American history at Yale, had launched the Yale Peruvian Expedition of 1911, which would begin in Cuzco, Peru, and cross the Andes Mountains (including Coropuna) to the Pacific Ocean. Bingham, the son of a poor missionary, had married the granddaughter of the founder of Tiffany & Co. As a part-time professor who made $1,000 a year ($27,300 today),

* For a picture of Annie in the mask, see https://www.granger.com/results.asp?image=0007811&itemw=4&itemf=0001&itemstep=1&itemx=1.

Bingham was looking to make a name for himself. Bingham had followed Annie's Mount Huascarán expedition with disdain. When he read that Mount Coropuna was estimated to be twenty-three thousand—higher than Annie Peck's record of 21,840—he decided to use his Peruvian expedition to climb Coropuna.

Bingham did not like women explorers, and he especially did not like Annie, who was old enough to be his grandmother and billed herself as "Queen of the Climbers." He was not about to let an old lady hold on to the record for the highest ascent in South America. As his son Alfred later wrote, "His male ego was undoubtedly offended" by such a thought. Not only would scaling Coropuna give Bingham the fame he craved, but it would "meet that aggressive female's challenge to male supremacy. The fact that he had no experience with serious mountain climbing did not deter him."

As she was getting ready to sail to Peru, Annie was interviewed by the *New York Times*. The reporter asked about women climbers. Annie responded curtly, "A woman who has done good work in the scholastic field doesn't like to be called a good woman scholar. Call her a scholar and let it go at that. Taking the figures given for Mount Huascarán by the triangulation, I have climbed 1,500 feet higher than any man in the United States. Don't call me a woman mountain climber."

In June, Annie boarded a steamer in Panama City en route to Peru. To her surprise, Bingham was on the same ship. In a letter to his wife, Bingham wrote about the chance encounter, describing Annie as a "hard-faced, sharp-tongued old maid." Bingham's son recalled, "It was easy for a male chauvinist like my father to make fun of Annie." But Annie was also at fault: she baited him when she told him that "she had been intending to climb Coropuna herself but was willing to let him accompany her." Bingham was furious.

He refused to demean himself by racing Annie up the mountain. He stuck to his itinerary. In Cuzco, he scouted out the land rumored to be the Lost City of the Incas. Within a week after his expedition arrived in Cuzco, the explorer found the lost Incan capital, Machu Picchu. It was well known to the area farmers who had cleared the terraces to plant crops. But he did not recognize it as the lost city. He returned to camp and told his colleagues about his day. The naturalist on the expedition, Harry Foote, noted in his journal for that day, "No special things to note." The next day, they moved on, and Bingham continued to search for the lost city in other regions. A week later, he began to suspect that Machu Picchu was the lost city, but then he discovered two more ruins of ancient cities, and he changed his mind.

Meanwhile, Annie headed for Coropuna. Newspapers caught wind of the unofficial mountain-climbing competition and announced that Annie had a head start in a race against Bingham to the top of Mount Coropuna. When Annie got to the foothills of Coropuna, she wrote to Bingham, ostensibly to offer him tactical information about the mountain. But it was a taunt: she claimed to have superior knowledge of the mountain because she was looking at it while Bingham was still one hundred miles away. Bingham chafed at her offer and suggested that if Annie was so intent on being a good sportsman, she could postpone her climb until he reached the summit.

On July 16, 1911, Annie ascended the eastern peak of Coropuna, where she planted a yellow and black Joan of Arc "Votes for Women" flag. Her instruments measured the elevation at almost twenty thousand feet. She knew there were higher peaks, but she was sure they were not higher than Huascarán, which she had already scaled. She thought she had won the race and headed home.

When Annie returned to the United States, throngs of

admirers greeted her. One man asked a reporter what was causing such a commotion. The reporter introduced the bystander to Annie: "This is Annie Peck, the mountain climber, who has ascended higher than any woman in the western hemisphere. Am I right, Miss Peck?"

"I would not put it that way," Annie replied. "Better say I have climbed higher than any man in the western hemisphere."

She may have recalled the words of her former porter and guide Julian: "The Senorita is neither a man nor a woman: she is a cat."

Two months later, Bingham climbed the western peak of Coropuna, which he thought was the mountain's highest peak. When they measured the summit, it was over twenty-one thousand feet. Bingham crowed with delight: he beat the old woman! He regarded the ascent as the most significant accomplishment of his expedition—more crucial than finding lost Incan cities.

Bingham had a lingering fear that he had not reached the highest peak, for he saw a neighboring peak that looked slightly higher. He took some measurements, and, according to his son, "he persuaded himself that the bothersome dome was really 250 below him." He placed a flag on the western peak.

Bingham wrote his wife, telling her that after he reached the western summit, Annie had become strangely silent. He interpreted her silence as an acknowledgment she had not scaled the mountain's highest peak: "No wonder she doesn't talk about it much."

The American Alpine Association credited Bingham with the first ascent, not Annie. In fact, neither Annie nor Bingham had reached the apex. The snowy dome that had worried Bingham was the true summit, fifty feet higher than Bingham climbed, and it was not reached until forty-one years later in 1952, by a team of male Spanish mountaineers. Although Bingham had climbed to a higher peak than Annie, he had not broken her record as the American who climbed the mountain in the Western Hemisphere then regarded as being the highest. (Fanny Bullock Workman, who was challenging Annie's record, held the highest record in the Eastern Hemisphere—about nine hundred feet higher than Annie's record.) Mount Coropuna was almost six hundred feet shorter than Mount Huascarán.

Later, when Amelia Earhart met Annie, she said, "Miss Peck would make almost anyone appear soft." And yet, climbers, porters, and other workers tended to ignore her instructions. Annie wrote, "One of the chief difficulties in a woman undertaking an expedition of this nature is that every man believes he knows better what should be done than she." This was a common assumption at the time. When Annie Peck asked Blair whether, as a married woman, she had experiences that allowed her to control an expedition team better than Annie could as a single woman, she heard a very different story. She learned that Blair embraced the idea that women could bridge the cultural divide in imperialist countries where the indigenous people distrusted the white men who had come to conquer or exploit them.

Illustration 8. Blair and Tandook (1910)

CHAPTER 4

A MERE WOMAN

Unexpected difficulties, I think, are at once the challenge and the charm of the lives of all explorers.

—OSA JOHNSON, EXPLORER, FILMMAKER, AND SOCIETY MEMBER

MAY 1911

San Francisco and New York

On May 27, 1911, Blair and Will Beebe stepped off the subway at Pennsylvania Station, completing their round-the-world pheasant expedition. The excursion had taken them through India, Ceylon (now Sri Lanka), Burma (Myanmar), China, Siam (Thailand), Malaysia, Borneo, Indonesia, Japan, and Singapore. Most of these countries were colonies of either Britain or the Netherlands or under their protection, making it easy for Will to obtain governmental assistance on his pheasant hunt. As historian Katherine McLeod notes, Will's "persistent racial categorizing," as evidenced by "the overtly racist and nationalist rhetoric of his travel writing created a way to validate labor practices of indentured servitude and below living-wage salaries" during his expeditions. The Asiatic pheasant expedition was no exception.

The trip had been funded by Anthony Kuser, a utility tycoon and president of the New Jersey Audubon Society. He had offered to underwrite an Asian expedition to collect pheasants for the New York Zoological Park (now the Bronx Zoo), where Will was curator of birds. Kuser also asked Will to bring back live pheasants for his aviary at Faircourt, his 250-acre estate in New Jersey. Kuser wanted Will to document his discoveries in a limited edition, four-volume book set, to be called *A Monograph of the Pheasants*, which would be published under the imprint of the Zoological Society at Kuser's expense. The monograph would feature large, colored plates showing pheasants painted from birds collected during the expedition.

When Will presented the idea to Blair, she was shocked that their next excursion would be to Asia, not to South America. She was still nursing a broken arm from a fall in Venezuela, where they had traveled to scout a location for a tropical research station. They had even told President Theodore Roosevelt, an explorer and amateur naturalist, about their plans for a South American field station when he invited them to visit him at the White House. Roosevelt knew of the Beebes through their book *Two Bird Lovers in Mexico* (1905) and Will's reputation as the curator of birds at the zoo. Roosevelt backed the idea and pressed it upon the zoo's executives. The zoo's executive board readily agreed, and Will and Blair had recently decided on a location in British Guiana (now Guyana). Blair was disappointed, but she knew they could not turn down the fully paid, seventeen-month expedition.

When Blair and Will returned from the pheasant trip, reporter Helen Dare interviewed them. She was particularly captivated by Blair. Dare described her as a dainty young woman who was "so exquisitely attuned to life—with little reaching tendrils of understanding going out so far that they gently touch even her remotest naked savage sister and win response." She asked Will, "How in the world can a woman be of use to a man threading his way into a jungle and its unknown dangers?"

Blair responded, "The women rule among the savage* tribes, directly or indirectly—as they do everywhere."† She smiled coyly. "And whenever I could meet them and make friends with them we were sure of the men's cooperation too. It was so essential for my husband to make friends with the natives for they were the ones who knew where the wild things were, and could show him the pheasants—or, if antagonistic, could make a journey futile, that, of course, I did everything to win their confidence."

When the *New York Times* interviewed Will and Blair in July 1911, the reporter included Will's comment that he could not have accomplished as much as he did without Blair, because she got along better with the indigenous people than he did. Will said that a diplomatic white woman did not remind the aborigines of the hordes of white men who had previously visited these countries and mocked or abused them. Will conveniently ignored the fact that he was one of the white men who made fun of the aborigines and bullied them. The reporter gave women a backhanded compliment when he said, "This tribute may well raise the value of women explorers. It is a lesson to scientists of an exploring turn of mind to choose wives who are plucky and tactful."

---

* "Savages" was not a term that Blair typically used. She preferred the term "primitive." This use of the word was probably a transcription error because the reporter used the word "savages" in her questions.

† Other explorers held this view. Carl Von Hoffman said that when he was in Rhodesia, during breakfast, a tribal chief called his wife "lazy like all women." When he returned home to the village that evening, the chief found that the women were on strike. No work had been done that day because of his insult. The women in the tribe were part of an organization called the "Society for the Protection of Women from Tyrant Husbands."

Blair recalled two incidents that shaped Will's views on imperialism and white supremacy. During a dinner in Ceylon, a British government official explained the necessity of dressing formally for dinner. He explained, "It is imperative to keep up certain standards of conduct, to make evident constantly the laws of caste which operate between an English master and a Singhalese servant. It is fatal for a white man to allow the slightest infringement upon these unwritten codes, else he loses the respect of the natives, and the foreign government which he represents becomes accordingly less powerful. If he makes any concessions to local conventions he is no longer considered a superior from a superior country, but a native, an equal."

During the trip, Blair recognized that Will began to take for granted his superiority as a white man. It was difficult to avoid falling into this trap because almost everyone he met accepted him as superior merely because he was white. For example, in Singapore, a British officer ordered people on a crowded wharf to get out of Will's way. When a Chinese man did not hear the order, a Malay trader leaned over to Will and pointed at the man: "Kick him into the water. It will help his ears."

These conversations impacted how Will treated the expedition members. He explained, "When Aladdin, our Singhalese guide, does something unselfish for our comfort—we accept it without comment, or with merely 'bagau' [good]. He makes an error in counting; he orders a rickshaw half an hour too early and I give it to him soundly, threaten him with all sorts of things which he accepts meekly." Will was afraid that if he treated Aladdin with more respect, then he would "leave him for a master whom he could respect, who verbally or physically, would kick him about."

In contrast, Blair understood that white superiority was not the result of innate supremacy, but rather was a consequence of British imperialism.

The journey had been difficult and dangerous. Like Annie, sometimes Blair encountered incompetent male guides. When that happened, however, it was Aladdin, their trusted Singhalese head porter and interpreter, who got them safely to camp. In Blair's opinion, Aladdin was more valuable than a British guide.

When they reached Fort Sadon, the last British outpost in Upper Burma, a border dispute between Burma and China was brewing. The conflict resulted from clashing perspectives of the British Burmese government and the Chinese Qing Dynasty. The British claimed the right to the region based on immutable geographic features such as mountains and rivers. In contrast, the Chinese claimed ownership based on sovereignty over Burmese tribes whose members had been acculturated into the traditions of the indigenous Chinese clans who lived near the border. The local Tusi (the Chinese chieftain) recently had ordered Burmese villagers to pay lapsed taxes to his clan. The villagers objected and sought the intervention of the British military. Blair and Will reached Fort Sadon at the same time the British troops arrived with instructions to force the Chinese from Burma.

Government officials at Fort Sadon advised the expedition to stay clear of the border to avoid being killed: "There is no telling what the hill people will do, let alone the cruel border tribes." Blair and Will had heard similar warnings before, and yet they had safely collected many pheasants en route. Will informed British officials that he planned to proceed to Yunnan, China, where he hoped to procure eight of the remaining genera of pheasants. The officials permitted them to continue but assigned six armed Gurkhas to escort the expedition. Lieutenant Colenso volunteered to lead them to the border. But neither the Gurkhas nor the British guide would prove effective in protecting them from danger.

As they set out, British caravans passed. The expedition team pulled their horses to the side of the trail. Hundreds of mules carried munitions to the border to stop the Chinese from burning the Kachin (the hill people of Upper Burma) villages and making them their slaves. As sixteen hundred Burmese soldiers passed them on their way to the border, Blair had an inkling of the horrors of war.

They were following Lieutenant Colenso to the border in a secluded forest when they came upon a fork in the trail. The lieutenant announced, "Our way lies to the right."

Will followed him unquestioningly since the officer was familiar with the area. The Gurkhas, muleteers, and Aladdin, however, went left.

They came to a shaky log bridge spanning a stream. At the lieutenant's suggestion, Blair dismounted and walked her horse over the dilapidated bridge. While crossing, Blair's horse slipped and fell through the rotten timber and crashed into the rocky, turbulent stream. Blair, though frightened, kept her balance and did not fall. The horse landed in deep water and was not hurt, and Blair later wrote, "Had I been on his back I should certainly have been dashed to pieces!"

Without the bridge, they could not cross the raging stream, and so they retraced their steps to the fork in the trail, where the Gurkhas were patiently waiting for them. The Gurkhas told the lieutenant that he had gone the wrong way, and he became enraged. He demanded Will's horse, gave it to his orderly, and commanded him to find a Kachin and ask for directions.

The orderly returned soaking wet. His horse had fallen through another bridge.*

They continued. At the next fork in the trail, the lieutenant

---

* Fifteen years later in *Pheasant Jungles*—the book in which Will sensationalized facts most liberally—Will would claim the accident had happened to him even though he knew this to be untrue.

insisted that they veer to the right, while once again, the Gurkhas, muleteers, and Aladdin went left. The path became so dense that Blair could barely see a foot in front of her horse, and she had to press her face into its neck to avoid being slashed by thorny branches. It was 3 p.m., and she was hungry and tired. In two hours, the sun would set, and she feared they would be lost in the cold, damp, dark forest. Blair shuddered at the thought.

Just as the route became nearly impassable, they entered a valley where a Kachin was waiting for them. He excitedly waved his arms to indicate that they were going the wrong way. The Kachin ran ahead, disappearing into the jungle, then reappearing "like some elfish sprite of the hills." As she followed him, Blair noticed a piece of paper attached to a freshly cut sapling. She dismounted and read the note. It was from Aladdin. It said, "Turn to write."

They took the right trail in good spirits, optimistic that the end of their trek was near. They continued up the steep mountain trail, the horses crawling, rather than walking. Tall shoots of bamboo lashed out at them as they scrabbled up the mountain. Suddenly, on a very steep pass, Blair slid off the back of her horse. She quickly rolled out from under her horse's hooves. When she stood up, she was astonished that her glasses were unbroken and relieved that she had no bruises.

She heard someone call out, "My word! It's all right! There are our tents!" As she looked down from the mountaintop, she saw their white tents dotting the landscape below them. She rejoiced, knowing that without Aladdin's note, they would have spent a wretched, cold night in the jungle.

When they reached the camp, Aladdin rushed over to them, grinning his toothless smile, and said, "You find my *chit*? [note]. I give Kachin money show me way; more money show you. I thought you in China by this time." He laughed. Blair appreciated Aladdin's resourcefulness.

Their next stop was at a *dâk* outside of Washawng, Burma. Government rest houses called *dâks* were scattered across the Burmese countryside, each about a day's trek apart. Blair considered the *dâk* "a blessed institution" for the weary traveler. Blair thought they meant warmth when one has been chilled to the bone by biting winds, or shelter from the driving rain and hail storms. The typical *dâk* has two bedrooms and a dining room. The kitchen is in a separate building, and there are sheds and stables for the porters, horses, and pack animals. Upper Burma is sparsely populated, and its *dâks* are in the wilderness.

After they settled in the *dâk*, Blair decided to walk to the village to get to know the local Shan people. She set out bearing her "passport to friendship" (gifts of chocolate) and a camera to take pictures of her soon-to-be friends. As she approached Washawng, a villager noticed her and cried out in alarm. Instantly, the villagers scurried away. Blair watched as "women with babies strapped on their backs, toddling youngsters, aged men and women—all disappeared as fast as their respective means of locomotion permitted." She stood alone at the settlement's edge, pretending to be unfazed by the villagers' rejection and untroubled by the wild dholes barking at her feet.

In fact, she was anything but calm. She was embarrassed. Feeling dozens of eyes on her, Blair studiously took pictures of a bamboo fence, pretending that had been the sole purpose of her visit. When she had snapped enough pictures to prove this pretext, she left the village, repeatedly reminding herself not to run. Being fond of chocolates, undoubtedly she ate some of them as a consolation when she returned to the *dâk*. Later she analyzed the situation: "Naturally such tribes have their own aesthetic standards and equally naturally such standards are not ours. Complacency about one's appearance is forever destroyed by the first village that flees in terror before one's strange white spectre."

A few days later, the Kuser expedition headed for Pumkahtawng, three thousand feet above sea level, where they planned to stop for a week to hunt silver and peacock pheasants. Blair drew her horse's reins and paused to gaze at the panoramic view of the Burmese countryside. Terraces brimming with golden rice stalks cascaded down the mountain steppes and tumbled into a basin filled with scarlet rhododendron bushes. Sunlight bathed the mountainside and glistened off a distant stream. "The air tastes like wine," Blair thought; it was crisp and light with floral tones. She glanced at Will, perched on his horse, his six-foot frame dangling over its flanks, his body angular and braced for the moment—which he believed to be imminent—when his horse would turn into a mountain goat, shake him off, and scramble across a gulch on its hocks.

As Blair scanned the mountains, clouds of butterflies fluttered around her. Hundreds more carpeted the ground like a tapestry. A pale blue butterfly landed on her soft blue dress, and she wondered if the butterfly had chosen it as camouflage. She recalled the Burmese belief that butterflies (*leikpyâ*) are spirits that reside within people, yet while the owner sleeps, they wander the countryside. A person awakened when his butterfly spirit is wandering will become ill or die. If the wraith is frightened, the person will become deranged. She was careful not to harm the butterfly.

Blair observed Will as he prodded his horse, and they continued their journey, parting the cloud of butterflies. Had his horse stepped on a butterfly?

Below, Blair could see a bright orange sun parasol bobbing as the expedition's Burmese guide wound his way down the dusty trail. Sixteen mules and three Chinese muleteers followed him.

Every chance they got, the three muleteer brothers delighted in antagonizing Aladdin. When Aladdin urged them to hurry, yelling, "*Jaldi, jaldi!*" Lanoo and his brothers provoked him by leaning back and puffing lazily on their pipes. They mocked him, saying that they could not understand him; his Hindi words reminded them of a yapping dog. When the surly cook translated this taunt, Aladdin hopped in rage. His white tunic fluttered about him, and his turban miraculously remained in place as he attempted to reassert his authority.

When they arrived at the Pumkahtawng *dâk*, Blair bustled about transforming it into a home, pleased with her ability to unpack rapidly. In a letter to her parents, Blair bragged about her talent: "If you could have looked in upon us after 24 hours, you would have said, 'That family has lived there for years.'" The veranda had a stunning view of the undulating mountain ranges, culminating in the snowcapped Cangshan mountains fifty miles distant in southwestern China. Blair designated the porch as a dining room with a scenic view. She went out to the yard to gather sprays of fragrant jasmine and lavender flowers to decorate the table.

When she left the *dâk*, Will was in good spirits, demonstrating his keen sense of humor and his friendly nature. But when Blair returned, she discovered that Will had locked himself in one of the bedrooms. She called him.

No response.

She called again.

He refused to come out.

Blair was familiar with Will's moods. Usually, he was personable and charismatic, approaching each discovery with childlike wonder. But he equally valued solitude. Blair knew this trip offered him enough time alone; Will spent hours by himself stalking pheasants, writing in his journal, or skinning birds. She doubted that he needed more seclusion. She wondered if he was having a bout of anxiety. She knew that, sometimes, he panicked at the start of an expedition, overwhelmed by the responsibility and a fear of failure. But they had been traveling for ten months. She may have wondered whether the problem was that he was fulfilling his patron's dream, not his own. She understood what that felt like. Birds were interesting to her but not as fascinating as people. Asia was an intriguing continent, but not as fascinating as South America, where she and Will had traveled to find a location for a tropical research station.

Blair kept busy unpacking their belongings. She set up Will's laboratory table, which he affectionately called *Gehenna*, the Greek word for *hell.* (In college, Will's summer landlord had nicknamed his workshop in Nova Scotia "Gehenna" because of its foul smell. The name stuck.) Blair laid out specimen bottles, scientific instruments, weapons, photographic equipment, and chemicals for taxidermy. She organized Will's papers and books.

While Will was resting, Blair amused herself by reading the magazines that Will's mother had mailed to them. She imagined what their life would be like when they got home. Where would they live? She thought of her friends at home and her thoughts lingered on memories of Will's friend, Robin Niles, an attractive young man who often went to the theater with them. He was smart, wealthy, and ambitious. And here she was in the middle of the wilds of Burma with an incapacitated, despondent, and unhinged husband.

Will unexpectedly emerged from the bedroom.

"The thought of going on is impossible," he announced.

Restlessly, he paced the bungalow, spewing pessimistic and vile thoughts.

Blair, ever the optimist, tried to reason with him. She reminded him of all he had accomplished. He had already observed pheasants from each of the four subfamilies of the *Phasianidae Horsfield* (pheasant) family.* Of the sixty-six types of pheasants they hoped to collect on this journey, they would ultimately collect or observe forty-two, and already they had encountered twenty-six. Most of the remaining pheasants were in Japan and China, which they had not yet visited. They had shipped hundreds of live birds and specimens back to the zoological park, where Will worked as curator of birds. They had even sent Kapit, a sun bear cub from Borneo.

Will cut Blair off: "I hate pheasants, the jungle and all its inmates."

Blair protested. This, too, was unlikely: after all, Will had obsessed over birds since childhood, and he had been the zoo's curator of birds for ten years.

"I want to go to America, to my home as fast as possible, and never think pheasant again," he snapped.

Although Blair had experienced Will's episodic bouts of depression, this attack frightened her. It was as though the light inside him had been switched off. He could no longer see the beauty in the nature surrounding him. He was no longer passionate about birds. The thought was inconceivable to Blair. She wondered why he was feeling such panic now when they only had seven months left on their trip. She could hardly believe that this was the same man who calmly accepted her decision to hire

* Perdicinae (quail-like pheasants), Phasiananae (pheasant-like pheasants), Argusianae (argus-like pheasants), and Pavoninae (peafowl-like pheasants).

the only cook she could find in Borneo willing to go into the land of the headhunters, a cook who had poisoned six people during a bout of "moon madness" during a full moon. He had responded, "It is not necessarily logical that having poisoned six, he should harbor further ambitions."

Frantically, Will rummaged through guidebooks and papers, madly trying to figure out the shortest route home.

He became verbally abusive and more agitated.

In desperation, Blair searched her medicine kit for a tonic that would sedate Will. Even with a sedative, he slept restlessly, haunted by sleeping terrors.

The next morning, Will emerged from his seclusion. Aladdin served him breakfast but quivered and slunk away in fear when Will swore at him.

Blair kept an eye on Will. She was horrified when he picked up a revolver and put it in his mouth, threatening suicide. She pleaded with him and eventually—after moments that seemed to stretch out into eternity—he put the gun away.

The next evening, Blair heard a crash. She peeked into the bedroom and saw Will sitting on the floor, surrounded by piles of penny dreadful novels that had cascaded onto him when he blundered into a closet. She watched as he picked up one of the yellow booklets that had been abandoned by previous tenants. Blair knew Will relished the adventure stories of his youth, which had influenced him to become a naturalist. Perhaps these stories would distract him. She quietly closed the door and left.

Will later told Blair that he had read about a handsome hero who killed a baboon and shot an aborigine. The story ended abruptly just as the hero found a fair maiden who, of course, was in mortal danger. The room darkened, and Will lit a candle and searched for the next installment. He was anxious to find out what happened. He read through the night with the breathless wonder of a child.

The next morning, Will joined Blair for breakfast, still reading. He read all day, then slept. The books seemed to keep the nightmares at bay, and so he continued to read. Blair continued to worry and minister to his needs as much as he would allow. She read a few of the books, but she preferred the classics over trashy serial novels.

Days passed. One morning, Aladdin brought Will a pheasant he had trapped. Will identified and measured it. He had forgotten that he hated pheasants.

His butterfly spirit had returned.

Blair was relieved: "In his battle with the lure of the Jungle, he has undoubtedly come off the conqueror. My relief tells me how uneasy I have been."

A few days later, Blair and Will were hunting pheasants. On the dense jungle floor, the pheasants cackled—*Chirrup! Chirrup!*—as they scratched and pecked the dense jungle floor for grubs. Between jabs, they lifted their ginger-colored heads and listened for danger. Hearing none, they continued to forage for food. But one bird sensed danger. He stood erect, cocked his head, and spread his wings half-open, ready to warn the other pheasants by vibrating his pinions like a feathered drumroll.

Blair stood nearby on a path worn into the jungle by deer, tigers, and wild boar. Her pulse quickened when she heard the thrash of the pheasants. *Whirrr-whirrrrr!* The whir-wing alarm of the lone pheasant hit her like an electric jolt. She glanced at Will, who was crouched on the muddy ground, his gun ready. He signaled Blair to flush out the pheasants. She crept down the path planning to circle the pheasants, flail her arms, and drive them into Will's lair. In the distance, she heard Will. He was insistently whistling for her to drive the pheasants toward him.

But before she entered the thicket, a water buffalo and her calf appeared on the trail. The mother buffalo brandished her three-foot curved horns at Blair and charged. Blair dashed to the nearest tree. Seconds before the buffalo reached her, she jumped into the crook of a cherry tree and pulled her long skirt out of the buffalo's reach. She climbed higher, her grip slipping on the mossy branch. Her heart pounded.

As she waited for Will, she concentrated on slowing her heartbeat and steadying her breathing. Below, the water buffalo snorted and pawed at the ground. From her perch, Blair surveyed the verdant Burmese jungle looking for Will. She was confident that Will would come to her rescue: he often said that the water buffalo was more dangerous than the leopard or elephant.

But she saw no sign of him. He had heard the rustle of a pheasant, yet he seemed oblivious to a snorting, pawing thousand-pound mother buffalo protecting her calf.

Dusk descended.

The longer she waited for Will, the more frustrated Blair became with him. All of her energy—previously devoted to worrying about the water buffaloes—became directed at Will. She contemplated her current situation for what seemed to be a very long time. Perhaps she should not have accompanied Will on this round-the-world pheasant expedition. To her dismay, the expedition was leaving a trail of wounded and dead people in its wake.

She did not like the person Will had become during this trip—a man without compassion or empathy for his fellow man—a man who truly believed that he is superior to indigenous people because he is white. Or, perhaps he was the man he always had been, but now the blinders had been lifted from Blair's eyes.

Will increasingly sounded more like his boss, William Hornaday. Four years earlier, ministers criticized Director Hornaday when he displayed Ota Benga, an African pygmy, in the primate cages at the New York Zoological Park. Ministers protested that the exhibition of a human being in a zoo was degrading, saying, "Only prejudice against the Negro race could explain the fact that Ota Benga was lodged in the monkey house." Hornaday erupted: "This is the most ridiculous thing I have ever heard of. Any person who criticizes a decent savage because he is in a zoological park is ridiculous."

And Will's other "boss," Madison Grant, was just as bad. He hated Jewish people.* It was just this type of prejudice and lack of compassion that Blair wanted to prevent.

Stuck in the cherry tree, Blair scanned the jungle for Will.

There was no sign of him.

The water buffalo and her calf stood guard at the bottom of the tree.

She thought of the way that Will stereotyped people. He had made fun of Walter Rothschild, who owned the third largest collection of bird skins in England, with 203,000 bird skins: "Rothschild is genial and cordial: a strange contrast of porcine build, about 350 lbs, interested in naming the most delicate of tiny moths! He is of Hebraic extraction and has his race's love of acquisitiveness." Back home, he referred to Black people as "niggers." With a few exceptions, he treated his hired help as inferior.

In contrast, Blair loved to meet people in their native lands,

---

* Grant stridently defended white supremacy employing the pseudoscience of eugenics. In 1916, he wrote *The Passing of the Great Race: Or, The Racial Basis of European History*.

especially aboriginal people: "Here is living history. I thought that this was how people lived in a distant age. Their dress, habits, customs, described in the school textbooks are here, before my eyes. I am fascinated by this primitive way of living here in the twentieth century."

Will, however, did not share this outlook. He assumed that people who could not speak English were inferior, even though English was not their native language. Blair recalled their expedition to Mexico in 1904. She had invited an old Aztec man to lunch every day when he shepherded his few scraggly cows past their camp to feed on the fresh grass and drink from the stream. The elderly man did not speak Spanish. Will delighted in imitating the man's words, assuring Blair that the man's greeting was "ping-pong racket." Each day, Will would eagerly greet him: "Ping-pong racket!" The man would reply joyfully and launch into an undecipherable monologue. Will responded to the man's constant yammering with German and Latin phrases, the multiplication table, or folktales. He pitied "this poor ignorant man, whose speech was that of long-gone centuries." Blair gave the man trinkets and spare change, perhaps embarrassed at the way Will made fun of him.

Another day, two curious Mexican children approached the campsite as Blair and Will were eating breakfast. Blair offered them food. The children stuffed themselves with so much food that Will feared that they would not survive their meal. While they were ravenously eating, a brusque Mexican man rode up to the camp on his horse, armed with guns and knives. Will thought he was a bandit, but Blair recognized him as the children's father. The man thanked Blair for feeding the children by helping Will find some birds that had been hard to locate. This scenario had been repeated throughout their marriage: Will would worry about the dangers that strangers might present, and Blair would win them over with kindness.

From the cherry tree, Blair saw Will in the distance. He was absorbed in some task. *He had simply forgotten all about her.*

An eight-year-old Burmese boy emerged from the dense, dark jungle and passed Will. The boy saw Blair's plight and ran over to her. Blair marveled as the mother buffalo allowed the boy to jump on her back. The buffalo, which had posed such grave danger to Blair, became docile in the hands of its master, an urchin. He rode away, and the calf trailed behind them. (Later, Will told a reporter that he was sick with fear when the water buffaloes trapped Blair.)

As she stared at Will, Blair felt like she was waking from a dream. It was as though someone had lifted a veil from her eyes. She did not want to be like the water buffalo, silently obeying her master—following Will's ornithological dream rather than her own. She would rather be in Latin America, where she felt she belonged, studying the rich cultural heritage of its people. The pheasant expedition had made it clear that Blair's interest in humanity had taken a backseat to Will's interest in birds.

Unlike the native Burmese, who accepted their fate, convinced they had little control over their destiny, Blair believed that fate provided her with the raw materials with which to weave the tapestry of her life. As a female explorer in a male-dominated profession, she had overcome many obstacles. She had lived among marginalized and subjugated people and had empathy for them. Now, Blair perceived that she could use these raw materials, these experiences, emotions, and callings, to sculpt her future. She realized that she could weave a new pattern for her life. By studying people and places that resonated with her, Blair could allay her insatiable fascination with other cultures. By writing about diverse people and how they have been misunderstood and exploited, she could model tolerance and encourage empathy in others.

As she climbed down the tree, steadfast in her decision to control her destiny, Blair's thoughts drifted to Will's friend, Robin Niles. Robin had many of the qualities that she loved in Will, but he was much more stable—financially and psychologically—and so much younger and more attractive.

Blair escaped Pumkahtawng without the threat of physical harm. She would not be able to make the same claim when they reached the border.

The expedition continued to the Sansi Gorge near the Burmese village of Sin-Ma-How, six miles from the Chinese border. It was the type of territory that the Chinese were trying to reclaim. Will was on edge. He wrote his expedition financier, Anthony Kuser, "We know that a most cruel death would overtake us if we went on, for we are at the boundary and our faithful soldiers will not go further with us, and we will be at the mercy of the yellow men—clever only in the ingenuity of the torture which they plan and execute on innocent travelers. Do you wonder that the more I see of men, the more I love birds?"

That night while Blair and Will slept, the Kachin hill people erected shrines around their tent to protect them from evil spirits called *nats*. The Burmese had feared *nats* for centuries; the most important *nats* are the spirits of thirty-seven enemies of kings whose violent deaths prevented reincarnation, but ordinary people, too, can become *nats*. They rule the skies, the water, and the mountains. Each tree has its own *nat*, as does each field and each village.

The Burmese live in perpetual dread of *nats* because, at night, the *nats* wander the trails looking for havoc to wreak. A Kachin explained, "We worship them only that we might be left alone." A *nat* will seek revenge if the villagers withhold their sacrifices or desecrate the shrines (knowingly or unknowingly) or simply because the *nat* whimsically decides to make trouble. Kachins spend their days trying to stay on the right side of the *nats* so that no bad luck will befall them. To prevent catastrophe and illness, they place offerings on *nat* shrines. Kachins erect these altars (which look like tiny bamboo chaise lounges on stilts) around the village to give the demonic *nats* a comfortable place to rest at night so they will stay put and not cause havoc. Blair treated the altars with respect, but Will, tempting fate, claimed they were useful as towel racks. He said that the shrines looked like "a topsy-turvy forest of music racks, deserted in wild confusion by the sudden flight of some insane orchestra."

To appease any inadvertently offended *nats*—for no Kachin would purposefully offend a *nat*—the Kachins hung eggs from the eaves of their thatched-roof houses. They also mounted sacrificial heads of animals on posts. One evening, after dinner, a local Kachin boy who helped Will hunt pheasants explained his nightly ritual. Blair listened with interest.

"I empty food and drink on the ground, so that the *nats* might be well fed and strong to fight out their quarrels among themselves and have no time to go meddling in the affairs of those who would sleep in peace."

Will replied, "Have you ever thought that you might be making them stronger and more capable of harming you?" Blair must have cringed, knowing that Will was intentionally stirring up trouble, much like a *nat*. Behind their backs, Will called the Kachin people "the most degraded creatures I have ever seen, filthy horrible rags for dress, living on anything, seeming half-witted, afraid of everything, and living only as pigs would live."

The Kachin boy became overwrought.

Remorseful, Will suggested, "A used bowl might be sufficient sacrifice at the shrine, since it symbolizes the rice, which is both expensive and scarce, and a few feathers would imply the flesh of the fowl which you ate."

The boy did not welcome the suggestion to the centuries-old *nat* problem.

Sometimes Blair felt unwelcome near the Chinese border. When boulders rolled down the sides of the mountain into their campground, she suspected foul play. One rock landed just ten feet from their tent. Will told Blair that when he was away from the camp, a bandit had rolled two large rocks down a steep slope at him: "I managed to fire my pistol, and that frightened him."

One night while they were lying on their cots in the tent, they heard a whooshing sound followed by a thud against the tent canvas.

"Did you hear that?" Will asked.

"It sounded just like an arrow shot from a crossbow!" Blair was familiar with the sound because she had recently learned how to use a crossbow.

They heard the sentry walk around their tent to check out the sound. Nothing happened, and they fell back asleep. Blair's philosophy was to trust the future, and she refused to worry needlessly about things she could not control. This philosophy, she believed, was necessary to stay sane during expeditions, especially as Will was prone to worry, mostly about finances, personal insults, and mutiny.

Each night, for three successive nights, they awoke when arrows bit into their tent. Each morning, they found arrows sticking out of their tent or lying nearby. Will told Blair that he thought the arrows were poisoned, reminding her that the local

Chinese chief had pantomimed the hill people rubbing their arrows in aconite, a poison derived from a local flower. Blair and Will decided the arrows probably were from a bandit on the trail.

As the expedition's medic, Blair was keeping an eye on 17-year-old Lanoo, one of the mischievous muleteers who liked to torment Aladdin. Lanoo had developed an abscess on his finger some weeks earlier, and it was not healing. Blair knew the infection was not life threatening. But Lanoo and his brothers were convinced that the ulcer was a sign that a *nat* had entered Lanoo's body. They expected him to die within three days. Each night, they rang bells to ward off the *nats*. Blair tended to Lanoo's wound. She hoped that "the medicine is stronger than his conviction that a *nat* poisoned him!"

On the fourth morning, Blair awoke to the flutelike trill of a thrush. She arose and saw Aladdin crouching outside their tent flap as he did each morning, waiting to tell them some startling piece of information, "like the scare-lines of a yellow journal. Sometimes it was the delinquencies of his enemies, the muleteers, who refused to feed the horses." At other times, it was a medical condition.

Aladdin was visibly frightened. He blurted out, "That China boy dead, sir! One horse dead, too, sir!" (In his agitation, Aladdin called Blair "sir.")

Blair rushed out of the tent. She found Lanoo sprawled on the ground, his horse laying nearby, stiff. She could see no visible cause of death, and no arrow, poisoned or not, lay nearby. Reluctantly, Blair concluded that Lanoo had been scared to death by fear of the *nat*. But that did not explain the horse's death.

Blair watched in despair as the villagers erected more nat shrines to appease the spirits that had taken Lanoo's life. She may have shuddered as she thought, "Towel racks!"

Lanoo was not the expedition's first death, nor would he be the last. In all, the excursion would claim eleven lives. Most were deaths by natural causes or accidents. But Will later confessed to killing two people during the expedition.*

Blair was overwhelmed with feelings of guilt and remorse over Lanoo's death: "It seems as though the expedition attracts death. Had we never gone a-pheasanting perhaps this would not have happened!" she wrote, referring to Lanoo's death. The Northern Burma portion of their expedition had been one of their most successful pheasant hunts in Asia. But Blair wondered whether the price they had paid for this success was too high.

On previous trips, Blair sometimes felt that she was an appendage, a "mere woman" who joined her husband's expedition. She felt this way even though Will doted on Blair and bragged about her. Perhaps it was because she helped him write books, and yet he refused to list her as a co-author. During the pheasant expedition, Blair wrote an article about their Burmese excursions. She noted that she was thankful that, on previous treks, she had performed well enough to be part of this round-the-world expedition "in spite of being labeled as a mere woman." It was a dreadful phrase, a mere woman; she had

---

* In a letter to Anthony Kuser, the sponsor of the pheasant expedition, Will wrote, without further explanation—in a statement which cries out for clarification—"I have told you how I got the splendid scarab ring which was picked out for me by M. Mspero; the first tragedy of the trip and the first man I have killed since the South American Caribe Indian of which I told you about. Blair bought a second greenish scarab..." More than fifteen years after the incident, Will would publicly confess the murder of the poisoned arrow shooter in his book *Pheasant Jungles*. Even more bizarre, he included a picture of the boy with the caption: "The evening following this photograph I shot and killed him." This candid admission of guilt dumbfounded a book reviewer: "We confess we were a little astonished at the calm way in which our author shoots at a Kachin who was said to have attacked his camp with poisoned arrows. The whole incident is recorded with the matter-of-factness and objectivity of one of the author's compatriot gunmen." It is unclear if Blair knew of the people Will said that he murdered. In *Wild Burma*, an article published by *Harper's*, Blair wrote that Lanoo's "death was the second death since we set forth on this Asiatic expedition."

never heard of a "mere man." It implied that women could never reach the level of a man. She decided that, when she got home, she would join the fight for equality in the suffrage movement.

When they retrieved their mail, Blair received some good news. Will's father sent them the *New York Sun*'s review of *Our Search for a Wilderness,* Will and Blair's book about their recent expeditions to Venezuela and Guyana to find a home for the tropical research station Will planned to create. The review was favorable, especially about Blair's contributions, which the reviewer discussed in detail. Will jokingly complained to his father, "Blair's head is swelling over the comments to her chapter." He told Kuser, "I think Blair is going to be a 50% better writer than I have ever been; taking after her grandmother who has just finished her 5th book—a novel! At 80!* Blair is a brick. She has helped me tremendously in every way." But perhaps Blair was happiest when she received praise from her grandmother: "We admired the chivalry of the senior partner in placing *first* the junior partner's name." Will had never before listed Blair as a coauthor, although he had once listed her as a chapter's author. It looked good to see her name before Will's on the first page of the book. Blair realized that she was finally getting the recognition she deserved.

As she reflected on how she had grown more confident and capable during the pheasant expedition, Blair decided to take charge of her fate. She would focus on her own writing career instead of assisting Will with his research. She would fund her own expeditions. And she would find a more suitable companion—one who was not racist, who did not rely on imperialist regimes

---

* Blair's grandmother, Sara Agnes Pryor, wrote her first book at age seventy-three. Before she died, she wrote five books.

to conduct his work, and who was not prone to anxiety and depression. She wrote to her mother-in-law and asked her to find a house on Sedgwick Avenue for her and Will.

Blair did not tell her that 23-year-old Robin Niles lived on Sedgewick Avenue.

Illustration 9. The Shooter of the Poisoned Arrows (1910)

CHAPTER 5

RENO-VATION

There was bondage in love; no one had told her that love took away freedom.

—ALICE TISDALE HOBART, AUTHOR AND SOCIETY MEMBER

MAY–AUGUST 1911

New York City

After the pheasant expedition was over, Blair and Will settled into their new home at 2291 Sedgwick Avenue in the Bronx. Robin Niles lived next door at 2265 Sedgwick, and Will's parents, Nettie and Charles Beebe, lived down the street at 2309 Sedgwick.

Blair relaxed for a short time and then wrote some articles for *Harper's Magazine*. Meanwhile, Will started working on the pheasant monograph that his patron, Anthony Kuser, had commissioned. First, he classified the 2,400 photographs that he and Blair took during the expedition. Because Will spent most of the week at the aviary on Kuser's New Jersey estate, Kuser gave Will a new car so that he could travel more easily from the Bronx to meet with him. Now a celebrity, Will spent weekends at Colonel Roosevelt's house in Long Island and Professor Osborn's estate in Connecticut. Blair often was left alone to work on her articles. She became increasingly lonely and sought out the company of her neighbor Robin.

Blair knew of Robert "Robin" Lyman Niles through Will. Robin was one of Will's earliest friends from the zoo. When he started working there, Will was twenty-one, and Robin was only fourteen. His uncle, William White Niles, was on the executive board of the Zoological Society. Robin lived with his family in University Heights, not far from the zoo, so he often visited there. As a rich, young man, Robin was impulsive. He often drove through the zoo in his car—he was an automobile fanatic—scaring the animals and earning Director Hornaday's wrath.

Robin's father, Robert Lossing Niles, was a wealthy stockbroker. His mother, Anna Cornelia Roma Lyman Niles, was born in Rome, Italy. As a young man, Robin was well connected in the social circles of the elite. He introduced Will to budding entrepreneurs who were potential patrons of the park.

Although Robin graduated magna cum laude from Harvard with a degree in architecture, his love of vehicles attracted him to mechanical engineering, specifically the transportation industry. After college, Robin traveled throughout Europe for a year. During his travels, he saw a road locomotive (similar to an eighteen-wheeler but powered by steam) in London. He thought that the manufacture of similar trucks designed to carry bricks to construction sites in the Bronx would eliminate traffic congestion and rubble at construction sites. He returned to the United States and entered business school, determined to figure out how to create a transport company that could deliver bricks across the city. In his Harvard alumni report, Robin joked that the only benefit of business school was that he now had a typewriter to write his report. But he also had designed carriage containers that could be filled with bricks at the kiln and stacked onto a flatbed truck.

After graduate school, Robin returned to live with his parents on Sedgwick Avenue. Like Will, Robin enjoyed going to the theater and often attended musicals with Will and Blair.

In June, Will told Blair that he had to return to Europe to do additional research on pheasants and to meet with his publisher. Blair and Will sublet their house for three months. Worried that Blair would become lonely while he was working long days at the museum, Will invited Robin Niles and his father to join them on the trip.

While Will was doing his research in London, he took some time off to go sightseeing with Blair and the Nileses. Robin's father left for Paris, but Robin stayed in London and escorted Blair to museums. When Will worked late, Blair and Robin dined together or went to the theater. Blair enjoyed Robin's attention. Will was so absorbed in his work that he was oblivious to the blossoming romance between Blair (now thirty-two) and Robin (age twenty-five).

In many ways, Robin was a more suitable match for Blair than Will. Like Will, Robin was smart, funny, adventurous, ambitious, and a good writer. He enjoyed traveling, but he was not prone to panic attacks and anxiety. Robin enjoyed people and was sociable. But unlike Will, he was financially stable. Will's family was middle class, perhaps upper middle class, but Robin's family was wealthy. Robin was Harvard educated and had been an excellent student. In contrast, Will did not have a degree although he studied at Columbia, where he was a mediocre student. Robin was attentive and loving. Will was sometimes affectionate and abusive at other times. Robin was kind, and Will was self-deprecating and acerbic. Robin was good-looking, while Will was gangly: "his high-domed bald head and quizzical eyes gave him the look of an alert egg." And Robin was rich and so very young. Blair realized that when she became forty, Robin would only be thirty-two, and so she decided to fib about her age.

Back in New York, Will continued to work obsessively while Blair and Robin fell in love. Blair researched divorce law. She read articles in the *New York Times* about the ease of getting a migratory divorce in Nevada, which required six months of residency and proof of one of seven grounds for divorce, including extreme cruelty. In contrast, New York had only one ground for divorce: adultery. In 1907, New York attorney William H. Schnitzer had moved to Reno to represent the growing number of New Yorkers who temporarily transferred to Reno to get a divorce. He was disbarred in Nevada after local attorneys complained that he violated the spirit of Nevada's divorce law when he advertised to out-of-staters. An article in the *New York Times* claimed that Reno's long-term residents resented the migratory residents "who come here to find easy and painless termination of marital infelicity." Only Reno's businesses, which profited from the short-term residents, were happy with the weekly influx of newcomers.

Cruelty was easy to prove in Nevada, perhaps too easy. In 1909, Lindley C. Branson, editor of Nevada's *Tonopah Daily Sun*, wrote, "Reno cruelty has a wide arc. It stretches from actual coarse brutality to the finest shades of annoyance. For instance, by a fine line of reasoning, if one's husband becomes obnoxious or tiresome or irritating, that irritation is cruelty." But others argued that society benefited from the state's lenient divorce laws. The editor of the *Reno Evening Gazette* wrote, "The law allows a mistake to be corrected, which permits sunlight to come again into a darkened, blighted life." One lawyer said, "I believe that marriage is a contract and that anyone twenty-one years old ought to be able to get out of it just about as easily as he gets into it." Nevadan Judge George A. Bartlett acknowledged that "flexible, far-visioned individuals who see life as an ever-changing, ever-progressing force" recognize that divorce is a natural and inevitable consequence of a tumultuous era.

On January 19, 1913, Blair was shocked when she read a front-page article in the *New York Times* that said that the Nevada legislature planned to lengthen the divorce residency requirement to one year. Ten days later, Blair placed her parting note to Will prominently where he would see it when he returned home. She took one last look around the room, then picked up her suitcases and headed for the train station to board the transcontinental *Divorcee Special* to Reno. She had come to Reno in time. In December, the legislature would extend the requirement to one year for all nonresidents who arrived in Reno after July 1, 1913.

On August 12, 1913, Blair fulfilled her six-month residency. Her lawyer filed a six-page complaint that alleged cruelty and indifference. He also alleged that Will was "hateful to her family and friends." This may have been boilerplate language that the lawyer used in every complaint, as it does not ring true.

When Will received the divorce papers, his attorney denied the charges, but Will did not contest the divorce petition. Perhaps Will's lawyer urged him to rebut Blair's claim that he never praised her. Will spoke with a *New York Tribune* reporter and lavishly praised Blair. He emphasized her importance on the expedition. "My wife was directly responsible for the success of my expedition. There are few women who could have done what she did on this trip, and I want the public to know she contributed fully as much as I did to the results we attained."

He did not mention that one of the reasons for his upcoming divorce was because he allegedly never praised Blair.

It appears that he also tried to rid Blair of the notion that he was insensitive to indigenous people. Yet he surely missed the mark when he told the *New York Tribune* that it is easy to get along with a native "if you realize from the start that he is a human and not an animal." Will—who had claimed that *nat* altars were suitable towel racks—incisively told the reporter, "If the native has a little shrine or idol that he venerates, take off your hat or show it some sign of reverence, which is not a difficult thing to do and which shows that you think, as you certainly should, that his religious beliefs are entitled to respect, even though they chance to be at variance with yours." He relinquished his opportunity to discard his cloak of white superiority when he told the reporter that his servants were so eager to please them that they reminded him of "splendid and faithful dogs."

Two weeks later, Judge Harwood heard the case. Blair entered the witness stand wearing dark glasses. She was not above a little theatrics if it would get her a divorce.

Her lawyer asked her to substantiate the extreme cruelty she endured during their marriage.

"My husband made me a nervous and physical wreck."

Her lawyer asked for details.

"Once he put a revolver in his mouth and threatened to shoot himself to frighten me. He also cut his throat with a razor and threw himself in a river." She said these suicide attempts had occurred between 1909 and 1912 when they were in Europe and Asia.

"For days at a time, he refused to speak to me."

Her lawyer asked why she was wearing sunglasses.

Blair explained that because their finances were tight, she

had assisted Will for six years with typing until it affected her eyesight.

"I have never regained good eyesight. When I could no longer help him, he became cruel and indifferent."

"Before we went on the pheasant expedition, Will was practically the master of his time, allowing him to thoroughly enjoy life, while I was compelled to be alone the entire time in a lonely flat with neighbors not of my own choice, and not even provided with the convenience of a telephone."

"He was very critical, jealous, and surly, humiliating me whenever another man chanced to hand me a glass of water or show me the slightest courtesy."

Judge Harwood granted the divorce on the grounds of cruelty.

The next day news of the divorce was splashed over the front pages of the *New York Tribune* and the *Reno Gazette-Journal*. Two days later, the *New York Times* announced the marital dissolution on the front page under the banner "Naturalist Was Cruel." Helen Dare, the reporter for the *San Francisco Chronicle* who had interviewed Blair and Will after the pheasant expedition, expressed her astonishment that the couple had divorced. They had been delightful when she interviewed them two years earlier. She titled her article "They Were Happy in Jungle and Came Home to Disagree."

On September 7, 1913, the nation was again astounded when newspapers announced Blair's marriage to Robin Niles. The *New York Tribune* reported the wedding as front-page news. The headline read "Mrs. Beebe Wed Again in Secret: Husband Near Neighbor." The newspaper stated that the ceremony took place on August 29, the day after the divorce, but Robin later said that their wedding was in September.

When family members refused to talk to the media, Director

Hornaday of the Zoological Park confirmed the news. The *Times* interviewed friends of the Beebes, who said, "Blair's action for divorce came as a surprise, and her quick remarriage is an equal surprise." The *Times* reported that the Niles and Beebe families are next-door neighbors. "Where Robin Niles and his bride are now is not known outside a very limited circle, and they are not talking." The paper also pointed out the age difference between Blair and Robin. Based on the Niles' maid's comment to reporters, the public speculated that they were honeymooning in Boston.

The unspoken question in the minds of the reporters was: Had Beebe loved birds better than Blair?

A week after Blair married Robin, Director Hornaday wrote to Theodore Roosevelt to update him on Will's side of the story, which the papers had ignored. "Mrs. Beebe's story of neglect and cruelty is unmitigated nonsense!" Contrary to Blair's divorce testimony, Hornaday told Roosevelt that during the marriage, Will had "constantly made the mistake of worshipping his wife *too much*, praising her *too much*, bringing her *too much* into the public eye and ascribing to her far *too much* credit for his own success in life." He claimed that the credit Will had given Blair after the expedition was "ridiculous and absurdly overdrawn."

Roosevelt immediately replied to thank Hornaday for clarifying the situation. He did not believe in divorce. Instead of divorce, Roosevelt seemed to recommend confrontation. He wrote to Hornaday, "I think that the man whose wife is taken from him by another should hold that other man to instant account."

As a newlywed, Blair's ideas about love were evolving. She realized that Will had placed her on a pedestal and loved his image of her. She wrote, "A woman would rather be loved for what she is than for something she isn't. Yet man is continually trying to clothe some particular woman's body with his own ideals, and he insists on believing in the verity of his idol, often with such tragic consequences to them both." Women, on the other hand, "want to be made love to, and they consider lovemaking to be an art, a thing worthy of study." She wanted a man who would love her, not the idea of her. Robin fit that bill.

Blair did not believe in bitter divorces. She thought that divorced couples should remain friendly. She often made characters in her books naturalists or other scientists, and in writing her books, she called upon the knowledge she learned while she was with Will, the people they had met, and the places they had traveled.

In the Victorian era, marriage was based on notions of duty. Minister Daniel Wise cautioned newlyweds, "Remember that, however unsuited to each other you may be, the irrevocable covenant has been uttered. You are bound to each other for life; and both prudence and duty command the concealment of your dislikes, and the strongest efforts to conform to each other's tastes." Marriage was patriarchal, in line with the deeply rooted American law of coverture that held that the husband and wife become one in marriage, and the husband controlled the assets. Except for small geographical pockets of divorce colonies around the country that permitted migratory divorces, in 1914 divorce was rare—less than .01 percent of Americans divorced. Yet, for members of the Society, the divorce rate was double the national average.

By 1914—the year after Blair divorced—this patriarchal attitude toward marriage was slowly starting to erode, but divorce was still a sensational, scandalous event. Future Society member Mary Austin, who described her marriage as a "pattern of male dominance and female subservience," separated from her husband in 1903 and finally filed for divorce in 1914. That same year, Gertrude Mathews divorced her husband, alleging that her husband's violent temper caused her to live in a state of constant anxiety. Anthropologist Margaret Mead married three times. She believed that Americans should "recognize that divorce is no longer a rare, socially repudiated tragedy, but the actual practice of our society." When a reporter asked Margaret why her marriages failed, she reportedly replied, "I beg your pardon, I have had three marriages and none of them was a failure." As a photographer and future Society member Margaret Bourke-White noted, "People seem to take it for granted that a woman chooses between marriage and a career as though she were the stone statue on the county courthouse, weighing one against the other in the balance of her hand. I am sure this is seldom so. Certainly, in my own case, there was no such deliberate choice. Had it not been for a red-gold ring that broke into two pieces, I would never have been a professional photographer."

Divorce was just one way that women were fighting for equality. Like Blair Niles and Annie Peck, many women explorers no longer accepted the designation of being a "mere woman." Nor were women content to simply tag along on an expedition as the wife of an explorer. They were explorers in their own right and viewed the adjective "mere" as a slight, an adjective used to keep women in their place, to reinforce the notion that a married woman was simply an appendage of her husband. Many members of the Society also found the doctrine of coverture to be unacceptable. Coverture proclaimed, "By marriage, the husband and wife are one person in law; that is, the very being or legal existence of the woman is suspended during marriage, or at least incorporated and consolidated into that of the husband, under whose wing, protection and cover she performs everything." In other words, when a woman married, she lost her status as a person, and instead was "covered" under her husband's personhood. Any legal actions she wanted to take, such as buying real estate, would have to be done in her husband's name. In response to this doctrine, which legally made them "mere," women began to campaign for suffrage.

Members of the Society took different approaches to suffrage. After her divorce, Blair was elected as one of the delegates for the lobbying group the Congressional Union for Women Suffrage. Mary Ritter Beard fought for a federal suffrage amendment, an alternative to encouraging each state to pass a suffrage act. Ellen La Motte moved to England to study the militant tactics of suffragette Emmeline Pankhurst. In the United States, Ella Riegel employed Pankhurst's radical tactics like picketing and hunger strikes.

PART 2
EARLY ADVOCATES FOR HUMAN RIGHTS

Illustration 10. Ella Riegel and Picketing Suffragists from Pennsylvania (1917)

CHAPTER 6

THE PRISON SPECIAL

Cows in India occupy the same position in society as women did in England before they got the vote. Woman was revered but not encouraged. Her life was one long obstacle race owing to the anxiety of man to put pedestals at her feet. While she was falling over the pedestals she was soothingly told that she must occupy a Place Apart—and indeed, so far Apart did her place prove to be that it was practically out of earshot. The cow in India finds her position equally lofty and tiresome. You practically never see a happy cow in India.

—STELLA BENSON, AUTHOR AND SOCIETY MEMBER

MAY 1912

New York City and Washington, DC

Ella Riegel was determined to win the vote for women. She was a proud alumna of Bryn Mawr's first graduating class, where she studied political economy under Woodrow Wilson. She cherished the college so much that when she died, she bequeathed it $45,000

($813,300 today) to establish scholarships in the department of archaeology. A leader in the Congressional Union for Woman's Suffrage and, later, the National Woman's Party, Ella would become known as an iron-jawed angel for her silent protests against the president's inertia on women's suffrage. After states ratified the Nineteenth Amendment, her attention was temporarily diverted from women's rights issues after being charged with vehicular manslaughter for running into a pedestrian who turned to wave at a friend while crossing the street. A jury found her not guilty. When asked about the verdict, Ella told a reporter, "The jury was fair but I am sorry there were no women on it."

Ella engaged in many of the same types of activities as other future members of the Society. She differed only in that she regarded her suffrage work as a full-time occupation.

Most women got their start in suffrage politics and campaigns by participating in parades. Like Annie Peck, Blair Niles, and many others, Ella probably marched with ten thousand in the New York City Suffrage Parade on May 6, 1912. Ella lived in Philadelphia, and Manhattan was a short train ride away.

The parade was organized by the Women's Political Union, under the direction of Harriot Stanton Blatch, the daughter of suffrage leader Elizabeth Cady Stanton. Harriot kept tight controls on the march. She distributed instructions: "Eyes to the front, head erect and shoulders back. Remember that the public will judge, illogically of course, but no less strictly, your qualification as a voter by your promptness." She instructed the women to wear white, preferably from Macy's, the official department store for parade attire.

At precisely 5 p.m., as the late afternoon sun shimmered off of the green at Washington Square, the women on horseback at the front of the parade signaled their horses to walk. A large banner near the front of the parade declared, "Woman suffrage has passed the stage of argument. You could not stop it if you would. And in a few years, you will be ashamed that you ever opposed it." Another banner read, "All This Is a Natural Consequence of Teaching Girls How to Read."

A reporter for the *New York Times* called it "a parade of contrasts." Women of every age and occupation marched. "There were times when fifty files of four women each would walk by in the space of sixty seconds. There were long pauses when nobody came at all, and the spectators would start to scatter to their homes until the faint sound of music far down the street gave promise of more marchers to come." Mothers pushed babies in strollers, a father held a small son's hand, young women dressed in lovely white gowns, and older women rode in carriages.

One thousand men joined the formal procession singing a marching tune. Bystanders jeered the men, yelling, "Aren't they cute? Look at the Mollycoddles." After the parade, one marcher wrote an article titled "How It Feels to Be the Husband of a Suffragette," which he dedicated to the "11,863 of you who requested me to go home and wash the dishes."

Annie Peck, then age sixty-six, walked in the two-hour march from Greenwich Village to Carnegie Hall, where representatives of the Women's Political Union gave speeches to an overflowing crowd. When the meeting was over, Annie jumped onto a chair in the lobby and waved her Joan of Arc Suffrage flag over the audience. She shouted, "This was the banner that I planted 21,000 feet above the sea on one of the highest peaks of the Andes!"

Everyone knew of Annie. One day, she went to the office of the Woman's Suffrage Party to buy tickets for an event. The ticket agent said, "I am sorry, but I have nothing left except the second gallery. Perhaps you would not care to climb as high as that."

"I don't know that I object to climbing to the second gallery. I'm Annie Peck."

The ticket agent laughed and handed her the ticket.

Annie wrote editorials for the *New York Times* that explained her reluctance to speak on behalf of all women: "The program of the woman suffragists of New York? Pardon me if I say that the question is absurd. What woman is authorized to speak for all suffragists? On one point only are we agreed: we desire the ballot. To suppose that we shall unite upon a definite program before or after obtaining the ballot in New York, is as absurd as to conceive of men doing so. We have too many men in politics who are better fitted for hoeing corn or selling ribbon than for settling the affairs of state or nation."

In March 1913, another future Society member, Ellen La Motte, then forty, joined a band of suffragists on a seventeen-day hike from Baltimore to Washington, DC, to march in the Women's Suffrage Parade. Ellen was an enigma. She grew up in Baltimore in the home of her cousin Alfred I. du Pont, of du Pont chemical fame. Although she identified herself as a radical feminist and a lesbian, ironically and to her dismay, she was simultaneously attracted to socialism and women millionaires. She was motivated, in part, to support suffrage because Baltimore judges issued decisions slanted in men's favor, even men who were sexual predators. She declared, "We want to be able to effect certain reforms, and we are prevented from doing so from lack of political power. It requires the ballot to accomplish the things that we wish." She fought for legislation on suffrage, maximum working hours, child labor, and compulsory education. She testified before Maryland's Senate Committee on Elections to promote a bill to allow tax-paying women the right to vote, which she described as "suffrage with its fangs drawn, since it admits tax-paying women only." She believed that the bill had a greater chance of passage if it limited rights to tax-paying women since they were in the minority. Legislators amended the bill to exclude Black people and then voted against the proposal.

A few weeks later, frustrated with the direction of the American suffrage movement, she traveled to Europe to study the tactics of Emmeline Pankhurst, who led the militant suffragette movement in Britain. She admired the British "women who have shaken off the conventionalities which have bound them down for years."

She was surprised that her cousin did not try to stop her from going to England, for she knew that Alfred du Pont "heartily disapproved of suffragetting and such things." She recalled Alfred's lack of response: "Not a word of objection. Not an 'Ellen, you are insane.'" When she got to London, she participated in some riots. When du Pont read about the riots, he sent her a check that said, "For Bail."

Ellen soon became a rabid suffragist. The *Baltimore Sun* reported that Ellen had "stepped over the line and become an anarchist." She wrote to a friend, "Outwardly I'm a good Socialist, and speak at meetings and all that, but inwardly I'm a free Anarchist—free—free." She was involved in four fights and one riot, not always as an innocent bystander.

Ellen was appalled when the police started arresting her friends, jailing them, and force-feeding them during hunger strikes. She told a *Sun* reporter that this caused "the rank of the suffragettes to thin until now there are not enough in England to create a proper impression. They can no longer intimidate, but, on the contrary, simply irritate the nation, and instead of winning converts to the cause of suffrage, they create the most violent opposition." Ellen slowly realized that the British suffragette fight was not her battle.

Many of the future Society members took leadership roles in the Congressional Union for Women Suffrage. In November 1915, the New York branch of the Congressional Union for Women's

Suffrage elected Blair as a delegate. A week later, she traveled to the District of Columbia with fifty other New York women to attend its national convention, which was preceded by a march for suffrage. Her friend, novelist Mary Hunter Austin, organized the parade. Twelve women on horseback led the procession down Pennsylvania Avenue holding an eighteen thousand-foot cloth suffrage petition signed by more than half a million people. After leaders gave speeches on the steps of the Capitol, the women presented their petition to Congress.

Afterward, the women walked to the White House, where Blair had visited President Roosevelt years earlier. Now, she was going to meet President Woodrow Wilson. When she arrived, the White House staff ushered Blair and the other delegates into the East Room. President Wilson listened to their pleas for suffrage at the federal level, a tactic that Mary Ritter Beard was pushing. Like Blair, Mary Ritter Beard's travels to Europe, China, and Japan to recover women's history would prompt an invitation from the Society of Woman Geographers.

Mary firmly believed that the Susan B. Anthony constitutional amendment was the only rapid means of achieving women's suffrage. Because each state had different requirements for changing the state constitution, she thought a federal amendment would be more expedient than passing laws state by state. In the 1912 presidential election, only six states had passed voting rights for women, and 1.3 million women were eligible to vote. The Congressional Union had not successfully leveraged the western women's votes to oust the Democrats, then in power. But they did send a clear signal to politicians: women's votes could influence the election.

When the delegates pressed President Wilson to pursue a federal constitutional suffrage amendment instead of state legislation, he replied, "I hope I shall always have an open mind, and I shall certainly take the greatest pleasure in conferring, in the most serious way, with my colleagues with regard to what is the right thing to do concerning this great matter." Blair left the White House encouraged.

Not content to rely on the president, who was notorious for his lukewarm interest in suffrage, the leaders of the Congressional Union organized the "Suffrage Special," a train that would travel from Washington, DC to the West Coast to rally voter support for the federal amendment, where women had the right to vote in six western states. The train held twenty-three suffrage organizers, including Ella Riegel, the campaign's business manager. Ella was responsible for the logistics of the five-week tour. A secondary purpose of the Suffrage Special was to drum up attendance at the Congressional Union's convention, scheduled for June 1916, when the leaders planned to announce the establishment of the National Woman's Party. Ella was so devoted to the Suffrage Special that, not only did she donate her time, but she contributed $1,000 ($24,000 today).

Ella had an office on board the train. While traveling across the country, the train made whistle-stops at towns to gather signatures for a new petition that they planned to present to Congress. Ella wrote, "If you Washington ladies could peep into the Suffrage Special when nine typewriters are pounding away, and Press reports and resolutions are being written, and literature being folded and counted, and membership cards listed, and the Business Manager receiving money, you would realize that this is no place for the graceful letter writer!" When they reached California, Ella noted, "My charges are busy and happy—not too much coddled—and so far no broken heads!" When they returned to the East Coast, the organizers led an automobile parade from the District of Columbia train station to the Capitol, where they presented the petition to Congress.

The Suffrage Special was a success, and so was the National Woman's Party, which only admitted women in enfranchised states. The creation of the Woman's Party allowed the Congressional Union's members to more effectively threaten to withhold, in future elections, votes from incumbents who did not support the constitutional amendment. As Florence Bayard Hilles, the Delaware state chairperson for the Congressional Union and one of the founders of the National Woman's Party, explained, "A party fears nothing but votes, and up to the time of the last presidential election there were not enough votes of women to frighten politicians." But by the 1916 election, women could vote in eleven western states and had the potential to control a fifth of the electoral votes. Doris Stevens,* a friend of Mary Ritter Beard and Ella Riegel, noted, "For the first time in history, women came together to organize their political power into a party to free their own sex. For the first time in history, representatives of the men's political parties came to plead before these women voters for the support of their respective parties." The National Woman's Party was determined to punish politically any party in power which did not use its power to free women. This allowed women to morph into a powerful political faction.

Women began to lobby legislators on suffrage. Blair and Annie called on U.S. congressmen in their New York offices and threatened to withhold women's votes from those who did not support women's suffrage, while Mary Ritter Beard paid them visits on Capitol Hill. Mary warned legislators, if they did not support a federal amendment, then women voters in the eleven states would vote for members of the Progressive Party instead of the incumbents.

---

* Unlike most of the other women mentioned, Doris Stevens and Florence Bayard Hilles were not members of the Society.

This strategy proved effective in the next election. The Democratic Party caved in to the Congressional Union's demands and announced that it would encourage states to give women the right to vote. This placed pressure on the candidates to address federal suffrage in their campaign speeches, even though they wanted to avoid the topic. As a result, President Wilson lost support: in the 1912 election, Wilson won sixty-nine electoral votes from suffrage states; in 1916, he got fifty-seven. The impact of women on the election was so obvious that no one ever seriously questioned the Congressional Union's claim that women had cost many of the congressmen their seats.

In January 1917, Ella Riegel and other members of the National Woman's Party began to employ the militant tactics of British suffragette Emmeline Pankhurst. Ella became a "silent sentinel" and picketed the White House. She told a newspaper reporter that she was only carrying out the principles she learned when she studied political economy at Bryn Mawr with Woodrow Wilson: "President Wilson instructed us that legislation depended upon the party in power, so I know he will be glad to see me on picket duty to prod Democrats to favorable action on the suffrage amendment."

At first, newspapers covered the picketing objectively, but when reporters realized that the women planned to picket every day until Congress passed the amendment, their reports became scathing. Critics called the protesters silly, unsexed, crazy, shameless, and pathological. Bypassers encouraged the picketers to keep up the protest. "I certainly admire your pluck—stick to it and you will get it," said an observer. Supporters brought the picketers mittens, hot bricks to stand on, hot coffee, and coats to ward off the bitter wind. A veteran told the picketers, "I've done sentinel duty in my time. I know what it is. And now it's your turn. You young folks have the strength and courage to keep it up. You are going to put it through."*

In April 1917, Congress voted to enter World War I in support of the Allies. Women were outraged. Why was Congress so willing to shed blood for democracy in Europe when it refused to grant equal rights to women at home?

In June, the president hosted Russian diplomats. Picketers held signs at the front of the White House: "President Wilson is deceiving Russia when he says 'We are a democracy.'" A large crowd gathered around the picketers. Doris Stevens, a lead organizer for the Congressional Union, recalled, "Of course it was embarrassing. We meant it to be. This was no time for manners." White House staffers met to decide how to react to this affront. They told the chief of police to order the National Woman's Party to stop picketing.

Alice Paul, the leader of the National Woman's Party, responded, "We have picketed for six months without interference. Has the law been changed?"

"No, but you must stop it."

"But we have consulted our lawyers and know we have a legal right to picket."

"I warn you: you will be arrested if you attempt to picket again."

The next day, two picketers showed up, and police arrested them before a large crowd gathered to be entertained by the protesters.

At the police station, the women asked what crime they had committed, but the officers who booked them were confused because picketing was not a crime. They consulted with their superiors. Doris Stevens recalled, "Doors opened and closed

---

* Not all the future members of the Society endorsed the picketing. Grace Thompson Seton, president of the Connecticut Woman Suffrage Association, resigned in protest against picketing.

mysteriously. Whispered conversations were heard. The book on rules and regulations was hopefully thumbed. Hours passed." Finally, the police charged the women with obstructing traffic. They released the protesters and dropped the charges.

Over the next week, the police would arrest twenty-seven women for picketing. Most were released. Those booked were shipped off to jail for the weekend. Among the women jailed were Anne Martin, Doris Stevens, Florence Bayard Hilles, and Matilda Gardner.† Anne Martin, a feminist and former history professor who studied militant suffragette tactics in England, had returned to Nevada to wage a successful suffrage campaign. Suffrage organizer Doris Stevens was a radical feminist who had graduated as a music major from Oberlin College six years earlier. Like Doris Stevens, she believed in militant tactics. Florence Bayard Hilles, a blue blood from Delaware, sported a suffragist tattoo on her arm. Before her arrest, she heckled the president by shouting, "What will you do for woman suffrage?" Matilda Gardner of Washington, DC, was a member of the executive committee of the National Woman's Party. She challenged a correspondent for the *New York Evening Post* who likened picketing to nagging the president by asking, "Is the President not wholeheartedly for that kind of democracy which recognizes women as people?"

On Monday, the judge held a hearing. Defendants Anne Martin and Doris Stevens acted as the attorneys for the prisoners. Anne explained the defense's position. "We were petitioning the President of the United States, for a redress of grievances; we are asking him to use his great power to secure passage of the national suffrage amendment. As long as the government prefers to send

† None of these women would become members of the Society, but they would later protest prison conditions with Ella Riegel.

women to jail on petty and technical charges, we will go to jail. We believe, your Honor, that the wrong persons are before the bar in this court."

The district attorney interrupted her: "I object, your Honor, to this woman making such a statement."

Defendant Florence Bayard Hilles rose to speak.

"This court has not proven that I obstructed traffic. During the months of January, February, March, April, and May, picketing was legal. In June, it suddenly became illegal."

Matilda Gardner spoke next.

"I submit that these arrests are purely political. We have been carrying on activities of a distinctly political nature, and these political activities have seemingly disturbed certain powerful influence."

Finally, Doris Stevens rose.

"We say to you, this outrageous policy of stupid and brutal punishment will not dampen the ardor of the women. Where sixteen of us face your judgment today, there will be sixty tomorrow, so great will be the indignation of our colleagues in this fight."

After two days of testimony, the trial concluded.

The judge rendered his decision: sixty days in a work prison or a $25 fine.

The women chose prison. They were sent to the Occoquan Workhouse in Virginia.

In anticipation of the women's sentences, the prison had transferred some of the Black prisoners to the "white section." When the picketers arrived, the guards placed them in cells with the Black women, hoping it would provoke the women. Doris Stevens said, "Not that we shrank from these women on account of their color, but how terrible to know that the institution had gone out of its way to try to humiliate us. But prison must be made so unbearable that no more women would face it. That was the policy attempted here."

Three days later, the president pardoned the picketers. As the suffragists were leaving, the prison warden warned, "The next lot of women who come here won't be treated with the same consideration."

Picketing resumed, but the police did not arrest the picketers. Stevens recalled, "Our fight was becoming increasingly difficult—I might almost say desperate. Here we were, a band of women fighting with banners, in the midst of a world armed to the teeth." The fact that the president was hypocritical in sending men to fight for democracy abroad while denying equality at home was lost on the administration. As the suffragists became more militant, the public became more violent.

After the United States entered World War I, servicemen regarded the continued picketing as unpatriotic, especially when Alice Paul, the founder of the National Women's Party, mocked the president by calling him "Kaiser Wilson." Two days after the "Kaiser Wilson" incident, a sailor pushed Alice Paul to the ground and dragged her across the sidewalk as he tried to tear off her suffrage sash. Soldiers attacked several other women. When a soldier knocked down future Society member Ellen La Motte's suffrage poster, she acerbically said, "He does not object to militancy when it involves wearing a uniform and 'being paid for taking a human life.' Yet he objects to the militancy of a guerrilla type, practiced by women" who are merely seeking equality.

The next day, the police joined in the attack.

The protests continued for a year and a half. After languishing in committee for years, the suffrage bill was reintroduced during a new congressional session. To assuage the protesters, President Wilson announced that he supported a federal amendment. The House passed the bill, and the Senate introduced a companion proposal. The bill lacked two votes to pass in the Senate.

The Congressional Union decided to ramp up their protests by burning effigies of the president in a cauldron at the picket site. In February 1919, on the night before the U.S. Senate met to vote again on the federal amendment—now only lacking one vote—Ella and Louisine Havemeyer,* the 63-year-old widow of a sugar trust king, a wealthy art collector, and a member of the Woman's Party, lead seventy-three picketers from the suffragist headquarters to the White House gates. Louisine was "an odd combination of self-assurance and naiveté." Twenty years earlier, when she signed a suffrage petition, she said, "I thought I would have my franchise by return mail."

At the front of the procession, Louisine carried the American flag, and Ella held the Congressional Union's purple and gold flag. Ella watched Louisine as they approached the White House. It was Louisine's first picket, and she was nervous. Alice Paul had asked Louisine to head the picket line because, as a wealthy, law-abiding citizen, her arrest would attract the media's attention. She told Louisine that to garner public support, she had to be arrested. The blue-blooded New Yorker was opposed to militant tactics: "No picketing and no prison for me. I don't like the thought of either one." Louisine once said, "I have often wondered what would have happened if there had been picketers in Egypt. We know that Pharaoh was visited by every plague under the sun, but history doesn't relate whether picketers were among them." But she had finally conceded.

Ella probably knew that Louisine was reluctant to do anything that might land her in jail. She watched as the last group of the picketers arrived, carrying a large clay urn, kerosene-soaked logs, and a two-foot paper effigy of Wilson. The fire was lit. A protester placed

* Louisine was not a future Society member.

the effigy into the fiery urn, and it burst into flames. The crowd of one thousand roared. Police immediately extinguished the fire.

Alice Paul handed Louisine paper parcels and matches to relight the fire. Louisine was frightened. She feared that she would receive a life sentence for such irreverence. She picked up a match and halfheartedly tried to rekindle the fire, but the match kept burning out. She began her speech: "No other people in the world have suffered as American women—"

A police officer grabbed Louisine by the arm, and she stumbled. He led her to a police wagon. Before she ducked to enter the carriage, she turned: "Every Anglo-Saxon government in the world has enfranchised its women. Even Germany has woman suffrage."

She continued, "We, American women, are taking this way of voicing our deep indignation that, while our government preaches democracy for Europe, we are still deprived of a voice in our government."

The police officer firmly pushed her into the wagon.

Another woman continued the speech.

The police arrested her as well.

When it was her turn, Ella proudly carried on the speech.

Police arrested her.

Thirty-nine women were arrested that day. The women refused bail and spent the night in a jail that, ten years earlier, had been discarded "as unfit to hold a human being." Although Ella seemed comfortable with the arrest, Louisine felt so degraded that she became a radical. She wrote, "Sparks of indignation snapped within. Where was my Uncle Sam? Where was the liberty my fathers fought for? Where was the democracy our boys were fighting for?" In prison, Louisine received telegrams from her wealthy relatives. "Oh those telegrams!" she wrote. "From them I gleaned I had stripped the family tree, broken its branches, torn up its roots and laid it prostrate in the dust. What had the whole treeful of innocents ever done that I should treat them thus?"

The next day, as the Senate sat down in legislative chambers to vote on the amendment, the protesters were being tried. When the Senate clerk tallied the ballots, the bill still lacked one vote.

When released from prison, Ella, Louisine, and twenty-two other women went on a "Prison Special" train tour to tell the stories about their incarceration for picketing. Editorials disparaged the women, describing them as "short-haired unreasonable and fanatical women" who have tried to become martyrs by violating municipal laws. The former convicts donned prison garb. From a platform on board the train, they spoke of the horrors of prison and their fight for equality. They explained how guards had handcuffed a suffragist to the bed and threatened prisoners with straitjackets and gags. During a hunger strike, an officer force-fed a woman who was being held down by five guards. An eighty-year-old protester was knocked unconscious by guards.

The spectacle of the Prison Special pressured the president into amending the suffrage bill to meet the concerns of one senator who had voted against it. The senator agreed to support the amended bill. But Congress ran out of time, and the bill expired when the legislative session ended a few days later. Congress adjourned until December 1919.

The National Woman's Party continued to picket. The White House administration turned its attention to the two recently elected Democratic senators. If they could get one of their votes, the bill would pass. The administration sent a request to the president, who was in Paris. One of the new senators, Harris, was nearby in Italy. Could the president meet with him about the suffrage amendment?

The president summoned the new senator to Paris and

convinced him to vote for the amended bill. A special session of Congress was called. On May 21, the House passed the bill. On June 4, the Senate enacted the law, and Congress submitted the Susan B. Anthony amendment to the states for ratification.

It took over a year for the states to ratify the amendment by the required 75 percent. In June 1920, Ella, Doris, and Louisine picketed the Republican National Convention in Chicago to pressure Republicans in unratified states to endorse the amendment. Two more states ratified the constitutional amendment, and on August 26, 1920, President Wilson signed the Nineteenth Amendment into law. Eight million women voted in November 1920. By 1928, seven women served in the U.S. House of Representatives.*

Mildred Adams was a journalist and a suffragist whose travels in Spain and whose work on philosopher Jose Ortega y Gasset would win her entrance into the Society. She described the right to vote as the Holy Grail for women. It was a means for women to get power. Adams believed that the suffrage campaign was "remarkably selfless." The suffragists worked for the common good. "They were working for the better status of women in a democracy and for the better conduct of that democracy. They honestly believed that women should have the right to vote because they were citizens." Voting rights gave women a tool to improve their legal status and the nation's laws.

After women's suffrage became law, Ella turned her attention to a problem that plagued one of her fellow Society members, Grace

---

* By 1940, a woman geographer had succeeded her late husband in the U.S. Congress, representing Ohio. Frances P. Bolton served as a representative until 1969. She was a member of the Committee on Foreign Affairs for almost thirty years. Bolton was the first committee member to travel to the Soviet Union, the first woman to lead an overseas congressional delegation, and the first woman congressional delegate to the United Nations. She fought against apartheid and for the decolonization of Africa. She advocated for women to serve the military in noncombat roles, stating, "I am afraid that gallantry is sorely out of date, and as a woman, I find it rather stupid. Women's place includes defending the home."

Thompson Seton, who had once hypnotized a donkey-keeper. Grace described herself as "one of those people who were born believing in suffrage." She joined the suffrage movement when she was seventeen and soon became the vice-president of the Connecticut Woman Suffrage Association. She refused to define herself by her marriage to a famous British naturalist, Ernest Thompson Seton. Her travels in Cuba, Egypt, and Asia to study suffrage movements abroad eventually helped qualify her for membership in the Society. In the 1930s, she would create the *Biblioteca Femina*, the largest library in the world of books and pamphlets written by women.

Grace got a rude awakening when she was arriving from Cuba by ship with her husband. When she left Cuba, she was an American. But when the ship docked in the United States, officials directed Grace to the immigration line for foreigners. Because she had entered the United States with her alien husband, the States revoked her citizenship.

Grace was livid: "I was born in California. I am a property holder and income taxpayer. The situation is ridiculous—a relic of the time when women had no legal existence." Something had to be done. She urged her fellow suffragists, "One of the first matters for us to tackle is the disenfranchisement and denaturalization of free-born American citizens, provided the sex be female, as a penalty for getting married."

Grace's denaturalization was a direct result of coverture, the concept that upon marriage, the husband and wife become one person under the law; for all legal purposes, the woman becomes part of the man. The wife no longer has a separate legal identity and has no power to buy real estate, bring a lawsuit, or sign a contract. The legal doctrine, which was not repealed until 1992, was based on the premise that women were incapable of making sound financial and political decisions. For example, when a woman married, the husband wielded control over the property his wife brought to the marriage, including her body. Coverture meant that a married woman could not be raped by her husband, and he could discipline her by beating her. When a woman married a foreigner, she also ceded her citizenship. The doctrine of coverture reinforced the patriarchal notion of society.*

In 1922, the United States stopped denaturalizing women who were married to foreign citizens. In 1930, Ella Riegel would attend The Hague Conference on the Codification of International Law to advocate the worldwide repeal of marital expatriation laws.

While women were fighting in the United States for suffrage, war was raging in Europe. Many of the Society's future members viewed World War I as an opportunity to combine adventure, danger, and patriotism. Harriet Chalmers Adams, who would become the Society's first president, was the first woman war correspondent to report from the front. In 1916, the French government issued her a permit to take battlefield photographs for *Harper's Magazine*. The petite, charming journalist spent three months interviewing the men and women who served the military abroad. Later, Helen Kirtland Johns reported from the Italian front for *Leslie Magazine*. Eleanor Roosevelt volunteered with the Red Cross, and Mickie Akeley entertained the troops in Europe. Ava Singer used her knowledge of languages to do intelligence work during the war, and Amelia Earhart joined the Voluntary Aid Detachment in Toronto, where she served meals to wounded warriors and worked in the pharmacy. But of these members, Ellen La Motte perhaps had the most lasting impact on the antiwar movement; that is, until she was muzzled.

---

* The effects of coverture are still felt today in lower pay for women, in the assumption that women will not work as many hours as men due to domestic duties, and in the cyclical news stories claiming that particular human behavior can be explained by innate traits, rather than cultural differences.

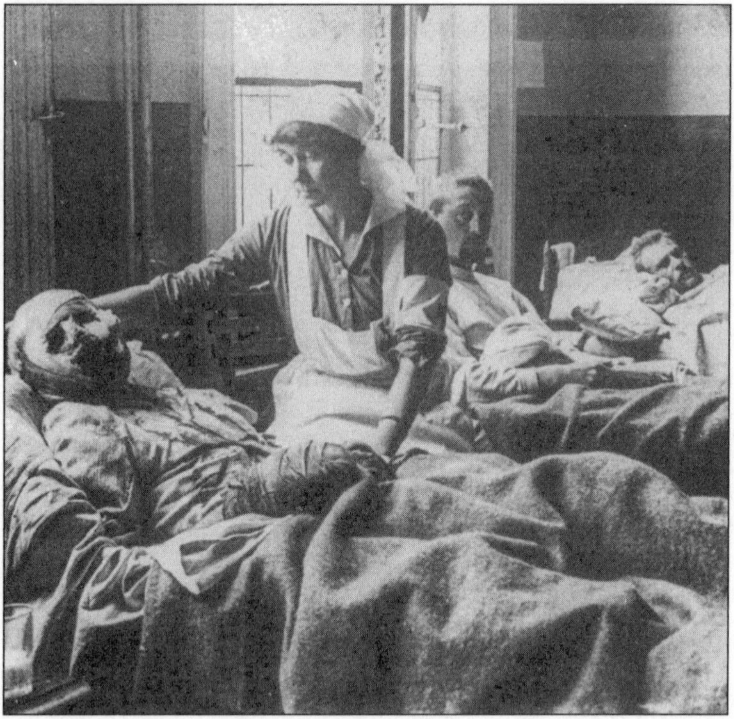

Illustration 11. The Horror of War; Possibly Ellen La Motte Attending Belgian Wounded (1915)

CHAPTER 7
THE BACKWASH OF WAR

We are witnessing a phase in the evolution of humanity, a phase called War—and the slow, onward progress stirs up the slime in the shallows, and this is the Backwash of War. It is very ugly.

—ELLEN NEWBOLD LA MOTTE, NURSE AND SOCIETY MEMBER

1914
Atlantic Ocean

Socialist Ellen La Motte stood on the deck of the *SS Minnetonka*, staring out at the Atlantic Ocean. She was dismal.

After she lost faith in the radical tactics of the Pankhursts, Ellen struggled to find the purpose of her life: "I feel singularly adrift. Singularly useless, and unattached, and with a curious sense of having finished—finished—finished. I'm in an almost desperate state of mind, when nothing seems to matter. I have no desire left. And I have so little money."

Her mood changed a few weeks later when her cousin Alfred came to visit. They took off for Paris, where they had a ripping time going to dinners and dances. She wrote, "Paris from the standpoint of a millionaire is a totally different place from Paris from the poor Latin Quarter." Back in London, Alfred convinced Ellen to move back to the United States. He bought two tickets on the *SS Minnetonka*, bound for Baltimore on August 1, 1914.

Three days later, England declared war on Germany. As Ellen stood on deck, she wondered, Why did I leave England? At age forty-one, Ellen was a fiercely independent woman, a trained nurse, an expert on tuberculosis, and the first woman to hold an executive position at the Baltimore Health Department. She felt compelled to return to Europe immediately: "I am leaving behind my chance to put my skill as a nurse to its greatest test—nursing, through all sorts of privations and discomforts, the victims of war back to life and vigor."

Ellen did not have to wait long for the discomforts of war. After the captain of the *Minnetonka* received the war cable, he ordered the ship to go silent and dark. On August 9, at 9 p.m., passengers were startled as a searchlight lit up the deck. They crowded the bridge to find the source of the light—a German cruiser. Just then, Captain Cannons received a wireless transmission: "Who are you?"

He replied, "Who are you?"

There was no answer.

The crew in the navigation room tensed as they waited for a reply.

The wireless tapped out a message.

"Sound your fog whistle twice."

Captain Cannons ignored the demand and increased to eighteen knots an hour (about 20 mph). For two hours, the German cruiser chased the *Minnetonka*. When they reached U.S. waters, the boat retreated.*

---

* A German U-Boat sank the *Minnetonka* in 1918.

Ellen arrived in Baltimore, excited about the encounter, and determined to return to Europe to volunteer as a nurse. She reached out to her contacts to find a job on the front in France.

On October 13, 1914, she received a cryptic cable from the American Ambulance of Paris: "Come—American Ambulance." Thrilled, she told her friends, "I will be gathering the wounded on stretchers, and conveying them to a waiting ambulance. I will be working night and day—eighteen-hour and twenty-four-hour stretches—worse even than that—and doing without food, sleep, and warmth." She packed and set sail for France.

Ellen was shocked on November 7, 1914, when she arrived at the American Ambulance in Neuilly, a Paris suburb. She discovered that the French used the term *ambulance* to refer to a military hospital. "I found myself on a comfortable ten-hour duty, with two hours off a day, and a half day off once a week, in a steam-heated, electric-lighted building, with excellent food and a handful of patients."

As she entered the dining hall on the first day, she saw dozens of nurses and auxiliaries each dressed in their professional garb—"or such adaptation of her uniform as she happened to fancy." She was profoundly disappointed: "Somewhere off, outside Paris, there is hell let loose." But she was stuck in the "grande finale of a comic opera, where the costumes of the entire show are gathered together in a kaleidoscopic climax."

From the dining room, she went to the recovery ward, where she set off a bureaucratic nightmare by breaking a soap dish. To replace it, she had to get signatures from three people. "I had to walk about a mile, from one department to another, 'til I finally found someone authorized to give me a new one." A few hours later, a patient broke an ashtray. This time, Ellen was prepared to deal with the "crisis": "I simply went to the cupboard and helped myself to one from a generous supply. After all, the importance of things is relative."

That afternoon, the administration assigned her to the receiving ward, where ambulances dropped off soldiers injured on the front. Four men arrived that day—"dirty, muddy, bloody little heaps of humanity, making no moan or outcry," even as she undressed and bathed them. Three of the men had been injured days earlier, and their emergency dressings were foul: full of blood and pus and stuck to their skin. One man's palm was missing; another had a shattered, gangrenous leg. A soldier with a shrapnel wound on his lower back had spent a month in a field hospital and "was emaciated and worn to a skeleton and filthy beyond words."

In her spare time, Ellen wrote about her experiences in the American Ambulance, and she did not mince words. She criticized the waste of hospital resources, especially personnel. "The volunteer attendants outnumber the wounded nearly two to one." Because the United States had not yet entered the war, the American Ambulance was "the one place in France where Americans could offer their services and have them accepted, where laymen and professionals, blundering or efficient, could work off their sympathies, their desire to help, or their desire to 'see things,' with no questions asked as to impelling motives."

Ellen thought that those motives were often superficial: "There are young society girls gathering experiences which will tell well in next year's ball-rooms. A few are pearled and jeweled, rouged, and scented till they are quite adorable. Some are animated by a genuine desire to be of service, others by nothing more lofty than a craving for new sensations. This is a mass of unskilled labor, some of which is useful, much superfluous, and some a positive menace to the patients themselves." She caught a woman trying to move a patient to a stretcher so she could make his bed. She wrote, "Had I not by chance appeared upon the scene, she would have undoubtedly dragged the patient from his bed to the stretcher, and killed him, for his life depended upon his being kept motionless." She recalled the British doctor who told her, "No war hospital can be run on the basis of efficiency or economy if a large or any portion of the nursing staff is entrusted to incapable hands. We do not trust our wounded to scented, painted ladies, or scented, painted men."

"The sting lay in its truth," she thought.

She also condemned the cruelty of the military and government: "The trains of wounded soldiers are often delayed by being sidetracked to let the fresh troops go through to the front. That seems barbaric, you say? Certainly, it is barbaric. War never was better than the uttermost horror of barbarism, and this war today is more brutal than any that has gone before it. We are sadly perfected in machinery to mutilate our men en masse. En masse, we bring them back and heal them with our expert knowledge, born of civilization, only to hurl them forward again to the firing line."

After a few weeks, she quit her job at the American Ambulance and started writing stories about her experiences while she sought a post on the front. The job outlook for volunteer Americans was very bleak.

While she waited for a job offer, Ellen visited Paris, where she continued to work with suffragettes. She also joined the circle of American intellectuals who frequented Gertrude Stein and Alice B. Toklas's apartment. Although Gertrude Stein seemed to be infatuated with her, Ellen was too busy admiring Emily Chadbourne, a wealthy American, to reciprocate Gertrude's advances. Soon she and Emily were lovers. They would become life partners.

Emily was her second wealthy lover, and Ellen wondered why she was attracted to millionaires: "I believe in millionaires, aristocracy, and idleness all at once, and those who are of them, or profess them, are no better or worse than anyone else!" She began to wonder what she stood for.

After five months, Ellen got a position as a nurse in Belgium, at a hospital less than ten kilometers from the front. There, she experienced the real horror of war.

She was assigned to Hôpital Chirurgical Mobile No. 1, in the Belgian village of Roesbrugge. The mobile hospital had 140 patient beds, a dozen nurses, and one operating room. It was halfway between Dunkirk and Ypres.

The nurses set out from Paris on June 20, 1915, and stopped in Dunkirk for the night. The trip, which would normally take three hours, took ten. Dunkirk was in the war zone, and upon entering it, Ellen felt like she was being locked in. She wrote, "Only through the most rigid formalities had we been able to enter; only through the same formalities would we be permitted to leave. Individual liberty was gone; we were not free to come and go how and where we liked, but, under observation in the zone of the armies, we must share with the armies whatever fate had in store." The longer she stayed in the military zone, the more she felt like a prisoner.

The next day, they went sightseeing. First, they surveyed the damage made by German siege guns, which Ellen described as "formidable and powerful cannons, which fire projectiles which rise eleven miles in the air before they fall to earth, each shell a ton of devastating steel." Despite the damage made by these guns, life in Dunkirk carried on as usual, except that soldiers and military transports crowded the streets. The Germans had not bombed Dunkirk in six weeks, and so the civilians were shopping, working, and strolling, confident that the "Allies had found and silenced the great guns." As they basked in the warm sunshine, they could hear guns in the distance: "Somewhere over there was 'war,' but here was harmony, tranquility, and peace." The nurses went to bed that night hoping that the hospital would be ready soon because Dunkirk was too comfortable and boring.

A few hours later, a terrible explosion woke the nurses. A

German plane had dropped a bomb outside of the hotel. Ellen and the other nurses rushed out of the hotel and swarmed to the beach in their pajamas. They joined thousands of civilians, soldiers, children, and mothers with strollers, who had rushed to the sand, believing that the Germans would not bomb the beach. Ellen waited, but nothing of consequence happened, and so she headed back to the hotel with the other nurses.

The proprietor was serving tea when they arrived at the hotel, and they sat down and visited. Tea was interrupted by another blast, this one so loud that the hotel shook. Ellen looked out on the town from the dining room balcony and thought, "A seventeen-inch shell, fired by a gun twenty-two miles away, had burst somewhere among those homes." For the next fifteen minutes, the Germans fired a shell at the town at five-minute intervals.

The proprietor, knowing that it took forty minutes for the guns to cool, sent the women to bed: "Get to sleep while you can, till they begin again. After all, it's practically three o'clock in the morning and we shall have a whole day of this." Ellen noted that no one was scared: "It was all merely an intensely interesting, an intensely exciting experience, but still, for all that, something quite apart from, something totally beyond, our hitherto sheltered lives."

After they woke up, they toured the city to see the damage. Suddenly, "a sickening sense of fear, of nervous dread, passed" over Ellen as she realized that they were entering the town in between bombardments. The streets that had been filled the day before were now desolate. Houses had collapsed, windows had shattered, and walls had been torn apart. For the first time, Ellen saw "war in the concrete, saw the havoc wrought by those awful guns, contrasted the peaceful workaday life of yesterday with this sunlit, silent, stricken scene of today." She was chilled when a "feeling of cold terror" washed over her.

As she approached the train station, a shell burst a hundred yards away. Ellen stood still, like a deer in headlights, not sure which way to run. Not to the railroad station, which was an obvious target. All of the houses nearby seemed abandoned. Ellen recalled, "Danger was everywhere, in the open spaces, under the walls of houses. There was no one to direct us. A military motor flew by and the occupants waved to us to run. Yes, that was it, run—but where? Out of range of those awful shells, that traveled twenty-two miles in a few seconds? As well wait here as a few hundred feet away. Why run?" Ellen was afraid—not of death "but an agonizing fear of the concussions, of a jaw torn off, of a nose smashed in." She tried to move but was paralyzed: "Right, left, forward, backward, there was no intellectual power to direct my steps."

Ellen saw a woman run across the square and bang on the door of a demolished house. Ellen thought, "They've got a cellar!" She ran to the house and frantically pounded on the door. After a bit, a man opened the door and said, "Enter quickly—there is not much time." He led Ellen and the other nurses to the cellar. As soon as she stepped into the shelter, Ellen heard a shell explode. She was relieved: "The wonderful relief of that cellar! The feeling of security in the blessed darkness, the comfort of companionship." Ellen counted as the shells exploded. *Two... Three... Four*. Ellen thanked the owners of the shelter, and the nurses left, hoping to return to the hotel in the forty minutes while the guns cooled.

They passed the "shattered houses; gaping walls open to the heavens," Ellen recalled. "It was terrible to pass through those hot streets, wondering, as we walked, whether we would reach the hotel before the guns began again. It was like walking in a nightmare, dragging leaden legs, with the terror that comes with dreams. A wrong turning, a false direction, and we should lose precious moments—those moments while the great guns cooled."

She heard a motor roaring behind her and turned to see the truck that had dropped them off. Ellen was overjoyed: action, not indecision! The nurses climbed into the truck and were back at the hotel before the next shells hit. The next attack was after lunch. Ellen had "nothing to do but sit on the balcony and watch them. So here we are, six of us, calm, smiling, apparently indifferent. Underneath, however, is a terrible tension as each shell falls, and the tension in the intervals of waiting is still more awful. And so we sit on the balcony and watch the bursting shells—and wait."

A few days later, they set out for the field hospital.

After six months of working in the hospital, Ellen began to write about the patients. The newest was a deserter who tried to commit suicide. Ellen described him with derision:

> When he could stand it no longer, he fired a revolver up through the roof of his mouth, but he made a mess of it. The ball tore out his left eye, and then lodged somewhere under his skull. To save his life, he must reach the hospital without delay, and if he was bounced to death jolting along at breakneck speed, it did not matter. That was understood. He was a deserter and discipline must be maintained. His life must be saved, he must be nursed back to health until he was well enough to be stood up against a wall and shot. This is War.

As Ellen looked around the ward, she wondered, "Was it not all a dead-end occupation, nursing back to health men to be patched up and returned to the trenches, or a man to be patched up, court-martialed and shot?"

In another bed lay a patient who received the Médaille Militaire for bravery. He had asked the army doctor for permission to smoke when he got his medal. The doctor refused, saying that it would bother the other patients. The man smoked anyway, and the patient in the next bed became violently nauseous. Ellen wondered, "How much honor lay in that?" Slowly she realized that France had imposed on him "an Ideal that was not his own." He was "harnessed to a great car, a Juggernaut, ponderous and crushing, upon which was enthroned Mammon, or the Goddess of Liberty, or Reason. Nothing further was demanded of them than their collective physical strength."

She recognized that the soldiers "had no Ideals, even though they fought for them" when she heard one patient whisper to another, "Dost thou know, mon ami, that when we captured that German battery a few days ago, we found the gunners chained to their guns?"

To work through her feelings about the war, Ellen wrote unflinchingly about it. She wrote of the absurdity of doctors working feverishly to save a quadruple amputee, and the indifference shown by patients irritated by the constant cries of a wounded ten-year-old boy. She introduced readers to the uncaring orderly who said he would "do anything" for a patient, that is, anything except change a fetid surgical dressing. The stench of the operating room permeated her stories.

In September 1916, Ellen's book of essays *The Backwash of War: The Human Wreckage of the Battlefield as Witnessed by an American Hospital Nurse* was released in the United States and Britain. A reviewer for the *Los Angeles Times* wrote, "If we were to compile an anthology of the ten best war stories, about eight of them would be listed under the name Ellen N. La Motte. It is the first realistic glimpse behind the battle lines that has been offered to a neutral public." Another reader praised the book, saying, "There is a corner of my book-shelves which I call my TNT library. Here are all the literary high explosives I can lay my hands on. So far, there are only five of them." La Motte's book was the only "TNT" book written by an American and the only one written by a woman. England and France quickly censored the book because of its negative portrayal of the war. In December 1918, the United States banned *Backwash.*[*]

Like Ellen, Blair Niles was maturing into a writer who did not spare her readers the facts, even when they were ghastly. She believed in telling the "unadorned truth." In this respect, her writing philosophy meshed with Ellen's, as Blair believed, "It is only in travel that history comes thus sensuously alive, that it appears with the reality of personal memory."

Back in the United States, another type of censorship was being used by a future member of the Society, Adelene Moffatt, to combat the rising tide of white supremacy. Many of the women who would join the Society of Woman Geographers were also active in the NAACP (National Association for the Advancement of Colored People). They advocated on behalf of people of color and other marginalized people. (It appears there were no Black women among the early members of the Society.) Although the Society of Woman Geographers was a much different type of organization than the NAACP, with different objectives, women—especially gay women—and Black people had much in common. They both felt the sting of discrimination and were determined to fight against it. Two future members of the Society, both white lesbians—Adelene Moffat and Zonia Baber—became members of the NAACP before 1915.[†]

* Although Ernest Hemingway is known for his writings on the war, Ellen La Motte was forgotten until 2019, when Cynthia Wachtell re-released *Backwashed*. Wachtell believes that Ellen La Motte influenced Hemingway's spare, declarative writing style. She hypothesizes that mutual friend Gertrude Stein (who was infatuated with Ellen) gave Hemingway a copy of *Backwash* to emphasize her editorial direction to "Cut out words. Cut everything out except what you saw, what happened."

† Blair Niles, Eleanor Roosevelt, and Pearl S. Buck supported the NAACP in the 1930s, although it is not clear whether they became members. Blair Niles met many of the Black leaders of the NAACP as a result of her book on Haiti. Walter White, executive secretary of the NAACP in the 1930s, hailed Pearl S. Buck and Eleanor Roosevelt as examples of white Americans who truly understood Black life. Pearl grew up as a white girl in China, where the Chinese fully embraced her. She encountered segregation and discrimination only after she moved back to the United States and adopted racially mixed children. As the first lady, Eleanor worked with Walter White to convince her husband, Franklin D. Roosevelt, to outlaw job discrimination and help prevent lynchings.

Illustration 12. NAACP Picket Outside Theater Protesting Movie "Birth of a Nation" (1947)

CHAPTER 8

BIRTH OF A NATION

> *The main barrier between East and West today is that the white man is not willing to give up his "superiority" and the colored man is no longer willing to endure this "inferiority."*
>
> —PEARL S. BUCK, AUTHOR AND SOCIETY MEMBER

1915

Manhattan and Boston

As she read the headline about a new silent film, *Birth of a Nation,* a racist depiction of the Ku Klux Klan's role in protecting Southern white women from being raped by Black men, Blair Niles thought of her grandmother. In 1907, Sara Agnes Pryor had published a book of the same title. Sara's book was undeniably about the birth of the United States; it chronicled the history of the Jamestown colony. In contrast, the movie was based on the book *The Clansman,* written by Thomas Dixon, a white supremacist who claimed to represent the Civil War and Reconstruction accurately. Actually, it was revisionist history.

Dixon hoped that the book would inspire whites to remove Black people from the United States. Director D. W. Griffith named the film *Birth of a Nation* to reflect his belief that the South had suffered trauma and agony after the Civil War so that a unified nation would be born. Blair's grandmother would be horrified at the use of her title for such an insidious movie about the rise of the Ku Klux Klan.

Adelene Moffat was also angered by the film. In her role as a leading member of the Boston NAACP, she had just seen the *Birth of a Nation* at the Tremont Theater. The film depicted "heroic" members of the Ku Klux Klan in their efforts to protect the nation from "savage" Black men as they attempted to marry white women.

Outside the Tremont Theater, Adelene listened to viewers' reactions. She felt like she had been punched in the gut.

"I've always hated niggers, but I never knew why 'til I saw *Birth of a Nation*," said one viewer as he walked by.

"You can't civilize Negroes—they are all savages."

"I think all the niggers ought to be sent back to the place they came from."

Adelene agreed with the assessment of the *New York Age*, a Black newspaper, which called the movie "an appeal to the baser emotions to degrade a people and incite race hatred."

Birth of a Nation was the first feature-length film. The three-hour silent movie, with an intermission and an orchestral accompaniment, was an epic event that instantly drew crowds accustomed to fifteen-minute movies shown in nickelodeon theaters. It featured new cinematic techniques such as color tinting, fade-outs, long panoramic shots, crosscutting between scenes, and total screen close-ups, all designed to tug at the audiences' emotions. One reviewer wrote, "When a motion picture can hold you in thrall for three hours, when in that time you feel all the emotions sway you and your breath comes in short gasps, when you know tears are near the surface and in another instance your face flushed, there comes the realization of the power of the silent drama." Tickets were sold out four weeks in advance.

Reviewers praised the film's cinematic effects, its strong narrative, and its impact on the audience's emotions. This reaction was typical: "It makes you laugh and moves you to hot tears unashamed. It makes you love and hate. It makes you actually live through the greatest period of suffering and trial that this country has ever known."* Upon leaving the screening, one critic said that it was like "coming out of a thunderstorm."

Adelene had grown up in Tennessee, the birthplace of the Ku Klux Klan, and she was familiar with Southerners' attitudes toward Black people. She believed that, unlike other white Southerners who accepted the fact that the Civil War put an end to slavery, members of the Ku Klux Klan remained imprisoned by "a fear of Negro Supremacy." This "evil band of lynchers" was "determined at all costs to preserve its own tradition, the exploitation of the Negro." The Ku Klux Klan fed on notions of white supremacy and masculinity.

Adelene described the members of the KKK as "strong in their prejudices, and limited in knowledge and foresight." They "cloaked their mental and moral timidity under a noisy bravado, stimulated by that other ready aid to valor, whiskey."

On April 17, Black leaders planned a demonstration at the Tremont Theater. Management was tipped off and stationed sixty

---

* Critics and viewers alike "praised the film as a benchmark of historical accuracy." D. W. Griffith claimed that the film was "a photoplay reproduction of what actually happened and what is down in black and white in the pages of American history." Actually, the film was propaganda designed to encourage white supremacy. By the 1910s, the history of the Civil War was being revised to be a white tragedy.

plainclothes policemen—fifty more than usual—inside the theater and two hundred police outside. On April 21, a Massachusetts court ordered the removal of a rape scene from the film. The same day, Adelene and others spoke before the Massachusetts legislature, seeking to give city officials the authority to censor films. Adelene testified, "I can see no way in which this film can be altered to make it either a desirable or safe influence in any community in America. I think the film should be withdrawn promptly and forever and from all places."

A few weeks later, twenty-five hundred people met at the Tremont Temple to protest the film. Adelene spoke before the crowd, calling the film "a loathsome calumny [slander] of the Negro race and an insult to the South as well as the North." Adelene believed that the film was a historically inaccurate and racist piece of propaganda.

Although Adelene and the Boston NAACP were able to get some of the most objectionable scenes removed, they failed to ban the movie in Boston. (Local chapters in several other states, however, convinced censorship boards to ban the film.) The city council passed an ordinance that gave police the authority to revoke a license to show a film, and the Boston police banned the movie one Sunday.

But not all future members of the Society were as supportive of the rights of people of color as Adelene. Some began their anthropological and ethnographic studies with the best of intentions, but when they realized that "a pot of gold could be found at the end of the publicity rainbow," as Blair was fond of saying, they changed course. Osa Johnson was a prime example of a Society member who pandered to racist misconceptions.

In 1921, Osa and her husband, Martin, left on a two-year expedition to Africa with Carl Akeley (Mickie Akeley's ex-husband) to film "a documentary about wilderness and wildlife as it must have looked thousands of years ago." The American Museum of Natural History offered to pay most of the $250,000 ($3.6 million today) price tag. During this expedition, Johnson learned filming techniques that would enhance his career. According to the Johnsons' biographers, Pascal and Eleanor Imperato, "a year and a half of intense experiences in the African bush [with Akeley] had transformed Martin and Osa Johnson into first-rate wildlife photographers. They had produced films that were truly unique and spectacular for their time." Although Akeley emphasized that scenes had to be authentic, Martin and Osa were entertainers, not scientists, and when necessary, they staged scenes by provoking animals into dangerous actions.

The resulting film was called *Trailing African Animals*. Akeley and Professor Henry Fairfield Osborn, the president of the museum's board of trustees, vouched for the authenticity of the film, saying that the film was neither staged nor misleading. In fact, the Johnsons had duped Akeley and the museum; the film was a fictional story, which used contrived scenes of dangerous wild animals.

As their careers progressed, the Johnsons became less wedded to accurate depictions of animals, and eventually, they gave up on any attempt to realistically portray the African jungles. Instead, they churned out films that portrayed indigenous people as "nothing more than objects of amusement for white audiences."

Blair would not have condoned Osa Johnson's exploitation of aboriginal people for the comedic relief of Americans. She admired travel narratives that "squared with the truth." She believed that nonfiction was always more interesting "than any of the deliberate misrepresentations which are unfortunately the currency of certain writers. It is only the poor in imagination who are tempted to falsify. And it is a gratifying fact that, although the sensational sometimes achieve a flurry of bestselling, they are essentially 'short-livers.'" Blair detested travel books and films that focused on "an immeasurable difference between black and white, between primitive and—God save the word—civilized." Instead, the goal of the writer or filmmaker was to chronicle spiritual travel "in which the national and racial soul is the object of study."

In many ways, Blair had more in common with Zonia Baber, a future member of the Society who shared her desire to celebrate both racial commonalities and cultural differences. In later years, they would both work to expose discrimination against people of color.

1917
Chicago

Zonia Baber, a professor of geology and geography, was a feminist, pacifist, and an advocate against racism and imperialism and for peace. One day in 1917, she was hunched over her desk at the University of Chicago, absorbed in her work. She looked up as a Black female janitor knocked at her door. Because she devoted her career to interracial understanding, Zonia was always pleased to talk with the custodian. They often talked about race relations.

The janitor handed Zonia a book called *From Superman to Man: A Fearless and Penetrating Discussion of America's Greatest Problem*. She told Zonia that she might find the book compelling since Zonia was always trying to get her students to discuss race in an intelligent and unemotional manner. Zonia believed that as long as the "white Race retains its childish or primitive belief that it is superior to all other peoples and consequently intended by God to dominate over all other races, there can be no hope for permanent peace." Zonia thought that many white men regarded white superiority as a fundamental belief, as absolute as gravity and the earth's rotation.

Zonia immediately read the book. The author was Joel Augustus Rogers, a Black Jamaican-American intellectual, writer, and former Pullman train porter. Dixon's *The Clansman* had motivated Rogers to write the book. He wrote, "As a young man I wasn't interested in 'race.' Then in Thomas Dixon's '*Clansman*,' I read that if you had a 'drop of Negro blood,' you were damned intellectually and I began to take notice." Zonia learned that as a Pullman train porter, Rogers had met many white passengers from different states, which exposed him to the arguments that whites commonly used to subjugate Black people.

When *Birth of a Nation* was released, Rogers was disturbed by the media's vicious attacks on Black people. He explained that history had ignored the accomplishments of great Negroes in order to bolster claims of Negro inferiority. Rogers believed that Blacks were as intellectually able as whites and that history proved this point. Zonia agreed wholeheartedly with Rogers on this point.

In all, Rogers wrote more than a dozen books that attacked the myth of Negro inferiority and highlighted the accomplishments of Black men. Most of the books were self-published. Rogers's first book, *From Superman to Man,* was a novel about the ignorance that fuels racism, written from the perspective of a porter on a Pullman train. In the story, a porter—a thinly disguised Rogers, ironically with the same last name as the author of *The Clansman*—is reading a book on racism when he meets a racist congressman who sees the book and asks the porter if he believes "all these impossible views on the equality of races."

"No sir, I do not believe in the equality of races. It is impossible."

The congressman asked why it is impossible.

Zonia must have laughed with delight as she read the porter's response: "Because there is but one race—the human race."

The porter, Dixon, then engaged the legislator in a candid discussion of race. The legislator tried to best him on each argument but could not win because the porter outsmarted him each time with well-researched and -reasoned arguments, facts, and recitations of extended passages from treatises. Dixon convinced the congressman that history has not always regarded Black people as inferior, by telling him of the illustrious achievements of Black men throughout history.*

After Zonia read the book, she wrote to Rogers to tell him it was "the finest bit of literature she had read on the subject." As a member of the NAACP, she wanted people of color to have their own voice, rather than having whites speak for them. Rogers was the perfect spokesperson for Black people because he could debunk pseudoscientific arguments about Negro inferiority with accurate historical and scientific authorities.

For years, Zonia had been trying to erase prejudice from her students, and so she assigned *From Superman to Man* as required reading. She also convinced her colleague George B. Foster to adopt the book for his classes. She ordered fourteen copies of *Superman* to send to professors at other universities and invited Rogers to her home to speak to her students about the book.

---

* Mary Ritter Beard would also use this tactic as she attempted to empower women by reminding them of their rich history as great leaders.

Zonia and Adelene were clearly ahead of their time with respect to fighting for equality among races. Meanwhile, Blair's ex-husband, William Beebe, was in South America, taking advantage of the imperialist colonization of British Guiana and exploiting six future members of the Society of Woman Geographers.

PART 3
THE "GIRLS" OF THE TROPICAL RESEARCH STATION

Illustration 13. Roosevelts at Kalacoon (1916): Clockwise from wicker chair: Edith Roosevelt, Sir Walter Edgerton (governor-general of British Guiana), Department of Tropical Research staff members Inness Hartley and Paul Howes, William Beebe (at far head of table), the Withers family, Anna Heyward Taylor, Theodore Roosevelt.

CHAPTER 9

WANTED: A CHAPERONE

No, I have never wanted to be a man. I have often wanted to be more effective as a woman, but I have never felt that trousers would do the trick!

—ELEANOR ROOSEVELT, FORMER FIRST LADY, EXPLORER, AND SOCIETY MEMBER

1915
Manhattan

A headline caught Blair's attention: "To Study Wild Life Near the Equator." The *New York Times* article explained that Will Beebe, Blair's ex-husband, was about to sail to Trinidad and British Guiana to observe wildlife there.

Blair put down the newspaper and reminisced. She knew that the purpose of the station was to establish a place where scientists could conduct year-round research. As Beebe's biographer Carol Gould noted, it was a place "where the same area could be mined...week after week, month after month, year after year, to yield...an in-depth portrait of the whole interdependent ecology of a region." Another reason was to convince scientists from institutions other than the Bronx Zoo that tropical research was neither dangerous nor expensive. Will did not have enough funding to work there year-round, and he anticipated that he would remain there six months at a time.

Blair recalled how she and Will had traveled to find the ideal place for the tropical research station in 1908, just two months after they met with President Roosevelt. They sailed out of the New York Harbor on the *Royal Mail* steamer bound for Trinidad. Their goal was to search for "wilderness wonderlands,—full of beauty, abounding in the romance which ever enhances the wild creatures and wild men, who were part of the great zoological 'dark continent' which they hoped to devote their lives to studying."

From Trinidad, they chartered a Venezuelan one-masted sailboat staffed by a rugged captain, two sailors, a mate, and a cook and equipped it with a month's supply of food and scientific instruments. In a chapter titled "A Woman's Experiences in Venezuela," published in their book *Our Search for Wilderness*, Blair wrote about the voyage. "The night we set forth in our tiny sloop from the tiny island of Trinidad, headed for an unexplored part of the Orinoco delta, it was hard to realize that we were at last bound for South America, the land of our dreams. The charm of exploration laid a spell on us both."

That night, they placed their inflatable mattresses on the cabin's bunks—Blair preferred to call the narrow sleeping areas *the catacombs*—and tried to sleep.

Rats had found a home in between the floorboards and outside planks of the boat. Blair thought that it sounded like the rats were hosting an Olympic event. Blair later described the tournament:

"A race would start near the stern, the contestants tearing around Will's bunk; then the footfalls would die out toward the bow to become audible almost at once on my side—a medley of sound indicating a mob of invisible rushing creatures, galloping down a mysterious homestretch. Then would follow a general mêlée and fight, punctuated with shrill squeaks and squeals and vicious blows and sounds of tumbling, rolling bodies. Were we in the mood we might have learned much of rat vocabulary." She hoped the rats did not have a secret entrance to her catacomb.

Later that night, Blair heard a rivulet of water coming from the bowels of the sailboat. She called out to the captain, asking about the trickling stream.

He called down in a deep, hoarse voice, "It's only a leak!" He had looked for the source, but he could not find it.

Blair hoped it was a slow leak and then fell asleep.

She dreamed that she was being buried alive. Sleepily, she sat up and banged her head. She thought she had hit her head on the coffin lid of her catacomb. Then she realized that she was in a narrow berth, not a coffin. In frustration, she grabbed her bedding, hauled it to the floor, curled into a fetal position, and tried to sleep.

When the sailboat pitched in the waves, she slid into the walls. Blair was glad that she did not have far to slide. The floor was only five-feet long and a few feet wide. By the third day, they abandoned the berth and set up camp on the ship's deck. The captain would tell them bedtime stories about snake charmers and black magic, only to be outdone by the cook's story, which featured ghosts, the angel of death, and the devil.

The crew members were hearty eaters. At the start of the voyage, Captain Truxillo bought one hundred pounds of beef. The maestro—*maestro* being the honorary title given to the cook—sliced it into long strips, salted it, and hung it on the rigging to cure. Blair wrote, "Whole entomological collections buzz noisily about us. I feel as though we are living in a butcher's shop; and a butcher's shop in a tropical climate is a thing to be avoided." But then she thought, "Suppose it were fish; and we were so grateful to be spared that, that we cheerfully submitted to a sloop draped with strips of meat, as a house is festooned with smilax* at Christmas."

In Venezuela, they sailed up the Orinoco River, past mudflats, and anchored near the mangroves. Blair enjoyed exploring the dense mangroves, where all sorts of fishes, crustaceans, and reptiles lived: "Life is delightfully new and strange, with the spice of danger ever attendant upon the exploration of unknown lands." The highlight of their river trip was when they saw a tree full of hoatzins, which are only found near the Orinoco and Amazon rivers. These leaf-eating birds sport a spiky red Mohawk crest tinged with black, shimmering cyan eye shadow, cape-like wings of serrated white and chestnut brown, and large reptilian claws that they use to climb trees.

The following winter, they headed to British Guiana, where they found two locations for the Tropical Field Station. Gaylord Wilshire, a millionaire Socialist who owned a gold mine there, liked the Beebes so much that he offered them the free use of a plantation, Kartabo, on the mine's premises.† Will also received an invitation from George Withers to use his rubber plantation, Kalacoon, for the research station. But their plan to establish the station would be interrupted by the pheasant expedition and the Beebes' divorce.

---

* Ornamental foliage used by florists to make garlands.

† Wilshire would become a real estate developer and give land to Los Angeles for Wilshire Boulevard.

By 1916, Will was ready to establish the Tropical Research Station in British Guiana. Although Will planned to set up the research station on Wilshire's property, he changed his mind and instead located it on Kalacoon. The house was in a hilltop clearing on the Bartica Rubber Company's estate, near a jungle and the junction of the Mazaruni, Essequibo, and Cuyuni rivers. Kalacoon offered the comforts of civilization at the edge of the wilderness. Mail, ice, and vegetables were delivered three times a week. Telegraph lines provided contact with Georgetown, British Guyana's capital city.

The station would attract many of the future members of the Society of Woman Geographers, including one of its founders: Gertrude Mathews. It would also attract one of the more outspoken members, Anna Heyward Taylor.

Will invited Anna Heyward Taylor to become one of the scientific artists at the soon-to-be-created Tropical Field Station in British Guiana. Anna was a brutally honest woman who never minced words. Anna's nephew, Edmund R. Taylor, described her as a person surrounded by the spirit of adventure: "She was as straight as an arrow, tall, strong, and very vigorous. She was quite social, and she loved to laugh." She was insulted when someone called her a "typical American." She responded, "I must say that to be a typical American is not my ambition." At age thirty-six, Anna was a young woman who loved to drink, smoke, swear, and travel.

Rowena Tobias, a contemporary Charleston art critic, described Anna: "There are no soft fuzzy lines to Anna Heyward Taylor. She has a forceful personality, a straightforward, unwavering approach to all things, both personal and artistic. If you know her work, you know her, for into it, she puts the strength and direction of her own personality."

Anna was born in Columbia, South Carolina. In 1900, she moved to New York City to study at the New York School of Art. In 1903, she met William Merritt Chase, a leading American artist, and traveled with his class to study art throughout Europe. Rachel Hartley was also on the class trip. In London, John Singer Sargent introduced them to the Japanese style of painting. She wrote to her sister Nell, "Now, for the best news of all! I have seen 'S a r g e n t.'" She was smitten with the six-foot, blond, blue-eyed, bearded artist. She told Nell that she shook his hand and talked with him. "I was so busy looking at him that I didn't have time to look at the pictures much." Referring to the English habit of saying "thank you" on every occasion, she told Nell, "If Sargent asked me to marry him, I am sure that for once I would get ahead on the '*Thank You.*' The whole class has been in a gale since leaving his studio, and all are ready to die now, and all ready to stop painting." After art school, she traveled throughout Europe, and when she returned, she taught painting at her alma mater, Presbyterian College for Women. In 1914, she headed for Tokyo to study Japonism, an artistic movement created when Western artists applied Eastern techniques to painting, printmaking, and gardening. The war cut short her trip. When she returned to the United States, Anna was delighted to receive an invitation from Will Beebe to join the upcoming British Guiana expedition as a staff artist.

The research station was staffed by Will, his assistant Inness Hartley, naturalist Paul Howes, animal collector Donald Carter, and two woman artists: Inness Hartley's sister, Rachel, and Anna. Will's friend, Gertrude Mathews, a divorcée then thirty-four, stayed with them for a few months. Anna described Gertrude as "an extremely clever woman with enough self-reliance and assurance to take her to the North Pole and back." She was an economic geographer who spent her seven-month honeymoon cruising on the Mississippi River to study the feasibility of a deep waterway from Chicago to the Gulf of Mexico. She had a "charming irreverence" for economic and scientific conventions and "she likes to see things as she sees them and write about them in her own way." This last characteristic would later cause friction among her fellow members of the Society.

In letters to her sister Nell, Anna grumbled about the lack of respect given to the women on the expedition: "Our party seems to be very well known and causing much interest. Accounts of it are in all the papers and scientific magazines. Rachel and I are offended because we don't seem to be mentioned." She also complained that in addition to her artistic work, she was the camp's housekeeper.

Initially, Anna was skeptical of Will. She admired Will's dedication to research but considered him to be a womanizer: "He is used to having women make a dead set for him." She thought that Will was rather fresh with women. "Inness told Rachel that he didn't believe that Mr. B had ever known women like us before, his wife and the ones he knew were just a little free, not fast but rather bohemian. He doesn't know it but he is rather *free* sometimes, doesn't mean a thing."

Anna immediately set to work finding out about Will's ex-wife: "Mr. Beebe is quite a study. He was married at dawn in an apple orchard! No wonder he is now divorced! They say his wife was always in search of sensations; so long as he was exploring, it was a happy match. He is very clever and companionable, and a delightful person to travel with for he enters into everything with his heart and soul, deck sports, a joke, or science. He's a man with lots of imagination which accounts for his writing as he does." She thought he was the most energetic and restless man she had ever met.

In February 1916, days after the expedition crew arrived at Kalacoon, Theodore and Edith Roosevelt visited for three days. Anna wrote to her sister, "Roosevelt is a great friend of Mr. Beebe's and really came this far down because of our party being here. We just about fainted when Will came over Sunday and broke the news that they would all be over to lunch Monday." Anna immediately connected with Edith Roosevelt, who she knew from her cousin. Anna did not filter her opinions about the ex-president in her letters home: "I think that he is physically one of the ugliest and most unattractive looking men I ever saw, but very virile and forceful. I never saw anyone so well adapted for caricature."

Roosevelt was surprised that the expedition included women. This is odd because he had met Blair and knew that she had traveled the world with Will. Roosevelt had also traveled on safaris with Mickie and Carl Akeley. Annie Peck had visited him at the White House. And he had traveled to British Guiana with Edith. Yet, when he got there, he was surprised that Will had hired two women artists.

During dinner, Rachel sat on Roosevelt's right, and Anna sat on his left. The women were pleased with the dinner they had arranged on such short notice: veal, rice, pumpkin, butter beans, asparagus, mayonnaise, rice pudding, and canned pears. Anna told Nell, "I have never seen people easier to entertain, and they 'spent the day' in true old-time fashion."

They employed Sam, a Black servant, to wait on them. Nightly cocktails became a routine. Will's favorite was the Demerara Swizzle:

1 Swizzle glass Gin—

1 teaspoon Angostura Bitters

1 pinch sugar

½ swizzle glass water
With plenty of crushed ice.

Swizzle all together in a glass jug and strain through the fine strainer. Sufficient for three glasses.

Rachel and Gertrude left after a few months but Will implored Anna to stay. She was undecided. Anna did not want to be the only woman at the station. She wrote to her sister Nell, "The chaperone question is difficult. Will has had a long talk with me. He says it is very necessary to have someone to do the painting as this is the beginning of the most important season." Will told her that he preferred to have a woman in the camp "because otherwise, the men will get entirely too lax." Although she agreed to stay until July, she left early because she contracted malaria. For the rest of the summer, Anna studied woodblock printing in Provincetown, Massachusetts.

When Will invited Anna to join the 1917 expedition, she told him that she had reservations about returning to the field station without a chaperone. The previous year, George Withers had started rumors about the female members of the Kalacoon expedition, "telling such horrid things and saying the meanest sorts of remarks" about them. This was embarrassing, especially in British Guiana, with its heightened sense of propriety among the expatriates. Anna told Will that Withers "had done everything he could to make the women never want to go there again."* But Will refused to believe that a chaperone was necessary and instead found a new location for the research station at Kartabo at Wilshire's plantation. (Will had visited Wilshire's gold mine nearly a decade earlier with

* Anna provided no details.

Blair.) Will told Anna, "I can tell the Withers man to go to hell. I intend literally to do so. Otherwise, after all he said this year, I shall explode." However, the new accommodations at Kartabo were not ready, and Will decided to return to Kalacoon. Anna wrote to her sister, Nell, "Withers talked horribly about Will and everyone at Kalacoon, yet has offered the place again! But more remarkable still Will has accepted it!"

Anna told Gertrude Mathews that they would be returning to Kalacoon, and Gertrude agreed that Will did not understand the social intricacies of the expedition. Gertrude said, "It struck me that last year—this is very frank of course—that Will didn't really understand what he should have done for the women in the party. He should, and very easily could, have made his position more impregnable by seeing to it that everyone pay the utmost respect to them." Gertrude said that she had told Will that he would be lucky if Anna agreed to return to Kalacoon. Anna had been a good sport about looking after the housekeeping, and was an excellent artist. Gertrude predicted that Will was not likely to find someone else as good as Anna.

Will asked Anna a few weeks later for her final decision. He wrote, "As for our living together down there & not understanding each other, I know it is true & I only am grateful to you for not resenting my attitude. The shreds and tatters that remain of my life for me after my little tragedy* must make me an exceedingly difficult person to associate with. I fear that most of my friends feel that keenly. But I make no pretense at being normal, or of living life more than on the edges."

He told her that he was unwilling to take a chaperone who was not also an artist because it would be costly and inefficient.

* The tragedy was Will's divorce.

Gertrude wrote to Anna, "Whatever Will's opinion, I think just what I did before, that if you had the right sort of woman [chaperone] along, you'd be more comfortable."

Gertrude met with Will and confronted him about the need for a chaperone. She gave Will the name of a woman to interview for the position. Gertrude thought that this woman would "make everybody just as comfortable as the law allows." Will agreed to meet the chaperone, but then he reneged on his promise. Gertrude wrote Anna, "I have repeatedly tried to get Will to see her, and he is completely indifferent. I am simply furious. He has been abominably rude. Of course, he did a long spiel about it being unnecessary, etcetera, etcetera. But just the same, it is better, and he knows it. But he refused to hire a chaperone—at least not anyone old enough, that is, to be the least restraint." After consulting with Gertrude, Anna decided to join the field station team without a chaperone, because the experience of working as a scientific artist was too rare and valuable to give up. But, at the last minute, Will canceled the expedition because of the war and Anna would not return to British Guiana for a few years.

Anna had legitimate concerns about the impact on her reputation of the loose environment at the Department of Tropical Research Station in British Guiana. The field station—which Will had transformed into a domestic site for the scientists—would soon become known as a place where Americans worked hard and partied hard.

In this manner, the atmosphere at the tropical research station violated established norms of social etiquette in the early 1900s, which mandated the presence of a married woman as a chaperone whenever unmarried women were in the company of men. A 1901 etiquette book, *Manners for Girls*, cautioned, "Men set little store by what is carelessly guarded. They undervalue the fruit that hangs over the garden wall, and long for what is beyond their reach. This is human nature." Women needed chaperones to protect them from rumor, scandal, sex, and fortune hunters. Chaperones reminded their wards "that three times are as often as a girl can dance with the same man in one evening without getting herself unpleasantly talked of. So-called emancipation is very often exchanging a gentle and kindly protection for an implacable tyranny, that of the world's malevolent gossip." Etiquette experts cautioned, "To be 'talked about' is extremely disagreeable, and it is seldom worthwhile to excite gossip merely for the sake of an evening's entertainment."

Emily Post assumed, in her famous etiquette book for Americans, that chaperones were nonnegotiable. She warned women that they should not become too familiar, too close, or too open with men. As more women entered the workplace, new problems emerged: workers "had to learn how to relate to each other more or less regardless of gender and sexual attraction. Therefore, many women would have experienced a tug-of-war between their old nineteenth-century sources of power and identity, and their newly gained, twentieth-century sources." Emily Post advised women to be impersonal in the workplace: "At the very top of the list of women's business shortcomings is the inability of most of them to achieve impersonality. Mood, temper, jealousy, especially when induced by a 'crush on' her employer, is the chief flaw of the woman in business." To become "one of the boys" was regarded as improper. It was not until 1942 that Post admitted that chaperones were an old-fashioned concept.

Until the 1940s, society placed the burden of maintaining propriety on the woman. Lilias Campbell-Davidson wrote in *Hints to Lady Travellers at Home and Abroad*: "Much has been said about the danger to women, especially young women, traveling alone, of annoyance from impertinent or obtrusive attentions from travelers of the other sex. I can only say that in any such case which has ever come within my personal knowledge or observation, the woman has only had herself to blame." The author of the 1933 book *No Nice Girl Swears* admonished women readers not to respond enthusiastically to the ill-bred overtures of any man who approaches them on the promenade deck of a ship. Further, "On no account permit a person whom you have just met to go with you to your cabin, even with the ostensible purpose of leaving a package or even a book. And at night, always lock your door, even if you've never done it before in your life." But if the woman was acquainted with the man before the trip, she could dine with him or sit with him on the deck: "The other passengers will probably die of curiosity wondering what their relationship is and will be certain they are traveling in sin, but we wouldn't worry about that!"

Scholar Laura Godsoe writes, "Danger and adventure were particularly gendered subjects in the realm of travel writing, and women who admitted to feeling threatened physically or sexually were potentially opening themselves up to charges of impropriety." As a result, most explorers "did not admit to any feeling of physical or sexual danger and made sure to stress that they traveled with proper chaperones and avoided placing themselves in harm's way." Even women traveling on vacation or for business needed chaperones. The need was so great that in 1855, Thomas Cook started marketing tours to women that would allow them to "safeguard their respectability in order to stay marriageable by traveling with a chaperoned tour led by an honorable man."

The necessity of a chaperone was, of course, primarily a concern for women travelers, not men, "because of their sexual vulnerability and objectification at the hands of men." Women who traveled were sometimes assumed to be sexually promiscuous. Women who lived abroad in the company of men were even more likely to become the subject of gossip, as some of the future members of the Society learned.

World War I interrupted the next British Guiana expeditions. When Will gathered members of the British Guiana expedition in 1919, their destination was Gaylord Wilshire's Kartabo. Will hired three women for the team: Ruth Rose, Isabel Cooper, and Helen Tee-Van. (Helen would later become a member of the Society.) Will fancied Ruth and hired her to be the expedition's historian and technicist. They churned out many popular articles together.

Once, while the women were walking through the jungle, they heard a cry for help. They followed the sound and found four indigenous people staring at a rainbow boa constrictor. The women took charge and collared the snake. Ruth recalled, "The natives fully expected to see all three of us disappearing into the reptile's mouth, as they had seen small pigs and rats disappear in the past. But while there was never any danger of that we were certainly given some rough treatment for a moment as the snake threshed its body up and down in an attempt to get loose. Finally, I managed to close my arms tightly about its head and with the other two girls dragged it back to the clearing." While they waited for the indigenous people to make a bamboo cage, Ruth held the boa behind its jaws, while Helen Tee-Van and Isabel Cooper sat on it.

When the capture of the boa hit the news, Will knew he had found the secret to publicity for his expeditions, for news reporters loved to emphasize the unusual activities of the women.

After several years in British Guiana, Will became intrigued with the Galapagos Islands and wanted to expand on the research Charles Darwin did there on natural selection. At the time, legislatures were enacting antievolution laws, which banned the teaching of evolution in schools. He convinced the Zoological Society's board to approve a trip to the islands off the coast of Ecuador to collect specimens for the zoo and, incidentally, to conduct research to support the theory of natural selection. Now he needed to find a patron to finance it.

Blair knew that since the pheasant expedition, Will had become quite adept at attracting significant donors. In 1923, he had told Harrison Williams, a utilities mogul and newly elected member of the Zoological Society's Board of Trustees, about his interest in taking a temporary sabbatical from studying birds to study ocean life. Williams offered to charter the 250-foot steam yacht *Noma* as long as he could invite his friends, so that Will could sail to the Galapagos Islands to explore the ocean there. After the expedition, Will wrote a best-selling book on the trip. He hoped to return to the Galapagos to continue his land-based research, but Williams had other thoughts. The following year, Williams convinced Henry Whiton, the president of Union Sulphur Company and a fellow member of the Bronx Zoo's board, to lend Will the *Arcturus*, his steam-powered yacht. Whiton agreed but said he preferred to visit the Sargasso Sea to trawl among the seaweed. Desperate for money, Will agreed to a Sargasso Sea expedition. It was a decision that would change his life: he would focus his research on marine biology for the next decade.

The ocean-going expeditions captivated the attention of the public even more than his jungle studies. They also attracted more generous donations. But he soon found out that, although the Zoological Society appreciated the increased publicity on its most famous curator (and the increase in financial support as a consequence), they wanted to tamp down any mention of the women members on the expedition.

Illustration 14. Gloria Hollister and Diving Helmet (ca. 1926)

CHAPTER 10

TOO MANY GIRL PICTURES

> ***The volumes which record the history of the human race are filled with the deeds and the words of great men but The Twentieth Century Woman questions the completeness of the story.***
>
> **—MARY RITTER BEARD, HISTORIAN AND SOCIETY MEMBER**

APRIL 1925

Metropolitan New York

When Blair opened the *New York Times*, she read the headline on the front page: *Beebe Ship Silent 11 Days as Radio Calls to Her in Vain.* The *Arcturus* had set sail for the Sargasso Sea two months earlier. The *Times* had started reporting on the expedition months earlier, with teasers about the fabled mysterious Sargasso Sea. The *Times* justified this advance press: "We are childishly delighted when one spirit among us, like William Beebe, stalks out of the ranks and sets sail for a region that has as romantic a name as the Sargasso Sea." The public was aware of this part of the ocean mostly through stories and novels, and many believed it to be a "tangled mass of yellow seaweed, so thick it looks like a meadow."

Blair read on: "Some Alarm Expressed. 51 Persons on Board." But the *Times* reassured readers that the New York Zoological Society was not concerned about the break in communication. Static, which was common near the equator, often interfered with wireless messages. Although the ship had two state-of-the-art radio receivers and two wireless operators, it was not unusual for there to be long silences in this area of the world where wireless stations were few and far between.

At least one future member of the Society was closely watching the *Arcturus* expedition: Gloria Hollister.

For as long as she could remember, Gloria wanted to be a deep-sea diver. When she was a young child, she experimented with ways to sit on the riverbed. As Gloria tramped into the house, a long glass air tube in her hand, her mother would say, "Dear me. Goodness, what a child." Gloria tied rocks around her waist and tried to sit on the basin of the Mahwah River. She found she could breathe through the hose but could not expel air.

"The tube won't work, darn it," Gloria complained to her mother. "I have another idea."

She rooted through the house until she found a large, rectangular tin can. She added a glass window and headed back to the river to try it out. Her mother sighed.

By the time she entered college, Gloria had read many of Will's books. She decided to major in zoology at Connecticut College. In the summer of 1923, as she was about to enter her senior year, the slim, athletic woman wrote to Will Beebe, now forty-six, most likely in her role as president of the student body, to invite him to speak at the college's convocation. She received a quick reply. Will suggested that Gloria call him and arrange a meeting, saying, "I find that 20 minutes of talk equals many hours of letters." After they spoke, Will agreed to be the speaker at the opening ceremony.

A few months later, Gloria was arranging the film projector and slide lantern at Connecticut College for Will's lecture *A Naturalist in the Guiana Jungle*. She recalled, "I was setting up the picture slides, and he came back to see that I didn't put them in upside down." They talked about her studies, and Will told Gloria that when she graduated, she should contact him. Gloria could hardly believe her luck. She had never been to the jungle but desperately wanted to work there.

When Will signaled Gloria, she started the film projector. Leaf-eating ants filled the screen. Gloria was mesmerized. Next, a magnificent waterfall filled the screen. Gloria longed to visit such a place.

Gloria knew that the scientists at Will's research station were specialists. So after college, to make herself a more attractive hire, she enrolled in Columbia University to get a master's degree in zoology. After graduation, Gloria contacted Will about a position on his next expedition. He told her to be patient as his team was already full.

Gloria knew how difficult it was for a woman to get a position on a scientific expedition. She also knew that Will had hired women before, although they tended to be scientific artists such as Anna Heyward Taylor. This probably strengthened Gloria's resolve to hound Will until he gave her a job.

Gloria was particularly interested in joining Will's latest expedition because the scientists were studying ocean life instead of birds. While she waited, she got a job in a research laboratory and followed the *Arcturus* expedition in the news.

Five of the fourteen members of the *Arcturus* expedition were women: artists Isabel Cooper and Helen Tee-Van, bacteriologist Lillian Segal, ichthyologist Marie Fish, and historian Ruth Rose. Although Will was smitten with Ruth, she would soon fall in love with Ernest Schoedsack, the expedition's cinematographer. At six-and-a-half feet tall, his friends called him Shorty. He had just returned from filming *Grass* with future Society founder Marguerite Harrison and Merian Cooper.

Reporters relished the large number of women in the expedition. Gene Cohn, a journalist for the NEA News Service, wrote about these "intrepid girl scientists": "And were it further necessary for woman to prove worthy of emancipation the story of this ages-old mystery [of the Sargasso Sea] will be jotted down by a dainty, sun-burned hand."

Many people would visit them on the *Arcturus* for part of the journey. Western author Zane Grey dropped by on his sailboat. Student Gregory Bateson, the future husband of Margaret Mead, assisted Will on the expedition. Dorothy Putnam and her twelve-year-old son David would join them later, increasing the number of women to more than 30 percent.

Dorothy was a fun-loving woman who loved to entertain and to organize brain games, such as charades. Her husband, George, Will's literary agent and publisher, knew that she loved parties and social crowds. He was lonesome when she went on the expedition. He wrote to her, "Oh dear girl, once in a while just pretend you like me better than anyone else, and that you prefer being with me all alone, to being in a giddy crowd." Although she may have been the life of the party, she also very much enjoyed doing the scientific legwork. George tried to goad her into feelings of guilt. He said that when he told her mother that she had decided to stay on board for an additional six weeks, she "was pretty surprised and critical." Dorothy's mother told George, "Can't see how she can do it. Leave you that long. Leave her new house. Leave the [four-year-old] baby. It's not fair." Sometimes, he laid the guilt on thick: "I want you to come back and love me ridiculously. There's an immense amount of work that you must do with the new house, but that's the small part of it all. The big job is to fuss over me, get that. I'm just played out playing solitaire. Now I'm going all in and going to bed, and I need you so much. Look, Hon, I didn't mean to make this note a wail."

Dorothy's participation in the *Arcturus* expedition made her realize that she was more than a wife. According to her granddaughter, Sally Putnam Chapman, Dorothy was "independent, self-sufficient not only physically, but emotionally. In discovering her own self-worth, Dorothy would no longer be satisfied as Mrs. George Putnam—hostess, wife, and mother—and she could no longer disguise her growing detachment." Dorothy's diary reflected her indecision: "I seem to have reached the exact spot in the general 'spottiness' of life, when I am undecided which road to take!"

George told Will that he was "fabulously courageous to go off on a floating wallowing steamer with so much femininity. Myself, I would kick seven of them in the teeth within the first fifty-six hours." He also told Will that Madison Grant, president of the New York Zoological Society, was not pleased with the Department of Tropical Research. Although Grant appreciated the fact that the team worked hard, produced more publications than the zoo's other departments, and generated more publicity, he did not appreciate the party-like atmosphere of the expedition. At sea, the U.S. rules on prohibition did not apply. One of Will's colleagues at the zoo said, "He was a severe task master and expected everyone who worked with him to work as indefatigably as he himself did." In particular, Grant probably detested Don

Dickerman, a pirate aficionado that Will hired as an artist. It did not take much for Dickerman to convince Will—who loved costume parties and games—that a pirate party on the high seas was just what the team needed to relax. It would be a perfect birthday party for David Putnam's thirteenth birthday. The group relaxed with vigor stimulated by booze.

The newly renovated *Arcturus*—retrofitted with a $250,000 ($3.8 million today) floating laboratory—had a new dance floor and state-of-the-art radio receivers. The *Brooklyn Daily Eagle* wrote, "The expedition is not to be all work and no play. In the party are three women,* all of whom, in addition to their scientific qualifications, can dance. After the day's work of dredging and diving and looking through the microscope is over the party will tune in on the best jazz music program in New York and there will be dancing under a tropical moon in the warm tropical climate." The reporter concluded, probably to Madison Grant's consternation, "Both scientifically and socially it should be a great success." And it was a social success: "Fancy dress costume parties, impromptu musical nights, equator-crossing ceremonies, alcoholic indulging, and goofing for the camera are in evidence throughout the trail of photos, films, and anecdotal evidence left by the Department of Tropical Research." A few years later, during the Depression, a reviewer, R. L. Duffus, wrote, "While stocks have been shooting the chute and governments tottering, Dr. William Beebe has been wandering over submerged reefs in a bathing suit and diving helmet. He has too much fun, he has more fun than a man ought to have in a world which is in as desperate condition as this one."

In an article about scientific artist Isabel Cooper, then

---

* Apparently, the scientific artists were not worthy of mention. There were actually five at the beginning and, later, eight, when guests joined them.

thirty-three, the *Philadelphia Inquirer* quoted William Beebe as saying that the ocean voyage to explore the unknown part of the ocean called the Sargasso Sea "was the multiplication of a dozen romances." The article said that Isabel was trying to decide whether to give up her life of adventure for a life of domesticity or whether to continue to follow her dream to travel throughout the world. The reporter described the second option as "far-off places where romance is supposed to lurk in waiting just around every corner, where the world is always flooded with sunlight and where men are either great lovers or daring rascals."

Newspapers cast the *Arcturus* expedition in a romantic light. And the aspersion was perhaps not too far off. Isabel wrote to Harrison Williams, the sponsor, "I expect we will all suffer acutely when we get back to civilization at having to dress in good form again. We have been living in bathing suits and other negligee garments. The men especially have been seeing how much surface they could expose to the equatorial sun and still survive."

In a letter to Will during the *Arcturus* expedition, publicist George Putnam said that Madison Grant was not happy with the undignified publicity that the expedition was receiving. George wrote to Will, "I reckon he means the pictures. Of course, as is inevitable, the papers use chiefly the photos of the charming young women. That is always the case."

George asked Will to send more pictures of the scientific work of the expedition. When he received them, he congratulated Will: "There practically wasn't a woman in them and they were all dignified as they could be." He asked Will to remind cinematographer Schoedsack to send more pictures of *Grass*, a reference to the film he had just completed. In this context, *Grass* was probably a code word for pictures of the expedition without women. Will was irritated by Madison Grant's criticism about the women explorers. He complained to George that on the next trip he was going to "ship off alone." George replied, "I don't blame you. In fact, I think a real he-man trip is exactly what you should do next. A trip alone, or with just a couple of men."

A month later, George met with Fairfield "Fair" Osborn Jr., a member of the board of trustees of the Zoological Society and the son of Professor Fairfield Osborn, who was William Beebe's mentor at the zoo. Osborn told George that they needed to be tactical about the women on the expedition. George conveyed the message to Will, starting with an apology:

> In the first place, I grant that I let too many girl pictures get by me in that first batch and I know you didn't like it. Anyway, henceforward the feminine element has been soft-pedaled satisfactorily. Fair and I want to help you on that head when you get back here. He and I undoubtedly will go down to the bay in a tug to meet you. Perhaps we will smuggle, say Dorothy and David [his wife and child] and one girl ashore in the tug. If that does not prove practicable, I think a stern order should go out from you, the commander, that the women are to be as little in evidence as possible at the landing. Certainly, tell them that none of them is to talk beyond the absolute necessities. (I can see you saying "for God's sake! This is coming from George.") The girls should say to the reporters, "Dr. Beebe* will give out all the informa-

* Will was not a doctor, except by honorary degrees. He left college early to work at the zoo. But he used the initials ScD and LLD after his name in the book *Half Mile Down* to the consternation of the registrar of Columbia University, who knew that he had not graduated from Columbia. In 1950, Will explained that he only had honorary degrees but that Professor Osborn, his mentor, had "pulled [him] out of his graduate work" to work at the zoo. Will never attended graduate school.

> tion." And then poor Dr. Beebe, whether he wants to or not, will have to calmly take half an hour and sit down with the reporters and answer every damn question they want to ask. You may as well face the realization of that necessity. And then the young ladies can all disburse in their several directions, and we will all be there to cooperate in soft-pedaling them as much as can be. Not that there is anything reprehensible in it, but *that*, from your standpoint, is wisdom.

Although many of the expedition's photographs managed to slip through George's grasp and leak into the media, Will's published writing tended to be devoid of intimate references to women or any other person: he wrote as if he traveled alone. He implied that his life was monkish. His biographer, Robert Welker, observed that "women are not noted as being present, or they are but distantly involved." But, as the photographs show, especially the unpublished ones, Beebe's implied monkishness is "something of a gentlemanly delusion." The pictures of women released to the news, however, probably encouraged Gloria, who was still patiently waiting for an opening on the staff.

When Gloria read the headline in the *New York Times* about the missing *Arcturus*, she fretted. Beebe was her future. She felt that she was close to reaching her childhood dream of diving underwater. What if something had happened to the *Arcturus*? The next day, she must have breathed a sigh of relief when the *Times* reported that the ship's wirelesses had been interrupted by static: the crew was safe, and had witnessed a double volcano in the Galapagos Islands that interfered with the radio signals.

After the *Arcturus* returned to New York, Gloria received a special delivery letter from Will Beebe. She opened it with excitement and read, "Please, Gloria Hollister, call me up and come see me as soon as you can. I have an idea.—Will Beebe" She immediately called him.

Will told Gloria that he had recommended her as a travel companion for Mrs. Roger Mitchell, "a society woman who had grown tired of the superficial and monotonous rounds of luncheons, dinners and bridge parties and wanted to do something entirely different and something which she considered worthwhile." Will suggested that Mrs. Mitchell travel to Trinidad and British Guiana with Gloria. Gloria accepted the job, although she was worried about traveling to foreign countries without a male escort. "I jumped at the opportunity like a race-horse at the word 'go.' Of course, my family circle was horrified, and my friends, too, expressed themselves in no uncertain language. The idea of two lone white women embarking for a distant land of jungle, wild animals, and Indians was shocking and awful. But criticism can never influence determination when you know what you want to do and are certain that you are right in doing it."

But the journey proved fruitful because in Trinidad, Gloria found a rare guacharo bird. She published a detailed record of her expedition and lectured on it. The feat of collecting the rare and difficult-to-get bird, writing an article about it, and traveling on the lecture circuit would prompt an invitation from the Society of Woman Geographers.

Although Gloria was grateful to Will for arranging the trip to British Guiana with Mrs. Mitchell, she still hoped to work for him. She read Will's most recent book, *The Arcturus Adventure*. When she read the opening paragraph, she must have felt an intense longing to be a member of Will's team: "I am floating in mid-space beneath a dense grape arbor with the sun shining through a mat of yellow-green leaves and the unripe fruit glowing like myriads of jade beads. Then the air becomes chokingly oppressive—I gasp—kick out violently with my feet and shoot up through the tangled mess of olive growth. Dripping like Neptune, wreathed like Bacchus, my head breaks water in mid-ocean in a mass of sargassum weeds—a thousand miles from land."

As she read on, Gloria probably imagined she was underwater with Will: "I am twenty feet underwater with a huge copper helmet on my head, tilting my trident against an olive green grouper over a yard long, who is much too fearless and inquisitive for my liking." Will was wearing a sixty-pound, copper-framed, conical diving helmet with two glass windows in the center. A hose was attached to the back and ran to a pump on board the boat. Gloria was reminded of her oilcan helmet.

Now, even more determined to be a member of Will's expedition team, she reminded him of her interest. He promised to give her the first available position. Again, she waited.

Two years later, in 1928, Will called Gloria.

"Dr. Beebe speaking. I am taking an expedition to Bermuda this summer, and there is a place for you, if you want it,"

"Want it?" Gloria nearly shouted with glee. "When do we start?"

Will hired Gloria as a general technician. The eight-person expedition team included four women, three of whom would later join the Society. Gloria described the invitation as "the answer to a maiden's prayer."

It did not take long for the 28-year-old woman* to develop a schoolgirl crush on the 51-year-old naturalist, especially since he was making her childhood dream of walking on the ocean floor

* Newspapers identified her as twenty-three years old, but she was actually twenty-eight. She looked twenty-three.

come true. Gloria took turns with the other scientists using the diving helmet. She would use an electric toy popgun to stun the fish so that she could bring them back to shore alive and study them. When she donned the helmet for the first time, she was surprised by its lightness: "It feels like a feather underwater."

One time, while she was looking at some lavender-colored snails on the ocean basin, the air to her helmet stopped flowing. She took a deep breath and inhaled the oxygen that had collected in the mask, and waited for the pump to start working. Water began to flood into the helmet. When it reached her chin, she stretched to move her head further up into the mask. The water reached her nose. Gloria grabbed the boat ladder and hauled herself up to the surface. She was stunned when she reached the surface. The entire crew was looking up at the sky, watching the migration of birds, totally oblivious to her emergency.

Despite this mishap, Gloria was falling for Will. He was a sucker for adoring young women, and soon they were romantically involved. Like a schoolboy, he wrote in his diary in a secret code: "I kissed Gloria and she loves me."

But Will was already committed to another adoring woman. The previous year, Will had married romance novelist Elswyth Thane on board a yacht moored in Oyster Bay at the Roosevelt home. Elswyth was twenty-seven, and Will was fifty. One reporter quipped, "Truth to tell, we had thought of Dr. Beebe as quite a settled old gentleman, but as so often, we find we were wrong."*

Although it was clearly inappropriate for Will to enter into a sexual relationship with Gloria and other woman employees,

---

* Reportedly, Will and Elswyth had an open marriage. On one of the few occasions when Elswyth visited Bermuda, she stormed off. Newspapers speculated that Gloria was the cause of the premature departure. The front-page headline in Elswyth's hometown paper read, "Report of Discord in Beebe Family 'Utter Rot,' Des Moines Woman Says." In public, Elswyth chose to ignore the affair.

even today his reputation remains relatively untarnished because he gave women career opportunities that they would not otherwise have had. As a result of her job at the Department of Tropical Research, Gloria would soon achieve worldwide fame.

On Nonsuch Island in Bermuda, Gloria worked on the difficult problem of how to observe a fish's skeleton without dissecting it. She and an assistant worked in the tropical research station's laboratory, which she affectionately called the Clearing House for it was where they made fish clear, and where they had many noisy discussions. The Bermudans called it the House of Magic, because Gloria mysteriously turned fish transparent there. Gloria thought, "History recalls that not many years ago a woman was burned to death on St. David's Island nearby, as a witch, for working minor magic; I could easily qualify if those days were not past."

Gloria found that "beauty is not skin deep" when she applied a combination of dyes, bleaches, and chemicals to the fish: "Every bone, tendon, muscle and fiber assumes an individuality, with a characteristic pattern." When she poured the dye concoction over the fish, its body faded away, and its bones became permanently visible for study.

The process was complicated. First, Gloria immersed the fish for hours in alizarin, a staining agent, which colored the bones scarlet. When the skeleton was stained, Gloria gave the fish a series of bleaching and ammonia baths to decolor the fish's skin and tissues. Then, she soaked the fish in potassium or sodium baths to rid the bones of scarlet and produce a "transparent, ghost-like form."

Gloria found the technique to be much more reliable than the X-ray, for it allowed her to study the specimen rather than a photographic plate. In addition, the dye produced a much cleaner and clearer image. It was also much easier than dissecting the fish.

By experimentation, she learned that, contrary to expectations, fresh fish produced a better result than preserved fish: "It was almost unbelievable to see the scarlet skeleton of a small trigger-fish, apparently suspended in mid-fluid, with the remainder of the fish wholly invisible—and to remember that only twelve hours before, the little fellow had been swimming, happy and opaque." She believed that she had set "a time record for producing a perfectly stained and cleared transparency." She recalled, "The skeletons tell us invaluable things about the habits of all these deep-sea fish, which we may never be able to study in the icy submarine haunts."

One of the reasons that the research station moved to Nonsuch Island was to test out the bathysphere designed by Otis Barton. In 1926, Will announced that he planned to descend a mile deep in a steel cylinder eighteen inches in diameter, seven feet high. The submersible would have a 7 × 12-inch window designed to withstand several tons of pressure per inch. Otis Barton, an engineering student, read about Will's plans and thought, "It won't work." He wrote to Will and offered his help. At first, Will rebuffed him: "Another gadget!" He was relentlessly pursued by crackpots with crazy ideas. But when Otis offered to finance the construction of the submergible, Will agreed to collaborate with him. The bathysphere cost $12,000, or nearly $176,000 today.

Otis convinced Will to change the design to a sphere, rather than a cylinder. A spherical design would more evenly disperse the ocean's pressure at great depths. Will recalled that once, when he and Theodore Roosevelt were talking about diving, Roosevelt drew a sketch of a spherical deep-sea vessel on a napkin, and declared that it was a better design. Now, a decade after the ex-president's death, Will decided to proceed with a spherical design. While Otis was supervising the construction of the sphere, Will thought up the name—bathysphere, named after the deep-sea fish *bathytroctes*. Will liked the Greek prefix *bathy*, meaning *deep*, and combined it with the shape of the submersible to create the name *bathysphere*. Otis Barton described the sphere as an "ungainly ball that looked rather like an enormous inflated and slightly cockeyed bullfrog."

Illustration 15. Gloria Hollister, William Beebe, and John Tee-Van with Bathysphere (1932)

The first test drive of the bathysphere occurred on May 27, 1930. Otis and Will only went forty-five feet on the first manned descent. On June 3, they lowered the unmanned bathysphere to two thousand feet with little problem, except the tangling of cables.

Three days later, they loaded the bathysphere onto a barge with the Arcturus' seven-ton winch and towed the barge eight miles off the coast, where the ocean was a mile deep. As Will climbed through the fourteen-inch hatch to the center of the four-and-a-half foot sphere, he scraped his bare legs on the steel bolts. When he landed on the bottom of the bathysphere, he was not ready for the cold, hard floor. He swore and yelled for a cushion, recalling how miserable sitting on a cold surface for an hour could be. Otis climbed in and they awkwardly disentangled their limbs.

A winch lifted the four hundred-pound door into place with a loud clang, and the crew secured the bolts with a sledgehammer. The sound was deafening inside the sphere. When the hatch was sealed, Will felt as though he was isolated from the world.

Gloria was the only person that Will could communicate with from inside the bathysphere. She was connected to the submergible by a telephone cord. A horn-shaped microphone allowed her to talk with Will. She spoke comforting words to calm Will, who was trying to remember Houdini's method of breathing in a closed coffin. At first, the inside of the sphere seemed huge, but the longer they were in it, the smaller it seemed to become.

Will glanced out of one of the portholes: three inches of fused quartz. Through his microphone, Will gave Gloria the command to descend.

"Lower the bathysphere," she told the winch operator.

The winch picked up the bathysphere. The bathysphere dangled for a moment, like a roller coaster pausing at the summit, ready to plunge. Although the winch gently lowered the steel ball, it caused a huge splash when it hit the water. Inside the 5,000-pound submersible, the impact was barely noticeable.

Gloria kept up a constant chatter with Will. Their protocol

was to avoid a silence of more than five seconds. If Will became preoccupied with examining fish or recording his thoughts, he was supposed to grunt to signal to Gloria that all was fine.

"100 feet," called Gloria through the telephone. "How's it look?"

"There's a slight twilighting and chilling of the blue," responded Will.

"200 feet."

Gloria watched as the winch lowered the submersible another one hundred feet. When it stopped with a gentle tug, workers attached a clamp to the cable.

"300 feet," she said.

They were now deeper than the sunken *SS Lusitania,* on which Will and Blair had sailed at the start of the pheasant expedition. In a few feet, they would be below the greatest depth reached by Navy divers.

Over the microphone, Gloria heard Otis yelp. Her heart lurched.

"What's happening?"

"There's a leak," Will told Gloria.

"Are you alright?"

"Yes."

"400 feet."

Gloria knew that they had surpassed the deepest submarine dive.

"Is the leak increasing?"

"No, it is not."

Gloria breathed a sigh of relief.

"600 feet. What does it look like around you?" Gloria asked Will.

"It looks like a very long twilight. Only by shutting my eyes and opening them again can I realize the terrible slowness of the deepening shade. There's luminous creatures here."

Gloria tried to imagine a twilight ocean twinkling with bioluminescent fish, appearing like the first stars of the night.

"What depth, now?" Otis asked Gloria.

"700 feet. Are you alright?"

"Yes." Gloria thought she heard some doubt in his voice. Or was it fear?

"It's as brilliant as ever." Will told Gloria.

"800 feet," Gloria reported.

"Halt the descent," Will told Gloria.

"Halting at 803 feet," she replied. She wondered what was wrong. She knew that sometimes Will's hunches were so vivid that he could not ignore them.

She continued to keep up a chatter as the bathysphere ascended.

"600 feet."

"400 feet." It seemed like the ascent was taking longer than the descent, but Gloria knew it was because she was worried about Will.

The winch deposited the bathysphere onto the deck and workers removed the bolts. Gloria stood by as Will tried to climb out of the sphere. When he stumbled, Gloria moved closer, ready to help. She thought that perhaps his feet had fallen asleep. He hurled himself onto the deck. Otis staggered out behind him.

After his legs began to obey his brain signals, Will leaned into the bathysphere and started rummaging around. Gloria wondered what he was looking for. He complained about a pain in his buttocks.

Will pulled a wrench out of the submersible and held it up for Gloria to see.

"I was sitting on the monkey wrench," he told her.

Gloria probably had a few days of fun teasing Will about the distinct impression of the tool on his backside.

Soon, Gloria started hounding Will for a ride in the bathysphere.

Four days later, the crew descended the unmanned bathysphere to two thousand feet. Then Will and Otis descended to 250 feet.

The next day, the weather held, and Gloria talked to Otis and Will as they descended to 1426 feet. After the dive, Will announced that Gloria and John Tee-Van would make a descent that afternoon. Gloria was elated! She would be a passenger on their fourth manned descent of the bathysphere. Gloria recalled, "I had forgotten it was my birthday. It was the strangest and most desirable birthday present in the world." On June 11, 1930, at 12:32 p.m., Gloria and John squirmed into the steel ball. The door was lowered, and Gloria heard the crew hammer the ten large bolts into place. As she looked out of the porthole, she could see the boat's large winch that would lower the bathysphere into the water. Through her headphones, she heard Will say, "You're off."

She felt a jolt, and suddenly she was swaying. The bathysphere halted for a moment. As the winch lowered the steel ball, Gloria saw air bubbles rising in the water, bathed in the sunlight. As she descended deeper, the sunlight disappeared, and the water became blue-green. Jellyfish and shrimp floated by, and "fish butted savagely against the window and darted away into blue space." It never occurred to her to be frightened: "I was far too interested in what I was seeing. Only once, when I felt a drop of water, did I even think of anything going wrong. When I realized it was moisture from condensed air, I again completely forgot about the bathysphere."

At 410 feet below the surface, she asked Will to lower them another one hundred feet. He refused, and she felt the winch start to pull up the bathysphere.

When the bolts were hammered out, and the hatch was opened, Gloria "emerged from her steel chrysalis, excited by the unforgettable experience of this hour."

It was not her only dive, but it was her most memorable.

That summer, Will hired two women to join the Bermuda team: twenty-one-year-old Jocelyn Crane and forty-seven-year-old Else Bostelmann. Both women would become members of the Society. Jocelyn met Will when he gave a lecture at Smith College. She was an adoring fan, much like his new wife Elswyth Thane and Gloria. Carol Gould, Beebe's biographer, explained Jocelyn's adoration of Will: "From her solitary childhood, she had lived a fantasy life through Beebe's tales of birds and people and fish and adventures in exotic locales. She had read and reread every single one of his books, reveling vicariously in his dangers and discoveries, and loving the natural history he canonized." Jocelyn did not find it easy to convince Will to hire her as an unpaid intern. She later recalled, "I had to work like blazes for eighteen months, through letters, three additional interviews, a deluge of good marks, copies of term papers, and my entire honors thesis to convince him it was worthwhile to give me a trial as a volunteer worker." But the deciding factor for Will seems to have been the sizable donation that Jocelyn's mother made to the expedition.

When Jocelyn was around, Gloria tended to be an "alpha female," because Jocelyn idolized Will. Gloria knew that Will had a weakness for young, adoring, pretty women, and she worried that Jocelyn might be a threat to her romantic relationship with Will.

When asked why he hired two women associates (Gloria

and Jocelyn), Will replied, "I am after adaptable scientific students who fall in with my plans, and sometimes women offer just those qualities. It's what is above the ears that I am after for the expeditions." A reporter noted, "Both young women have sleek permanent waves above the ears, incidentally, and complete and very feminine wardrobes, including formal dresses for parties at the Governor's house in Bermuda." Jocelyn Crane recalled, "Will was one of the first to have women assistants. First they came as wives—the wife of the artist, or some other worker. Then the women came on their own. If they could do the job, that was the criterion, and that's it." But a telegram to Gloria supposedly from Gypsy Rose Lee, the famous striptease artist—but most likely a pseudonym for Will—tells a different story. Alluding to Gloria's work with chemically induced bone transparency, "Gypsy Rose" propositioned Gloria: "In the interest of science, how would you like to tint my osteological structure, babe?"

Else Bostelmann was a German-born divorcée. Her paintings were striking, colorful, and bold. Within days after she was hired, she "dazzled Will and everyone else with her renditions of the strange creatures of the abyss. She had a gift for visualizing the dead or living specimens that were her subjects as though they were swimming in the deep ocean. Their anatomies signaled motion and vitality to Bostelmann, and her interpretations of them leaped from her easel."

Will and his crew would trawl for fishes and sea life at a thousand fathoms and then give the fish to Else to draw. When the fish was removed from its ice-cold waters and dragged up thousands of feet at a reduced pressure, it changed color. As the fish decompressed, its swim bladder expanded and pushed its way out of the fish's mouth. They had to find a better way to paint fish from the deep.

One of the difficulties the expedition crew faced was that sea creatures did not look the same above the surface as they did in their natural habitat. Else noticed immediately—even thirty-six feet under—that "there was no red to be seen anywhere, nor the delightful purples of the sea-fans which I had seen two fathoms higher up during my descent. At this depth those two colors have already disappeared as far as human observation is concerned and my red bathing suit, the red sea anemones and the purple gorgonians all appeared just gray."

It would have been enormously helpful if Else had descended in the bathysphere to see the fish that Will asked her to paint. But Will refused to let Else descend. She explained to a reporter, "Doctor Beebe would not take me in the Bathysphere because I had a teenage daughter and he didn't want me to be in danger." Instead, she contrived a way to paint twenty-five-feet underwater with oil paints. She would climb down a boat ladder. Once she was in the water, the boat crew would lower the sixty-pound copper diving helmet onto her head and hand her drawing supplies: a zinc engraver's plate and a steel pen to draw the underwater world. As she descended to ten feet, a pain pierced her ears, and she remembered the admonition: swallow. She recalled, "Possibly I did swallow—I do not remember; but looking down, I saw the seascape was coming to meet me. I gazed into a magnificent valley with peaks of tall coral reefs, swaying sea-plumes, slender gorgonians, purple sea-fans. Forgotten then was all the pain—I must go down just a few steps more, and a few more." She continued to descend into "a fairyland, six fathoms below the surface—thirty-six feet as landsman know them." Painting the coral reefs was one of her favorite tasks. It was "her own underwater 'fairyland.'"

It was not easy to draw on her zinc plate with her steel pencil: "It seemed almost unbelievable how slowly I was able to bring my right hand up to the left one which held the zinc plate so I could make my notes." Else enjoyed painting underwater:

> After I descended, my painting outfit was lowered by ropes from the boat. Generally, I used an iron music stand for an easel on which was tied my frame covered with stretched canvas. My palette was weighed with lead and on it were squeezed gobs of color in all the rainbow hues. The use of wet colors under water in this way might at first strike one as impossible, unbelievable. But oil colors have never yet mixed with water. My brushes were securely tied to the palette and, as one can imagine, floated with their wooden handles upright, tugging lightly at their strings and bobbing in the gentle current.

Will began a new practice: when he returned from a bathysphere dive he would review his telephoned notes. Often, Else Bostelmann would record the telephone log. They would review the log and go "into an artistic huddle." Will would scrawl some pictures of fish, and Else would make tentative sketches, and then he would make changes. He called the fish that no one saw but he and Otis, "brain fish" because they seemed to exist only in their brains. "Little by little," he recalled, under Else's brush, "my brain fish materialized, its proportions, size, color, lights, finally interdigitated with those of my memory."

Will "viewed marine life as an altogether mad world, full of paradoxes and as fantastic as the whimsical characters in *Alice in Wonderland*, his favorite book." Else brought to life Will's verbal caricatures of sea creatures such as the resident of Lobster Alley, whose "antennae are forever protruding from the window of her apartment." Else's pictures were like a porthole into another world. Will said, "Else Bostelmann gave her best in the colored paintings of deep-sea creatures, and when there is only my memory to assist and check, the artist must indeed be good."

Numerous scientists challenged Will's claims that he had seen unusual fish from the bathysphere. And, indeed, some of the fish were bizarre. Carl L. Hubb challenged the bioluminescent fish that Will called the *Bathysphaera intacta* because no one other than Will had ever seen a bioluminescent fish.* He speculated that Will had seen a photophosphorescent fish "whose lights were beautified by halation in passing through a misty film breathed onto the quartz window by Mr. Beebe's eagerly apressed face." Even Otis suspected that Will invented the *Bathysphaera intacta*: "His description sounds a little fishy to me. I'm not calling him a liar; he had a better view than me. But this species hadn't been seen before and I don't think since."

Fortunately, Will's bad reputation among scientists did not rub off on his woman staff.

In 1932, Gloria Hollister became famous throughout the world when NBC broadcast a live transmission of William Beebe's half-mile descent into the ocean in the bathysphere. Gloria was in radio communication with Will the entire time. Unfortunately, newspapers identified her as Will's stenographer. Her agent set up a series of lectures. Soon everyone was talking about Gloria Hollister, the beautiful ichthyologist.

Brushed under the carpet was the fact that the Department of Tropical Research's field stations operated almost exclusively in British colonies or overseas territories. Will located the station in British Guiana, "a colonized country with the reputation of being

---

* Will readily admitted that it was difficult to identify the fish because either the fish or the bathysphere would move.

rich in natural resources." Historian Katherine McLeod notes, "The field stations Beebe established in South America answer Roosevelt's call to enter the South American wilderness in the name of U.S. progress." His patrons included the Aluminum Company of America and the Standard Oil company, both of which had a strong investment in South America.

Not only did Will assist the United States' interest in the mining of natural resources, he exploited the "intellectual and physical labor of the local populations." For example, he used convicts to clear trails through the jungle. One of the countries he visited in his undersea explorations was Haiti, which was under U.S. occupation. He sailed there soon after his ex-wife, Blair, wrote a bestselling book about the racism that permeated Haiti.

PART 4

ADVOCATING FOR BLACK PEOPLE, GAY MEN, AND FRENCH PRISONERS

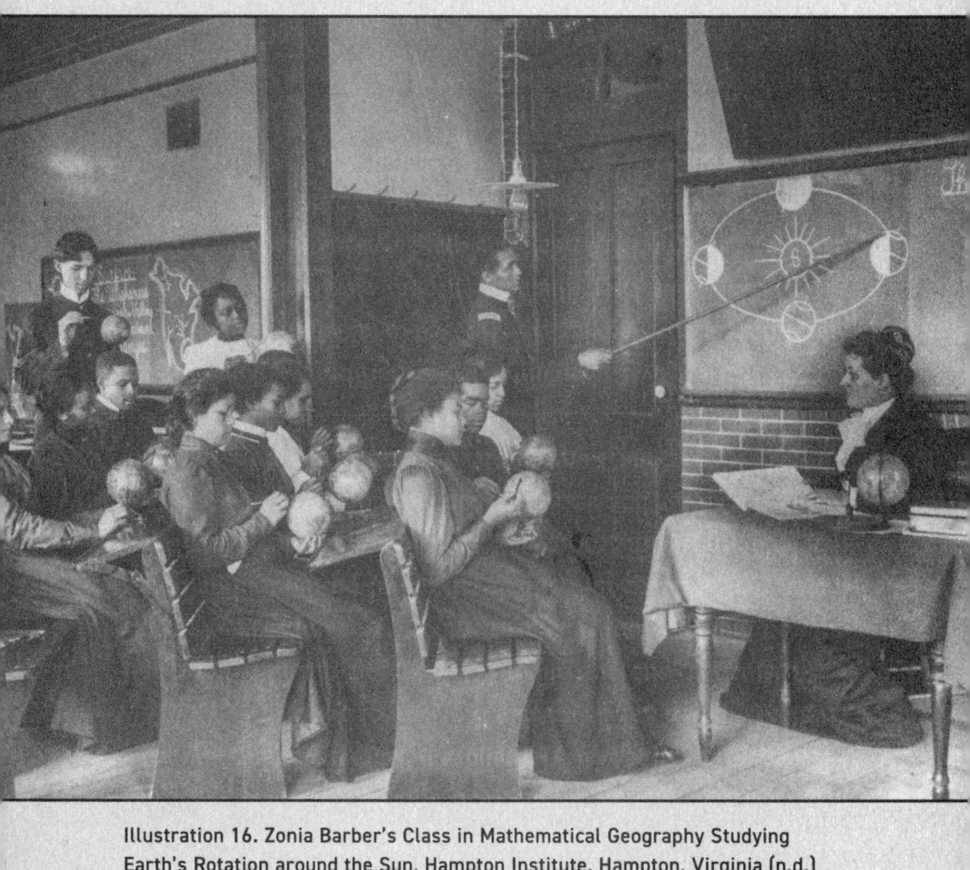

Illustration 16. Zonia Barber's Class in Mathematical Geography Studying Earth's Rotation around the Sun, Hampton Institute, Hampton, Virginia (n.d.)

CHAPTER 11
IMPRISONED BY WHITENESS

Thus, to the Haitians, their heroes are not law figures stuffed with noble sawdust, but men—Africans of extraordinary personality.

—BLAIR NILES, AUTHOR AND FOUNDER OF THE SOCIETY

1924
Manhattan

Blair walked home from the New York Public Library, where she spent her days researching Haiti. As she turned the corner of Lexington Avenue onto 49th Street, she smiled when she saw her pink stucco townhouse surrounded by drab brownstones. She was glad that Robin had converted the five-story apartment building into a tropical refuge. It was a constant reminder of their travels to South America, "a flash of Southern color, a concrete bit of Latin America in New York." Blair hurried toward the building, anxious to get home. She unlatched the wrought iron gate and carefully closed it, then walked up the flight of stairs to the arched entrance.

Inside the lobby, she checked her mailbox and headed for the elevator. The elevator operator was a ruddy ship captain, temporarily landlocked in a small lift. He stood before the elevator crankshaft, his stance wide, as though he were standing before a ship's wheel.

Blair had told the captain that she was going to Haiti. The last time they talked, she was surprised to discover that he was biased against Black Haitians. Today, she was ready to confront him. She asked him why he was prejudiced.

"When I was in Haiti, last March, a big nigger came up to me. 'If I could get you alone,' he told me, 'I'd cut your heart out and eat it.' And, what's more, he meant it too."

Blair thought, "My captain with the blue Nordic eyes takes the matter of eating hearts quite seriously. He remains convinced that in Haiti, fearful things might happen to the hearts of white men. He is credulous because it is so easy to believe what has been countless times said, to believe what many before you have credited, for reputation greases the ways of belief."

Disturbed, she got off the elevator on the fifth floor and entered their penthouse apartment. She was immediately comforted by the decor the Himalayan mural on the folding doors that led to the dining room wall, the Chinese window that Robin had designed for her, and the wallpaper copied from a tapestry she had seen in the Kensington Museum in London. She was going to Haiti.

As she put away her notes from the library, Blair thought about the captain's advice. She refused to take him at his word.

A few weeks later, Blair and Robin were walking down a narrow street in Haiti when Blair spied a young Black boy sitting on the edge of the sidewalk, sounding out words.

Ca-lam-i-té.

Mo-ral-i-té.

He was wearing hand-me-down overalls several sizes too big and a straw hat that was too small. "He cannot have possibly seen more than seven rainy seasons fall upon the thirsty streets of Cape Haitian," she thought.

The recitation of the young Haitian interrupted her reverie.

Ti-mid-i-té.

Sé-gur-i-té.

Blair was enchanted by the intensity of the tiny boy. "Robin!" she cried to her husband. "I must have a picture!" Robin was the official photographer for the expedition.

Robin prepared to take the picture. The child posed and smiled, and just as Robin was about to release the shutter, a Creole man intervened.

"I oppose!"

"But why?" Blair asked, astonished.

"Because I will not have it! I will not have the child put on a postcard and labeled a 'monkey'! That is why you want the picture. And I will not have it!"

"Ah, no! It was because he was so small and so studious, and the words so long—"

"That is only your bluff." The man shook his head in sorrow.

Blair took some candies from her pocket and asked if she could give them to the boy. The man nodded.

The boy, who was now hiding behind a shop door, poked his head out and smiled. Blair held the candies in her outstretched hand, and the boy ran over to her, grabbed the candy, and ran off.

Blair worried that the experience had scarred the boy for life. "What must such an incident do to a plastic human ego? The idea of race animosity has been planted in his mind. The child will remember what the man said about being labeled 'a monkey on a postcard.' And remembering, he might someday accost a great blond captain walking ashore. It might amuse him to threaten such a captain with cannibalism."

An image from that day would be "branded on her heart forever; that figure of a little man, shaken like some withered yellow leaf which had been scorched in the searing flame of humiliation"—scorched enough to defend a small child from a photograph. She realized that ten years of the American occupation had revived the racism that Haitians had felt under French rule.*

In Port-au-Prince, Blair noticed signs of the white invasion: "The white face of the foreigner is everywhere. The American Club, American drivers in the narrow streets, the great homes of the Haitian aristocracy, leased by American officers. In Port-au-Prince you realize there is an opposition as well as an occupation."

As she stood looking at the street filled with Americans whom she feared were racist, Blair may have thought of her mother, Gordon "Gordy" Pryor Rice, who believed that prejudice was the result of a narrow, uneducated perspective. When Blair and her brothers were old enough to go to school, her mother tutored them for three hours each day and read to them at night. Gordy wanted to expose her children to diverse viewpoints, but the family could not yet afford to send them away to school. As a temporary solution, in the 1890s, Gordy started a night school and invited the sharecroppers' and neighbors'

* The United States occupied Haiti in 1915, after the start of World War I, ostensibly to prevent a German invasion. This justification was a pretext; the real reason was that a revolution had begun in Port-au-Prince in 1915, and the Americans were eager to establish order.

children to attend. She welcomed all children, Black and white, girls and boys. The diverse student body met three nights a week in the plantation's main house. This stopgap measure proved so successful that Gordy continued it for more than a decade. She wrote, "My plan of helping and teaching both races has had a most excellent effect." Gordy believed that when white and Black students got to know each other, prejudice was likely to dissolve.

Blair doubted that integration by means of an American occupation would teach the American soldiers to be more tolerant of the differences between them and the Haitians. Nor was it likely to teach them that there are "as many standards of beauty as there are races," a concept she firmly embraced. Blair knew that "race memories die hard, and somewhere in everyone are beliefs which shrink into the cellar of the subconscious mind, hiding from reason."

Nearby, a drunk policeman read a novel by Alexandre Dumas. He told Blair that his distant cousin had written the book, for Dumas's father was born in Haiti. Blair chuckled as she recalled an interview with Dumas.

"You are a quadroon, Monsieur Dumas?"

"I am, sir."

"And your father?"

"Was a mulatto."

"And your grandfather?"

"A Negro."

Dumas was running out of patience.

"And may I inquire what your great grandfather was?"

"An ape, sir! My pedigree commences where yours terminates."

Blair wondered whether Marie Cessette Dumas, his Black grandmother, of one hundred years ago, would have laughed at such a story or whether she would have been puzzled to understand why the subject was worthy of mention, there being in those days so many children in Haiti whose fathers were French and whose mothers were African?

After she studied Haiti's history, Blair concluded that Americans are ignorant about Haiti's history and its people. "Haitians have little regard for the white race. Why should they?" she thought.

Black Haiti: Africa's Eldest Daughter was Blair's breakthrough book. It told the story of the Toussaint L'Ouverture, the former slave who led the largest uprising of slaves in history, the Haitian Revolution. The Spanish had brought the first African slaves to Haiti (then Saint-Domingue) in 1517. The last slave ship arrived in 1804. After a ten-year war in Saint-Domingue, in 1801, Toussaint became the former French colony's first governor-general and freed the slaves. Within a year, the French military under Napoleon Bonaparte's rule took back control of the island. Napoleon deported Toussaint to France and imprisoned him in the French Jura mountains. Poet Aime Cesaire wrote a poem about Toussaint's experience of being Black:

What is mine too: a small cell in the Jura,
The snow lines it with white bars
The snow is a white gaoler who mounts guard in front
of a prison
What is mine
a man alone, imprisoned by whiteness
a man alone who defies the white screams of a white
death

Blair wrote of the dignity and pride of Black Haitians. Even though Black Haitians had been torn from their native country for generations, they still "gloried in the traditions of the ancestors who won the country for him. It is the memory of their magnificently brave struggle, it is the sense of a subject race having gained for themselves their independence, that expresses itself in their dignity."

The book catapulted her to a new level of fame. Portions of her book were translated into French by the Haitian poet Dominique Hippolyte. The *New York Times* book review was favorable, and over the next few years, the *Times* would publish two of Blair's page-and-a-half articles about Haiti.

Helen Fitzgerald, of the *Brooklyn Daily Eagle*, lavishly praised *Black Haiti*: "Blair Niles has not shirked the truth. Fearlessly she has tackled the ugly as well as the lyric and dramatic. No writer would tell the whole story of an insular Black group evolving a startling patchwork of brutality and heroism. One admires the courage with which Blair Niles deals with this ghastly subject; her judicial fairness in presenting the truth as she sees it." Fitzgerald reported that Blair had recently received a letter from "a member of the black intelligentsia asking for her picture in order that the writer may show it to the incredulous to prove that the author of *Black Haiti* is a white person!" Mary White Ovington, chair of the NAACP, praised the book as an accurate depiction of Haiti under the American occupation. But Blair must have felt the most pride when she discovered, nearly twenty-five years after the publication of the book, that it was among African American poet Langston Hughes's favorite books on Haiti.

Like Blair, Zonia Baber, who recently joined the Society of Woman Geographers, had a strong interest in Haiti. In 1926, she traveled to Haiti with an interracial delegation to investigate and report on conditions in Haiti under the American occupation. The Women's International League for Peace and Freedom (WILPF), a nonprofit organization organized after World War I to unite women in their fight for peace, sponsored the delegation. The commission had six members, four white and two Black. Five were women. Zonia made sure that all committee members were treated equally.

The committee spent three weeks in Haiti, interviewing a wide range of people, including businessmen, educators, physicians, and government workers. In the United States, they met with Haitians and Americans who held differing perspectives on the role of Americans in Haiti. They authored a report that addressed the influence of the American occupation on health, education, government, race relations, and the criminal justice system. The committee recommended that the U.S. military withdraw and stop violating Haiti's right to self-determination. During the occupation, the United States had interfered with the right of Haitians to govern their nation, "the second oldest independent nation in the Western Hemisphere." Historian Mary Renda describes other means by which the United States held the Haitians hostage: "Marines installed a puppet president, dissolved the legislature at gunpoint, denied freedom of speech, and forced a new constitution on the Caribbean nation—one more favorable to foreign investment." The WILPF delegation cited some of these abuses as evidence that Americans had usurped power from the Haitians.

Even worse, the committee reported that the occupation had made the Haitians feel inferior: "There was almost nothing before the Occupation to make Haitians racially self-conscious or to create an 'inferiority complex.'" But, after the occupation, prejudiced Americans made the Haitians feel inferior. The committee challenged the American intervention as "imperialist." As the chairwoman of the committee, Emily Greene Blatch wryly noted, "There are more ways of helping a neighbor who is in trouble than knocking him down and taking possession of his property and family." The committee report cited Blair Niles's book on Haiti as a reference.

Despite these criticisms, the United States would not withdraw from Haiti until 1934, thus ending nearly twenty years of paternalistic rule and domination.

After Blair had completed her book, *Black Haiti: A Biography of Africa's Eldest Daughter*, she turned her attention to another Caribbean island: Guadalupe, a French territory that had recently freed the indentured servants whom plantation owners had culled from India. But when she opened the *New York Times* and read the headline "Passengers for Eternity Board the Martinière—Broken Men Sail for Devil's Island—Condemned to a Living Death," she felt a strange pull.

Blair put down the newspaper, dumbfounded. Although she had read many similar articles written by journalists who had traveled to France to report on the embarkation of prisoners exiled to French Guiana, she realized that she had never read an article that told about what happened when the convicts arrived. She longed "to know what lay behind the silence."

Blair poked her head into the bathroom where Robin was shaving.

"Let's go to French Guiana!"

Robin stopped shaving. He looked at Blair with a puzzled expression on his face. But he was not surprised.

"All right!"

Since the late 1600s, France had been trying to figure out a way to populate its overseas territory of French Guiana, a dense South American jungle surrounded by shark-infested waters. It was a place no one wanted to live. In 1852, Emperor Napoleon Bonaparte decided to civilize its territory by shipping its convicts there and forcing them to build roads and other infrastructure. Napoleon also conceived of *doublage*, which required the ex-prisoners to remain in French Guiana after they served their sentence until they served a sentence of equal length. It was Napoleon's solution to the problem of populating French Guiana, which had been under French rule for over two hundred years, and yet was still a desolate country. He hoped that the men serving *doublage* would marry and have a family—or at least impregnate the woman convicts the government sent to French Guiana. This was not as successful as Napoleon had hoped, as the women routinely had abortions. Eventually, the government halted the sentencing of female convicts to Guiana. In thirty years, no child had survived.

Blair was drawn to French Guiana because it offered a "startling contrast between the primitive and the civilized." There, "the drama of the criminal is staged against a backdrop of tropical jungle, where descendants of escaped Negro slaves live the jungle life of Africa, dancing the African dances and worshipping the African gods while, locked behind the bars of prison, are criminals sent from highly civilized France."

Blair set to work getting permission to visit the penal colony. When she discovered that no foreigner had ever visited the prison on Devil's Island, she feared that her plan was a mad impossibility. Undeterred, she asked the recently appointed governor of French Guiana, Gabriel Henri Joseph Thaly, for permission to visit. To her delight, the governor gave her full access to the penal colony, including the three penitentiary islands.

Illustration 17. Part of Detention House on Devil's Island (1934)

CHAPTER 12

CONDEMNED TO DEVIL'S ISLAND

> *I wanted to see for myself the dangers that they are willing to face, knowing all the time that, should they succeed in [escaping], it is only to be apprehended, sent back, and subjected to drastic punishment. But such is their desperation.*
>
> —BLAIR NILES, AUTHOR AND A FOUNDER OF THE SOCIETY

1926

St. Laurent, French Guiana

On April 29, 1926, Blair and Robin stood on the dock in St. Laurent, French Guiana, impatiently awaiting the arrival of the *La Martinière*, which had sailed from France twenty days earlier. A white pith helmet shielded Blair's eyes from the tropical sunlight as she craned her neck to see the garish ship cruising down the Maroni River. The old German freighter was a study in contrasts, painted with "flaming bars of red and yellow mingled with stripes of black and white to produce a weird effect of cubist painting or wartime camouflage."

The bright, festive day seemed like a holiday. Nearly the entire town of St. Laurent-du-Maroni had turned out for the "town's great (and only) occasion": the annual arrival of the *La Martinière*. Chinese women dressed in colorful frocks, and soldiers donned bright white tropical uniforms and helmets. The former Dutch slaves and Creoles wore bright-colored clothing and showed their gold-capped teeth when they laughed. Maroons* had arrived from inland, wearing loincloths. Even the women had dressed up: they were wearing brassieres—usually shunned apparel. In contrast, Blair thought that the French women looked "like fashion plates sketched at Deauville or the races," and the Black women of French Guiana copied "the Paris mode in every violent hue."

Blair, too, had dressed for the occasion. The sailor's tie of her stylish middy blouse and matching skirt flapped in the soft trade winds. Wisps of her black hair broke loose from the Dutch boy bob hidden beneath her helmet.

The passengers had affected gaiety when they embarked on this grand voyage in Marseilles, France. But Blair knew that the journey spelled doom for the passengers. Their pretense at joie de vivre was a form of bravado. They were not cruising to a tropical destination for pleasure. This was no ordinary ship. It was a floating prison. Blair thought, "They are entering a world where a laugh or a song is as rare as a meteor passing across the sky. The French government has relegated these prisoners to a living death in its South American territory."

The floating prison held 687 prisoners and 90 guards. Inside the steamer's hold were four tiers of cells and two large cages measuring sixty-six-feet long by twelve-feet wide and twelve-feet

* Maroons are the descendants of slaves who escaped into the bush to live in freedom.

high. Each pen could accommodate ninety convicts, allowing each convict less than a square yard of space. Hammocks hung from the ceiling, but the strongest men claimed these beds, leaving the vomit- and excrement-encrusted floor for the weaklings.

Guards observed the prisoners twenty-four hours a day from a central location and enforced progressive discipline. The unruly convicts sat on the "bench of justice," their backs arched into the cage's steel bars, their hands locked to the rods behind them, and their legs dangled high above the floor. Guards herded the most disruptive prisoners into a "hot cell." These cells, less than six-feet tall and enveloped in darkness, were made of sheet iron, and were strategically placed near the ship's boiler. To quell a mass rebellion, "pipes from the steamer's boilers led to all the cages, so blasts of scalding steam and boiling water could be pumped among them, subduing uprisings or fights, but burning the innocent as well as the guilty."

The prisoners were as diverse as the waiting crowd, for France sent not only the French to Guiana but also criminals from its colonies such as Chinese from French Indochina, Black men from Madagascar, Arabs from North Africa, and "occasionally a Spanish, a Belgian, a Briton, or a German caught somehow in the web of the French convict system." These men were convicted murderers, thieves, forgers, traitors, and defectors. The *fort-à-bras*, sinister tattooed men wise from their years in French African military prisons, became the bullies of the cages and soon selected young convicts as their sexual partners.

As the *La Martinière* docked and blew its whistle, the crowd on the dock stirred. Under the watch of armed guards dressed in white khaki, the convicts poured out of the cages in the ship's hold. Eager to see their new home, they rushed down the gangway. Blair thought, "They look like gray rats, in the thick woolen uniforms of the French prisons. But they are confused by the crowd that has gathered to greet them. They do not understand that in the monotony of Guiana, the arrival of a convict convoy is like a Roman holiday."

Blair watched as the men stopped at the end of the gangway and lined up four abreast, "blinking in the strong tropic sun, with rivulets of perspiration trickling down their faces." After twenty days at sea, they were relieved to disembark. "But they know little of the land where most of them have come to die. Surrounded by miles of dense and unexplored tropical forests and shark-infested waters which make escape nearly impossible, it will not be long until one of them, in desperation, dies attempting escape."

A guard yelled, "March!" and the convicts surged forward to the end of the pier and through the streets of St. Laurent. Blair followed as they passed the Palais de Justice and the wardens' houses, which the inmates had landscaped with ornamental walls, shrubs, and trees. Soon, they arrived at the Camp de la Transportation, where the administration would register them in the prison system.

The roll was called, and the prison director welcomed the convicts.

"You have arrived here to pay for crimes committed against France. You are all criminals and do not deserve the least bit of mercy. For those who behave themselves, life will not be made unbearable. For those who cause trouble, we have excellent methods of punishment at our disposal. I know that most of you have ideas to escape—forget them! You will be given a great deal of freedom in the camps and in town. Don't ever forget that the real guards are the jungle and the sea."

After this "welcome," the inmates were stripped, processed, and assigned a number. The authorities inventoried "the men's bodies, recording every distinguishing mark, every wart or mole, every birthmark blotch and every tattooed design, making measurements, and adding these things to his name and age and birthplace, and to the individual crime histories to facilitate emergency reference." As she watched a man go through the registration process, Blair thought, "He is no longer a man; he scarcely has the individuality of a number." She suddenly realized that the prisoners were being cataloged and thought, "It is as though the officials are amputating and preserving part of each man in card catalogs much like Will, in Burma, had impaled upon pins all that is mortal of once living insects, classifying them as Hymenoptera, Lepidoptera, and so on and so on, the brittle remains of creatures who had known life. And standing naked in the room, man after man looks on with a sense of horror while an integral part of his ego is inventoried, impaled for all time in the criminal archives of Guiana, their human rights struggling there on a merciless pin."

Later, W. E. Allison-Booth would extend Blair's analogy, describing the paradox of "one branch of government which goes to great expense to capture some wild animal for the national zoological collection" and takes great care to ensure that the specimen arrives alive in France. Simultaneously, another branch of the French government cages human beings and sends them to the jungle to rot "with apparently no thought for their comfort." Allison-Booth concluded that "it is as though they seek to repopulate the jungle with an inferior type of beast."

With dread, Blair predicted, "Soon, each prisoner will understand that he has lost everything but the tortured physical body and his troubled spirit. And so faint, so uncertain will be his contact with the world that he will soon wonder which it is that has died—himself or the world."

In St. Laurent, Blair and Robin took up residence in the

prison commandant's house. They hired a servant who had been a prisoner for almost forty years. Under the French penal law of *doublage*, convicts sent to French Guiana had to serve their sentence of up to eight years in prison there and then serve an equal sentence as "free" men or *libérés* in French Guiana. Prisoners with sentences greater than eight years must remain in French Guiana for life as *libérés*. France also sent *doudous*—prostitutes—to ensure that the *libérés* would stay in Guiana and populate the country. After the government abolished slavery in 1848, the French abandoned the plantations and moved to Cayenne, the capital. Although coastal villages had emerged, they were only accessible by boat. The dense jungle quickly devoured any land that was not continuously cultivated.

The massive prison compound in St. Laurent, the Camp de la Transportation, housed barracks and offices. The prisoners preferred to call the prison "The Dry Guillotine" because "imprisonment in French Guiana was, to them, only a degree less fatal than the descending knife itself." Mounted perpendicular to the interior walls of the barracks were 160 wide wooden planks where men slept with their feet chained to a giant iron rod that ran the length of the building. Nearby was a hospital and the dock for the disembarkation of prisoners.

When prisoners arrived in the Camp de la Transportation, they were classified for light work, jungle work, or road work. The administration sent most of the inmates to the jungle prisons, where they chopped trees (1 cubic meter per day) or planted vegetables. Convicts assigned to road building worked on grading a coastal road from the country's borders: from Brazil to Dutch Guiana. The task was so abominable and deadly that a French journalist who visited the capital city of Cayenne wrote, "The question is whether this is a project to build a road or a project to kill convicts. If it's a project to kill convicts, don't change anything. All goes well."

About one thousand prisoners assigned to light duty stayed in Cayenne in three-story barracks about five blocks from the center of town. There was an iron fence around the buildings. During the day, the convicts built elegant houses for the prison officials on wide boulevards and with extensive gardens. The grounds were immaculate: *transportés*—prisoners allowed to work in town—clad in vertically striped red and white pajamas and straw hats swept the streets, weeded the gardens, and carried packages for women. If they were trustworthy, they could sleep at their employer's home. They made enough money to buy tobacco and rum and perhaps to sleep with a mistress. The *libérés* were dressed in rags and pushed wheelbarrows, hoping to catch the attention of one of the women who might pay them to carry some packages. It was an impressive city, built off the sweat of prison labor.

Less fortunate convicts were sentenced to one of the three islands that "lay like green leaves on the sparkling tropical ocean" seven miles off the coast of South America. A convict approaching the islands by boat would marvel at the beauty of the emerald islands, with brown cliffs, surrounded by azure water and blue skies. Maritime law decreed that no foreign ships could sail within a mile and a half of the three islands.

Île Royale was the largest of the Salvation Islands. It held about 650 convicts sent over from St. Laurent because they were dangerous. A steamship arrived twice monthly from Cayenne to deliver supplies. The island held a hospital, a church, the guards' houses, the administrative offices, a guillotine, and a cemetery for the children of the guards. (The prisoners were buried at sea.) Île Royale also held the prison barracks. Prisoner René Belbenoît wrote about the bathrooms: "*Dans cet endroit, plus de meurtres ont été commis que dans n'importe quel endroit du monde dans un espace aussi restreint.*" In that one spot, more murders have been done than in any place on earth of such restricted space.

Île St.-Joseph was an island several hundred feet off the coast of Île Royale. It held fifty-two underground dungeons with metal grate ceilings that allowed the guard to observe the incorrigible convicts in solitary confinement. No talking was permitted. No personal belongings were allowed. Each dungeon consisted of a plank, which was lowered at night for a bed, and buckets for water and waste. The only sounds that emanated from the island, save for the breaking waves, rustling palms leaves, and screeching gulls, were the screams of the insane prisoners.

Île du Diable, Devil's Island, was on the other side of Île Royale, separated by strong currents. A cable stretched across the channel between the two islands. Although the island was accessible by sea, often the waters were too rough, and food, wine, and supplies were delivered from Île Royale to Devil's Island by a basket hooked onto the cable and sent zipping across the ocean. Less than thirty *deportés* (political offenders) lived on Devil's Island.

When Blair and Robin visited Île Royale, they lived in a guard's house near the prison barracks. The beauty of the island surrounding the guard's village camouflaged the death, corruption, and stench of the prison barracks.

On several occasions, Blair and Robin boarded the rowboat bound for Devil's Island only one hundred yards across treacherous shark-infested seas. But sometimes they had to wait for hours until the current was safe.

While she waited, Blair saw sharks. She shivered.

When the current was safe, she boarded the rowboat. Six prisoners pulled the oars as a guard cried, "Now pull, all together!" Blair hoped that the clatter of the oars would keep the sharks at bay,

The boat lunged close to the sharp rocks. "This is not the moment to give up!" the guard yelled.

As the boat rose and fell in the waves, and inched its way through the current to Devil's Island, the guards in the boat's stern kept an eye on the water. "Oh-la-la! But there are sharks!" one remarked. Blair thought, "I could think of more aesthetic ways to die!"

Twenty minutes passed.

A guard yelled, "All together," and with a last heave, the boat landed, nestled between large slippery boulders.

Blair recognized the cabin that had imprisoned Captain Alfred Dreyfus, a French officer, for treason against France. The Dreyfus Affair had occurred in 1894 when Blair was a teenager. It lasted for twelve years and was often sensationalized in the news. The French court-martialed Dreyfus, a person of Jewish faith, claiming that he was spying for the Germans. Dreyfus maintained that he was innocent and that he had been convicted because of anti-Semitism. He was imprisoned on Devil's Island.*

When Blair visited the island, nineteen political prisoners lived there as "aristocrats of the condemned" because they were exempt from hard labor. The guards told Blair and Robin that they had converted Dreyfus's cabin into punishment cells for political prisoners who interfered with the convicts who commuted from Île Royale to work on the island. Blair glanced up the stone path to the watchtower: "When Dreyfus was imprisoned there, a guard kept watch day and night, searching the sea.

---

* The real traitor was found but a rigged court martial found him not guilty. Five years after Dreyfus's arrest, the government returned him to France and retried him and again declared him guilty despite the mounting evidence in his support. The French president pardoned Dreyfus to avoid an international reputation as an anti-Semitic country. In 1906, the military exonerated him and reinstated him. He received the highest award of the French government, a Knight of the Legion of Honor.

He was afraid that an outraged world might send a rescue ship," thought Blair.

On their second visit to the island, Blair and Robin walked its length to a bench on a cliff where Dreyfus, when he was released from solitary confinement, liked to sit in the evenings and enjoy the sea breeze. "It was as if he sat at the world's end," Blair thought, "with everything earthly behind him; and before him—to the north, the east and the west—a universe of sea."

They walked past the armed sentries, down a stony path to the cabins where prisoners lived. As they approached, prisoners ran out of their little huts. "They remind me of Jack-in-the-Boxes, popping out of their houses. It is the first time they have seen a woman on the island. I am almost as strange a sight as though I had descended in a parachute from the moon."

There, Blair met the prisoners who would provide some of the material for her book and the five front-page Sunday magazine articles she would write for the *New York Times*. Robin would also publish a full-page photo spread.

Blair took a new approach when writing her book about Devil's Island. She decided to write a "fictional biography," which would allow her to write in the collective voice of the prisoners: "It does not seem to me important how I personally feel about this tragic Penal Colony but immensely important how the convicts, themselves, feel about it." She wrote the fictitious biography of René Belbenoît, a real prisoner, whom she called Michel in the book. She met him in St. Laurent. He had served time in most of the prisons in French Guiana, including Île St.-Joseph and Île Royale. She altered facts only enough to conceal his identity. She also took the liberty of referring to the collective penal colonies of French Guiana as Devil's Island.

In 1921, at age twenty-one, René Belbenoît was arrested in

Paris for stealing a pearl necklace from the Countess of Entremeuse, while he was working as a valet at her chateau. A judge sentenced him to eight years of hard labor in French Guiana. For eighteen months, he was held in a French prison at Saint-Martin-de-Ré, an island off the coast of France. In June 1923, he arrived in Saint-Laurent-du-Maroni and became Prisoner 46635.

During his incarceration in Guiana, René made five attempts to escape. Soon after he arrived, an opportunity to escape presented itself. His first attempt was in August 1923 from Camp Nouveau, a jungle camp fourteen miles from St. Laurent. When they arrived at the camp, he was assigned to braid palm, which would be used to weave straw hats for the prisoners. It took him several hours each day to braid his allotment, and then he was free to roam the surrounding forests. He decided to escape on August 14 because it was a Dutch holiday, and he thought that the police would not bother him when he crossed the mile-wide river on a raft to Dutch Guiana. The current dragged the raft to Albina, the Dutch city opposite St. Laurent. There, he was captured by some Caribe Indians, who reported him to the police for the ten-franc reward. The police returned him to the Camp de la Transportation. For this 39-hour escape, prison officials confined him for sixty days. When released, he was sent back to Camp Nouveau.

On Christmas Eve, René and eight other convicts attempted to escape by stealing a canoe and rowing down the Maroni River. Three men were murdered along the way—the first for lying about his ability to sail a boat, the second for his can of condensed milk, and the third as punishment for murdering the second. The men were starving, so they agreed to eat the murderer. The police in British Guiana arrested them and sent them back to French Guiana. Prison officials sent René to Charvain, a camp where prisoners were forced to log timber naked in the jungle.

In the spring of 1926, René was released from the hospital in St. Laurent after a stay in solitary confinement on Île St.-Joseph. After an afternoon of losing money gambling, René's friend asked him if he had seen the Americans who were staying in town—Mr. and Mrs. Niles. René decided to visit them to see if they wanted to buy some of his prison stories. He walked over to the house where they were staying, carrying a bundle of his stories.

Robin answered the door. In broken English, René asked Robin if he wanted to buy some stories. Robin asked him to wait while he took the stories upstairs to show Blair.

When Blair came downstairs, she saw a small, malnourished man in ragged prison clothes. "But there is an appeal in his straightforward eyes," she thought. "In his gallant young smile, there flutters the dauntless spirit which says, 'Do not pity me! *C'est peu de chose* [It's a small thing].'"

Blair greeted René and asked, "How much do you want for these writings?"

"Whatever you wish to give me, Madame."

She handed him a folded bill. "Come again tomorrow morning. I might want to talk to you."

René thanked her and left. When he got outside, he opened the bill and was shocked to find it was for 100 francs. He had been hoping for twenty-five francs. He went to the Chinese market and bought some sardines and bread because the prison administration systematically underfed the prisoners to pocket the money. He also bought tobacco and then paid off his gambling debt. With eighty francs left, he visited a machine lathe operator and ordered a new *plan* (an aluminum suppository used to hide a prisoner's bills).

The next day, René returned to the Niles. Blair invited him to join them for a light breakfast. She took notes while he ate, and he told her about his life history. She asked questions about his stories and gave him another 100 francs. They continued to meet. René was working as a bookkeeper in the prison's administration building and could visit in the mornings. Blair rewarded him with more money, a poker set, and a small pocketknife.

As they were finishing a session, René told Blair, "Ah, now that you know everything, you will think, 'How black is his soul.'"

"That may not be said of any soul," Blair responded.

She felt compelled to tell his story so that readers "may look into the abyss of prison, coming thus to understand something of the effect of prison upon man, and something of what happens to man when suddenly woman is taken from life, and stripped of all." She wanted her readers to sympathize with him, not intellectually but with their hearts. When, after five escape attempts, René escaped in 1937, he published several books about his life in, and escape from, French Guiana.*

Part of Blair's research for the *Condemned* book was to travel through the jungle using a map of secret routes that René drew. She wanted to experience a prison escape and understand the dangers the escapees felt. She was much more prepared than the average escapee: she was well nourished, fit, and had considerable experience hiking through jungles. Plus, she hired fourteen porters to carry her gear, make camp, and cut a path through the jungle with a machete. She noted the isolation of the jungle: "Few

* Later, when Henri Charrière wrote *Papillon* (Butterfly), several French journalists claimed that Charrière had stolen some of René's stories. In a 1970 review, John Weightman wrote, "Far from being one of the outstanding tough guys in the penal colony, Charrière was a comparatively well-behaved convict, who was contentedly employed for a long time on latrine duty. He never escaped from Devil's Island. The majority of the anecdotes he relates did not happen to him at all but are adaptations of stories he heard about other people." Journalist Georges Ménager discovered that Charrière had never been imprisoned on Devil's Island. French journalist Gerard de Villiers claimed, "Only about 10 percent of Charrière's book represents the truth."

people realize how little civilized French Guiana is. Out of 32,000 of its square miles only 14 are said to be under civilization. The rest is dense, unmapped jungle networked with streams" with names like Try Me, God Knows, and Don't Touch Me.

Also scattered around the jungle are the villages of the Ndyuka Maroon people, former Africans who escaped after being sold as slaves to the Dutch-owned plantations. In Moengo Tappo, they lived among the Ndyukas, where Blair noticed that "there is no nonsense about white superiority. They are proud to the point of savage arrogance. Hatred and distrust of the white man are as much a part of their inheritance as their jungle lore." These descendants of slaves were so bold that they were able to negotiate treaties with the Dutch that required the government to pay them annual reparations for being enslaved.

"As among the Negroes of Haiti, you must win your way. But when you are finally accepted, not as a superior being, but as an equal, then how warm and charming a thing their friendship is!"

She refused to bring a gun with her and, instead, made a white flag that read, "*Nous sommes vos amis*": We are your friends. The flag was directed at any fugitive prisoners who were wandering through the jungle. She knew the escapees were desperate and would not hesitate to kill them if they thought the expedition posed a threat. At night they kept a fire burning under the flag to illuminate it and to keep away vampire bats and jaguars. She told a reporter, "We took few precautions outside of careful eating and drinking and always brushing our teeth with boiled water. Although we wore cork helmets and stout clothes, we soon ceased to bother with raincoats and umbrellas as we grew accustomed to incessant downpours."

The last few weeks of the trek occurred during the rainy season. When the jungle floor flooded with water, Blair and Robin climbed into a canoe and paddled their way through the jungle: "We glided along often lying down in the boat to avoid the low-hanging branches and trailing lianas." Deep in the forest, they were so isolated that "civilization seemed an impossible dream."

"The jungle is perpetually vigilant," Blair thought. "There are its armies of fire-ants, its mosquitoes, its serpents, and its vampire bats. There is the terror of its vastness: the sense that for uncounted miles to the east and to the south it marches to the Amazon; that to the west it proceeds across the Guianas, across Venezuela and Colombia, to the foot of the mighty Andes, while to the north the sea threatens where the jungle ends. Death lurks in the jungle."

As they traveled, Blair thought, "The lush beauty of the jungle beckons the prison-weary man. Are they ready for the terror of its vastness? Do they realize that the guards may drowse a little in the shade of his bread-fruit tree, dreaming, confident that the jungle is playing its part in the relentless game of checkmate?"

In her book, *Condemned to Devil's Island*, Blair candidly addressed the issue of opportunistic same-sex relationships, true same-sex love, sexual abuse, and rape. A historian noted, "It is not possible to write of the convict stations of Guiana and not mention the perversion of morals and the effect of the whole question on convict behavior. Not to mention homosexuality and the dramas it caused would be like describing a motor car without mentioning the motor." Blair received international acclaim for her book. The *New York Times* reviewer Perch Hutchinson described the book, in a full-page review, as "amazing. Not to be duplicated anywhere. Fathoms the psychology of the convict with uncanny accuracy. An epic of the living dead." The *Saturday Review of Literature* described it as a "poignant study of the cruelty of justice in a dreadful tropic, and an exciting novel of accumulating movements, queer types, and exotic background. The system reeks with sodomy, grafts, sadism. Blair Niles has spoken adequately for the thousands who have perished on Devil's Island."

Once Blair returned to the United States, it was not long until a Hollywood producer approached her to make a movie of the book. She traveled to Hollywood to consult on a screenplay for *Condemned* (1929), starring Ronald Coleman and Ann Harding. She stayed a month in Hollywood and quipped that she no longer needed any backs to her clothing because, in Hollywood, the backsides of everything are wood and chicken wire.

Condemned became a blockbuster, and Blair soon became a household name. Her comings and goings were reported in the gossip columns from Kokomo, Indiana, to Harlingen, Texas. When *Condemned* was released, a reporter commented, "Mrs. Niles is probably the only author who ever had a book produced as a picture in Hollywood without claiming that the whole thing had been ruined." When, as a result of Blair's book on Devil's Island, the Salvation Army decided to open a post in French Guiana to monitor conditions in the penal colony, this news was reported under the banner "Book Has Influence." Her second book on Devil's Island, *Free*—this one about an attempted escape—was hailed as a "powerfully realistic novel written in a beautiful and artistic style." When Blair traveled to Guatemala, newspapers reported that she was greeted by a flamboyant sign advertising "THE COLOSSAL! THE MOVING! THE VIRILE! All talking motion picture of '*Condemned*.'"

Some of the gossip column observations were more personal. When she sunbathed on her balcony, a reporter noted that she wore a red bathing suit. When she and Robin spent the weekend in Delaware visiting Robin's cousin, a newspaper reported that the Niles returned home by airplane, certainly interesting news during the Depression. But reporters also wrote about more serious matters, such as when Blair agitated for a female in President Roosevelt's cabinet, and the president appointed Frances Perkins, who would become a member of the Society.

In 1933, while a bill to outlaw the practice of *doublage* was pending, the *Washington Post* gave credit to Blair for calling Americans' attention to the penal system. The last prisoners were sent to French Guiana in 1937. But World War II delayed the closure of the penitentiary. In 1946, the French government began to repatriate the inmates. The prison was finally closed in 1952, and France declared its efforts at colonizing French Guiana through *doublage* a failure. And, in the mind of the public, which is fraught with images portrayed by Blair Niles and others, French Guiana remained "a land of death inhabited by the unfortunate, the misunderstood, and the wrongfully convicted."

By the stock market crash of October 1929, Blair was already looking for places closer to home to explore. She found the subject for her next book in Harlem.

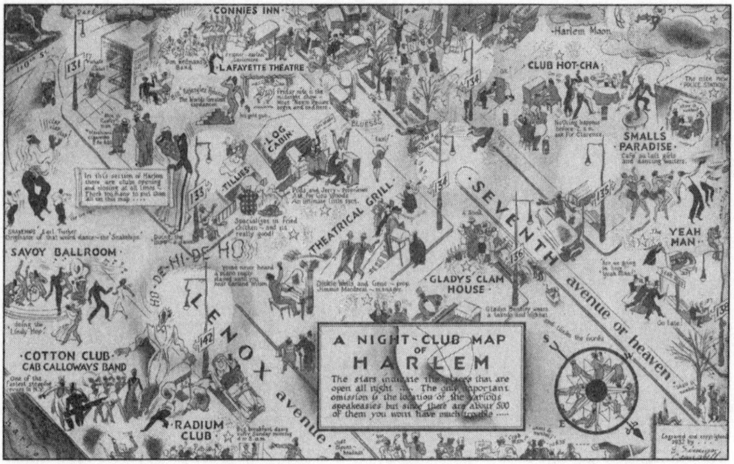

Illustration 18. A Night-Club Map of Harlem (1932)

CHAPTER 13
GAY HARLEM

I want so much to make people understand others and thereby come to a better understanding of themselves. Mutual understanding would banish half the sorrow and cruelty from the world.

—BLAIR NILES, AUTHOR AND A FOUNDER OF THE SOCIETY

DECEMBER 1929
Harlem

In late December 1929, Blair attended a party hosted by A'Lelia Walker, a wealthy African American patron of the arts. Walker, whose mother was reputedly the first African American millionaire, used her inheritance—money made from marketing hair-straightening products—to throw lavish parties at her Hudson River mansion and her Sugar Hill apartment in Harlem. She enjoyed the company of artists, musicians, writers, and actors, especially gay men.

Author Carl Van Vechten also attended the gathering. He

was "the undisputed downtown authority on uptown night life," a frequent Harlem visitor, where he felt comfortable as a white gay man. Van Vechten had previously introduced Blair to Leland Pettit, a young, white gay man who also frequented Harlem. Blair was fascinated by Pettit's identification with Black men in Harlem. According to historian Eric Garber, "Pettit frequented the homosexual underworld in Harlem because he found social acceptance, and because he identified with others who were outcasts from American life. This identification and feeling of kinship, undoubtedly shared by other white gay people, may have been the beginnings of homosexual 'minority consciousness.'" When Pettit committed suicide in September 1929 over the loss of affection from Harlem Renaissance poet Countee Cullen, Blair was inspired to write a fictional account of his struggle with his sexuality so that others would treat gay people with tolerance and respect.

At age twenty-four, when Pettit was living in Milwaukee, he learned that Cullen, a twenty-one-year-old Harlem poet, had won a national poetry prize. He read the poem, became infatuated with the poet, and invited him to give a reading at the Atheneum in Milwaukee. It is not clear whether they started a sexual relationship in Milwaukee, but soon after he returned to Harlem, Cullen wrote a poem for Pettit, a tradition he observed with most of his lovers. Scholar Alden Reimonenq interpreted the poem, *Colors*, as alluding to the "insignificance of color," the fear caused by the unseen such as racism and homophobia and Cullen's relationship with Pettit.

Within a few months, Pettit and his mother moved to New York City, where Pettit became the organist and choir director at Grace Church. In Harlem, he continued his relationship with Cullen. Pettit was a "negrotarian"—a word coined by writer Zora Neale Hurston to describe white people who were fascinated by

Negroes and Harlem life. Pettit often visited a rooming house where poet Langston Hughes, novelist Wallace Thurman, and artist Bruce Nugent rented rooms and Zora Neale Hurston often dropped by. In *Infants of the Spring,* Wallace Thurman portrayed Pettit as an "indelible conservative who was innocently conscripted into the radical movement" of socialism. "He became a white hope, battling for the cause of the American Negro. No Negro ever had the welfare of his race so much at heart as did the alien Pettit." In this role, most Blacks admired him, and most whites denigrated him.

It is unclear how long Pettit's affair with Cullen lasted. In 1926, Cullen moved to Massachusetts to attend Harvard for graduate school. In 1927, at the urging of W. E. B. Du Bois, author and founder of the NAACP, Cullen proposed to Du Bois's daughter, Yolande, perhaps to disguise his affinity for men. Within a few months, the marriage was on the rocks and in April 1929, Yolande filed for divorce. Cullen occasionally returned to the United States, but it appears that he did not resume his relationship with Pettit, who must have been devastated.

In September 1929, Pettit committed suicide at the age of twenty-eight. Right after his death, Harold Jackman wrote to Cullen, "There is a rumor in Harlem that Pettit committed suicide—I spoke to your father about this and he said it wasn't true. But the niggers have it that Pettit committed suicide over some boy." Scholars today believe that Pettit committed suicide over Countee Cullen.

During the party at A'Lelia Walker's house in December 1929, Carl Van Vechten decided to leave to go to the Clam House, a Harlem speakeasy, where Gladys Bentley, a stocky, Black gay singer performed in a top hat and tuxedo. It is not known if Blair tagged along, but it is likely, as she was anxious to see more of

Harlem's gay shadow world to set the stage for her book about Pettit, and Van Vechten was an excellent tour guide.

Blair knew that upper-class whites frequently visited Harlem to see entertainment targeted at white heterosexual men and women. Whites owned most clubs. Shows featured light-skinned Black entertainers and edited out material that might be considered too offensive. They featured bands such as Duke Ellington, Cab Calloway, Fletcher Henderson, and Fats Waller. "Everyone rushed up to Harlem at night to sit around places thick with smoke and the smell of bad gin, where Negroes danced about with each other until the small hours of the morning." Visitors were fascinated with what many perceived to be the primitive nature and unbridled passion of Black people, especially concerning sex. African American writer Richard Fisher complained of the intrusion. "I am actually stared at. I frequently feel uncomfortable and out of place, and when I go out on the floor to dance I am lost in a sea of white faces." The whites' fascination with Harlem seemed to "smack of 'sexual colonialism;' whites used Harlem as a commodity, a stimulant to sexuality." Poet Langston Hughes, who disapproved of the white invasion, wrote, "Harlem nights became show nights for the Nordics."

But, as usual, Blair wanted to see the "real" Harlem—the Harlem where Leland Pettit came to experience "the epitome of the forbidden." Even before the 1920s, black-and-tan clubs and speakeasies catered to folks who appreciated explicit sexuality. Harlem welcomed everyone: Black gay people and "stigmatized white groups" who were exploring their sexuality, as well as heterosexuals. White gay men preferred Harlem to the rest of Manhattan because there they could openly pick up other gay men. Most speakeasies and nightclubs tolerated prostitution, as it drew men to the clubs.

Blair found out that although some gay Black men were overt, flaunting their bleached, marcelled hair and red ties, which announced their sexual status, most Black men were more cautious about their sexuality. The social lives of Black gay people revolved around private parties such as rent parties, which featured a jazz band, sold bootleg liquor, and charged entrance fees to raise money for rent. Blair explored Harlem, going to rent parties, to gambling dens, to a Harlem debutante's charity ball, and to a drag ball. She discovered that drag balls were also safe public places for gay people to meet. For example, the Harlem Masquerade Ball attracted gay people from as far away as Boston, Philadelphia, and Atlantic City. Blair's friend Taylor Gordon, a Black male singer, noted that the drag ball at the Savoy in Harlem cost $1 but "would have made a twenty-five dollar George White's *Scandals* opening look like a side show in a circus." White and Black gay people participated in the event. Thousands of spectators watched from the balcony.

She learned about men who cruised for sex in parks, at the zoo, movie houses, bathrooms, and clubs, while others identified their long-term partnerships as marriages. These marginalized men formed hidden gay social circles—shadow worlds of gay culture they could live in—while they hid their sexual identity from their families and co-workers. They "developed a highly sophisticated system of subcultural codes—codes of dress, speech, and style—that enabled them to recognize one another on the streets, at work, and at parties and bars, and to carry on intricate conversations whose coded meaning was unintelligible to potentially hostile people around them." Blair was unable to identify the gay men who presented themselves as masculine. In a scene in *Strange Brother*, the protagonist (i.e., Blair) attends the opera with her gay friend, Mark. He tells her which cast members are gay. "How on earth do you know?" she exclaims. Mark tells her that it is "an undefinable something, hard to explain." Later, when she sees her ex-husband at a drag ball, she understands the "undefinable something," that the undefinable something "of radio and electricity—had been there, of course, all along." Many of the Harlem intelligentsia were openly gay. A resident of Sugar Hill said, "Of course they had not come out of the closet back then. They didn't have to. We all knew they were homosexuals. We admired them for their intelligence and work during a very difficult time." Black gay men had a difficult time throughout the United States. They faced discrimination, mockery, and arrest for their sexuality. But Harlem showed more tolerance than other parts of the country and carved out a place for gay people to feel safer.

Additionally, law enforcement tended to be lax in Harlem; arrests—at least for whites—were unheard of. Elsewhere, a criminal charge of disorderly conduct was punishable by a fine of up to $50 ($761 today) and six months in prison. But perhaps more importantly, white gay people felt welcomed in a more tolerant community.

In *Strange Brother*—initially, the book was titled *Queer*—Blair tells a fictionalized story of Pettit, a gay white man disguised as the protagonist Mark Thornton. June Westbrook, a wealthy white divorcée (i.e., Blair Niles), is dancing with her boyfriend, Seth, at a Harlem speakeasy, when she sees Mark sitting in the segregated Black section with two Black men. She gets to know Mark and learns that he frequents Harlem bars because he feels that he is accepted there because Black people who have been the target of racism understand the suffering of white gay men and women. Their status as minorities who suffered discrimination bound them together. Mark explains, "I can be myself there. They know all about me and I don't have to lie."

June and Mark become friends. Mark becomes obsessed with Nelly, a gay Black man, who is arrested by the police just because he is effeminate. Mark attends Nelly's trial, and when the judge sentences him to jail, Mark wonders how difficult his own life as a gay man will be. While June explores her relationship with Seth (a companionate relationship as was in vogue at the time),* Mark explores the biological "naturalness" of same-sex relationships. This allows Blair to introduce the reader to the medical and psychological literature about sexual orientation at the time, which Blair describes in the method of an anthropologist.

The book, which was the first book to depict gay people in Harlem compassionately and to discuss gay profiling, received mixed reviews, although comments were mostly favorable. The *New York Times* refused to review it. The *Saturday Review of Books* commented that "a panorama of abnormality is unrolled with the utmost tolerance and sympathy, though never with approval." The *Cincinnati Enquirer* said, "Blair Niles is a woman. She has chosen for the theme of her book an "unwomanly" subject—and she has handled it well. Blair Niles has entered a dark and mysterious cavern and we may go with her." The *Newark Advocate* of Ohio wrote, "It is a delicate theme, handled with skill and perfect taste." The reviewer cautioned, "Probably this book will titillate the suburban bridge clubs. That is unfortunate. It is no cheap shocker. It was written for the civilized adult." But another

---

* After World War I, societal thoughts about marriage changed. Women had a taste of equality during the war, and they wanted more. Americans stopped considering marriage as a duty and began to see it as a "path to personal happiness and fulfillment," an equal partnership. Branded as the "companionate marriage" by authors Ben Lindsey and Wainwright Evans in their 1927 book of that title, this new type of bond "stressed marital sex for intimacy and pleasure." Women would begin to reject the nineteenth-century notion that "I'd rather be a free spirit and paddle my own canoe" and begin to think of the world as being inhabited by couples. Author Stephanie Coontz argues that this new form of marriage bound the wife to the husband even more securely than before because marriage became the emotional center of most women's lives.

reviewer noted that, as she did in *Condemned to Devil's Island*, Blair "is not so much telling a story as she is exposing suffering."

Retailers had difficulty getting enough copies of *Strange Brother* because it was so popular. At the time, booksellers did not have a section for books with gay themes, so they placed it in the African American section, thus reinforcing historian Eric Garber's hypothesis that the "borders between black and homosexual geographical spaces were blurred by clandestine crossings." The book was also popular in England.

The book has withstood the test of time. In 1979, the book was hailed in *Gay News* "as a monument of good reporting." In 2001, Lisa Walker described it as "a novel of historical importance because it synthesizes an early and self-consciously liberal use of this analogy between blacks and gays in defense of homosexuality."

When the Depression was over, Blair would return to her studies of the people of Latin America. For now, she had completed her trio of books on Black people, prisoners, and gay men: *Black Haiti*, *Condemned to Devil's Island*, and *Strange Brother*. She would not return to any of these subjects for a decade.

While Blair was studying gay men in Harlem, other members of the Society were rushing to study aboriginal cultures, fearful that the "dual ideologies of imperialism and racism" combined with Darwin's theory of the survival of the fittest, would doom these cultures to extinction. The fear of extinction thrust some future members of the Society of Woman Geographers into a frenzy to record these people before they disappeared. Ethnologist Margaret Mead explained, "The work of recording these unknown ways of life had to be done now—*now*—or they would be lost forever." In *Coming of Age in Samoa*, Mead wrote, "I feared [in 1925] that the grace and zest and gaiety of the Samoans, carried only by them as a people, without the kind of art and literature which has left us something of Greece and Egypt after their civilizations were gone, would disappear forever, transmuted beyond recognition by the difficulties of Euro-American culture around the world. I did not know then, could not know then, how extraordinarily persistent Samoan culture would prove, and how fifty years later the grace that I had attempted to record as something that was surely going to vanish would still be there."

Unlike Osa Johnson, who preserved aborigines on film to make a buck in the entertainment industry, these women wanted to transport the world to the United States so that Americans could appreciate the beauty, dignity, and humanity of these elusive cultures. For example, Frances Densmore collected and transcribed twenty-four hundred Indian songs for the Bureau of Ethnology of the Smithsonian Institution to preserve their work. But in 1929, Malvina Hoffman was given a unique opportunity to not just memorialize one "dying" culture but to record, in bronze, the characteristics of almost all "subspecies" of the human race. Her artistic work up until that point had paved the way.

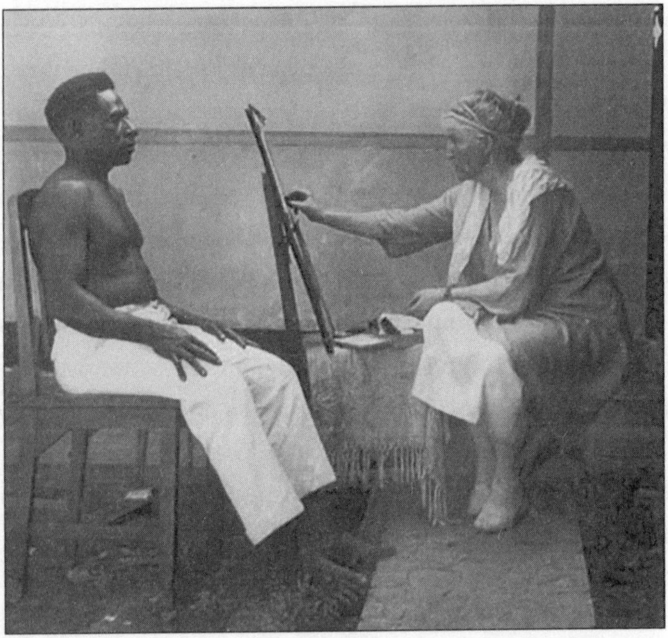

Illustration 19. Malvina Hoffman Sketching a Man Named Mare for a Bronze Sculpture for the Races of Man Exhibit (ca. 1929)

CHAPTER 14
RACES OF MANKIND

> ***Won't all the primitive people in the world soon be extinct? Or won't the cultures of the surviving peoples be so changed, so transformed by contact into various versions of the emerging worldwide culture, that they no longer will be of interest?***
>
> **—MARGARET MEAD, ANTHROPOLOGIST AND SOCIETY MEMBER**

1910
France

Malvina knocked at sculptor Auguste Rodin's door. It was the fifth time that she had tried to meet the sculptor, and each time she had been rebuffed. The 25-year-old art student had traveled to Paris in 1910 with her mother to arrange to study with the prodigy; so far, she had not met him. But Malvina, who had the persistence and tenacity of the woman geographer that she would later become, was determined to study with him.

When Rodin's assistant opened the door, Malvina was ready. This time, she summoned her courage. In halting schoolgirl

French, she announced, "Tell Monsieur Rodin that if he does not see me today, I must return to America, but I came to Paris to study with him, and that I must deliver a message to him from his friend Madame Simpson."

Malvina was shocked when she heard Rodin speak from behind the door.

"Wait, wait, mademoiselle. Why didn't you mention Mrs. Simpson? How is my dear friend?" Kate Simpson was one of Rodin's most enthusiastic patrons, one who had believed in him when the art world maligned him.

Rodin opened the door and asked Malvina what she was holding.

Malvina handed Rodin an envelope that held photographs of her sculptures.

"I am just a beginner and find that I cannot escape it. Sculpture seems to have taken possession of me, and my desire is to be your pupil, if you would be willing to guide me and criticize my work."

Rodin opened the envelope and studied the photographs, busts of her father and friend.

"Character seems to interest you. You have studied these men well."

Rodin turned his attention to several visitors in the studio who were asking about a figure of a fallen angel that had been inspired by a poem. He started to recite the poem, but he faltered. At seventy, Rodin's memory was failing. He became angry.

Malvina softly touched his arm and told him that she knew the poem. She had memorized it when she was studying French. Unlike her clumsy dialogue with Rodin, Malvina quoted the poem flawlessly in French.

The room was silent. Malvina could hear her heart pounding.

Rodin walked to the door and told Malvina he was having lunch with his visitors. He pointed to keys that were hanging by the door.

"Here. This is where my keys hang. You may use them to open the other studios and examine the trays of plaster studies and I will see you when I return."

When Rodin returned several hours later, Malvina was sitting in a cold room, sketching an arm. She was concentrating so hard that she did not realize that the fire had died. Rodin glanced at her drawings, relit the fire, and told her that he would accept her as a student. He gave her a sculpted arm to take home as a model and instructed her to spend her days at the Louvre. On Sundays, she was to take a carriage to Rodin's house in Meudon and show him her work.

Malvina studied with Rodin for over a year. He taught her the concept of physiognomy: that "an individual's character and soul are imprinted on one's facial features." When she drew Russian dancers, Rodin asked her what emotion she was trying to convey.

"Joy! Intoxication!"

Rodin was silent.

"The difference between ecstasy and tragedy is no greater than the thickness of a sheet of tissue paper. When you carry joy to its full intensity like this, you are already on the borderline of exquisite pain. Don't forget these dancers could be drunk with joy or mad with despair. It is all so closely interwoven in human life! Socrates once said that joy and pain should have a fabled creature with one head and two bodies, so inevitably do they go together and follow each other."

In London, she met Emanuele de Rosales, a sculptor who convinced her to visit the foundries so that she could learn about metals. Ivan Mestrovic, a sculptor, warned her, "The first thing you must do as a woman is to learn the principles and technical side of your work better than most men before you can start *even,* without the handicap of a preconceived idea that women are amateurs in art and generally take up sculpture as a diversion or pastime." She took his admonition earnestly because she knew he was right: "What a serious obstacle this femininity becomes in the field of sculpture—and with good reason, for the work itself demands that we stand on our feet from morning until night, lifting heavy weights, bending iron, sawing wood and building armatures; we must know how to use carpenters' tools and plumbers' tools and be able to calculate the strains and necessary supports to build up the clay figures. These last are often treacherous and collapse at just the moment when we are enthusiastically bringing them to completion." Later, when she turned sixty and reflected on her career, she told a reporter: "Sculpture is definitely not for women, nor is it a lazy man's job."

She refused to be called a sculptress: "To begin with, there's no such word. Secondly, why should there be? A woman sculptor can and ought to do just as much hard physical labour as the men of her trade."

Rodin proved to be her first challenge. He was a known womanizer, and so Malvina was prepared when he locked the studio door and chased her around. She told him that she was there to learn, not to play. He controlled himself and gave her artistic advice that he wished he had received as a young sculptor. Foremost, among this advice, was to take an anatomy class.

Malvina was not looking forward to learning anatomy and dissection, but when she returned to New York, she asked a professor, George S. Huntington, to teach her. On her first day, the smell of formaldehyde overwhelmed her.

"Well, well, Malvina, you look pretty green this morning—can it be that you regret having asked me to teach you how to dissect and learn the principles of anatomy? Remember you are the only woman up here and medical students are likely to jeer at you if you give any signs of funking."

Malvina covered her nose, took several deep breaths, and stepped closer to the dissecting table.

Dr. Huntington uncovered the corpse and made an incision. Malvina felt the contents of her stomach seize.

"Now watch me closely as I reveal to you the beautiful mechanism God built into our knees. Here are the basic principles on which all bridges and levers are constructed!"

Malvina was hooked. It was like revealing the interior of a sculpted figure. Dr. Huntington left her alone to examine the body. Soon she was dragging other artists such as Helen Tee-Van to anatomy lessons.

1930
Chicago

In February 1930, sculptor Malvina Hoffman was stunned when she received a telegram about a potential commission from Stanley Field, president of Chicago's Field Museum: "Have proposition to make, do you care to consider it? Racial types to be modeled while traveling 'round the world."

Malvina was intrigued: "Sudden vistas of remote islands and mysterious horizons flooded over my imagination—escape from city life, discovery of new worlds, conflict with the elements. Infinite new windows of life seemed to open before me."

She traveled to Chicago to meet with Stanley, his employees, and the museum trustees. She learned that the museum wanted to create a new type of exhibit that was the brainchild of Henry Field, an anthropologist who was Stanley's cousin and the nephew of the museum's founder, philanthropist Marshall Field (of Marshall Field & Co.). As conceived by Henry, *Races of Mankind* would be a permanent exhibit of the world's races that would "preserve vanishing primitive races." Henry Field viewed race as hierarchical, with European races in the supreme position. Museum visitors would meet with their "own images portrayed in imperishable bronze." The exhibition would debut in the summer of 1933 when the Century of Progress Fair opened its gates in Chicago.

Henry's boss, Berthold Laufer, envisioned the show as a humanitarian effort. He hoped that the exhibit would demonstrate that "race prejudice is merely the outcome of ignorance" and that visitors would "leave with their sympathy for mankind deepened and strengthened." He distinguished race from culture: To him, race "referred to the physical traits acquired by heredity, not the total complex of habits and thoughts acquired from the group to which we belong." Laufer believed that people of other nationalities are not radically different than Americans: "Armenians, Arabs, Persians, Indians, Chinese, and Japanese are as shrewd, keen and enterprising industrialists and merchants as any in the Western world. The fundamental divergences are not between individuals or classes of people, but are deeply sunk in the thoughts of the folk mind fostered by a different background of civilization." Because Germans had recently elected Hitler as chancellor under a platform of racial superiority, Laufer also reminded visitors that Aryan was not a race.

When the Field Museum approved the exhibition, Stanley Field recommended Malvina, whom he had met at a Chicago dinner party, and discussed sculpture and travel. Marshall Field III, grandson of Marshall Field and one of the project's sponsors, agreed that Malvina was the right choice. Conveniently, he was married to Malvina's cousin. But familial connections aside, Marshall was impressed with Malvina's sculptures, which were filled with humanity, and he knew she was capable of traveling under harsh conditions.

During her meeting with the museum's representatives, Malvina learned that they wanted an exhibit that was vastly different from the usual type of presentation, filled with skulls, bits of pottery, and diagrams. They told Malvina that those types of displays were boring. The trustees believed that an exhibition that showed life-size replicas of each of the subspecies of the human race would attract more visitors. Stanley asked Malvina if she could create waxen models of people, true to color, with false hair and eyes and authentic clothing. They proposed 164 statues, modeled by four or five artists. Malvina was astonished that there were so many different racial types. Could she do such a large project?

Her knees began to shake. She summoned her courage.

"I cannot work under those conditions, but I would like to present you with an entirely different scheme tomorrow morning."

She returned to the Drake Hotel to consider how she would approach the commission.

She sat down in an armchair and held her head in her hands. How could she meet the trustees' expectations without reducing the quality of her work? Was she physically able to do that many sculptures in three years?

As Malvina worked on the proposal, she wandered over to the phone, tempted to call her husband. But she refrained. Later she wrote, "I felt this would be a lack of courage on my part. After all, it was my own risk and my own responsibility, and I knew that I could count on his loyalty and complete cooperation." She knew it would be a strain on their marriage as well as her health. "And yet—something stronger than doubt and more inevitable than calculations overtook me in the wee hours of dawn, and I started drafting the many pages of my proposed scheme." She felt like a spirit had taken control over her life.

She rejected the idea of multiple sculptors; it would cause artistic disagreements and create a hodgepodge of sculptures rather than a homogeneous group. She wanted the medium to be bronze, not wax models with wigs. She shuddered as she envisioned "dummies of sawdust or painted plaster with staring glass eyes and dusty false hair which has become unglued partially because—'there is never enough money for upkeep. The '*Races of Man*' should *look alive*.'" She was confident that, based on her training in the foundries, she could apply the right patina to indicate color variations among the races. She was determined to get the commission and then negotiate for bronze. Later, Malvina wrote, "I sensed that if I insisted at this point upon the sculptor's dream of bronze or marble, I would lose the chance of exploring the world, and that the museum would immediately turn to other artists who would gladly carry out the plan of painted plasters. Something told me I could prove this conviction by the first months of work."

At 10 a.m., Malvina returned to the Field Museum. As she walked across the soft carpet in the executive suite, she felt as though she was on the fairway of the ninth hole at a golf course: "Everything seemed to my distorted vision to appear over-life-size and ominous in the extreme." Objects loomed around her, dwarfing her in her imagination. She felt as small as an atom.

She presented her counterproposal: she would create over 150 sculptures in plaster for $125,000 (2 million today). She assured the museum representatives, "If I am chosen to do this work, I will be ready to assume all of the risks and complete the task to the limit of my physical endurance." They asked for time to consider her proposal.

When Malvina departed, Stanley Field, president of the museum, reacted sharply to her initial estimate, "a six-figure sum of such proportions that it sounded like a national debt." The Field Museum could not afford a budget of that size, especially after the stock market crash. He cut the project by more than a third and ordered his curators to "cut out some of the less important types" of racial hybrids. Malvina's biographer, Didi Hoffman (whose husband was Malvina's great-nephew), commented, "It was the most ever paid to a man or woman. Had she been a man, there might have been celebration, but because she was a woman, there was pushback."

The museum countered with an offer for Malvina to sculpt one hundred figures. Each sculpture would depict a race and a particular individual of that race, although the exhibit would not identify the person. A fifteen-foot monument in the center of the display would depict three idealized men (Caucasoid, Negroid, and Mongoloid), symbolic of the unity of mankind. The trustees commissioned life-size sculptures of the thirty principal racial types and full-size busts of important subdivisions of those racial types.

After Malvina finalized the agreement, she went back to New York with instructions to begin the project. In June, she traveled to Paris to study European and Asiatic types at museums and to consult with anthropologists. She attended anthropology lectures to learn more about the races she was going to sculpt.

Her first clay sculptures were the full-length Blackfoot Indian and the Nordic man. She used clay to mold the hair and eyes. Stanley Field was impressed and quickly rescinded the requirement that Malvina use fake hair and eyes. "Half the battle is won," Malvina thought.

She set to work on two African figures. At her own expense, she had them cast in bronze and patinaed them the same color as her models.

Stanley Field flew to Paris to see her work. She convinced him that metal was more durable and would need less upkeep. He telegrammed the museum and directed them to find additional money to finance bronze. The project ended up costing $158,000 (almost $2.5 million today).

Malvina used her study of anatomy and physiognomy to make her figures for the *Races of Mankind* realistic. She became a conduit for the expression of the races: "To register accurately just these subtle gestures and poses, I had to efface my own personality completely, and let the image flow through me directly from the model to the clay, without the impediment of any subjective mood or conscious mannerism on my part." For many of the races, Malvina observed indigenous people working, hunting, praying, and resting: "Then I chose the moment at which I felt each one represented something characteristic of his race, and no other." For example, the Hawaiian is surfing. The position of his arms and the intense expression of his face suggests his sense of balance. At first, Laufer objected to the inclusion of accessories such as surfboards and weapons, but Stanley Field quickly silenced him: "If Miss Hoffman wants to put something in the hand of one of these figures which adds life, avoids monotony, what harm can it do?"

Malvina was accompanied by her husband, Sam Grimson, a violinist whose hands had been crushed during an accident while on a 24-hour leave during World War I. These injuries made it impossible for him to continue as a classical musician. They made several trips to Europe, Africa, and Asia to find models for the exhibit. Sam was the expedition's photographer and general manager. Malvina worked at "concert pitch" to complete the project. They filled metal cans used in World War I with plaster, clay, and plasticine. They packed lead pipes, wire, ropes, and other supplies into trunks, and cameras and other sensitive equipment into hermetically sealed containers. Malvina packed a medicine kit. On October 2, 1931, they set sail with twenty-seven boxes. All told, they traveled in forty types of ships and boats and spent nights in hotels, thatched huts, and once in a broken car.

Reporters portrayed Malvina as a zoologist of sorts, "traveling around the world to find her subjects in the wild and appropriate their life (in clay, rather than through taxidermy)." Her statues were presented to visitors as authentic, a "peephole into reality." The *New York Times* described the world tour as "a scientific expedition that is believed to be the first of its kind. She will combine art with science and record in bronze for future generations all the types of people living on the earth today." The *Times* stated that Malvina was working "under the guidance and with the collaboration of leading anthropologists." Her biographer wrote that the museum's staff "nipped at her heels for three years like angry Chihuahuas." They challenged her artistic choices and overrode her decisions about the installation of the exhibit. Finally, she put her foot down and told them how the show was to be installed and asked Field for his support. He complied.

Race experts reviewed and authenticated the sculptures. Most scientists recognized three primary races: Negroids, Mongoloids, and Caucasoids, with numerous subspecies based on the work of Carl Linnaeus, the father of taxonomy, in the 1700s. Linnaeus divided *Homo sapiens* into four categories, which corresponded to geographic regions and which were identifiable by racist physical and behavioral characteristics: *Homo sapiens europaeus* (White Europeans), *Homo sapiens asiaticus* (Asians),

Homo sapiens americanus (Native Americans), and *Homo sapiens afers* (Africans). Linnaeus's typology was not hierarchical. Still, the behavioral characteristics that he assigned to the races implied the superiority of some races: Europeans were brawny and inventive, Asians were melancholic and greedy, Native Americans were stubborn and free, and Africans were crafty and sly. Later, race experts dropped these prejudiced descriptions.

Often, the professional race experts disagreed on racial differentiation. In those circumstances, Malvina chose the model. When she created the *Kalahari Bushwoman*, she received so many different opinions on the size of her model's buttocks that she threatened to make them "in a thick flexible rubber, which could be easily inflated or deflated according to which anthropologist was expected to visit the museum!" In an introduction to the booklet that the Field Museum prepared for visitors, Arthur Keith claimed, "We are all anthropologists"—even the "man on the street." In contrast, Ralph Bunche, a political scientist at Howard University, claimed that the problem lay not with scientists but with the "average man in the street, who will demonstrate an ability to expound at length on the term [race] at the slightest provocation." Courts were increasingly adopting this commonsense approach. In *U.S. v. Bhagat Singh Thind*, the U.S. Supreme Court found it unnecessary to decide whether the Japanese are from the Mongolian or Malay race because the answer did not matter legally, as neither race is white. Harlem Renaissance author Jean Toomer believed that, although anthropologists had a dynamic, changing view of race, in America in the 1920s race was becoming "more and more fixed and crystallized." Prejudice was reinforced by immigration laws, which excluded the Chinese, Japanese, and Pacific Islanders from immigration while allowing some Europeans.

Malvina created 101 figures (full nudes, busts, and heads).

She thought it was "a miracle that we were given the physical strength to endure such continuous strain. I felt the premonition of eventually being declared a complete physical bankrupt. The mysterious power of rejuvenation must have come at night through the benediction of sleep, and through the realization that our efforts were counted upon."

Malvina described the project as "a first attempt to combine scientific data with an interpretation according to the traditions of sculpture and art." Although Malvina traveled to find her models, she also used some foreign attendees at the French Colonial Exposition in Paris as models, changing their clothing and artifacts as necessary.

A press release announced that the exhibit was "a unique plan of combining art with science without sacrificing either the beauty of the former or the exactness of the latter. While the strictest scientific exactitude in regard to the details and measurements govern the creation of these sculptured figures, the highest degree of artistic expression is being permitted with the restriction that no license shall be taken with the facts."

Illustration 20. Races of Mankind Exhibit, installed in 1933 (n.d.)

On June 6, 1933, Malvina Hoffman's *Races of Mankind* exhibit opened with little fanfare. Workers installed eighty-four sculptures and would add seventeen more in the following year. In the first year, the show attracted 3.2 million visitors, mainly because of its proximity to the world's fair.

The Field Museum published a booklet to introduce readers to the display. Berthold Laufer wrote the preface, which explained that race, nationality, language, and culture are different and that much harm occurs when people confuse the terms. He defined race as the "physical traits acquired by heredity." Race does not define a nation; culture—"the total complex of habits and thoughts acquired from the group to which we belong—determines a nation's behaviors." When the exhibit opened, French art critic Louis Vauxcelles wrote, "One does not know which to admire most—the dauntless courage of the explorer or the forceful talent of the artist." Others were not as complimentary.

In *Constructing Race*, contemporary author Tracy Teslow describes the resulting exhibit as imperialist-sanctioned voyeurism: "Museum patrons could examine exotic people unable to respond or return the look." But in 1932, most people did not think that way. The public relished this opportunity to see three-dimensional images of people from around the world—people whom they would never have had an opportunity to see if it were not for the exhibit. They saw it as beautiful artwork.

Malvina Hoffman's work on *Races of Mankind* was labeled racist forty years after its premiere. During the civil rights movement, the *Races of Mankind* exhibit became an embarrassment for the Field Museum. Poet Amari Baraka (then Leroi Jones) criticized the museum's Map of Mankind, which included a world map, with a photograph of each of her sculptures, because it was "full of consistent and glaring inaccuracies, which can only be the result of ignorant white nationalism." He described the map as "white pseudo-anthropology." In 1969, the museum closed the exhibit, claiming that it needed the space for other purposes. Despite Baraka's charge of racism, in 1975, Malcolm X College borrowed replicas of eleven pieces and displayed them on its campus until 1995 "to promote the humanism of traditional Africa."

Malvina's biographer argues that Malvina was not prejudiced and that her participation in the exhibit did not show racist tendencies. She quotes Malvina: "The primitive instinct, that motive power of our real selves, is the one most sternly embedded in all of us—black, white, yellow, and red—brothers and sisters under the skin. It is the eternal cosmic consciousness which binds all the races of man together." Art historian Linda Kim agrees. She quotes letters from exhibit attendees such as Bertha Bennet, who wrote, "You have shown the racial differences so clearly, yet through such a sympathetic and respectful approach that many feel that you have contributed immeasurably to interracial fellowship and understanding."

Blair was impressed with the *Races of Mankind* exhibition, and the Society invited Malvina to become a member. Soon, Blair would snag an even more famous explorer, one who would bring national attention to the Society.

PART 5
NETWORKING WOMEN

Illustration 21. Amelia Earhart (ca. 1936)

CHAPTER 15

ONLY A PASSENGER

Surely, of all the wonders of the world, the horizon is the greatest.

—FREYA STARK, AUTHOR, EXPLORER, AND SOCIETY MEMBER

APRIL 1928

Boston and New York

In April 1928, Amelia Earhart was working as a social worker at the Denison House, a settlement house outside of Boston that provided support services for immigrants. Amelia had been flying for more than five years, but she was stuck doing an acceptable "woman's job" instead of making a living as a pilot.

Each afternoon, as Amelia directed the children to their after-school activities, they swarmed around her, begging her for special consideration.

"Miss Earhart, I'd rather paint than play games. Please can't I change period just this once?" a little boy asked her. The boys were assigned to play games while the girls had to paint. Amelia knew that education divided students by sex, "putting them in little feminine or masculine pigeonholes." As she considered whether to grant the request, an older student politely interrupted to tell Amelia that she had a phone call.

"I'm too busy to answer just now. Ask whoever is calling to try again later."

"But he says it's important."

She sighed and reluctantly answered the phone.

"Hello. You don't know me, but my name is Railey—Captain H. H. Railey." The caller got straight to the point. "Would you be interested in doing something for aviation which would be hazardous?"

"What?" she asked.

He refused to describe the task over the phone.

Amelia probed his credentials and found that they were excellent. Admiral Byrd, who had attempted to fly over the North Pole, was one of his references. Curious, she agreed to meet him that evening at his office. She brought along her supervisor, Marion Perkins, from the Denison House.

Captain Railey told Amelia that Admiral Byrd had sold his tri-motor Fokker plane to a woman who planned to fly across the Atlantic as the first woman passenger. But her family was trying to dissuade her from going. She told book publisher George Putnam, who was organizing the expedition, that if he could find "the right sort of girl," she would cede the honor to another woman. The "right sort of girl," according to the woman, would be "a pilot, well educated; preferably a college graduate. She should be physically attractive and have manners that would be acceptable to members of English society, who would undoubtedly welcome her on arrival there." George had sent Railey to find the right girl, but he did not give him permission to reveal the woman's identity.

"I may as well lay my cards on the table," the captain said. "Would you like to fly across the Atlantic?"

"Yes, if—"

Captain Railey interrupted her. He was simply the scout: Amelia would have to negotiate in New York with George Putnam and the attorney for the project.

When Amelia arrived in New York for the interview, she was put off by George. "When I first met Mr. Putnam, I just didn't like him. He seemed brusque." He kept her waiting long after their scheduled appointment time. By the time that George saw Amelia, she was "sore as a wet hen."

George told Amelia that he represented Amy Guest, who was offering her the chance to fly across the ocean. Born in the United States, she was the fifty-six-year-old wife of a British politician, Frederick E. Guest. Amy had renamed Byrd's plane the *Friendship*, to symbolize the relationship between her country of birth and her adopted country.

Amelia was not keen to be a passenger. She wanted to take her turn at the controls, but this was unlikely because she had little experience piloting tri-motored planes like the Fokker. The attorney explained that the pilot and mechanic who would travel with her would be paid, but Amelia would not be compensated.* She was not surprised because she never expected to be paid.

Amelia considered the offer for a few weeks. She did not want to be extra weight: she wanted to fly the plane. But when Charles Lindbergh flew *The Spirit of St. Louis* across the ocean in May 1927, he had inadvertently triggered a race to see who would be the first woman to cross the Atlantic—as either a passenger or a pilot. Eight flights by men had been successful; none of the pilots or passengers had been women.

---

* Pilot Bill Stultz was paid $20,000 (almost $300,000 today), and the mechanic Lou Gordon received $5,000 ($75,000 today).

So far, five women had attempted to fly across the ocean. Three died, one was rescued at sea, and one gave up.

Passenger Princess Lowenstein-Wertheim and her two-man crew became lost at sea in September 1927. While the princess's fate was still undetermined, Frances Grayson announced that she planned to command a flight to Europe. The 35-year-old pilot told reporters that she was not in a race: "I don't believe in rushing a thing like this. There will be nothing hasty or haphazard in my flight. This is not to be a stunt." Soon the media dubbed Frances the "Flying Matron."

A few days later, twenty-five-year-old Ruth Elder announced that she would attempt a transatlantic flight with copilot George Haldeman. Ruth told reporters, "I've been dreaming and planning this ever since I first learned to fly two years ago. Then Lindbergh did it—and I was more determined. I want to be the first girl to turn the trick. I'll do it—I and Captain Haldeman."

Ruth had to wait a month for good flight weather.

On October 12, Ruth and George took off from Long Island. Her plane, *American Girl*, developed a broken oil feed line about thirty-six hours into the flight, about a thousand miles from Spain. Ruth crash-landed in the ocean, and a Dutch oil tanker rescued them. As the tanker's crew was attempting to hoist the *American Girl* onto the deck, the plane burst into flames.

On October 17, Frances Grayson took off from Maine but was forced to return fifteen minutes later because the weight had not been properly distributed, and the plane was nose heavy. She made a second attempt on December 24, this time from New York with a crew of three men. The plane disappeared en route to Newfoundland. It was never found.

On the other side of the Atlantic, Austrian Actress Lilli Dillenz attempted to cross the Atlantic westbound on October 4, 1927, but her propeller was damaged. She made other attempts to take off but eventually gave up. A few months later, Elsie Mackay left England headed for the United States with Captain Walter Hinchliffe as her pilot. They were reported lost at sea in March 1928.

Amelia knew of all these attempts to cross the Atlantic. Also, she knew that passenger Mildred Doran and her crew had died trying to cross the Pacific. Amelia weighed her options. Did she want to take the risk, only to be a passenger?

Finally, she decided to accept the challenge. Julie, Captain Railey's wife, spoke to Amelia by phone to make sure Amelia was not being pressured to take the flight.

"No," Amelia replied. "This is the way I look at it: my family's insured, there's only myself to think about. And when a great adventure's offered you—you don't refuse it, that's all."

Captain Railey swore Amelia to secrecy, a condition imposed by Amy Guest, the plane's owner. She did not want to encourage a race across the ocean, which might result in more tragic deaths. Additionally, if the press learned of their plans, they would be "submerged in a deluge of curiosity making it impossible to continue the preparation in an orderly fashion." Amelia could not even tell her parents about the flight, although her boss at the Denison House knew. Nor could she risk being seen near the *Friendship*. Amelia wrote a letter to her parents. She gave it to George Putnam to deliver in the event she did not survive the flight. She wrote, "Even tho' I have lost, the adventure was worthwhile."

In May 1928, Amelia, pilot Wilmer Stultz, and mechanic Lou Gordon waited with George Putnam in Boston for the perfect flight weather. After four days, George called his wife, Dorothy, and asked her to come to Boston to befriend Amelia and to comfort her as she waited for the flight. Dorothy agreed. She admired Amelia: "*What* nerve, courage, intelligence and *faith*! Or perhaps it's *fatalism*."

Dorothy hung out with Amelia for six days until the weather cleared. At 4 a.m. on May 28, 1928, Dorothy drove Amelia to the *Friendship* and waited in the car for clearance. The two women lingered for hours, talking about their childhood and their common interests. After four hours, they heard that the flight was canceled due to weather. Dorothy thought, "How *does* this astonishing girl stand the strain?" On June 3, 1928, the *Friendship* took off in Boston, but it was forced to land in Nova Scotia because of fog.

Weather delayed the flight for another two weeks. Finally, on June 17, 1928, they took off. During the flight, they encountered bad weather. The water was visible for only two hours of the twenty-hour flight. Stultz had to fly by instrument, a task that Amelia was not qualified to do.

Twenty hours and forty minutes later, the *Friendship* landed near the coast of Wales.

In London, Captain Railey met the crew of the *Friendship*. When he saw Amelia, he called out, "Congratulations! How's it feel to be the first woman to fly the Atlantic?"

Amelia moved her hand listlessly.

"What's the matter? Aren't you excited?"

"Excited? No. It was a grand experience, but all I did was lie on my tummy and take pictures of the clouds. We didn't see much of the ocean. Bill did all the flying—had to. I was just baggage, like a sack of potatoes."

"What of it? You're still the first woman to fly the Atlantic and what's more, the first woman pilot."

Amelia smiled ruefully. "Oh well, maybe someday I'll try it alone."

Despite her disappointment, Amelia accepted honors from the flight—not on her behalf, but to honor all women aviators.

George, the master publicist,* orchestrated Amelia's every move in London, from shopping expeditions to guest appearances. She was on the front page of newspapers around the world. All this for merely being a passenger.

When the *Friendship*'s crew returned to New York, George, Dorothy, and various friends took a tugboat to meet Amelia's ship. Amelia's face lit up when she stepped aboard the tug and saw Dorothy, her new friend. She rushed to hug her.

New York City and Boston put on ticker-tape parades for the *Friendship* crew, and Dorothy and George accompanied Amelia to various social events. Amelia's conquest of the sky was a significant milestone in women's achievements. Author Sidonie Smith noted, "The sky was male territory and its conquest a male prerogative. To enter the cockpit of the airplane required the aviator to be technically skilled, courageous, death-defying, and dogged." Although Amelia had not flown the plane, in the public's eye, she was still a hero.

George, who had just published Charles Lindbergh's book *We*, convinced Amelia to write a book about her flight. She moved into the Putnams' house for six weeks while she worked on her memoir. Amelia wrote the book in two months, and two weeks later it was on the shelves of bookstores. George later recalled, "In the routine meaning of the term I was, I suppose, Amelia Earhart's manager. Philosophically, she felt no human being of normal

---

* One of George Putnam's clients, Corey Ford, described him as a friendly man with a "hard, calculating glance behind his steely spectacles, an eye that was as cold as an undertaker's night bell." Ford said Putnam "had a knack for showmanship and published the memoirs of page one celebrities who sparkled briefly and then as they began to fizzle, were discarded for the next headline hero; his instinct for the spectacular was almost occult. When another front-page notable popped up his eyes fairly snapped with electricity, his fingers coiled and writhed like live wires, his voice had the hum of a loaded power line. He was always calculating, always figuring out how to make use of people, always with the commercial end in mind. Everything was for sale."

intelligence should be managed by anyone else. Temperamentally she had a healthy distaste for the implication of being led around by the hand." Dorothy's granddaughter, Sally Putnam, claimed that it was "mainly due to Putnam's brilliant management of the name Amelia Earhart that she is still remembered." George made hero worship into an art form. He used the same simple formula he had used to generate public interest in Will Beebe: write a book, go on a lecture tour, set another record, and then repeat.

Dorothy knew that her husband was infatuated with Amelia, but she didn't care. Although they were still married, she had given up on their marriage and was having an affair with her older son's tutor, George Weymouth, a college student, nineteen years her junior. And she knew that her husband was having an affair because she found a love note in his suit pocket. Yet, George clung to their marriage, insisting on intimacy that Dorothy did not want to give.

In August 1928, Amelia and George were flying together when Amelia crashed on landing in Pittsburgh. George was terrified that the press would start rumors about them. Newspaper reporters rushed to the scene. He begged them to keep it off the presses, then made a last-ditch effort to reclaim Dorothy. George proposed that Dorothy join him, Amelia, and their teenage son David on an Arctic trip the following summer to deflect suspicion. He thought Dorothy would like this because she had enjoyed taking David on Will Beebe's *Arcturus* expedition. Dorothy was outraged that her husband was inviting her to be his chaperone for the sake of the press, and, in her diary, she called George a "passion-scalded pig." Two days later, Amelia announced that she was no longer engaged to her fiancé. For Christmas, the Putnam family went on a Caribbean cruise together—an attempt to convince the press that Amelia did not break her engagement so she could marry George.

When the Society of Woman Geographers invited Amelia to

join them, Amelia was already a member of the Ninety-Nines, an organization of women pilots* who bonded after they participated in the first Women's Air Derby. The race was held as part of the 1929 National Air Races and Aeronautical Exposition. The competition started in Santa Monica, California and ended in Cleveland. Twenty women participated, and fifteen finished the nine-day race. When Marvel Crosson fatally crashed after her plane leaked carbon dioxide, the public demanded that the race be stopped, but the women continued in homage to her. Pancho Barnes and Ruth Nichols crashed their aircrafts. Several women had mechanical problems and dropped out of the race. Amelia came in third in the heavy class.

By Cleveland, the women had bonded. Amelia and five other contestants gathered under the grandstand in Cleveland to discuss creating an organization for women in aviation. In October, a letter was sent out to women pilots inviting them to an organizational meeting in Long Island. Twenty-six women attended. The women were disappointed with the attendance and scheduled a second meeting for December. They explained to their sister pilots that the organization "need not be a tremendously official sort of organization, just a way to get acquainted to discuss the prospect for women pilots, from both a sports and breadwinning sort of view." They did not want to compete with men; they simply wanted to be treated as equals "rather than spoiled as something rare and very precious. We believe that our girls can and will learn to fly as well as the average man, better than many, but it does not seem likely that we will ever equal the remarkable skill of countless men fliers both in our own country and abroad." Amelia countered, "If enough of us keep trying, we'll get someplace."

---

* In 1929, 119 women were registered as pilots. Nearly 9,100 men were licensed.

They met in a maintenance hangar and agreed that the organization would admit all women with pilot licenses in good standing. Its goal would be to provide "good fellowship, jobs and a central office and files on women in aviation." They tossed around a few names: Gadflies, Homing Pigeons, Noisy Birdwomen, but Amelia Earhart proposed a name that stuck: the Ninety-Nines. It was the number of women who attended the meeting plus the number of women who ultimately expressed interest in joining.

In July 1929, Transcontinental Air Transport hired Amelia to educate women about the safety of air travel. She invited Dorothy to be the first woman passenger to fly round trip from coast to coast. Dorothy accepted. Although she did not blame Amelia for the demise of her marriage, she decided she would rather keep Amelia as a friend than keep George as a husband. Sixteen years after Dorothy's friend Blair got divorced in Reno, Dorothy and her younger son packed and left for a Reno-vation. George threatened Dorothy, saying he possessed certain information that could prevent a judge from granting a divorce to her. But he did not carry out the threat. The divorce became final before the end of 1929.

But Amelia was reluctant to marry. She had turned down George's proposals five times. She told him, "You must know my reluctance to marry, my feeling that I shatter thereby chances in work which means most to me. I feel the move just now as foolish as anything I could do." Years later, when Amelia finally agreed to marry George, she wrote a prenuptial agreement:

> In our life together, I want you to understand I shall not hold you to a medieval code of faithfulness to me, nor shall I consider myself so bound to you. Please let us not interfere with the other's work or play, nor let the world see our private joys or disconnections. In this connection,

I may have to keep some place where I can retreat from even an attractive cage to be myself. I must extract a cruel promise, and that is you will let me go in a year if we find no happiness together. (And this for me too.)

When Amelia married George in February 1932, she did not promise to obey her husband.* She was determined to fly her own plane across the ocean. Amelia thought, "There's more to life than being a passenger."

In 1932, Amelia received an invitation to join the Society of Woman Geographers. She demurely replied, "I am very much honored but doubtful of my qualifications. However, if the other members will bear with me a while, I'll try to make up the deficiencies." She attended the first annual dinner in New York and announced that she had scheduled a transatlantic flight to coincide with the fifth anniversary of Lindbergh's flight. Amelia still held the record as the only woman to fly across the Atlantic as a passenger, although two more women had attempted transatlantic flights since her flight as a "sack of potatoes." Edna Newcomer's plane had disappeared off the coast of the Azores Islands, and Beryl Hart had gone missing after a fuel stop in Bermuda.

---

* Blair's ancestor, Sarah Harrison, may have been the first woman to refuse to obey her husband in her wedding vows. She wed Reverend James Blair in 1689. Following the dictates of the *Book of Common Prayer*, the officiating pastor asked Sarah, "Wilt thou obey James, and serve him, love, honour, and keep him, in sickness and in health; and, forsaking all other, keep thee only unto him, so long as ye both shall live?"

Sarah replied in a clear, firm voice, "No Obey."

He asked her a second time.

"No Obey."

Shocked, he asked Sarah a third time, but she still refused to say that she would obey her future husband. The pastor glanced at Reverend Blair. Blair did not object—perhaps because the connections the marriage would bring were more important than Sarah—or her obedience—and the ceremony continued.

Governor Francis Nicholson, who attended the wedding, enjoyed the spectacle. He said that in Reverend Blair's case, "marriage begins with 'Dearly beloved' and ends with 'amazement.'"

Illustration 22. Members of Society Meeting Harriet Chalmers Adams in Washington, DC, for Amelia Earhart Luncheon at White House (1932): Gertrude Mathews Shelby, Marjorie Turnbull, Lucille Sinclair Douglass, Blair Niles, Delia Akeley, Grace Barstow Murphy, Gertrude Emerson, Harriet Chalmers Adams

On May 22, 1932, Amelia became the first woman to successfully fly solo across the Atlantic. She took off from Newfoundland bound for Paris. Amelia was forced to land early because of a broken exhaust manifold, a broken gasoline gauge, and a fuel leak. She landed in a field in Ireland.

The aviator climbed out of her plane and asked a farmhand who was approaching, "Where am I?"

"In Gallagher's pasture. How far have you come?"

"From America."

She told Mr. Gallagher that she needed to call her husband.

"You needn't worry about that. I will see you through," replied Mr. Gallagher. He drove her into town to make the call.

The flight had not been smooth. She told reporters, "I had this trouble with the exhaust manifold for about 10 hours and for a lot of the way I was flying through storms—mist, rain, and a little fog." For four hours, she flew blind in pitch black.

Amelia would assert that her achievement proved that women were equal to men. She was right. In their 1938 book on great

Americans, Gillis and Ketchum would profile her. They would comment on the gradual emancipation of women and ask, "What more appropriate declaration of independence can be offered than these solitary flights?" Amelia had shown another sign of independence when she married George Putnam: she had insisted that her "flying name" remain Amelia Earhart.

When Amelia landed in Ireland, Blair swung into action. She knew that it was essential to keep the Society in the news, and the presentation of medals to prestigious members was an effective way to get publicity. She was determined to make sure the media recognized Amelia Earhart and the Society in connection with Amelia's transatlantic flight. The flight broke several records. Amelia was the first woman to fly solo across the Atlantic and the only person to fly it twice (once as a passenger, once as a pilot), and she achieved a record for the longest nonstop flight by a woman. She had bested Charles Lindbergh's record, reaching the British Isles in less than fifteen hours, half Lindbergh's time.

Blair, Mickie, and Marjorie Trumbull boarded the Goodyear blimp *Resolute,* which Amelia had christened before her record-breaking trip. They flew to Sandy Hook, New Jersey, to meet Amelia and George Putnam as they returned from Europe on the ocean liner *Ile de France.* They planned to drop a notice onto the ship's deck that notified Amelia that the Society had awarded her its first gold medal. They cabled Amelia and told her to be on the lookout for the blimp. Blair placed the certificate in a waterproof container and tied it to a length of twine so she could lower it onto the *Ile de France.* The scroll read, "The Society of Woman Geographers awards its first medal to Amelia Earhart in commemoration of her solo flight of the Atlantic, May 20, 1932, and recognition of what her courageous achievement means to all women."

Unfortunately, the blimp could not find the ship through the dense fog. Although Blair was disappointed, she had achieved her goal for the Society to be the first organization to honor Amelia. She had distributed press releases in advance, and so, although the Society did not physically award Amelia the medal straightaway, it managed to upstage President Hoover and the National Geographic Society with this feat. A few days later, the White House held a luncheon to honor Amelia. Blair, Mickie, the two founding Gertrudes, Marjorie Trumbull, Lucille Douglass (who designed the medal), and Grace Murphy flew down to Washington, DC, to meet Harriet and attend the luncheon. During the bumpy flight, Mickie wished she had taken a train. She was "terribly afraid," but screwed up her courage, saying, "If Amelia Earhart can fly to Ireland, I guess I can be flown from New York to Washington."*

On January 5, 1933, Harriet presented the medal to Amelia at the home of Lena Richardson Arents, an associate member of the Society. Guests included Captain Railey and George Putnam. Harriet addressed the small group:

> Among our members are women who, like Miss Earhart, have greatly adventured off the beaten path, explorers who have toiled to high mountain tops, struggled through virgin forests, crossed bleak deserts, descended to the depths of the sea, leaving a written record of the trails they have blazed. It was a small group of women of this sort who founded this Society eight years ago. Yet we know that one only, among

---

* This fear remained with Mickie long after the plane ride. She told a reporter that she was afraid of elevators because she was in an airplane when it plummeted downward: "Ever since I have the same horrible sinking feeling when I go down in an elevator. I feel safer if I can get hold of something, but I clutched a woman's dress one day and she thought I was trying to pick her pocket. So now I walk." She once missed a meeting of the Society because she did not realize that she would have to take an elevator sixty-five floors to get to the Rainbow Room in Rockefeller Center.

us, greatest of our adventurers, has ever gone quite alone. There have been companions, or guides, on mountain trails, in jungle, and in desert. But out into the night and across the great ocean, Amelia Earhart went alone.

Harriet turned to Amelia:

Miss Earhart, many nations have acclaimed you. You have won a place for yourself among the immortals.

And perhaps no others can so fully understand and appreciate, as we Fellow Geographers of your own sex, whose background and battles have been similar to your own, not only the most stupendous courage, but the intelligence and the energy, the grim determination through the years which made possible this crowning achievement of yours.

The design on the medal represents Winged Victory standing on the arc of the world, and above are the clouds in the sky, whose clouds and that sky which you have conquered.

Will you accept this medal, woman Geographer of ours, from this Society whose shining glory you are?

Blair was thrilled with the publicity that Amelia brought to the Society members. But she valued their friendships and contacts even more. The Society was indeed turning out to be the organization she hoped it would become: one that brought women together to support each other. But tensions would soon become apparent.

Illustration 23. New York Members of the Society of Woman Geographers, 1930–1931 Season: Standing, left to right: Ena L. Yonge, Helen Johns Kirtland, Fannie M. Chapman, Margaret Mead, Blair Niles, Gertrude Mathews Shelby, Ruth Crosby Noble, Gertrude Emerson, Mae Mott-Smith, Grace Thompson Seton, Millicent Todd Bingham; Seated: Grace E. Barstow, Florence Morden, Jean Kenyon MacKenzie, Annie S. Peck, Isabel F. Dodd, Lucille Sinclair Douglass

CHAPTER 16
FRICTION

Unexpected difficulties, I think, are at once the challenge and the charm of the lives of all explorers.

—OSA JOHNSON, FILMMAKER, EXPLORER, AND SOCIETY MEMBER

1929
Washington, DC

Harriet continued to lead the Society as president, but she hoped to resign so she could travel. Like all of the members of the Society, she yearned to travel, and she had not been abroad in years. Harriet thought that the other members would understand her restlessness. Perhaps they understood, but no one who was qualified to be president stepped up to take over. Normally cheerful, Harriet became bitter.

Harriet's last overseas trip was to the Balearic Islands in the Mediterranean Sea off the coast of Spain. She was walking along on a cliff when she slipped through an unguarded opening in the seawall and broke her back.

With her usual optimism, Harriet tried to stand, but she could not move. The tide was rising. She watched as the waves crashed closer and closer to her.

Several fishermen saw her and brought her to the hospital. A journalist reported, "The medical care was better in intention than in scientific skill. No one knew how badly she was hurt; no one had an x-ray to find out."

She returned to the United States by ship, strapped to a board. Her husband, Franklin, met her, and they traveled to Kellogg's Battle Creek Sanitarium in Michigan. Doctors placed Harriet in a plaster cast and steel braces and told her that she would never be able to walk again.

When she was out of danger, Franklin brought her home to their Washington, DC, apartment. Harriet spent more than two years confined to her bed in a plaster cast. During her convalescence, she unrelentingly worked on the business of the Society.

But Harriet had not yet completed her goal of visiting every country once held by Spain; she had not been to Morocco. When she was finally able to walk, she announced, "I will travel again." Marguerite Harrison noted, "Physical limitations never shut out Harriet's view of the far horizon; she was always planning and looking out, not in." Marie Ahnighito Peary Stafford* recalled that Harriet's "fierce energy and indomitable will carried her triumphantly through so many difficult undertakings and enabled her not only to survive but to forget a crippling accident which would

---

* In 1931, the Society approved a flag with the North Star, the Southern Cross, and the globe. Marie Ahnighito Peary Stafford, who signed her correspondence MAPS, was the first member to carry the flag on an expedition. She carried it on the 1932 Peary Memorial Expedition to Greenland, to honor her father, Robert Peary. Marie was born 848 miles from the North Pole and christened the "Snow Baby." Her mother, Josephine, was also a member of the Society. Blair planned a reception for the presentation of the flag. Marie was thrilled that she was the first member to carry the flag on an expedition: "I can't tell you how proud I am."

have made a helpless invalid of almost any other woman." Now that her back was healed, she planned another long journey. But when Frances Carpenter Huntington resigned as vice-president, Harriet canceled her trip in anger. She was worried that if she died, "the Society would be rudderless." Grace Barstow Murphy volunteered to complete Frances's term, and the Society moved its headquarters out of Harriet's apartment and into an office at the Barr Building. Harriet was relieved. Soon she would be able to resign. After serving as president for seven years, she was feeling landlocked.

In March 1929, Harriet Chalmers Adams put on her back brace and walked out her apartment door with her husband, Franklin. They boarded a ship to Spain. An editorial in the *Asheville Citizen-Times* noted that her goal of following the trail of the conquistadors around the world had been "interrupted several years ago by her broken back, caused by falling off a cliff. But what's a little thing like a shattered spine among lady explorers?" At the beginning of her voyage, she was in nearly constant pain.

When Franklin returned to the United States to continue his work for the Pan American Union, Harriet started her journey to twenty countries that bordered the Mediterranean in Europe, Asia, and North Africa. Before the end of her seven-month trip, she said, "I am as good as new."

When she returned to Washington, DC, Harriet was determined to find a successor. She groomed Grace Barstow Murphy of New York to assume the presidency. Because Grace was deaf, Harriet tutored Grace in the intricacies of the organization by correspondence. Harriet thought they had reached an understanding: Harriet would resign, and Grace would take over her duties. She started to plan her next trip.

In February 1932, Grace's mother fell ill, and she advised

Harriet that she could not assume Harriet's responsibilities without an understudy who could take over for her while she traveled. Harriet was devastated. She knew how hard it was to get an understudy. Once again, Harriet had to cancel her travel plans because of the Society. She wrote to Grace, "After reading your letter, I was greatly distressed. In spite of the fact that my letter of resignation is already drafted and plans for my own personal work made, I cannot now resign."

Friction had always existed between the New York members and the other branches of the Society, but now it escalated. During the Society's early years, the New York women dominated the group. By 1933, the power had shifted to Washington, DC. Four of the Society's five officers were from the Washington, DC, branch, leaving only Ruth Crosby Noble from the New York chapter. Blair was the only founding member on the nineteen-person executive council, which consisted of nine DC members, seven New York members (including Mickie), and three Midwestern members. Blair and Gertrude Mathews Shelby were the only founders who remained active. Gertrude Emerson (now Gertrude Emerson Sen) had moved to India and married. Marguerite Harrison [Blake] had remarried and would soon move to California. When the Washington, DC, members took control of the Society, the founding New York members pushed back. Mabel Cook Cole observed, "It was not an easy task, mothering and nurturing this group from a tiny nucleus to a widespread organization, unifying the widely separated members into a whole."

Although members had passed the rigorous entrance requirements, the women tended to undervalue their accomplishments. When Dorothy Graham Bennett, former curator of Hayden Planetarium and editor of the Golden Guide nature series, was in her seventies, she admitted, "I have always felt unworthy in the company of the distinguished fellow members." Society member mountaineer Arlene Blum explained this phenomenon: "Women do such wonderful things, but are so apologetic. They say things like, 'Well, I didn't do anything much this summer. I just visited the pygmies and was kidnapped.'"*

Margaret Mead usually did not favor sex-segregated organizations, but she agreed to join because "the future aims of the society seem to me sufficiently valuable to dim that objection." In later years, she proudly proclaimed, "I've always felt this is my gang." But other women were more straightforward about the need to exclude men. Marion Stirling said, "Frankly, we don't feel the necessity for men." But Lucille Quarry Mann put it best when she said, "Who'd want to belong to a club where you're not wanted?"

Although some of the members were wealthy, many were not. During the Depression, members often complained that they could not afford the $5 annual dues (about $95 today)—they spent every cent they could on their work. To keep dues as low as possible, the executive council decided to encourage wealthy women travelers to join as associate members. These women were exempt from the scholarship requirements. Their dues were $25 a year, five times the price for active members. Their experiences were valuable but, more importantly, they had the means to support the less financially fortunate members. They could not vote or hold office, but they could attend meetings. In 1932, there were thirty-four associate members, mostly from New York.

Gloria Hollister, Amelia Earhart, Malvina Hoffman, and Osa

---

* Mary Russell contends that women tend to belittle their accomplishments to "disarm their critics in advance." This "understatement of their own accomplishments directly led to a lack of public recognition."

Johnson were examples of illustrious members who may not have technically met the Society's stringent entrance requirements. When admitted, Gloria had written one scholarly article on the guacharo bird. And yet she blossomed into a serious biologist. Amelia Earhart had flown across the ocean, a magnificent feat to be sure, and had written a book about her *Friendship* flight, but was this really a work of a serious geographical nature? Yet, she exemplified the image the New York members of the Society wanted to project.

When Malvina was nominated for membership, the executive council had to decide whether her artwork was the equivalent of a serious book of a geographical nature. Malvina had contributed more to geographical and racial understanding than most members, but she had not yet written a book. They agreed that art could substitute for a book if it was of a serious geographical nature.

When the executive committee was deciding whether to admit Pearl S. Buck, they were confronted with a similar issue. Should fiction writers be admitted?

Blair had strong feelings about geographical fiction and nonfiction. She wrestled with the ethics of travel writing and travelogues such as *Simba* and the Johnsons' latest film *Congorilla*. She placed travel writing and travel films on a continuum of ethics. At one end were the impeccable classics of great explorers such as Mungo Park and Cunningham Greene. Marguerite Harrison's film *Grass*—minus the silly intertitle cards—was close to this end.

At the other end of the continuum were the chronicles of explorers (like the Johnsons) who contrived hairbreadth escapes and included deliberate misrepresentations to win over audiences at the theater or bookstore. Blair thought that this "literature of escape—narratives of incredible tales which have been brazenly put forth as historical or scientific"—was the reason that travel writing "lost its reputation and became a term of opprobrium." She believed that many writers and filmmakers "are frankly 'jazzing up' their material in the hope of catching an inferior market. There are a few who stoop to what they enigmatically call 'fictionalizing'—although nowhere in their volumes do they admit the fact, preferring to flaunt a masquerade of truth. For of course, were a book plainly labeled 'Fictionalized,' more would be expected of it, both in craftsmanship and invention."

The Johnsons were now soundly in this "fictionalizing" category. Osa Johnson had started out producing serious ethnographic films. As their careers progressed, the Johnsons became less wedded to accurate depictions of animals, and by 1928, they gave up on any attempt to realistically portray the African jungles. That year, the Johnsons' film, *Simba*, opened in New York. Ticket prices were staggeringly high: $1.65 (more than $25 today), and the film grossed $2 million ($30 million today). Not only was *Simba* fictitious and inauthentic, but the Johnsons gave the animals human characteristics. This kind of sensationalism disturbed Blair, who was careful not to include misrepresentations in her books. She would spend up to seven months studying the region before she traveled there, and then spend many more months visiting the country and talking with its people.

In the middle were fiction books of merit, where Pearl S. Buck fell. She was born in the United States to missionaries while they were on a brief leave from China. Her primary language was Chinese. Pearl recalled, "I grew up in a double world. When I was in the Chinese world, I was Chinese, I spoke Chinese and behaved as a Chinese, and ate as the Chinese did, and I shared their thoughts and feelings." When she left China to attend college in Virginia, she was American. Then she returned to China.

But she always regarded herself as Chinese. The executive committee decided that her fiction books met the Society's requirement because they were steeped in accurate geographical and cultural detail.

In 1933, Harriet resigned as president of the Society and nominated Blair for president. She wrote to Marjorie Trumbull, Blair's close friend, "We should drop all petty criticism and meet on the big ground of contacts which are really of value; we should try to overlook the little human mistakes we all make. It requires infinite patience and a little generosity, which can rise above personalities to hold together a group like ours. Blair could do this. Help me persuade her to make the sacrifice." But to her disappointment, the New York members did not put much effort into persuading Blair. Even if they had, it is unlikely that Blair would have agreed to be tethered to New York. No doubt influenced by Harriet, she was now starting her research into the conquistadors and was planning to travel to Peru. District of Columbia member Mary Vaux Walcott stepped up and assumed the presidency, leaving Harriet free to resume her travels.

Soon after Harriet resigned, New York members discussed whether to award Malvina a gold medal for her *Races of Mankind* exhibit. Mickie Akeley objected. She questioned whether the award of the medal was premature and whether the exhibit was truly geographical. In response, the New York members asked President Mary Vaux Wolcott whether Malvina was entitled to an award as a geographer. Mary replied, "As an anthropological sculptor, creating types of the races of the world, she is indeed a geographer." Armed with this information, the key New York members met to discuss whether the Society should give a medal to Malvina. Again, Mickie disagreed. The Society had just given Amelia a medal. She said, "The Society is too young to give medals. We have no money for the purpose. Begging from members is undignified. It tends to cheapen and creates a bad impression and often ill-will among the members." She also believed that it was "unwise and a bad precedent to honor any member before her work is finished. Why are we in such a hurry to confer this honor?" The other members overruled Mickie and asked Ruth to convey the New York group's desire to Mary Walcott.

Mary put the issue to a vote with the Washington group, who sided with Mickie. They vehemently opposed the idea and suggested that the Society should confer a medal once every five years. The Society would not award its second gold medal for another eight years because the award was such a contentious issue.

Although the members of the New York branch of the Society enjoyed their social outings such as birthdays, they sometimes butted heads when it came to the business of the Society and its relationship with the Washington, DC, and Chicago branches. During the early years of the Society, Blair and Harriet could keep things in line. But now that Harriet had resigned, Blair thought it was time to turn the leadership over to the younger members. She discussed this with Mickie, and they agreed: "It is time others took our place." Mickie thought Blair was adorable and "deserved a special place in the Hall of Fame for being so self-sacrificing and faithful to the interest of the club." She regarded Blair as a thoroughbred who always "worked like a soldier" to make Society events a success. Ruth Noble, chair of the New York group, had a long conversation with Blair, and she agreed to serve on the council another year. Mickie followed suit.

The Washington group tended to describe the New York group as peculiar and rather difficult. The new president, Mary Vaux Walcott, regarded the New York group as more social-minded, while the Washington group was more professionally oriented. The New York group got most of the media's attention, with superstars such as Amelia, Blair, Mickie, Malvina, Osa, Gloria, Margaret, Annie, and Pearl. Former New York members who had relocated, such as Mary Austin and Mary Ritter Beard, also got a lot of publicity. In contrast, the Washington group had few public media magnets—only First Lady Eleanor Roosevelt and Secretary of Labor Frances Perkins (both former New Yorkers), and these women were not actively involved in the organization.

Mary Vaux Walcott rationalized that the Washington members could not maintain a heavy social calendar like the New York women, implying that because the Washington members tended to have government jobs rather than freelance jobs, their time was more precious. But she also implied that Washington, not New York, was the center of American science and exploration: "Perhaps we have so many interesting things transpiring in Washington, we do not need the social angle to keep us stirred up."

Blair firmly believed that the local meetings allowed members "to begin the friendships which are such an outstanding part of the Society's benefits," a concept that Mary may not have understood because she had not been invited to join the Society until 1931. Blair did not consider the Society to be a purely academic society, but rather, "membership implied active work in fields for which travel is essential."

Ruth Crosby Noble, chair of the New York group and second vice-president, explained to Mary that the New York group's "differences of opinion really revolve around the fundamental concept of our Society. Most of the old-timers, the more genuine explorers, feel that the Society should be kept primarily social and should offer a distinct contrast to the individual societies which they all belong to. They feel that the informal association of vivid personalities of similar interests and experience is a sufficient goal in itself; that any considerable increase in our membership, or even too ardent a missionary zeal, would defeat this end."

Another faction, with less support, pushed for growth. These women wanted more members and a clubhouse, so they could "command recognition in the world." Allied with this faction was a more conservative group—the missionaries—who believed that the Society "should be the standard-bearers for the advancement of women. The financing of a dignified annual publication would be an immediate objective with hopes of thus attaining recognition by a foundation or by persons of wealth." The problem was that "those who are most enthusiastic over such grandiose schemes would probably be the ones who could give the least time to their development."

A peace offering came in 1935 when the Washington group invited the New York group to an impromptu tenth anniversary party. Blair, Ruth, and six other members of the New York contingent traveled to Washington to attend a dinner. Soon afterward, Helen Strong, a geographer in the Washington group, participated in a meeting in New York at the expense of the New York group. She wrote to Ruth, "Your meetings are worthwhile, and you should not give them up. The inspiration of the luncheon is with me yet, it was splendid, and by this token I realize what these affairs mean to others." Helen brought the issue of expenses up to the Washington council members, and they agreed to set aside $50 a year (about $1,100 today) for the costs of the New York group.

But within a month, the pot was being stirred again. Helen discovered that the New York group had used the reserved fund for flowers and cigarettes purchased for a Society luncheon. She pointed out that the Society had $1,000 (almost $20,000 today) in reserve only because Harriet had been careful with finances. Ruth angrily responded:

> The New York members of the Council feel (and have long felt) that individuals should not be financially responsible for Society expenses, be they for flowers and cigarettes or for telegrams and postage. I made a serious mistake in not making it clear that our request for $50 was not to meet the usual running expenses but just for such incidental expenses as flowers, birthday cakes, telegrams of courtesy, and operator's fees. We really don't care in the least whether you hold the purse-strings or we; whether we are paid before or after. I assure you that the New York group in the course of a year probably contributes hundreds of dollars toward the Society in the form of entertainment, telephone calls, stationery, etc. The New York Council sincerely believes that it is penny-wise and pound-foolish to economize too closely on running expenses, including entertainment. Most of our new members, especially the Associates, are attracted by our interesting meetings and activities. We feel that a policy of liberal entertainment would bring in more than enough new members to make up for the extra $50 which we requested.

Although the older members appreciated Harriet's savings, they "looked upon her contribution as an unasked-for gift, which the Society should appreciate deeply but not regard as a precedent for present-day policies." Mary Walcott objected to this use of funds: "The New York people seem to think that the object of having money is to spend it," but she continued to set aside funds for the New York group's miscellaneous expenses.

In 1936, Grace wrote a letter to Ruth expressing concern over the members of the New York group who were grousing about the organization. She suggested that if women "of breeding, and background and geographical attainment are brought to the fore, the carping will die out. An earnest interest in geographical research and a mutual cooperation, hardly seem to be the order of the day." Grace pined for the old days when the meetings were dignified, and members were interested in each other's work. The newer members were pressing for cocktail parties, without an intellectual element.

But it was precisely these social events that bound the New York members.

Illustration 24. Members in Exploring Costumes at the Tenth Anniversary Dinner of the Society of Woman Geographers (1935): Blair Niles, Marjorie Trumbull, Lena Richardson Arents, Amelia Earhart, Marie Peary Stafford, Grace Barstow Murphy

CHAPTER 17
NETWORKING

> ***Women often focus more on staying friends, which is as important as climbing the mountain.***
>
> **—ARLENE BLUM, BIOPHYSICAL CHEMIST, MOUNTAINEER, AND SOCIETY MEMBER**

In March 1935, the New York group met at the home of Lena Richardson Arents to honor Amelia Earhart's 2,400-mile flight to Hawaii. They wore costumes. Blair wore her pith helmet and knickerbockers, Amelia wore her flight outfit, and Marie Peary Stafford, nicknamed the "Snow Baby" because she was born in Greenland, wore Arctic clothing. In April, Marguerite showed the film *Grass*, and in May, they welcomed Gertrude Emerson Sen, who was visiting from her home in India. In December, Gloria and Helen Tee-Van spoke of their expedition to British Guiana.

Members coached each other, always giving each other practical advice. In speaking of the Society, Harriet told reporters: "Society members helped each other in a myriad of ways." Twelve members who were artists had a collective art exhibit at the Argent Gallery. Members often traveled together. While in China, Lucille Douglass met Titanic survivor Helen Candee* and sinologist† Florence Wheelock Ayscough, and they traveled together throughout Asia for a year. Lucille illustrated four of Florence Ayscough's books, one of Helen Candee's books, and a book by Pearl S. Buck.

Other members had a mentoring relationship. Dorothy Bennett studied with Margaret Mead. While Margaret lived in Papua New Guinea, Dorothy taught her courses at the Metropolitan Museum. Blair orchestrated Annie's appearances, such as her well-publicized eightieth birthday celebration: "You will speak for about thirty minutes; after that, we will have tea and congratulations. Yes, indeed, I did know that it was your birthday as well as the birthday of your book, and the tea is given in honor of both those occasions. I have arranged to have the *New York Times* and World Wide Syndicate photograph you at 4 o'clock."

Blair Niles and Annie Peck were good friends. Blair's flying experience convinced Annie to fly over South America. Blair believed that a person could not fully know a country until she had flown over it: "Studying a country without the aëroplane is like examining a human countenance bit by bit; an isolated eye, a detached mouth, an eyebrow and then by an act of memory adding all together in the effort to see the face as a whole. Through flight, the vision of the mind is extended." Blair learned this in 1923—five years before Amelia Earhart's "sack of potatoes" flight over the Atlantic—when she took a seven and a half

* Filmmaker James Cameron allegedly modeled the love scene between Jack and Rose on the bow of the *Titanic* on Helen's reminiscences. She described a trip to the prow of the boat, in which she swayed in the wind with a beau. Helen recalled, "As the ship's bow cut into the waves, throwing tons of water to the left and right in playful intent, her indifference to mankind was significant. How grand she was, how superb, how titanic."

† A person who studies the Chinese language, history, customs, and politics.

hour flight (twelve hours with mail stops and a two-hour stop to fix the engine) from the coast of Colombia to the Andes. Blair thought, "Nine days or seven and a half hours! That is an easy choice, especially with the spectacular view from the plane, especially when I poked my head out of the window!" After hearing Blair describe the flight, Annie was desperate to fly over South America. In 1929, at the age of eighty, Annie flew twenty thousand miles as a passenger in a series of flights over the continent. Ironically, the plane never reached an altitude higher than Annie had climbed. Shortly before Annie left, she asked Blair what she should bring. Blair recommended a waterproof coat and a wool sweater. She suggested, "I would get a nice sporty aviation cap, with goggles and fastening under the chin. Pictures of you taken in it would be good for publicity."

Writers supported each other. Pearl Buck wrote an introduction to Gertrude Emerson Sen's book, *Voiceless India*. Nobel prize winner Rabindranath Tagore, the author of *Gitanjali*, also wrote an introduction. Pearl won the Nobel prize in 1938. Gertrude was pleased that two Nobel laureates provided the introductions to her book, which she wrote about her small village in India. Amelia Earhart endorsed Annie Peck's book, *Flying over South America*.

Members visited each other at their worksites. At least seven members visited the tropical research station, where Gloria Hollister, Helen Tee-Van, and Else Bostelmann worked.

The women geographers also provided emotional support for each other. When Harriet Chalmers Adams broke her back, Benita Harris helped her. When Te Ata's husband died, Dorothy Bennett helped her through her mourning during a trip to Guatemala.

When Malvina Hoffman traveled, she rented her house to

Pearl S. Buck, who at age forty-two, had recently returned to the United States for a visit.* It did not take long for Pearl S. Buck to realize that American women were not valued. Growing up in China, where sons, not daughters, were revered, and knowing that in the United States children of both sexes were cherished, she had assumed that American women were treated with respect. Pearl was astounded to discover that American women are mistreated: "A few of them know it, more of them dimly suspect it. The reason for this unhappiness is a secret sense of failure, and this sense of failure comes from a feeling of inferiority, and the feeling of inferiority comes from a realization that actually women are not much respected in America." Pearl wrote sarcastically, "Your home ought to be enough for you if you are a nice woman. Your husband ought to be enough—and your children. But if they aren't enough, we say, 'Go and have a good time, that's a nice girl. Get yourself a new hat or something, or go to the matinee or join a bridge club. Don't worry your pretty head about what is not your business.'" She urged her readers to "face the fact

---

* When she attempted to return to China, the government refused to grant her a visa. The Chinese did not tell her why she was not permitted to enter China. For decades, she sought permission to return.

In 1972, she finally received a definitive answer: Chinese officials banned her because they thought she had smeared and vilified the Chinese people and their leaders in some of her books. She was outraged when she received the letter of explanation. Pearl wrote, "The letter—the letter! It lies there like a living snake in my desk—a poisonous snake. It threatens me now and refuses to allow me to return to the country where I have lived most of my life. It is an attack, not a letter. It is violent, it is uninformed, it is untruthful." When people asked her if she planned to return to China, she replied, "I have never left China. I belong to China, as a child, as a young girl, as a woman, until I die." She died the following year.

Historians later credited her with "single-handedly changing the distorted image of the Chinese people in the American mind." She also was a force behind the repeal of the Chinese Exclusion Act in 1943, which had banned Chinese emigrants to the United States since 1882. Thirty years after her death, in 2004, Oprah Winfrey selected *The Good Earth* (Pearl's Pulitzer Prize–winning book) as a selection for her book club. The *China Daily* reported that although Pearl Buck once was controversial, she is now "a friendly cultural bridge between the East and the West."

that as a nation we are in a medieval state of mind about the place of women in society."

Te Ata, Eleanor Roosevelt, and Dorothy Bennett provide an excellent example of how networking enriched the lives of the members of the Society.

Te Ata was a Chickasaw Indian, born Mary Frances Thompson. Until she went to high school, she had never met a white child. During college, she learned that she had a talent for acting. In 1922, Te Ata traveled to New York City to break into acting. While waiting for callbacks after auditions, she made a living performing Indian folklore at private parties using the name Te Ata, which means *Bearer of the Dawn*. Wealthy women such as Eleanor Roosevelt hired her to perform at parties. Soon, she and Eleanor became friends. In 1932, the commissioners of a state park about eighty miles north of Manhattan renamed a lake after Te Ata, likely at the suggestion of Eleanor Roosevelt, who attended the dedication of the lake and whose husband was governor of New York.

In the fall of 1932, Franklin Delano Roosevelt was elected president. Te Ata sent the Roosevelts a note of congratulations. Although Eleanor did not reply to most letters, she wrote Te Ata, "I hope sometime that it will be possible for you to come to the White House after we are settled there." In April 1933, the first lady asked her to perform at a dinner honoring Britain's prime minister.

At the White House, Eleanor introduced Te Ata as a long-standing friend. Te Ata performed in the Blue Room wearing a white buckskin dress with long fringe and bells that jingled when she walked. Te Ata walked with quiet beauty and elegant grace. Her fluid movements brought to life the Indian stories she was performing. Soft light danced across her supple buckskin dress.

Effortlessly, she transformed from an arrogant young brave to an older woman, changing her voice and posture to portray each character. She hoped her stories would give the prime minister an accurate impression of Native Americans.

In 1933, Te Ata married Clyde Fisher, the curator of astronomy at the American Museum of Natural History. When the Hayden Planetarium was completed, he became the head of the planetarium. His assistant was Dorothy Bennett.

In 1937, Dorothy Bennett discovered that a seven-minute eclipse would be visible in the Southern Hemisphere that summer. Fisher had no plans for the planetarium to celebrate the eclipse. Dorothy recalled, "Well, I told him we ought to do something. I traced the path of the eclipse and found that the mountains of Peru would make an excellent vantage point from which to observe the eclipse. After learning there were American-run mining camps in Peru, I looked up one in the phone book and called for an appointment. I told this executive all about these distinguished astronomers setting out on this important scientific expedition and asked if the mining company would be willing to put them up." When Dorothy finished this preliminary work, Fisher contacted the Grace Line shipping company and convinced them to provide transportation. The Hayden Planetarium-Grace Peruvian Eclipse Expedition was ready to set sail. When Te Ata found out that they planned to view the eclipse from an area near Incan ruins, she was intrigued and joined the team.

As the Grace Line ship crossed the equator, Te Ata was reading Blair's book *Peruvian Pageant*. When she got to Peru, Te Ata used Blair's book as a guide and visited many places that Blair wrote about, including Guayaquil, Lima, Cuzco, and Machu Picchu.

She also met Dr. Julio Tello, the first indigenous Peruvian

archaeologist whom Blair had interviewed for her book. In *Peruvian Pageant*, Blair stated, "His profession is woven into the memory of his family and is inseparable from a deep love of his native land." A few years earlier, Blair had spent much time trying to win the trust of Dr. Tello. Finally, Tello invited Blair to observe the unwrapping of a mummy, an eye-opening, two-day experience that she wrote about in her book. Tello unwrapped the mummy at the Museo Bolívariano, where Blair met Rebeca Carrión Cachot and invited her to become a corresponding member of the Society. Te Ata likely met Rebeca while she was in Peru, as she was still assisting Dr. Tello.

But with friendship comes heartache at the loss of friends.

Annie Peck died before her eighty-fifty birthday. After a fellow Society member accused Gertrude Mathews Shelby of being a "warlike" person, she started to disassociate from the Society. She died not long afterward. Ella Riegel, the staunch advocate for women's rights who participated in the Prison Special, died in 1937.

On June 1, 1937, Amelia Earhart took off from Miami on her round-the-world flight. Before she left, she pointed to the South Pacific on a map near the Solomon Islands and told Gertrude Emerson Sen, "If I don't come back, I will be lost here."

She left a note for her husband: "Please know that I am quite aware of the hazards. I want to do it. Women must try to do things as have never been tried. When they fail, their failure must be but a challenge to others." She packed the Society's flag and headed for her plane.

She traveled twenty-two thousand miles, stopping in South America, Africa, India, Southeast Asia, and New Guinea. She had seven thousand miles left—which required flying over the Pacific Ocean—when she departed New Guinea for Howland

Island, her next stop. The island was tiny, only a few miles long. As she approached the island, she radioed *Itasca,* the Coast Guard cutter assigned to assist her on this part of the flight. She told the *Itasca* that she was low on fuel. The *Itasca* sent out black smoke to aid Amelia in locating the ship. She circled for hours, looking for the cutter.

"One half-hour fuel and no landfall," she told the *Itasca* and gave them her coordinates.

She lost contact with the ship and was never heard from again.

Archaeologist Marjorie Trumbull would later write of the last flight:

> It was our flag—the flag of the Society of Woman Geographers—she took with her on those swift journeys which made her name a comet in the sky. On those solo flights across wide desolate waters, there must have been times when she was lonely. There must have been times when those thin, strong arms tired, and mind and body felt the strain. But although Amelia played a game where there was room for only one mistake, she took her chances willing and boldly. It was the game she chose to play. All who felt her charm, knew her simplicity, her bravery, and her independence of thought, all who loved her, through dark days clung to the hope that she was still somewhere alive. We have faith that God let her find her wings.

Two weeks later, another tragedy hit the Society. Harriet Chalmers Adams died before she achieved her goal of providing endowed scholarships to young women and developing a mentoring program. The Society members immediately set to work to establish a memorial fund. Blair explained that the fund was designed to meet Harriet's dream: "Financing expeditions is expensive and botanists, archaeologists, and sociologists do not command big salaries. A great many young persons must be discouraged from the work because they lack funds. I hope that sometime we will be able to endow them."

Blair became ill. She realized that as she aged, "some expeditions would be too arduous for her." She began preparing for the time when her detailed field notes would allow her "to pursue her career to the end of her days."

When a reporter asked her to give advice to young women who wanted to become explorers, Blair answered, "Discouragement must never have a place in the vocabulary of an explorer, for the very essence of the profession lies in attempting the more or less impossible!" An explorer must be "versatile enough to earn her pennies in various ways, to have boundless energy and to be quick to grasp at opportunity on the wing."

Blair began to cut back on her work within the Society, hoping that the younger women would assume responsibility so that she could travel more and introduce her readers to marginalized people around the world and expose the discrimination and exploitation they faced, much like she did in her book on Haiti. But like so many women of the twentieth century, and like so many of the Society members, Blair's contributions would be downplayed and ignored in history.

PART 6
PAVING THE WAY FOR WOMEN TODAY

Illustration 25. Margaret Mead with Manus Mother and Child (1953)

CHAPTER 18

THE MATILDA EFFECT

With the passage of time—as so often happens with women's careers—the names and contributions of these explorers tended to sink from sight, their achievements questioned or minimized.

—ELIZABETH FAGG OLDS, NEWSPAPER CORRESPONDENT AND FORMER PRESIDENT OF SOCIETY

In 1883, Matilda Joslyn Gage, an early suffragist, wrote an article in which she asserted that historians routinely write women out of history. She pointed out that women had invented "a volcanic furnace for smelting ore," the gimlet-point screw, and the baby carriage, among other inventions. She also claimed that Eli Whitney, the supposed inventor of the cotton gin, actually made the machine according to the specific instructions of Catherine Littleton Greene. Matilda explained that Greene did not file for a patent because it would have subjected her to ridicule for engaging in a "male" activity. Instead, Eli Whitney took credit.

Over one hundred years later, science historian Margaret Rossiter coined the phrase the Matilda Effect to describe the cognitive bias that blots out the achievements of women in science.

Many of the early members of the Society of Woman Geographers suffered from the Matilda Effect.

For example, Annie Peck experienced the Matilda Effect when newspapers congratulated four German men who climbed the north peak of Mount Huascarán twenty-six years after she ascended the slightly lower neighboring peak. Annie's feelings were hurt. The fact that Peru had given her a gold medal for the accomplishment and renamed the ridge Cumbre Aña Peck was ignored. Reporters did not even mention that Annie held the record for the highest altitude ever climbed by an American in the Western Hemisphere.

Mickie Akeley suffered from the Matilda Effect because she was in the same line of work as her ex-husband, Carl—hunting specimens for museums—and because she was divorced. It was rare that a newspaper article would fail to mention Carl in an article about Mickie. Of course, the converse was not true. Even after their divorce and his death, reporters still identified Mickie as Carl Akeley's wife.

Carl had left his estate to his new wife, Mary Jobe. He had changed his will before the divorce to pass on everything to Mary. A friend asked Mickie about Mary: "And what about No. 2, is she still seeking the limelight?" She was, and she effectively erased Mickie from Carl's life in the books she wrote about him. The king of Belgium awarded Jobe the decoration of the Cross of the Knight of the Order of the Crown, Belgium's highest honor for the work she did in the Belgium Congo during the two years she was married to Carl. In contrast, Mickie got little recognition for her nearly twenty years of safaris with Carl.

Mary Ritter Beard's contributions were also erased, both by

others and herself. Although she wrote many books in collaboration with her husband, Mary did not get credit for her contributions. Critics identified *The Rise of American Civilization*, which included both Charles's and Mary's name on the cover, as Charles's masterpiece. In 1947, Merle Curti, who was writing an article about Charles, wrote to Mary and said he would "have to" include her in his essay. Mary was livid: "You say you will 'of course have to include me' with respect to writings which we have both signed. I can ease you out of that difficulty by saying you don't have to include me. You might indicate merely that I was 'also there'—in a respectable manner." Then she implied that it was no one's business how they wrote together: "We prefer to have the writing stand on its own ground instead of that mysterious intimacy." Historian Howard K. Beale wiped out Mary's contributions with two sentences: "No one knows the nature of their collaboration. Hence, I have always spoken of the joint works as Charles Beard's." Yet, when Mary authored books alone, she was still slighted. A reviewer called Mary's solo work inferior to a two-authored book simply because only one author wrote it.

Like many other women, Mary diminished her contributions, telling a friend, "I would not allow my name to be placed on our co-authorship if I could prevent it because the major contribution is his." Yet, while she permitted publishers and reviewers to dismiss her contribution, she "characterized women's history as a tale of oppression and invisibility." Scholar Alice Alvarado notes that Mary worked her whole life "to reconstruct history to include women, and merely received credit for being Charles' wife."

After filmmaker Martin Johnson died in a plane crash, agents were reluctant to book Osa on a lecture tour, fearing that she would not draw a crowd, even though she had been the anchor of her husband's wildlife films. Some refused to book her unless she was advertised as "Mrs. Martin Johnson." Her fame had faded with her husband's death.

When Will Beebe wrote about the pheasant expedition in *Pheasant Jungles,* he erased all mention of Blair. He appropriated some of her experiences, such as when the water buffaloes treed her, and when her horse fell through a dilapidated bridge. Not content with merely stealing her escapades, Will also plagiarized her words, placing large sections of her *Harper's Magazine* articles into his book without giving her credit and erasing all mention of her existence. Blair was a triple victim of the Matilda Effect: erased, plagiarized, and appropriated. Later, he had affairs with some of his female colleagues and did not provide a safe workplace for other women.

By 1936, Will had discarded Gloria Hollister as a lover and had begun a romantic relationship with Jocelyn Crane. Their relationship would last for over thirty years until Will's death. Elswyth, his wife, did not interfere with the affair.

Not only did Will aggressively pursue sexual relations with his female employees, but he also exploited them monetarily. Always operating on a shoestring budget, Will convinced many of his scientists and artists—men and women—to work for no pay. Some were graduate students who spent their summers interning for Will. Artist Helen Damrosch Tee-Van came from a wealthy family, and her family subsidized her work and her husband John's work at the center. Jocelyn worked for a "pittance" for eight years until the zoo recognized her as a research associate and began to pay her $1,800 a year ($33,700 today). Through rose-colored lenses, she recalled, "Yes, salaries at the Zoological Society were minuscule, but that was all right, for you were just having the most heavenly time."

Not only did Will fail to pay some members of the team when finances were tight, but he also required them to pay their travel expenses and room and board. In 1920, Will wrote Anna Heyward Taylor to ask her to join the expedition: "No wage money will be available until next year, so we will have to crawl along as best we can." He charged her $20 a week ($260 a week) for room and board. She spent one entire season owing Will for the ship fare to British Guiana, and in every letter that she wrote to her sister, she complained that money had not arrived from the United States, which she needed to pay him back and purchase her passage home. She told her sister, "I have spells of getting up in the air because I have no money. My relations with Will are not such that I can feel I am living on him and be comfortable." One can only guess her response if she heard Will grouse years later, "I wanted to make one brief sea venture, then one millionaire gave me a yacht, another millionaire gave me a yacht, and the Governor of Bermuda gave me an island. I spent ten years underwater."

Will also used many of the women to help him meet his publishing goals, often without giving them credit. During his life, he wrote eight hundred articles and twenty-one books. For him, writing was almost as natural as breathing, but he lacked the patience to revise his works. During his marriage to Blair, Will relied on her to edit his work. Blair typed and edited as Will dictated. Blair's editing skills accelerated Will's already-rapid writing pace. After they divorced, Will relied on women to edit his articles to keep up his prolific pace.

Perhaps the person he exploited the most was Jane Anderson, a writer. After Blair divorced Will, he was depressed and unable to write. Within a few months, he began a relationship with Jane, the wife of his friend Deems Taylor, a journalist and a future music composer. Not only was Jane a temporary solution to Will's depression, but she was also the answer to his writer's block. She wrote many of his articles.* With Jane's assistance, in 1914, Will published twice the number of columns as in 1913, all while writing his four-volume *Monograph of the Pheasants*. Jane complained to her college friend Kitty Crawford, "I am to do a whole book for Will, now. This is to be a book† about all the countries I have never seen—the Lord only knows what I would write if I had been there. I'm going to try and get the book out before spring." She wrote, "I know I'm getting a rotten deal—what with everybody believing that I've flunked in my work, and Beebe getting all manner of credit for the stuff."

Margaret Mead faced a different kind of erasure.

Five years after Mead's death, New Zealand anthropologist Derek Freeman sought his moment of fame by debunking her anthropological work of the Samoan people. Many anthropologists found his attack of Margaret cowardly and unsubstantiated. One of his colleagues said that Freeman "seemed to have a special place in hell reserved for Margaret Mead, for reasons not at all clear at the time." Freeman later described January 31, 1983, the day the *New York Times* ran a front-page story about his book on Margaret, as the day that "all hell broke loose." Freeman wrote in his diary, "Now the matchless deed's achieved: determined, dared, and done." He predicted that his matchless deed would cause Margaret Mead's reputation to plummet at the speed of a "falling body."

---

* Will inscribed in his diary, "The last week I have written and had accepted by Atlantic Monthly Jellyfish & Equal Suffrage. Have written half of a Geographic lecture & Geographic Magazine article; reviewed two books, given a Buffalo lecture, and kept up my other work." Below this entry is a cryptogram: "Jane really wrote them."

† It does not appear that she wrote a book based on the pheasant expedition, although she may have written several articles for *Atlantic Monthly* that Will later included in *Pheasant Jungles* (1925) or *Jungle Peace* (1918). Jane could have easily written these articles based on Will's detailed diary, although the pieces sound like Will wrote them.

In *Margaret Mead and Samoa: The Making and Unmaking of an Anthropological Myth*, published by Harvard University Press, Freeman claimed that Margaret had been the subject of an adolescent prank, and because of her limited field experience in Samoa, she had believed the hoax. One of the pieces of evidence that Freeman cited for his contention that the villagers had duped Margaret was a sentence in a 1931 book called *All True: The Record of Actual Adventures That Have Happened to Ten Women of Today*. Members of the Society of Woman Geographers authored the book. In her chapter, Margaret stated that she had become acquainted with Samoan girls and received "their whispered confidences" to learn the answer to her anthropological questions. Freeman contended that the whispered confidences were lies about sex, even though the chapter did not mention sex.

In a second book about Margaret, Freeman wrote that this hoax had widespread ramifications because Margaret convinced the world that Samoans were promiscuous as a result of their culture: "That a Polynesian prank should have produced such a result in centers of higher learning throughout the Western world is deeply comic. But behind the comedy there is a chastening reality. It is now apparent that for decade after decade in countless textbooks, and in university and college lecture rooms throughout the Western world, students were misinformed about an issue of fundamental importance. Never can giggly fibs have such far-reaching consequences in the groves of Academe." Freeman attacked Margaret professionally and personally, alleging that she had an affair with a Samoan. (Margaret indeed considered having an affair, but she told a friend that she decided not to because she represented Columbia University, where she was getting her PhD.) Conservatives, who attributed the moral decline of American values and "free love" to Margaret, sided with Freeman.

The debunking had an immediate impact on Margaret Mead's posthumous reputation. The *Wall Street Journal* wrote, "It now appears that Mead was bamboozling readers with her tales of sexual permissiveness in Samoa." When Freeman's second book was published in 1999, the *Journal* was so impressed with Freeman's discrediting of Mead that it concluded that she must have been a charlatan. That same year, when *Time* magazine named Margaret as the century's "foremost woman anthropologist," it deferred to Freeman's assessment of her: "It seems Mead accepted, as fact, tribal gossip embellished by Samoan adolescent girls happy to tell the visiting scientist what she wanted to hear." A few years later, the Institute for Intercollegiate Studies named *Coming of Age* "the worst nonfiction book of the century." In 2009, Benjamin Wiker named Mead's book as ninth in a list of *Ten Books That Screwed Up the World*, behind Hitler's *Mein Kampf* and Marx and Engel's *The Manifesto of the Communist Party*.

In 2009, Paul Shankman, author of *The Trashing of Margaret Mead: Anatomy of an Anthropological Controversy*, noted, "Although Mead's personality and motives were scrutinized by Freeman, both the media and professional anthropologists have been less interested and more reluctant to consider Freeman's motives and personality." Ellen Goodman, a liberal columnist, described Freeman's book as "one academic shade short of nasty, full of the muckraker's delight, and more than a little patronizing. There's a touch too much glee in watching people whack the great off their pedestal." She quoted Professor Michael Lieber, who speculated that the different perspectives of men and women were at the heart of the Mead-Freeman controversy: "Mead's conclusions were based on her observations of adolescent girls, Freeman's on his close association with the Samoan male power hierarchy." Of course their views would be different. Goodman also chastised the *New York Times'* coverage, which referred to Freeman as "Professor Freeman" and Mead as "Miss Mead." A corollary of the Matilda Effect must include the erasing of women's academic accomplishments to make male claims credible.

Paul Shankman continued to research the controversy. In 2013, he wrote an article that showed the dispute was not a mere difference between men and women, but rather that Freeman had purposely misled his readers, "not simply to revise the ethnographic record but to damage Mead's reputation in a deliberate and personal manner."

Even the *New York Times* suppressed the accomplishments of women. It was not until 2018 that the *New York Times* debuted *Overlooked*, a column of obituaries of remarkable women and people of color ignored by history (and by the *Times*). When *Times* reporters Amisha Padnani and Jessica Bennett introduced the new column, they noted that the newspaper published obituaries for white males such as the inventor of Stove Top stuffing and the person who named the Slinky but ignored author Charlotte Brontë and Ida B. Wells, an African American writer who reported on lynchings. They rectified this omission by belatedly publishing the obituaries of famous women. At the time of their deaths, the *Times* ran extensive obituaries of Blair and Mickie and a short blurb about Osa's death. All three obituaries mentioned their ex-husbands. The *New York Times* did not acknowledge Mary Ritter Beard's death, although the byline in her husband's obituary read "Collaborated with Wife." Her double omission by the *Times*—once at her death and again in the *Overlooked* column—seems ironically fitting for a woman who dedicated her life to empowering women by reporting their forgotten history.

As Blair approached the end of her life, she thought more about her childhood in Virginia. Although Blair was proud of her grandmother's literary achievements, such as her book *Birth of a Nation,* she felt a need to atone for her grandfather's role in the Civil War. Roger Atkinson Pryor was a member of the U.S. House of Representatives, elected by the citizens of Virginia. He was convinced that the North and South could not reconcile on the issue of slavery. On the evening of April 10, 1861, he spoke before a crowd in Charleston, urging South Carolina to start the war so that Virginia would join the seven states that already had seceded from the Union. The *New York Times* later claimed Roger's speech was the "match that exploded the powder magazine and brought on the war." Southerners telegraphed a transcript of the speech to the Confederate capitol offices in Montgomery, Alabama, and pressured President Jefferson Davis into declaring war. Not only did her grandfather incite the Civil War, but he was given the "honor" of firing the first gun of the war. He refused, and a soldier fired the first gun.*

Blair clung to the fact that although her grandfather was a secessionist, he did not order the firing of the first gun, and he did not fire the first gun. It was some solace. But she still felt the need to atone for her grandfather's involvement in precipitating the Civil War. Her first attempt to atone was to travel to American-occupied Haiti to learn about the largest slave revolt in modern history and to see how the Haitians, who had ruled themselves for a century, were faring under the American occupation.

---

* Confederate General Beauregard designated Roger Pryor as one of his aides-de-camp. He ordered the aides to row to Fort Sumter to demand that Union commander, Major Robert Anderson, surrender, and instructing that "all orders transmitted through them will be obeyed." Major Anderson refused to surrender immediately. As instructed by General Beauregard, the emissaries delivered the general's order to fire upon Fort Sumter to Captain George S. James. The captain had long admired Roger, whose passionate speeches, editorials, and antics on the floor of Congress were well publicized. He asked Roger to fire the first cannon of the war, telling him, "You are the only man to whom I would give up the honor." Roger's bravado disappeared. He replied huskily, "I would not fire the first gun of the war." Captain James fired the shot, and the Civil War began.

On the centennial of the Supreme Court's *Amistad* decision, Blair wrote a novel that introduced a new generation to the court's decision, which held that kidnapped Africans were not the property of their "owners." The book, called *East by Day*, was selected as one of twenty books by readers of the *New York Herald* for Great Britain readers. It served as her atonement for her grandfather's role in the Civil War.[†] She also won the Constance Lindsay Skinner Award for *The James*, a book about the James River that told of her childhood on *The Oaks* plantation.

In 1944, the executive committee of the Society of Woman Geographers had no difficulty agreeing to award its third medal, this time to Blair, for her research and travels in Latin America. The Society's president at that time, Mary A. Nourse, an expert on China, presented the medal at the 1944 annual dinner. She told the audience that the government of Ecuador regarded Blair's book *Casual Wanderings in Ecuador* as the best English-language book on the country. The City of Lima had awarded Blair a gold medal for her book *Peruvian Pageant*, and the U.S. Department of the Navy ordered sixteen hundred copies of *Passengers to Mexico* for their fleet libraries. Blair continued to write until her death in 1959.

But despite Blair's amazing accomplishments and her desire to curb prejudice of all kinds, history has almost completely ignored her. Blair did not keep any of her recorded history. Except for her published books and one manuscript, her records

---

† After the war, Roger renounced his anti-abolitionist views and fought for reconciliation between the North and South. In 1865, he moved to New York, passed the bar examination, and became licensed to practice law in New York. He enrolled his daughter, Gordy, in the Packer Institute. He was one of the few carpetbaggers who successfully integrated into New York's political arena. In later years, he would become a New York supreme court judge. Likely, Blair did not know of his role in the war until after his death in 1919, when obituaries mentioned it. In *East by Day*, Blair wrote about a young woman who learns of her grandfather's role as a slave trader immediately before his death and atones for his participation in slavery by moving to Africa.

can only be found in the archives of others. Fortunately, Blair wrote dozens of articles, seventeen books, and hundreds of letters, from which her life could be pieced together. Otherwise, she would continue to sink into oblivion like so many of the other founders of the Society. When researchers unearth and publicize the accomplishments of Blair, Annie, Malvina, and other overlooked members of the Society, women become empowered and society benefits. In the words of Mary Ritter Beard, "Without documents; no history. Without history; no memory. Without memory; no greatness. Without greatness; no development among women."

Illustration 26. Gloria Hollister, William Beebe, and Jocelyn Crane Looking at Eclipse (1937)

CHAPTER 19

SEEING WITH BOTH EYES

> *What women have to stand on squarely is not their ability to see the world in the way men see it, but the importance and validity of their seeing it in some other way.*
>
> —MARY AUSTIN, AUTHOR AND SOCIETY MEMBER

1940S

New York City

Fifty percent of the world population is female, but only .05 percent of recorded history relates to women. Textbooks are "almost wholly written from a masculine point of view." Mary Ritter Beard regarded these texts as "less than half a book." In 1917, she objected to the prevailing view that "men still count most" and "what is feminine is hysterical, frenzied or just idiotic—in a man's world." She also condemned the "folly of pretending to be a neutral human being, which was neither man nor woman," for society benefits from seeing civilization from multiple perspectives.

In 1918, Mary's contemporary, Mary Austin, claimed, "Civilization as we now have it is one-eyed and one-handed. It is kept going by man's way of seeing things and man's way of dealing with the things he sees." She noted that because "for so many centuries, man's intelligence was the only kind of intelligence that was heard, women are accustomed to judging intelligence by the masculine standard." Mary believed that women's failure to "know their own prophets is rather a serious predicament for women." She encouraged women to understand the importance of seeing the world differently than men and supporting other women in their attempts to do so.

She also believed that women were silenced by a "wall of men, a filtered, almost sound-proof wall of male intelligence, male reporters, critics, managers, advertisers, men editors, men publishers, and men reviewers." Novelist Gertrude Atherton believed that women did not leave an impression on history because "man had the power to wring her neck, and the legal backing to treat her as a partner or a servant, whichever he found convenient."

Like Mary Austin, her sister geographer Mary Ritter Beard argued that women have an essential role in achieving democracy: they need "to bring a feminine perspective to the debate." Equality with men was not her goal; she rejected social Darwinism as a male-oriented concept. Instead, she worked to empower women by increasing their understanding of the rich historical legacy of their foremothers who fought for the common good. She believed that because the accomplishments of women were erased or downplayed, history portrayed a lopsided, inaccurate view of women's roles in society. Mary argued that American education firmly placed women in the role of inspiring men to do great things, rather than achieving greatness themselves. She believed that women's new recognition of their low social status was "the most encouraging fact of the twentieth century."*

Mary Ritter Beard is relatively unknown today outside of women's studies circles, but her plea for a woman-centered history of the world has not gone unnoticed. In recent years, there has been a deluge of children's books in the "herstory" category, indicating a desire for parents (and grandparents) to make sure children understand the significant role of women in history. There has also been a proliferation of history books about forgotten women.

Mary Ritter Beard would be pleased that her fellow members of the Society are beginning to make their way into the public eye. Since 2015, women have written biographies of mountaineer Annie Peck (Hannah Kimberley, 2017), Arctic explorer Louise Boyd (Society member Joanna Kafarowski, 2017), musicologist Frances Densmore (Joan M. Jensen and Michelle Wick Patterson, 2015), Mary Vaux Walcott (Marjorie G. Jones, 2015), Marguerite Harrison (Elizabeth Atwood, 2020), and sculptor Malvina Hoffman (Didi Hoffman, 2018). Books by Ellen La Motte (Cynthia Wachtell, 2019) and Osa Johnson (Kelly Enright, 2019) have been reissued with new biographical material. In 2017, the Chickasaw Nation released the Hollywood film *Te Ata*.

In 2017, Michelle Westmorland, a member of the Society of Woman Geographers, won the best international documentary film at the LA Femme International Film Festival. The movie, *Headhunt Revisited: With Brush, Canvas and Camera*, followed Westmorland as she retraced Caroline Mytinger and Margaret Warner's 1926 expedition to Melanesia to paint pictures of the indigenous people. The film shows how art captures "evolving traditions and cultures,

* Mary Austin and Mary Ritter Beard's view on history is similar to Joel Roger's belief that white supremacy has erased the history of people of color.

and how crucial the role of artists can be in recording history, especially in societies such as Papua New Guinea's, where history is mainly passed down orally through the telling of stories."

In 2015, the Field Museum restored thirty-seven of Malvina Hoffman's *Races of Mankind* sculptures and opened a new exhibit called *Looking at Ourselves: Rethinking the Sculptures of Malvina Hoffman. Wall Street Journal* reviewer Edward Rothstein labeled the retrospective "an exhibition that goes out of its way to find racism where none exists." Jennifer Schuessler of the *New York Times* disagreed: the 1933 exhibit's "overall thrust—driven home by diagrams showing different nose types and the like—was unmistakable: The world's peoples could be arranged in a hierarchy, from the primitive to the most civilized." Alaka Wali, the museum's anthropologist, explains, referring to the taxonomy, "You can forgive the scientists for looking just at your physical characteristics and trying to classify you. That's what scientists do." She added: "But the Social Darwinists of that time who guided this exhibit said that human cultural evolution was progressive, so that we went from primitive to barbaric to civilized. And the civilized were always the Europeans." Until the 1960s, texts and encyclopedias reproduced the sculptures, and a miniature version of the exhibit toured the United States. Wali believes that "the scientific racism that underlaid this exhibit has continued to influence us to the present day." But visitors continue to praise the aesthetic beauty of the sculptures.

In recent years, museums have hosted art exhibitions on Helen Tee-Van and Else Bostelmann (Drawing Center), Anne Heyward Taylor (Gibbes Museum), Caroline Mytinger (Hearst Museum of Anthropology), and Malvina Hoffman (Field Museum). When Edith Widder, a McArthur fellow who specializes in bioluminescence, was researching Bostelmann she uncovered three hundred of her paintings, some never published. Widder arranged for an exhibition of those paintings in 2011, and as a result, interest in Bostelmann's art has resurged.

Exhibits at the Drawing Center and Sloan Museum of Moving Images featured diver Gloria Hollister. The America Museum of Natural History holds an annual Margaret Mead Film Festival. The Osa and Martin Johnson Safari Museum is dedicated to the work of filmmakers Osa and Martin Johnson, and in 2019, the museum held an exhibit on their travels to South America one hundred years earlier. Mickie Akeley's elephants are exhibited at the Museum of Natural History and the Field Museum. Robert Ballard's unsuccessful rescue effort, Expedition Amelia, was jointly funded by the National Geographic Society and National Geographic Partners. A film of the same title was produced by Chad Cohen and Christine Weber in 2019.

Margaret Crocco, a professor of education, says, "If women have had half the world's experience, there's a truth value associated with teaching and writing history in a way that reflects those experiences. If you aren't telling the broader story about all human beings, then what you are representing is partial and flawed." To change these perceptions, society must see with both eyes or at least acknowledge that other perspectives exist.

Both the Explorers Club and the Society award gold medals, and not surprisingly, many of the women whom the Society has honored have also received the Explorers Club medal. Dual recipients include paleontologist Mary Leakey, primatologist Jane Goodall, marine biologist and conservationist Sylvia Earle, astronaut Kathryn Sullivan, archaeologist Anna Roosevelt, and ichthyologist Eugenie Clark. These women have had a lasting impact on exploration.

In 1964, Sylvia Earle was the only woman on an oceanographic team of seventy-one for six weeks in the Indian Ocean. An article in the *Mombasa Daily Times* about her was titled "Sylvia Sails Away with 70 Men. But She Expects No Problems." In 1970, she and several other women lived underwater for two weeks in the Tektite Project, an underwater housing unit. The first time Sylvia applied for the project, she was rejected because the government sponsors did not want women and men living together. The next year she was selected for an all-women team. The director told her, "Well, half of the fish are female, so I guess we can put up with a few women as aquanauts." A naval officer later told Sylvia that she did an "OK job, but I did not really approve of having you involved. It wasn't that I was opposed to having women, but I just didn't think you should be involved, because you're a mother. None of the other women was a mother."

Sylvia replied, "Well, there were dads..."

"That's different. If something had happened to you that would have been a real problem for us."

Men used derogatory terms to refer to the women aquanauts. Sylvia recalled, "After Tektite, we were called aquanetts, aquabelles, aquachicks, aquababes, aquanaughties." But the Tektite Project made her a public figure. When Sylvia later became the chief scientist for the National Oceanic and Atmospheric Administration, she was dubbed "the Sturgeon General," a nickname she embraced. Now, she is called "Her Deepness," out of respect for her record-setting walk a quarter mile beneath the ocean's surface.

Astronaut Kathryn Sullivan also faced hurdles because of her gender. Initially, NASA excluded women from becoming astronauts because they did not have a background as military test pilots. (The military did not then allow women to become pilots.) Astronaut John Glenn explained, "It is just a fact. The men go off and fight the wars and fly the airplanes. The fact that women are not in this field is a fact of our social order."

In 1978, when Kathryn Sullivan and five other women became the first women astronauts, NASA engineers were bewildered: "The notion that women might menstruate in orbit drove the whole place up the wall." (Amelia Earhart faced the same problem fifty years earlier when she was grounded for menstruation.) The women told the engineers that one hundred tampons were excessive for two women on a one-week voyage and that they did not need makeup in space.

Women astronauts still face gender bias. In 2019, NASA scheduled astronauts Anne McClain and Christina Koch for a 6.5-hour spacewalk. It was to be the first all-female spacewalk. Less than a week before the scheduled event, Anne McClain was pulled from the walk because there was only one medium-sized spacesuit aboard the International Space Station. Nick Hague was sent in McClain's place because the spacesuit fit him better. It was to be McClain's second spacewalk and Koch's first. Investigative reporter Fatima Syed tweeted, "I'm still not over the fact that NASA spacesuits aren't designed appropriately for women even though the 1st solo female spacewalk happened 35 years ago & the 2 women set to do the all-female spacewalk Friday were part of NASA's 2013 class, which was 50% female. They. Had. Time."*

---

* But IFC Dover, the company that makes the spacesuits for NASA, said it is not that easy. The space station had a second medium-sized suit, but it could not be used until the astronauts tested the oxygen tank, a day-long procedure. Jinny Ferl of IFC Dover said, "I am the first to say that STEM [Science, Technology, Engineering and Mathematics] is so important to get women into. But in this case, I have to say, this is not an issue of discrimination or shortsightedness or a system that doesn't represent women well." It would be dangerous for McClain to walk in space in the large suit, even though she trained in it. When she tried out the suit on a spacewalk, she realized the medium-sized suit fit better and did not want to use the large suit. So, NASA decided to switch the astronauts instead of reconfiguring the suits. McClain tweeted, "Leaders must make tough calls, and I am fortunate to work with a team who trusts my judgment. We must never accept a risk that can instead be mitigated. Safety of the crew and execution of the mission come first." Collins Aerospace is developing a spacesuit that can adapt to the size of the astronaut. They expect it to be ready for the lunar landing scheduled for 2024. Progress is being made, although it is slow.

Ben Barres, a transgender professor who worked at Stanford, understood the reluctance of women to recognize sexism in the workplace early in their careers. Before he transitioned, Ben attended MIT, where his professors interacted with him as a woman. When Ben solved a mathematical problem that none of his classmates could solve, his male professor refused to accept the fact that Ben had solved the problem—because the professor "knew" that women were not as strong in math as men. He accused Ben of submitting work done by his boyfriend. But Ben did not have a boyfriend, and he had solved the problem by himself.

After he transitioned, Ben recalled:

> Even when it was implied that I had cheated on that computer science exam because 'my boyfriend must have solved it for me,' it was many years before it even occurred to me that this was sexism. I see this same belief in meritocracy in young women today; the idea that their womanhood confers barriers generally occurs only as they reach mid-career and see less competent men being promoted or given leadership positions while they are passed over. When I look at mid-level and senior women at Stanford, I do not think that most are thriving the same way that their male counterparts are. They are all too aware of the barriers and they are resentful (sadly, one woman put it this way in a Stanford survey, 'I feel like if I failed to stop showing up for work, no one would notice').

Ben believed that men are generally unaware of the barriers faced by women. Only when he transitioned did he truly grasp the harm that these barriers cause. He recalled that after he gave a seminar, a male faculty member said, "Ben Barres gave a great seminar today, but then his work is much better than Barbara's [the name Ben used pretransition]." Ben researched the literature and discovered that, when applying for a research grant, a woman has to be 2.5 times more productive than a male to be considered equal. The most significant change when Ben transitioned was that "people who don't know I am transgendered treat me with much more respect: I can even complete a whole sentence without being interrupted by a man."

Jane Goodall, one of the most popular members of the Society today, has overcome these barriers, although it was difficult. In 1960, a male anthropologist offered twenty-six-year-old Jane Goodall a job living among chimpanzees so that she could study them. She had no experience, but she eagerly took the ethology job. Author Karen Karbo explains, "Jane's credentials were: I love animals. What's ethology?* She presumed herself to be qualified and capable of doing things that the world insisted she had no business doing. She gave herself over to learning what needed to be done."

Zoologist Tamar Ron explains, "It is precisely because Goodall did not come from a structured school of thought with a scientific theory that she was able to discover the most impressive innovation, new interpretations. She succeeded in seeing and transmitting things that many did not want to hear."

She assigned names and personalities to chimpanzees, a practice that was derided by other scientists. Jane was shocked that chimpanzees were so similar to humans. She recalls, "Today there is no argument that animals express emotions. Then it was forbidden to talk about it, because you knew they would ridicule

* The study of animal behavior.

you. And they really did ridicule me many times. And also criticized me endlessly because I gave the chimpanzees I observed names, such as Mike, Flint, Flo, or David Greybeard. It was considered unscientific and not serious. The fact that I bonded emotionally with the subjects of the research, the chimps I observed, was considered at the time to be problematic behavior." Tamar Ron says, anthropomorphism "is seen as an illegitimate tool for understanding chimpanzees, even if they are the closest animals to us. If we publish assumptions about thoughts and emotions of animals it will turn you into an outcast in the scientific community. Jane succeeded in convincing the fixated scientific world to accept findings that show that chimpanzees are similar to us."

In 1963, when *National Geographic Magazine* ran an article about Jane Goodall, she became a celebrity. She has inspired millions. Marc Bekoff, an editor of *The Jane Effect: Celebrating Jane Goodall,* said, "I was, and continue to be overwhelmed, by how many people around the world Jane has influenced and touched in myriad ways as a mentor, role model, and friend."

Vicki Constantine Croke, nature writer, said, "For me, and countless other girls, she also profoundly changed the definition of 'woman.' She showed the world that going to Africa and studying animals wasn't just for boys. She had made a life among the wild chimpanzees of Gombe in Tanzania, and lots of us wanted to be just like her. Jane is part of my soul and comes with me everywhere. A little piece of her is with me in everything I write."

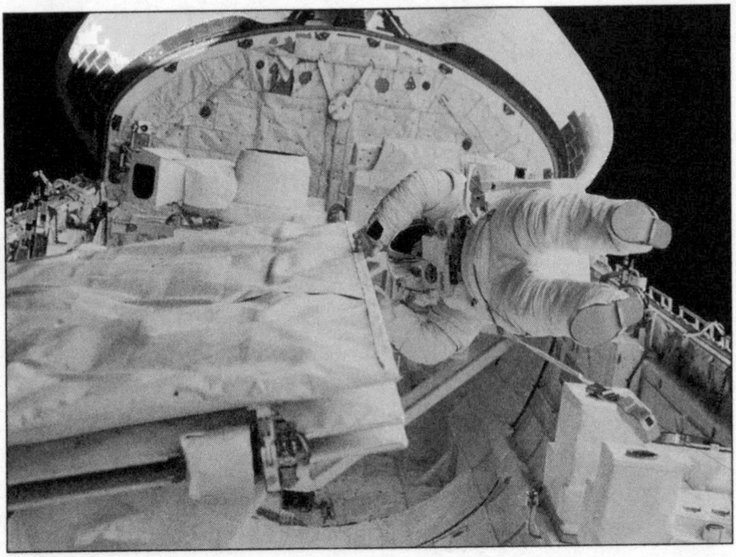

Illustration 27. Kathryn Sullivan on Spacewalk (1984)

EPILOGUE

THE LOSS WILL BE OURS

It is natural anywhere that people like their own kind, but it is not necessarily natural that their fondness for their own kind should lead them to the subjugation of whole groups of other people not like them.

—PEARL S. BUCK, AUTHOR AND SOCIETY MEMBER

1981
Manhattan

In 1981, Kathryn Sullivan, the first woman to walk in space, was surprised when she received a speaking request along with an invitation to join the all-male Explorers Club.

Although she did not know it, the invitation was prompted by astronomer Carl Sagan, who urged his fellow explorers to lift the ban on women. Like Mary Ritter Beard, Sagan understood true inclusion and the need to see out of both eyes—women's and men's. In a letter to his colleagues, Sagan tried to convince the members that it was time for a change.

"When our organization was founded in 1905," Sagan wrote, "men were preventing women from voting and from pursuing many occupations for which they are clearly suited. In the popular mind, exploration was not what women did. Even so, women had played a significant but unheralded role in the history of exploration."

Sagan acknowledged the importance of traditions, but he argued that the Explorers Club's ban on women members was an "accident of the epoch in which it was institutionalized." To prove that women were worthy of membership, he pointed to the archaeological discoveries of Mary Leakey, the ground-breaking primate studies by Jane Goodall, and the undersea depth record of Sylvia Earle. Like Kathryn Sullivan, these women were at the forefront of exploration. "If membership in the Explorers Club is restricted to men, the loss will be ours," he wrote. Sagan asserted that the primary purpose of the club was not "to promote male bonding or to serve as a social club—although there is certainly room for both." The primary purpose was "the conquest of the unknown and the advancement of knowledge," a goal that could be met by all members of the human race, regardless of gender, sexual orientation, or ethnicity.

After much discussion, the board of directors agreed to hold a vote on the admission of women. The issue was divisive. Although the club's president, Charles Brush, urged members to vote for change, he did not expect a favorable vote. John W. Flint, who sat on the board of directors, told a reporter, "You have no idea how strongly some men feel about this." Another member said, "Even a single female would destroy the quality (camaraderie) for which the organization exists."

On April 12, 1981, the ballots were counted. The ban was

lifted by a vote of 753 to 618.* The club's officers were stunned. They predicted that three hundred members would immediately resign in protest. But they were wrong.

Reporters praised the news. The headline of the *New York Times* read, "The Explorers Club Discovers Women." The *New York Daily News* announced, "The walls of another male bastion have crumbled." The editors were surprised the change took so long given the fact that Osa Johnson, Amelia Earhart, Margaret Mead, and so many others had obviously met all of the qualifications for membership except gender. As to the three hundred members rumored to quit the club in protest, the editors joked, "We don't know where they will go—unless perhaps it will be the Museum of Natural History, where they would make excellent additions to the fossil collection."

When Kathryn Sullivan received her invitation, she thought,

* In 2020, the Explorers Club reached another milestone when it created a Diversity and Inclusion initiative. It launched a virtual lecture series of LGBTQ explorers featuring, among others, the first openly gay woman (Silvia Vasquez-Lavado) and the first openly gay man (Cason Crane) to ascend the Seven Summits. Crane applauded the Explorers Club, saying: "It's fantastic that the Explorers Club is taking on new steps to encourage diversity and inclusion amongst its members and, importantly, in the broader community. Exploration has historically had many negative connotations—associations with colonialism, white supremacy, and exploitation of indigenous people, among others. That history can't be ignored, and so it's critical that these sorts of proactive steps are taken to address that and chart a new, more inclusive path."

In contrast, the all-male Los Angeles Adventurers' Club, which René Belbenoît joined when he came to the United States, has not admitted women. In 1995 and 2014, the members voted against opening the club to women. Scuba diver Ken Lee opposed the inclusion of women because he values the all-male camaraderie: "We can let our hair down on men's only nights and use different language than we would when ladies are present." He believes that the dynamic would be different if the club admitted women. Andrea Donnellan, a geophysicist at NASA's Jet Propulsion Lab regularly attended the club on Ladies' Night, which is held at least monthly. In 2014, Marc Weitz tried to get the club to admit women, as he thought Donnellan would be a good member. The proposal failed, 32–30, a majority, but not enough under the two-thirds vote the bylaws require. Donnellan felt profoundly disappointed. Once, after the vote was taken, she mistakenly visited the club during a men-only night. Club members turned her away at the door. She has not been able to overcome this feeling of rejection and reportedly has not visited the club since then.

"Maybe I'll go meet these guys who are on the verge of figuring out there are these 50 percent other people in the world."

But first, she joined the Society of Woman Geographers.

The accomplishments of Kathryn Sullivan, Amelia Earhart, Margaret Mead, Jane Goodall, and Sylvia Earle already have been recorded in the history books. As more authors write about the overlooked members of the Society, and as more museums showcase their accomplishments, the stories of these invisible women are finally being written in indelible ink. Their stories change our history and give a new generation of women the courage to chisel away at the glass ceiling until it shatters. Only when the male bastions crumble will society be whole and history be complete.

MEMBERS OF THE SOCIETY OF WOMAN GEOGRAPHERS DISCUSSED, DATE ADMITTED TO SOCIETY OF WOMAN GEOGRAPHERS, AND AREA OF EXPERTISE

Harriet Chalmers Adams, 1925, explorer, former Spanish territories
Mildred Adams, 1935, journalist, translated works of Spanish philosopher Jose Ortega y Gasset
Delia "Mickie" Akeley, 1927, explorer and African big game hunter
Lena Richardson Arents, 1931, world traveler
Te Ata, 1939, Chickasaw storyteller
Florence Ayscough, 1926, explorer and author, Chinese art and literature
Mary Hunter Austin, 1929, novelist, Native American culture
Mary Ritter Beard, 1931, historian, women's history
Zonia Baber, 1927, geographer and geologist, Haiti
Dorothy Graham Bennett, 1931, editor and curator, nature and astronomy
Else Bostelmann, 1939, artist, Bermuda
Louise Boyd, 1933, Arctic explorer
Mary Hastings Bradley, 1926, author, Egypt and Belgian Congo
Pearl S. Buck, 1932, author, China
Helen Churchill Candee, 1930, Cambodia
Eugenie Clark, 1950, ichthyologist
Jocelyn Crane, 1936, marine biologist, Latin America
Frances Densmore, 1928, ethnomusicologist, Native American music
Elizabeth Dickey, 1928, explorer, South America
Lucille Sinclair Douglass, 1928, artist, China and Cambodia
Amelia Earhart, 1932, author and aviator
Sylvia Earle, 1981, deep-sea diver and marine conservationist

Marie Poland Fish, 1928, ichthyologist, Latin America
Jane Goodall, 1983, primatologist, animal behavior, Gombe
Marguerite Harrison, 1925, journalist and spy, Russia
Malvina Hoffman, 1930, sculpture, world races
Gloria Hollister, 1929, marine biology, Latin America
Frances Carpenter Huntington, 1927, geographer and editor, folklore
Osa Johnson, 1932, filmmaker, South Pacific, Asia, Africa
Muna Lee, 1928, poet, Pan America
Ellen La Motte, 1931, nurse, China opium trade
Lucille Quarry Mann, 1931, naturalist
Margaret Mead, 1928, anthropologist, South Pacific
Adelene Moffat, 1931, social worker and activist, archaeology, China
Grace Barstow Murphy, 1929, author and naturalist, conservation
Caroline Mytinger, 1930, artist, South Pacific
Alexandra David-Néel, 1926, Tibet
Blair Niles, 1925, author, Latin America
Ruth Crosby Noble, 1929, biologist, animal behavior
Annie Smith Peck, 1929, author and mountaineer, South America
Ella Riegel, 1931, suffragist, archaeology, Latin America
Eleanor Roosevelt, 1933, world traveler
Gertrude Emerson Sen, 1925, editor, Asia
Grace Thompson Seton, 1927, author, American West, Egypt, India, China
Gertrude Mathews Shelby, 1925, Gullah people
Marie Ahnighito Peary Stafford, 1930, Greenland
Helen Strong, 1929, applied geographer
Anna Heyward Taylor, 1939, artist, British Guiana, Japan
Helen Damrosch Tee-Van, 1934, British Guiana
Marjorie Trumbull, 1930, anthropologist, American Southwest
Mary Vaux Walcott, 1931, artist and naturalist, wildflowers
Margaret Bourke-White, 1938, photographer, Russia
Michelle Westmorland, 2004, underwater photographer

SELECTED BIBLIOGRAPHY

Society of Woman Geographers, in general:

Dole, Gertrude E. *Vignettes of Some Early Members of the Society of Woman Geographers in New York*. New York: New York Society of Woman Geographers, 1978.

Eppinga, Jane. *They Made Their Mark: An Illustrated History of the Society of Woman Geographers*. Guilford, CT: Globe Pequot Press, 2009.

Olds, Elizabeth Fagg. *Women of the Four Winds*. Boston: Houghton Mifflin, 1985.

Society of Woman Geographers. *All True! The Record of Actual Adventures That Have Happened to Ten Women of Today*. New York: Brewer, Warren and Putnam, 1931.

HARRIET CHALMERS ADAMS:

Davis, Kathryn. "Harriet Chalmers Adams: Remembering an American Geographer." *California Geographer* 49 (2009): 51–70.

Rothenberg, Tamar Y. *Presenting America's World: Strategies of Innocence in National Geographic Magazine, 1888–1945*. Hampshire, England: Ashgate, 2007.

MARY AUSTIN:

Davis, Cynthia J. and Denise D. Knight. *Charlotte Perkins Gilman and Her Contemporaries:*

Literary and Intellectual Contexts. Tuscaloosa: University of Alabama Press, 2004.

ZONIA BABER:

Fitzgerald, Helen. "All Humanity Her Kinsfolk." *Brooklyn Daily Eagle*, October 20, 1929, 89.

MARY RITTER BEARD:

Trigg, Mary K. *Feminism as Life's Work: Four Modern American Women through Two World Wars*. New Brunswick, NJ: Rutgers University Press, 2014.

DOROTHY BENNETT:

Bennett, Dorothy. "Oral History." May 19, 1994, transcript, Bennett File, Records of the Society of Woman Geographers, Library of Congress, Manuscript Division.

ELSE BOSTELMANN:

Widder, Edith. "The Fine Art of Exploration." *Oceanography* 29:4 (1916). https://doi.org/10.5670/oceanog.2016.86.

LOUISE BOYD:

Kafarowski, Joanna. *The Polar Adventures of a Rich American Dame: A Life of Louise Arner Boyd*. Dundurn, Toronto. 2017.

PEARL S. BUCK:

Buck, Pearl S. *My Several Worlds: A Personal Record*. New York: John Day, 1954.

HELEN CHURCHILL CANDEE:

Candee, Helen Churchill. "Sealed Orders." *Collier's Weekly*, May 4, 1912. Reproduced at https://www.encyclopedia-titanica.org/sealed-orders.html.

FRANCES DENSMORE:

Jensen, Joan M., and Michelle Wick Patterson. *Travels with Frances Densmore: Her Life, Work, and Legacy in Native American Studies*. Lincoln: University of Nebraska Press, 2015.

ELIZABETH DICKEY:

Dickey, Mrs. Herbert Spencer. "My Thrilling Honeymoon among the Savage Head Hunters." *Star Tribune*, Minneapolis, May 22, 1927, 63.

AMELIA EARHART:

Chapman, Sally Putman. *Whistled Like a Bird: The Untold Story of Dorothy Putnam, George Putnam, and Amelia Earhart*. Boston: Grand Central, 2009.

Earhart, Amelia. *20 Hrs, 40 Mins., Our Flight in the Friendship. The American Girl, First across the Atlantic by Air, Tells Her Story*. New York: Putnam, 1928.

Earhart, Amelia. *The Fun of It: Random Records of My Own Flying and of Women in Aviation*. Chicago: Academy Chicago Publishers, 1984.

JANE GOODALL:

Bekoff, Marc. *The Jane Effect: Celebrating Jane Goodall*. San Antonio, TX: Trinity University Press, 2015.

MARGUERITE HARRISON:

Atwood, Elizabeth. *The Liberation of Marguerite Harrison: America's First Female Foreign Intelligence Agent*. Annapolis, MD: Naval Institute Press, 2020.

MALVINA HOFFMAN:

Hoffman, Didi. *Beautiful Bodies: The Adventures of Malvina Hoffman*. Meadville, PA: Fulton Books, 2018.

Hoffman, Malvina. *Heads and Tales in Many Lands*. New York: Scribner, 1936.

Kim, Linda. *Race Experts: Sculpture, Anthropology, and the American Public in Malvina Hoffman's Races of Mankind*. Lincoln: University of Nebraska Press, 2018.

GLORIA HOLLISTER:

Hollister, Gloria. "I Couldn't Help It." 1933, Hollister File, Records of the Society of Woman Geographers, Library of Congress, Manuscript Division.

Hollister, Gloria. "Birthday in the Ocean Depth." 1958, Hollister File, Records of the Society of Woman Geographers, Library of Congress, Manuscript Division.

OSA JOHNSON:

Johnson, Osa. *I Married Adventure: The Lives and Adventures of Martin and Osa Johnson*. Toronto: Lippincott, 1940.

MARGARET MEAD:

Shankman, Paul. *The Trashing of Margaret Mead: Anatomy of an Anthropological Controversy*. Madison: University of Wisconsin Press, 2009.

Shankman, Paul. "The Public Anthropology of Margaret Mead: *Redbook*, Women's Issues, and the 1960s." *Current Anthropology* 59:1 (February 2018): 55–73.

ELLEN LA MOTTE:

La Motte, Ellen N., and Cynthia Wachtell. *The Backwash of War: An Extraordinary American Nurse in World War I*. Baltimore: Johns Hopkins University Press, 2019.

CAROLINE MYTINGER:

Mytinger, Caroline. *New Guinea Headhunt*. New York: Macmillan, 1947.

BLAIR (BEEBE) NILES:

Beebe, Mary Blair, and William Beebe. *Our Search for Wilderness*. New York: Holt, 1910.

Beebe, Mary Blair. "A Quest in the Himalayas." *Harper's Monthly Magazine*, March 1911.

Beebe, Mary Blair. "Wild Burma." *Harper's Monthly Magazine*, April 1912.

Niles, Blair. *Colombia, Land of Miracles*. New York: Century, 1924.

Niles, Blair. *Black Haiti: A Biography of Africa's Eldest Daughter*. New York: Putnam, 1926.

Niles, Blair. *Condemned to Devil's Island: The Biography of an Unknown Convict*. New York: Grosset & Dunlap, 1928.

Niles, Blair. *Strange Brother*. New York: Liveright, 1931.

Niles, Blair. *The James*. Toronto: Farrar & Rinehart, 1939.

Niles, Blair. *East by Day*. Toronto: Farrar & Rinehart, 1941.

Niles, Blair. *Journeys in Time: From the Halls of Montezuma to Patagonia's Plains*. New York: Coward-McCann, 1946.

Rice, Marie Gordon. "Reminiscences." ca. 1920, Virginia Historical Society, Mss5:1R3652:1–2.

ANNIE SMITH PECK:

Kimberley, Hannah. *A Woman's Place Is at the Top: Biography of Annie Peck, Queen of the Climbers*. New York: St. Martin's Press, 2017.

GERTRUDE EMERSON SEN:

Sen, Gertrude Emerson. "Oral History." Sen File, Records of the Society of Woman Geographers, Library of Congress, Manuscript Division.

GRACE THOMPSON SETON:

Seton, Grace Thompson. *A Woman Tenderfoot in Egypt*. New York: Dodd, Mead, 1923.

ANNA HEYWARD TAYLOR:

Taylor, Edmund R., and Alexander Moore, eds. *Selected Letters of Anna Heywood Taylor, South Carolina Artist and World Traveler*. Columbia: University of South Carolina Press, 2010.

TE ATA:

Green, Richard. *Te Ata: Chickasaw Storyteller*. Norman: University of Oklahoma Press, 2006.

Green, Richard. "Crossing Paths: Te Ata and Eleanor Roosevelt in the Twenties and Thirties." *Journal of Chickasaw History* 4 (1994): 13–30.

Nonmembers of the Society of Woman Geographers

WILLIAM BEEBE:

Beebe, William. *Pheasant Jungles*. New York: Blue Ribbon Books, 1927.

Beebe, William. *Half Mile Down*. New York: Harcourt, Brace, 1934.

Gould, Carol Grant. *The Remarkable Life of William Beebe, Explorer and Naturalist*. Washington, DC: Island Press, 2004.

Welker, Robert Henry. *Natural Man: The Life of William Beebe*. Bloomington: Indiana University Press, 1975.

RENÉ BELBENOÎT:

Belbenoît, René. *Dry Guillotine: Fifteen Years among the Living Dead*. New York: Blue Ribbon Books, 1938.

ABBREVIATIONS

AMNH: American Museum of Natural History

BU: Boston University (Thane Collection)

HRC: University of Texas, Harry Ransom Center (Belbenoît Collection)

LOC: Library of Congress (Hollister Collection)

PU: Princeton University (Beebe Collection)

SWG: Society of Woman Geographers Collection at LOC (SWG Member Collections)

TRC: Dickinson State University, the Roosevelt Center Online (Roosevelt Collection)

UC San Diego: The Harrison Williams Collection on Expeditions of William Beebe and George P. Putnam

USC: University of South Caroliniana Library (Taylor Collection)

VHS: Virginia Historical Society (Rice and Bartlett Collections)

WCS: Wildlife Conservation Society (Various Collections)

ILLUSTRATION CREDITS

Illustr. 1: Map from the New York Section of the Society of Woman Geographers, ca. 1932, Dorothy Bennett File, Container I:3, Records of the Society of Woman Geographers, Manuscript Division, Library of Congress, Washington, DC 20540.

Illustr. 2.1: Marguerite Harrison, ca. 1921, (Jeanne E. Bennett, photographer), Marguerite E. Harrison, *Marooned in Moscow* (New York: George H. Doran Co.), frontispiece.

Illustr. 2.2: Blair [Beebe] Niles, 1910, Department of Tropical Research Collection, Photo Collection, Media Services Building, Box 15, Expeditions: Himalayas, Various, Darjeeling, Jorepokri, Tonglu, #4, Wildlife Conservation Society Archives, Bronx, NY 10460.

Illustr. 2.3: Gertrude Emerson, Passport Photo, 1921, Image adapted from photo by Dave Miller on Flickr, https://www.flickr.com/photos/puzzlemaster/37648243656.

Illustr. 2.4: Gertrude Mathews [Shelby], 1922; "Likes Ford Cooperation; Likes Ford Car She Won", *The Evening World*, Oct. 19, 1922, 4.

Illustr. 2.5: Harriet Chalmers Adams, 1918, Harriet Chalmers Adams File, Container I:1, Records of the Society of Woman Geographers, Manuscript Division, Library of Congress, Washington, DC 20540.

Illustr. 2.6: Te Ata, Performing Interpretive Dance, 1920, Chickasaw Nation.

Illustr. 2.7: "Mrs. Mary Beard of New York is a member of the Executive Committee of the Congressional Union for Woman Suffrage, Mrs. Beard is the wife of Professor Charles Beard of Columbia University and is joint author with him of his recent book on American Political History," New York, United States, ca. 1914 [to July 24, 1915]. Photograph, https://www.loc.gov/item/mnwp000085/.

Illustr. 2.8: Amelia Earhart, 1928, Underwood and Underwood, LC-USZ62–20901, Library of Congress, Prints and Photographs Division, Washington, DC 20540.

Illustr. 2.9: Malvina Hoffman, 1928, (Artist: Clara Sipprell), Smithsonian Institute, Malvina Hoffman, 1928, NPG 81.12, National Portrait Gallery, Smithsonian Institution, Washington, DC 20540.

Illustr. 2.10: Gloria Hollister, ca. 1930, Department of Tropical Research Collection, Wildlife Conservation Society, Bronx, NY 10460.

Illustr. 2.11: Osa Johnson, 1917, The Martin and Osa Johnson Safari Museum, Chanute, KS 66720.

Illustr. 2.12: Ellen La Motte, 1902, Alan Mason Chesney Medical Archives of the Johns Hopkins Medical Institutions, Baltimore, MD 21209.

Illustr. 2.13: Margaret Mead, half-length portrait, facing right, reading book, ca. 1930, World-Telegram photo by Edward Lynch, LC-USZ62–120226 (b&w film copy negative), Library of Congress, Prints and Photographs Division, Washington, DC 20540.

Illustr. 2.14: Annie Peck, 1893, Frances E. Willard, Mary A. Livermore, A Woman of the Century (Buffalo: N.Y.: Charles Wells Moulton), 1893, 563.

Illustr. 2.15: "Miss Ella Riegel, of Bryn Mawr, PA, finance chair for the joint conventions of the Congressional Union for Woman Suffrage and the National Woman's Party, to be held at Washington, March 1–4 inclusive," ca. 1918, Harris & Ewing, Photographer, http://hdl.loc.gov/loc.mss/mnwp.156008, National Woman's Party Records, Group I, Container I:156, Folder: Riegel, Ella, Library of Congress, Manuscript Division, Washington, DC 20540.

Illustr. 2.16: Mrs. [Grace] Ernest Seton-Thompson, ca. 1901, William Wallace Whitelock, Ernest Seton-Thompson, *The Critic*, 29:4, Oct. 1901, 322.

Illustr. 2.17: Anna Heyward Taylor, 1918, Anna Heyward Taylor Files, South Caroliniana Library Archives, University of South Carolina, Columbia, South Carolina, 29208.

Illustr. 3: Don't Take a Woman—When You Go Exploring, *Public Ledger*, 1932.

Illustr. 4: Osa Johnson with Crocodile in Borneo, 1917, The Martin and Osa Johnson Safari Museum, Chanute, KS 66720.

Illustr. 5: Osa Johnson and Nagapate, 1916, The Martin and Osa Johnson Safari Museum, Chanute, KS 66720.

Illustr. 6: Marguerite Harrison with Bakhtiari Men, ca. 1924, Getty Images.

Illustr. 7: Annie Peck, 1911, Library of Congress Prints and Photographs Division, 97504565, Washington, DC 20540.

Illustr. 8: Blair and Tandook, 1910, Department of Tropical Research Photo Collection, Media Services Building, Box 15, Expeditions: Himalayas, Various, Yak Hybrids, People #2, Wildlife Conservation Society, Bronx, NY 10460.

Illustr. 9: Shooter of the Poisoned Arrow, Department of Tropical Research Photo Collection, Media Services Building, Box 14, Expeditions: Burma, Various #4, Image 2053, Wildlife Conservation Society Archives, Bronx, NY 10460.

Illustr. 10: Pennsylvania on the Picket Line, Washington, 1917, Harris & Ewing, Washington, DC (Photographer), National Woman's Party Records, Group I, Container I:60, Folder: Pickets, 1917, Manuscript Division, https://www.loc.gov/mms/mnwp/16002, Library of Congress, Washington, DC 20540.

Illustr. 11: The Horror of War, Ghastly Glimpse of Belgian Wounded, Antwerp Hospital, ca. May 18, 1915, Prints and Photographs Division, Reproduction Number LC-USZ62-62662, Library of Congress, Washington, DC 20540.

Illustr. 12: NAACP Picket Outside Theater Protesting Movie "Birth of a Nation", 1947, "NAACP members picketing outside the Republic Theatre, New York City, to protest the screening of the movie *Birth of a Nation*, close-up view of demonstrators and sign reading 'Birth of a Nation revives KKK,'" www.loc.gov/item/95519951/, Getty Images.

Illustr. 13: Roosevelt Luncheon at Kalacoon, 1916, Department of Tropical Research Collection, Wildlife Conservation Society Archives, Bronx, NY 10460.

Illustr. 14: Gloria Hollister and Diving Helmet, circa 1926, Department of Tropical Research Collection, Wildlife Conservation Society Archives, Bronx, N.Y. 10460.

Illustr. 15: William Beebe with Bathysphere Owners [Gloria Hollister, William Beebe, John Tee-Van with Bathysphere, 1932], Bettmann Collection, Getty Images.

Illustr. 16: A Class in Mathematical Geography Studying Earth's Rotation around the Sun, Hampton Institute, Hampton, VA, Frances Benjamin Johnston

Collection, Prints and Photographs Division, Reproduction Number LC-USZ62–62376, Library of Congress, Washington, DC 20540.

Illustr. 17: Part of Detention House on Devil's Island, Bettmann Collection, Getty Images.

Illustr. 18: A Night-Club Map of Harlem, E. Simms Campbell, Dell Publishing Company, 1932, Control Number 20165955261, Beinecke Library, New Haven, CT 06520–8330.

Illustr. 19: Malvina Hoffman, Sketching a Man Named Mare for Bronze Sculpture for the Races of Man Exhibit, ca. 1929, © The Field Museum, Image No. A79996, Photographer Samuel Grimson.

Illustr. 20: Races of Mankind Exhibit, © The Field Museum, Image No. CSA77747, Cat. No. 336972, Photographer Charles Carpenter.

Illustr. 21: Amelia Earhart Portrait in a Plane, Getty Images.

Illustr. 22: Members of Society Meeting Harriet Chalmers Adams in Washington, DC, for Amelia Earhart Luncheon at White House, 1932, Society of Woman Geographers, Washington, DC 20003.

Illustr. 23: New York Members of the Society of Woman Geographers, 1930–1931 Season, Society of Woman Geographers, Washington, DC 20003.

Illustr. 24: Members in Exploring Costumes at the Society of Woman Geographers, Society of Woman Geographers 10th Anniversary Meeting, 1935, Image No. 0175700, Granger Historical Picture Archive.

Illustr. 25: Margaret Mead with Manus Mother and Child, 1953, Getty Images, Bettmann Collection.

Illustr. 26: Gloria Hollister, William Beebe, and Jocelyn Crane Looking at Eclipse, 1937, Department of Tropical Research Collection, Wildlife Conservation Society Archives, Bronx, NY 10460.

Illustr. 27: Astronaut Kathryn Sullivan on October 11, 1984 Spacewalk, NASA.

NOTES*

Unless otherwise noted:

All letters from William Beebe or Blair Beebe [Niles] are located in Thane Collection BU Box 82, except letters to Anthony Kuser or Madison Grant, which are in BU Thane Collection Box 78.

All letters between Gordon Rice and Franklina Bartlett are in VHS Bartlett Collection.

All letters between Anna Heyward Taylor and Ellen Elmore "Nell" Taylor and William Beebe are in the USC Taylor Collection.

All letters between members of the SWG are located in the SWG files, typically under the name of the receiver, unless otherwise noted.

All of William Beebe's diary entries are located in the PU Beebe Collection.

---

* This mark indicates that a quotation has been altered in order to fit better into the quote. It indicates places where I have changed the tense, corrected a spelling error, capitalized the first letter of the sentence, added a comma or other punctuation, or omitted phrases without altering the meaning. These changes were made to make the book more readable. Significant changes are noted by brackets within the text.

Introductory Quotes:

*From the days of the mythical Argonauts**: Elizabeth Fagg Olds, *Women of the Four Winds* (Boston: Houghton Mifflin, 1985), 2.

*My shock lies**: Kaya Purchase, "We Need to Talk about Women Explorers," *Aurelia*, June 13, 2019, accessed March 11, 2020, https://www.aureliamagazine.com/2019/06/women-explorers.html.

Author's Note:

Studying the national soul: Blair Niles, "Travel Books and the Travel-Reading Public," *New York Tribune*, January 24, 1926, E5.

"One of the results": Blair Niles, "Setting Up an Easel in Papua," *New York Herald*, December 12, 1926, F23.

*"both were essential"**: Kathryn Davis, "Harriet Chalmers Adams: Remembering an American Geographer," *The California Geographer*, no. 49 (2009): 66.

"The world of humanity": Blair Niles, "Main Street Travel," *New York Herald*, September 25, 1925, D15.

"How can a discipline": Margaret Edith Trussell, "Five Western Women Pioneer Geographers," *Yearbook of the Association of Pacific Coast Geographers*, vol. 49 (1987): 8.

Prologue: Banned

OPENING QUOTE:

"In exploration, more": Catherine Filene, ed., *Careers for Women: New Ideas, New Methods, New Opportunities—to Fit a New World* (Chicago: Riverside Press, 1934), 81.

BLAIR NILES'S EXPLORATIONS:

In general: "A Woman's 50,000-Miles World Tour through Jungles and over Mountains," *Washington Post*, November 19, 1911, 5; Harry Hansen, "The First Reader: Devil's Island," *Minneapolis Morning Tribune*, May 10, 1928, 10.

ROY CHAPMAN ANDREWS:

In general: Douglas Preston, *Dinosaurs in the Attic: An Excursion into the American Museum of Natural History* (New York: St. Martin's Press, 1993), 98; Kaitlin Boettcher, "Roy Chapman Andrews: A Real Life Indiana Jones," *Mental Floss*, March 25, 2013, accessed March 11, 2020, https://www.mentalfloss.com/article/49186/roy-chapman-andrews-real-life-indiana-jones.

Blair was always suspicious: Blair Niles, "Ninety-Five Per Cent True," *New York Herald Tribune*, January 8, 1933, H2.

*"to a Munchausen"**: Blair Niles, "Forbidden Afghanistan," *New York Herald*, January 3, 1916, E16.

ANDREWS'S SPEECH AT BARNARD COLLEGE AND EDITORIALS:

"Women are not adapted": "Mr. Andrews' Statement about Women Belied at Recent Dinner of Female Geographers," *Barnard Bulletin*, February 9, 1932, 1.

*"The secret's out."**: E. K. Titus, "Women Explorers Call Forth Wail from Men Adventurers; Only Sea Jobs Left to Them," *Brooklyn Daily Eagle*, March 6, 1927, 23.

"With them, it is" ... "Take, for example": Carol Bird, "Don't Take a Woman With You When You Go Exploring, Says Roy Chapman Andrews," *Honolulu Advertiser*, April 24, 1932, 39.

*"When Roy Chapman Andrews"**: *New York Sun*, *Baltimore Sun*, January 27, 1932, 12.

"This is no time": Editorial, "The Lure of Exploration," *Newark Advocate*, Newark, OH, January 12, 1932, 4.

"This should be evident": "Women Explorers," *Albuquerque Journal*, January 16, 1932, 6.

*"Men excel women as explorers"**: Editorial, "Not Conclusive," *The Gazette*, Cedar Rapids, IA, January 13, 1932, 6.

MISS ANNIE PECK:

broken three ribs: Katherine Beebe, "Daring Woman Enjoys Fame," *Salt Lake Tribune*, February 28, 1932, 11.

"women be firmly harnessed": Olds, *Women*, 8.

*"The same spirit"**: Walter Trumbull, "Lights of New York," *Monmouth Democrat*, Freehold, NJ, April 21, 1932, 3.

BLAIR'S BELIEFS ABOUT SEX:

In general: Blair Niles, "Whither Flaming Youth?" *Charlotte Observer*, December 14, 1932, 12.

GLORIA HOLLISTER:

zoology degree: Glenn Fowler, "Gloria Hollister Anable, 87, Dies; An Explorer and Conservationist," *New York Times*, February 24, 1988, 26.

"Like the fading" ... "Fish Magic": Gloria Hollister, "Fish Magic," *Bulletin New York Zoological Society* 30, no. 2 (1930), 72.

410 feet: "Women Who've Been Places Get Together to Brag," *Star Tribune*, Minneapolis, February 6, 1932, 1.

"But for the telephone" ... "This has opened" ... "only girl"*: Letter from Gloria Hollister to Harriet Adams (June 15, 1930).

"more like one of Ziegfeld's": "Women Who've Been Places," 1.

"She looks like a musical": Circular, James Pond, "With Beebe in Bermuda" (1930) (SWG—Hollister file).

Gloria, the beautiful ichthyologist: "Gloria, the Beautiful Ichthyologist or Some Blondes Have Brains," *Family Circle*, June 29, 1934, 14.

Will Beebe was known: Joanna Klein, "They Mixed Science, Art and Costume Parties to Reveal Mysteries of the Sea," *New York Times*, March 27, 2017, accessed March 12, 2020, https://www.nytimes.com/2017/03/27/science/william-beebe-department-of-tropical-research-illustrations.html.

sexual liaisons: Carol Grant Gould, *The Remarkable Life of William Beebe, Explorer and Naturalist* (Washington, DC: Island Press, 2004), 279–280.

ELIZABETH DICKEY:

"Here's one" ... "This is a particularly beautiful": "Women Who've Been Places," 1.

"The Jivoro headhunters" ... "At once"**: Mrs. Herbert Spencer Dickey, "My Thrilling Honeymoon among the Savage Head Hunters," *Star Tribune*, Minneapolis, May 22, 1927, 63. Her husband's version of the story, which is slightly different, appears in Herbert Spencer Dickey, *The Misadventures of a Tropical Medico* (New York: Vail-Ballou Press, 1929), chap. 13.

Process of Shrinking Head (All quotes from)*: Mrs. Herbert Spencer Dickey, "A Yankee Girl's Honeymoon among the Savage Head-Hunters," *Indianapolis Star*, May 1, 1927, 103.

AMELIA EARHART:

*"When I plan my trip southward"**: Hannah Kimberley, *A Women's Place Is at the Top: Biography of Annie Peck, Queen of the Climbers* (New York: St. Martin's Press, 2017), 314.

ANDREWS'S LETTER TO SOCIETY:

"I am skeptical about the possibilities": "Andrews Rules Out Women Explorers: Wonderful in Crises, but Not Physically Fitted for the Task, He Tells Barnard Girls," *New York Times*, January 6, 1932, 23.

"What I said was this" ... "I also said"*: "Women Explorers Recall Their Feats," *New York Times*, February 6, 1932, 19.

"I know of no" ... "One woman": Bird, "Don't Take a Woman with You," 34.

SYLVIA EARLE:

"Sometimes people find": "Sylvia Earle: Marine Biologist and Aquanaut," July 9, 2009, Women in Science

Blog, accessed March 11, 2020, https://blog.sciencewomen.com/2009/07/sylvia-earle-marine-biologist-and.html.

MARY RITTER BEARD:

"Without documents; no history":* Mary K. Trigg, *Feminism as Life's Work: Four Modern American Women through Two World Wars* (New Brunswick, NJ: Rutgers University Press, 2014), 168.

Chapter 1: Reckless

OPENING QUOTE:

Kimberly L. Smith, *Passport through Darkness: A True Story of Danger and Second Chances* (Colorado Springs, CO: Cook, 2011), 20.

BLAIR NILES:

"we-white-men": Blair Niles, "A Frenchman in Africa," *New York Herald Tribune*, May 12, 1929, J5.

"seek expression in heroics": Blair Niles, "For the Love of the Game," *New York Herald*, April 17, 1927, F13.

*"to swap the usual soiled"**: Blair Niles, *Light Again* (New York: Liveright, 1933), 91.

"the heroes of their own volumes," *: Niles, "For the Love of the Game," F13.

"come forward with narrow escapes" ... *"the exploits of the old Conquistadors"** ... *"Those women even"*: Blair Niles, "The West Again," *New York Herald Tribune*, August 29, 1926, F9.

"'the first white woman'": Blair Niles, "Letter to the Editor," *New York Tribune*, December 7, 1924, F20.

"If you are near enough": Blair Niles, "Polar Stampede," *New York Herald Tribune*, May 3, 1926, F11.

MICKIE AKELEY:

crack markswoman ... Lion Incident (All quotes from): Olds, *Women*, 84.

*"With only three birds"**: Harold W. Belcher, "Mrs. Delia J. Akeley, Crossing Africa, to Write of Experience," *Calgary Herald*, October 4, 1924, 13.

"It is not necessary to be a man": Art Arthur, "Off the Beaten Path: Pygmy Patroness," *Brooklyn Daily Eagle*, September 21, 1935, 11.

"In a country where anything" ... *"I do not feel especially"** ... *Elephant Story* (All quotes from): Stella Burke May, "She Feels Safer in the Jungle," *Baltimore Sun*, July 8, 1928, 112.

*"I was delirious half of the time"**: Arthur, "Off the Beaten Path," 11.

Sultan's violence (All quotes from)*: Olds, *Women*, 141–146.

*"No wonder the sky sheds"**: Olds, *Women*, 146.

Armand Georges Denis (All quotes from, except as otherwise noted)*: Helen Welsheimer, "Women Explorers Are Bravest—But Timid Man Feels He Must Always Go to Their Rescue!" *The Province*, Vancouver, BC, October 22, 1938, 41.

"One woman can cause": Kelly Enright, *Osa and Martin: For the Love of Adventure* (Guilford, CT: Lyons Press, 2011), vix.

OSA JOHNSON:

*"energy of purpose"** ... *"disarm antagonism"**: Nellie Simmons Meier, "Interesting Character Sketch from Hand Impressions of the Late Martin Johnson and Wife, Osa Johnson," *Indianapolis Star*, January 24, 1937, 60.

Trip to Islands (All quotes from)*: Osa Johnson, *I Married Adventure: The Lives and Adventures of Martin and Osa Johnson* (Toronto: Lippincott, 1940), 116–170.

GRACE THOMPSON SETON:

"The manager looked astonished": Grace Thompson Seton, *A Woman Tenderfoot in Egypt* (New York: Dodd, Mead, 1923), 150.

*"I was absolutely dependent"**: Seton, *Woman Tenderfoot*, 177.

*"When I caught"**: "Mrs. Seton's Hypnotic Eye Held Love-Crazed Desert Arab," *Boston Globe*, May 15, 1923, 22.

Desert Scene (All quotes from, except as otherwise noted)*: Seton, *Woman Tenderfoot*, 179–186.

"It seemed most strange": Winifred Van Duzer, "How She Cooled the Ardor of a Sahara Sheik," *Morning Call*, Allentown, PA, June 24, 1923, 25.

*"You may search through"**: "Uses Hypnotism on Sheik to Stop His Desert Wooing," *Baltimore Sun*, May 15, 1923, 1.

MARGARET MEAD:

New Guinea Scene (All quotes from)*: Louise Michele Newman, "Coming of Age, but Not in Samoa: Reflections on Margaret Mead's Legacy for Western Liberal Feminism," *American Quarterly* 48, no. 2 (1996): 233, 255 (quoting Margaret Mead and James Baldwin, *A Rap on Race: a Recorded Conversation between Margaret Mead and James Baldwin* [New York: Bantam Doubleday, 1971], 28).

See also Jean Walton, *Fair Sex, Savage Dreams: Race, Psychoanalysis, Sexual Difference* (Durham, NC: Duke University Press, 2001), 180–181.

SAFETY OF JUNGLE:

"A babe in a hammock": "Scientist Goes Today to British Guiana," *Rutland Daily Herald*, Rutland, VT, January 20, 1916, 4.

*"You're going to Africa"**: "Dr. Akeley, Gorilla Expert, Dies in the Jungle," *San Francisco Examiner*, December 26, 1926, 87.

*"But it isn't as mad"**: Mary Hastings Bradley, "American Woman Hunts Gorillas and Takes 5-Year-Old Girl along with Her," *Washington Times*, DC, May 21, 1922, 19.

MARGUERITE HARRISON:

In general: Olds, *Women*, 158–227.

*"I have absolute"**: Olds, *Women*, 163.

"I have no doubt": Olds, *Women*, 164.

*"So far as possible"**: Olds, *Women*, 168.

Arrest and Imprisonment (All quotes from): Olds, *Women*, 177–179.

Chapter 2: A Place of Their Own

OPENING QUOTE*:

"Where Women Go First," *Washington Post*, December 16, 1985, accessed November 11, 2019, https://www.washingtonpost.com/archive/lifestyle/magazine/1985/12/15/where-women-go-first/c59c8197-8102-490d-b9b0-adc24aae4c78/.

GRASS:

"sightseeing tours" … "do something different": Olds, *Women*, 197.

King Kong: Scott S. Smith, "The Larger-Than-Life Career of 'King Kong' Producer Merian Cooper," *Investor's Business Daily*, July 17, 2017, accessed March 11, 2020, https://www.investors.com/news/management/leaders-and-success/the-larger-than-life-career-of-king-kong-producer-merian-cooper/.

"they filmed the breathtaking": Product Description, "Grass: A Nation's Battle for Life," Milestone Films, n.d., accessed March 11, 2020, https://milestonefilms.com/products/grass-a-nations-battle-for-survival.

"I piled onto": Olds, *Women*, 218.

In general: Jeffrey Ruoff, *Virtual Voyages: Cinema and Travel* (Durham, NC: Duke University Press, 2006), 119–120; Dennis Doros, *Grass*, July 27, 2016, Library of Congress Online, accessed March 11, 2020, https://www.loc.gov/static/programs/national-film-preservation-board/documents/grass.pdf.

"Br-r" ... "Everywhere that Mary went" ... "I wanted": Olds, *Women*, 227.

"become synonymous": Blair Niles, "The Apostasy of William McFee," *New York Tribune*, December 6, 1925, E24.

banks, not publishers: Niles, "Human Travel Books," *New York Tribune* (December 7, 1924), F20.

"Such books will" ... "compel a reader": Blair Niles, "For the European Tourist," *New York Tribune*, February 18, 1926, E8.

*"Travel, after all"**: Blair Niles, "Information Plus," *New York Herald Tribune*, August 1, 1926, F1.

"I can't see any reason": Blair Niles, "Not a 'Mere' Travel Book," *New York Herald*, August 2, 1925, D3.

"human travel book": Niles, "Human Travel Books," F20.

CLAVER:

Colombia, Land of Miracles: Blair Niles, *Colombia, Land of Miracles* (New York: Century, 1921).

In general: "Saint Peter Claver, Saint of the Day," *Franciscan Media*, accessed July 23, 2019, https://www.franciscanmedia.org/saint-of-the-day/saint-peter-claver.

"slave of the slaves forever": "Slave of the Slaves: Saint Peter Claver," *The Word among Us*, accessed July 23, 2019, https://wau.org/resources/article/slave_of_the_slaves/.

"Did he not realize" ... "Claver may have brushed aside": Niles, *Colombia*, 3.

BLAIR NILES:

Letter to the Editor (All quotes from): Blair Niles, Letter to the Editor, "Human Travel Books," *New York Tribune*, December 7, 1924, F20.

MARGUERITE HARRISON:

"My Adventures among the Wild Persian Nomads." *Sioux City Journal*, April 19, 1925, 44.

Merian Cooper: "Twice Shot Down from Clouds, and Twice Sentenced to Death, Minneapolis Boy Lives to Astonish the World with New Exploit," *Minneapolis Star*, May 16, 1925, 13.

"I am annoyed": "The Founders, A Review of the Society of Woman Geographers in Two Decades (1925–1945)," 25th Anniversary Number (December 1950), 5 (SWG).

*"Even in prison"**: Anne H. Oman, "True Grit: Woman Adventurers," *Washington Woman*, February 1988, 22.

*"The charms of face"**: "A Modern Pocahontas," *Buffalo Sunday Morning News*, January 22, 1911, 14.

*"This I insisted upon"**: Stephens, "My Adventures," 44.

"I am quite eager" ... organizations were sexist: "Society Is Formed," 16; Catherine Filene, *Careers for Women: New Ideas, New Methods, New Opportunities—to Fit a New World* (Chicago: Riverside Press, 1934), 83.

The film officially debuted: Daniel Eagan, *America's Film Legacy: The Authoritative Guide to the Landmark Movies in the National Film Registry* (New York: Continuum, 2010), 99.

"Men have organizations": Helen Fitzgerald, "Women Now Become Geographers," *Brooklyn Daily Eagle*, February 23, 1917, 81; "Women Explorers Put Adventures On Screen," *Morning Call*, Allentown, PA, September 8, 1929, 21.

"were still regarded": Olds, *Women*, 4.

isolation ... "Look up a man explorer" ... "I've often thought"*: Isabel Foster, "Women Answer the Call of Adventure," *Hartford Courant*, June 24, 1928, 1E.

"Let's found one" ... "An Explorers Club": "Founders," 8 (SWG).

GERTRUDE MATHEWS SHELBY:

economic geographer ... honeymoon: Helen Fitzgerald, "The Whole World Is Her Office," *Brooklyn Daily Eagle*, April 24, 1927, 93.

1922 Ford: "Like Ford Co-operation; Like Ford Car She Won," *Evening World*, New York, October 19, 1922, 4.

*"might have saved" … "an unsexed"**: Heywood Broun, "It Seems to Me," *Boston Globe*, September 28, 1922, 14.

GERTRUDE EMERSON:

"90 pounds of courage" … "five feet of sheer determination": Lowell Thomas, "90 Pounds of Courage," *Woman's World*, August 1936, 10, 11.

Gandhi and Building House in India (All quotes from, except as otherwise noted): Gertrude Emerson Sen, Oral History, Sen File, Records of the Society of Woman Geographers, Library of Congress, Manuscript Division, 8–11.

INITIAL MEETINGS TO ORGANIZE SWG:

indignation meeting: April White, "The Intrepid '20s Women Who Formed an All-Female Global Exploration Society," *Atlas Obscura*, April 12, 2017, accessed September 8, 2018, https://www.atlasobscura.com/articles/society-of-woman-geographers.

"We were not organizers": Ada Currier, "An Evening with Gertrude Emerson Sen," Triennial Banquet, April 29, 1978, 16 (SWG).

HARRIET CHALMERS ADAMS:

most enthusiastic responder: "Founders," 8 (SWG).

"This wonderful journey": Durlynn Anema, "Adventuring beyond Civilization: Harriet Chalmers Adams, Early 20th Century Explorer," *Labrys, Etudes Féministes*, January/June 2014, accessed March 11, 2020, https://www.labrys.net.br/labrys25/aventura/harriet%20chalmers.html.

"solved the age-old": Kathryn Davis, "Harriet Chalmers Adams, Remembering an American Geographer," *California Geographer* 49 (2009), 56.

took a long, historical: Tamar Y. Rothenberg, *Presenting America's World: Strategies of Innocence in* National Geographic Magazine, *1888–1945* (Hampshire, England: Ashgate, 2007), 158.

"dispel many of the myths": Joyce Duncan, *Ahead of Their Time: A Biographical Dictionary of Risk-Taking Women* (Westport, CT: Greenwood, 2001), 4.

on a quest to visit: Davis, "Harriet Chalmers Adams," 60.

"as a conquering race": Edith Ogden Harrison, *Below the Equator: The Story of a Tour through the Countries of South America* (Chicago: McClurg, 1918), 3.

"whom we regard" … "there is no greater"*: Rothenberg, *Presenting America's World*, 131.

When riding horseback: Davis, "Harriet Chalmers Adams," 72.

"petite, dainty": Michele R. Willman, "Mimic-Women: Twentieth-Century American Women on the Edges of Exploration," Thesis, University of North Dakota, 2017, accessed March 11, 2020, https://commons.und.edu/theses/2381, 2.

"It seemed incredible": Alison Mary Blunt, "'Only a Woman': Women Travel Writers and Imperialism," Thesis, University of British Columbia, 1992, accessed March 11, 2020, 143, https://open.library.ubc.ca/cIRcle/collections/ubctheses/831/items/1.0058318.

*"This pretty woman"**: "Woman Explorer: Laughs at Peril," *Richmond Item*, December 19, 1908, 7.

*"What I would like most"**: Rothenberg, *Presenting America's World*, 134.

"their hide-bound": "Women Who Penetrate Wilds United for Further Exploits," *News-Review*, Roseburg, OR, March 16, 1928, 6.

"woman's place is anywhere": *Every Week*, January 17, 1916, 10.

"I've wondered why men" … "in tight places": Brooke Sutton, "Harriet Chalmers Adams: The Original Adventure-lebrity," *Adventure Journal*, January 28, 2016, accessed March 11, 2020, https://www.adventure-journal.com/2016/01/harriet-chalmers-adams-the-original-adventure-lebrity/.

"That sounds like rather": Davis, "Harriet Chalmers Adams," 66.

THE SOCIETY:

*"We all had our different fields"**: Currier, "Evening with Gertrude Emerson Sen," 16.

"distinctive work": Susan Ware, *Letter to the World: Seven Women Who Shaped the American Century* (New York: Norton, 1998), 95.

"Women cannot merely": "Society Is Formed by Lady Explorers," *Windsor Star*, February 9, 1927, 16.

"only women who have really done": Letter from Marguerite Harrison to Harriet Chalmers Adams (April 1, 1925) (SWG).

"No matter": Earnestine Evans, "Penelope Is Travelling," *The Guardian*, August 4, 1925, 4.

"woman who has done the most": Letter from Harrison to Adams (April 1, 1925).

"pool lore about baggage": Evans, "Penelope Is Travelling," 4.

*"a comradeship"**: SWG, In Memory of Harriet Chalmers Adams (SWG, 1938), 8–9 (Blair Niles's tribute).

"building personal relationships" ... "secure dignified": Jane Eppinga, *They Made Their Mark* (Guilford, CT: Globe Pequot Press, 2009), x.

Ida Pfeiffer: Society Is Formed, 16.

MEMBERSHIP REQUIREMENTS:

"two requirements": SWG, Annual Bulletin (August 1929), 1.

"published or produced": SWG, Annual Bulletin (August 1930), 1.

ALEXANDRA DAVID-NÉEL:

David Guy, "Alexandra David-Néel," *Tricycle* (Fall 1995), accessed January 6, 2020, https://tricycle.org/magazine/alexandra-david-neel/.

Sue Aran, "The Extraordinary Alexandra David-Néel: First European Woman to Travel to the Forbidden City of Lhasa," Bonjour Paris, the Insider's Guide Blog, January 24, 2018, accessed January 6, 2020, https://bonjourparis.com/history/women-who-shaped-paris/alexandra-david-neel/.

MARGARET MEAD:

"storm and stress": Helen Herbert Foster, "Life Nearly Perfect in Polynesia," *Brooklyn Daily Eagle*, February 13, 1927, 83.

"attitude toward sex" ... "mercy of God"*: "Youth in Samoa, A Land with No Neuroses," *Honolulu Star-Bulletin*, September 8, 1928, 32; Dale Debakcsy, "The Complicated Legacy of Famed Anthropologist Margaret Mead (1901–1978)," *Women You Should Know*, June 7, 2017, accessed December 17, 2020, https://womenyoushouldknow.net/the-complicated-legacy-of-famed-anthropologist-margaret-mead/.

MUNA LEE:

"Muna Lee, Sooner Poet, Compiles Spanish Verse," *Sooner State Press*, Norman, OK, October 10, 1925, 1.

"cage full of birds": Jonathan Cohen, *A Pan-American Life: Selected Poetry and Prose of Muna Lee* (Madison: University of Wisconsin Press, 2004), xv.

*"an extremely vigorous mind"**: "H. Elaine Boylan, Sooner State Girl Rises to Top in Poetry," *Daily Oklahoman*, Oklahoma City, October 14, 1923, 44.

Chapter 3: Go Home Where You Belong!

OPENING QUOTE:

Julie Cummins, *Women Explorers: Perils, Pistols, and Petticoats* (London: Puffin Books, 2015), 22.

ANNIE PECK'S BIRTHDAY:

All quotes from: "Women Explorers Honor Miss Peck at 84," *New York Times*, October 20, 1934, 17; "Celebrate 84th Birthday of Annie Peck," *Burlington Free Press*, October 20, 1934, 2.

DICKINSON'S SPEECH:

"Idiots and women!": "Idiots and Women: Lecture of Anna E. Dickinson before the Library Association," *Chicago Tribune*, February 21, 1868, 4.

"as clear as the tone": Kimberley, *Woman's Place*, 14.

*"They say woman"** ... *"Would it be fine"* ... *"If such a thing"* ... *"had been considered"* ... *"I wish I were"*: Kimberley, *Woman's Place*, 15–17.

EDUCATION:

$700: Kimberley, *Woman's Place*, 36.

*"The regimen of our schools"**: Edward H. Clarke, *Sex in Education; or, A Fair Chance for the Girls* (Boston: Houghton, Mifflin, 1874), 79.

*"never worried about"**: Kimberley, *Woman's Place*, 42.

*"I do not esteem"** ... *"In the end"**: Kimberley, *Woman's Place*, 43.

"Years ago": Kimberley, *Woman's Place*, 44–45.

not enough of them ...*"mere appendages"*: Kimberley, *Woman's Place*, 48.

"kind of disaster insurance": Paul Shankman, "The Public Anthropology of Margaret Mead: *Redbook*, Women's Issues, and the 1960s," *Current Anthropology* 59, no. 1 (February 2018), 57.

*"undoubtedly better qualified"**: Kimberley, *Woman's Place*, 76.

"very charming personality": Kimberley, *Woman's Place*, 83.

"without the discomfort": Kimberley, *Woman's Place*, 84.

MOUNTAIN CLIMBING:

*"When I first saw this"**: Kimberley, *Woman's Place*, 70.

"If you are determined to commit suicide": Kimberley, *Woman's Place*, 88–89.

Ascent of Matterhorn:

*"We saw nothing"** ... *"I found this"* ... *"The rocks were so"* ... *"The descent is"**: "One of the Most Notable of Feminine Mountain Climbers," *San Francisco Chronicle*, November 20, 1898, 3.

"Go home where you belong!": Joan Marlow, *The Great Women* (New York: Galahad Books, 1981), 154.

"I dare assert" ... *"I do not do"**: Linda Peavy, "Mountains That Matter," *Rutland Daily Herald*, SM 9, 10.

bike: "One of the Most Notable of Feminine Mountain Climbers," *San Francisco Chronicle*, November 20, 1898, 3.

"peaks of prejudice" ... *"today, there is scarcely"** ... *"Is a new world"*: "New Places for Women," *Harrisburg Daily Independent*, Harrisburg, PA, December 15, 1897, 4.

*"Climbing is unadulterated"**: Corrine Gaffner Garcia, *Trail Mix: Wit and Wisdom from the Outdoors* (Guilford, CT: Falcon Guides, 2019), 23.

*"Self-denial and labor"**: Kimberley, *Woman's Place*, 99.

Ascent of Mount Popocatépetl:

Sunday World Article (All quotes from)*: Alice Fahs, *Out on Assignment: Newspaper Women and the Making of Modern Public Space* (Chapel Hill: University of North Carolina Press, 2011), 173–174 (quoting Elizabeth Jordan).

Male Guides:

"To manage three men": Kimberley, *Woman's Place*, 146.

"If it hadn't" ... *"I'll tell you why I failed"*: "Miss Peck Lays Blame on Professor Tight: Noted Mountain Climber Gives Her Reason for Failure to Reach Summit of the Mountain," *Newark Advocate*, Newark, OH, December 14, 1903, 2.

"merely confirmed": Kimberley, *Woman's Place*, 153.

*"often described her male"**: Kimberley, *Woman's Place*, 166.
"managed to alienate": Rothenberg, *Presenting America's World*, 147.

Ascent of Mount Huascarán:

*"I was filled with dismay"**: Kimberley, *Woman's Place*, 170.
*"was so seamed" ... "He had proved"**: Kimberley, *Woman's Place*, 172-73.
"I cannot sympathize": Kimberley, *Woman's Place*, 179.
"We seemed to proceed" ... "cruel to ask"**: Kimberley, *Woman's Place*, 175.
*"If I had not accomplished"**: Kimberley, *Woman's Place*, 176.
*"To reach a higher"**: Kimberley, *Woman's Place*, 178–179.
turn into stone: Kimberley, *Woman's Place*, 182.
"I am the one paying": Kimberley, *Woman's Place*, 187.
*"There was nothing"**: Kimberley, *Woman's Place*, 188.
"Very well" ... "Why Ramos did not": Annie Smith Peck, *A Search for the Apex of America: High Mountain Climbing in Peru and Bolivia Including the Conquest of Huascaran, with Some Observations on the Country and People Below* (New York: Dodd, Mead, 1911), 256.
"To have deserted": Kimberley, *Woman's Place*, 211.
"I am sure that my peaceful death": Kimberley, *Woman's Place*, 212.
"I was angry": Kimberley, *Woman's Place*, 214.
"Once more I resolved": Kimberley, *Woman's Place*, 216.
"monster of persistence": Olds, *Women*, 8.
*"Persistence is worthy"**: Kimberley, *Woman's Place*, 180.
"I shall have the honor": Kimberley, *Woman's Place*, 234.
"I am not concerned": Kimberley, *Woman's Place*, 236.
"$13,000 seems a large sum": Michael Elsohn Ross, *World of Her Own: 25 Amazing Women Explorers and Adventurers* (Chicago: Chicago Review Press, 2014), 11.

Climbing Apparel:

"I suppose you expected": Kimberley, *Woman's Place*, 235.
"I have never found it": Kimberley, *Woman's Place*, 236.
"Men, we all know": Dorcas S. Miller, *Adventurous Women: The Inspiring Lives of Nine Early Outdoorswomen* (Boulder, CO: Pruett, 2000), 40.
"until out of sight of the hotel": Hannah Scialdone-Kimberley, "Woman at the Top: Rhetoric, Politics, and Feminism in the Texts and Life of Annie Smith Peck," Dissertation, Old Dominion University, 2012, 95.
*"a rather superfluous"**: Peck, *Search for the Apex*, 445.

Race with Hiram Bingham:

"I am sorry to have you": Kimberley, *Woman's Place*, 243.
Bingham: Alfred M. Bingham, "Raiders of the Lost City," *American Heritage* 38, no. 5 (July/August 1987), accessed March 15, 2020, https://www.americanheritage.com/raiders-lost-city.
"Queen of the Climbers.": Kimberley, *Woman's Place*, 246.
*"His male ego" ... "meet that aggressive female's challenge"**: Bingham, "Raiders."
"A woman who has done": "Miss Peck Goes out to Climb the Heights," *New York Times*, June 3, 1911, 11.
"hard-faced, sharp-tongued" ... "It was easy for a male chauvinist" ... "she had been intending" ... "No special things to note"*: Bingham, "Raiders."
"Votes for Women": Kimberley, *Woman's Place*, 266.
"This is Annie" ... "I would not put it": "Miss Annie Peck's Triumph," *Anthony Bulletin*, Anthony, KS, February 16, 1912, 8.
"The Senorita": Kimberley, *Woman's Place*, 199.

"he persuaded himself": Bingham, "Raiders."

*"No wonder"**: Kimberley, *Woman's Place*, 265.

INSUBORDINATION AS A COMMON PROBLEM:

"Miss Peck would make": Ross, *World of Her Own*, 1.

"One of the chief difficulties": Peck, *Search for the Apex*, 317.

Chapter 4: A Mere Woman

OPENING QUOTE:

Osa Johnson, *I Married Adventure*, 274.

IMPERIALISM AND RACISM IN WILL'S WORK:

"persistent racial categorizing" ..."the overtly racist": Katherine Fenn McLeod, "Beyond the Biological: William Beebe, the Bronx Zoo, and U.S. Biological Field Stations in British Guiana," Master's Thesis, City University of New York, 2017, 41, 12.

ANTHONY KUSER:

In general: Meryl Gordon, *Mrs. Astor Regrets: Betrayals of a Family beyond Reproach* (Boston: Mariner Books, 2009), 53; John K. Turpin and Barry Thompson, *New Jersey Country Homes: Somerset Hills*, Vol. 1 (Far Hills, NJ: Mountain Colony Press, 2004), 87, 90.

VISIT WITH PRESIDENT ROOSEVELT AND HORNADAY'S REACTION:

In general: Gould, *Remarkable Life*, 117.

INTERVIEWS:

"lazy like all women" ... "Society for the Protection": "Wives Rule Homes in Primitive Africa, Carl Von Hoffman Says," *Hawaii Tribune-Herald*, Hilo, October 18, 1931, 1.

Helen Dare articles (All quotes from)*: Helen Dare, "They Were Happy in Jungle and Came Home to Disagree," *San Francisco Chronicle*, September 13, 1913, 7; Helen Dare, "Scientist's Wife Who Was Not Excess Baggage in the Jungle," *San Francisco Chronicle*, May 15, 1911, 7.

New York Times article (All quotes from)*: "An Ornithologist and His Wife among the Brown Men," *New York Times*, July 11, 1911; Amisha Padnani and Jessica Bennett, "Overlooked," *New York Times*, March 8, 2018.

VIEWS THAT SHAPED WILL'S IMPERIALIST VIEWS:

Dinner in Ceylon (All quotes from): W. Beebe, "Pagan Personalities," *Harper's Monthly Magazine* 132, no. 792 (May 1916), 939; William Beebe Diary, March 2, 1910, PU.

Scene at Singapore Wharf ... "When Aladdin" ... "It is difficult to learn" ... "leave him for a master"* (All quotes from)*: Letter from William Beebe to Henrietta Beebe (September 20, 1910).

CHINESE-BURMESE BORDER:

In general: Letter from William Beebe to Anthony Kuser (November 24, 1910); *see generally*, Thomas McGrath, "A Warlord Frontier: The Yunnan-Burma Border Dispute, 1910–1937," *Ohio Academy of History Proceedings* (2003), 10–12; Zhidan Duan, "At the Edge of Mandalas: The Transformation of the China's Yunnan Borderlands in the 19th and 20th Century," Dissertation, Arizona State University, 2015; William Beebe, *Pheasant Jungles* (New York: Blue Ribbon Books, 1927).

"There is no telling": Beebe, *Pheasant Jungles*, 110.

TURN TO WRITE INCIDENT:

(All quotes from): Mary Blair Beebe, "Wild Burma," *Harper's Monthly Magazine*, April 1912, 768; Beebe, *Pheasant Jungles*, 110–112.

DÂKS:

"a blessed institution" ... "They mean warmth": Mary Blair Beebe, "A Quest in the Himalayans," *Harper's Monthly Magazine* 122, no. 730 (March 1911), 496.

WASHAWNG VISIT (CALLED WAH-HSAUNG BY BLAIR):

"passport to friendship" ... "women with babies": M. B. Beebe, "Wild Burma," 761.

PUMKAHTAWNG (CALLED PUNGATONG IN DIARY):

"Naturally such tribes": Blair Niles, "A Plucky Trip," *Saturday Review of Literature*, October 24, 1925, 239.

In general: Mary Blair Beebe, "Wild Burma," 763–767; Beebe, *Pheasant Jungles*, 105–110.

*The air tastes**: Beebe, "Wild Burma," 764.

"Jaldi, Jaldi" ... muleteers: Letter from Blair Beebe to Susan Kuser (February 24, 1910); Beebe, "Wild Burma," 763.

*"If you could"**: Letter from Blair Beebe to Gordon and Henry Rice (April 17, 1910).

Gehenna: Gould, *Remarkable Life*, 78; Letter from William Beebe to Henrietta Beebe (November 14, 1910).

*"The thought of"**: Beebe, *Pheasant Jungles*, 107.

progress with pheasants: William Beebe, *Pheasants: Their Lives and Homes* (New York: Doubleday, Doran, 1927), Introduction.

Kapit: Letter from Blair Beebe to Susan Kuser (July 21, 1910); Letter from William Beebe to Charles Beebe (August 17, 1910).

"I hate pheasants" ... "I want to go to America": Beebe, *Pheasant Jungles*, 107.

"It is not necessarily": Adolph Gillis and Roland Ketchum, *Our America* (Boston: Little Brown, 1938), 4.

threatened suicide ... In his battle: Blair Niles, "Cheating the Jungle," *Scribner's Magazine* 69, no. 3 (March 1921), 366.

THE WATER BUFFALO SCENE:

In general: Beebe, *Wild Burma*, 763; Beebe, *Pheasant Jungles*, ch. 4; William Beebe, "The Living Leaf and Water Buffaloes," *Scribner's Commentator*, December 1939, 144; "Bird Hunt in Borneo and Southeast Asia," *Evening Republican*, Columbus, OH, October 23, 1911, 2; C. William Beebe, "The Gates of the East," *Atlantic Monthly* 117, no. 3 (March 1916), 343.

trail of wounded and dead: "A 50,000 Mile Trip to Study Pheasants," *New York Tribune* (July 20, 1913), 60.

OTA BENGA:

"Only prejudice against the Negro": Daniel E. Bender, *The Animal Game: Searching for Wildness at American Zoos* (Cambridge, MA: Harvard University Press, 2016), 165.

"This is the most ridiculous thing": "Row over Pygmy: Minister Declares Zoo Exhibition Is Brutalizing," *Wilkes-Barre Record*, Wilkes-Barre, PA, September 11, 1906, 2; "African Pygmy's Fate Is Still Undecided: Director Hornaday of the Bronx Park Throws Up His Hands," *New York Times*, September 18, 1906, 9.

MADISON GRANT AND JEWS:

In general: Madison Grant, *The Passing of the Great Race* (New York: Scribner, 1916).

WILL'S PREJUDICES:

*"Rothschild is genial"**: Letter from William Beebe to Anthony Kuser (January 16, 1910).

"niggers": Letter from William Beebe to Charles Beebe (November 27, 1892); letter from William Beebe to Charles Beebe (November 8, 1892); letter from William Beebe to Nettie Beebe (February 27, 1908).

WILL'S ATTITUDES TO STRANGERS:

*Here is living history**: Jacob Deshin, "Adventuring with a Woman Explorer," *Hartford Courant*, October 9, 1927, E1.

In general: C. William Beebe, *Two Bird-Lovers in Mexico* (Chicago: Riverside Press, 1905), 167–169, 173, 195.

"ping-pong racket" … "this poor ignorant man": Beebe, *Two Bird-Lovers*, 168.

survive their meal: Beebe, *Two Bird-Lovers*, 173.

bandit: Letter from William Beebe to Anthony Kuser (December 24, 1910).

BLAIR'S AFFINITY TO LATIN AMERICA/HER LIFE'S TAPESTRY:

In general: Blair Niles, *Journeys in Time: From the Halls of Montezuma to Patagonia's Plains* (New York: Coward-McCann, 1946), 3–4; letter from William Beebe to Henrietta and Charles Beebe (postscript by Blair Beebe) (February 26, 1909); Helen Fitzgerald, "Women *Now* Become Geographers," *Brooklyn Daily Eagle*, February 13, 1927, 81.

*"We know that a most cruel death"**: Letter from William Beebe to Anthony Kuser (December 26, 1910).

NATS AND BURMESE SPIRITUAL BELIEFS:

In general: Beebe, *Wild Burma*, 764–770; Beebe, *Pheasant Jungles*, 122–129; John Nisbet, *Burma under British Rule—and Before*, Vol. 2 (Westminster, Scotland: Constable, 1901); Louis Vossion, "Nat-Worship among the Burmese," *Journal of American Folklore* 4, no. 13 (April–June 1891); Rev. O. Hanson, *The Kachins: Their Traditions and Customs* (Rangoon, Burma: American Baptist Mission Press, 1913); Bénédicte Brac de la Perrière, "'Nats' Wives' or 'Children of Nats' from Spirit Possession to Transmission among the Ritual Specialists of the Cult of the Thirty-Seven Lords," *Asian Ethnology* 68, no. 2 (2009).

SANSI GORGE:

"We worship them only" … "a topsy-turvy forest" … "I empty food" … "Have you ever thought" … "A used bowl": Beebe, *Pheasant Jungles*, 121, 126.

POISONED ARROW INCIDENT AND LANOO'S DEATH AND MURDER:

"I managed to fire": "Hunting Pheasants in Yunan a Thrilling Sport," *Press and Sun-Bulletin*, Binghamton, NY, July 7, 1911, 13.

"Did you hear that?" … "It sounded" … "the medicine is stronger" … "Like the scare-lines" … "That China boy": Beebe, "Wild Burma," 771.

eleven servants died: "50,000 Mile Trip to Study Pheasants," 60.

"I have told you how": Letter from William Beebe to Anthony Kuser (February 9, 1910).

"The evening following": Beebe, *Pheasant Jungles*, 128a.

"We confess": Arthur Shipley, "Pheasant Jungles by William Beebe," *Discovery: The Popular Journal of Knowledge* 8 (1927), 202.

"death was the second death": Beebe, "Wild Burma," 771.

"It seems as though": Letter from Blair Beebe to Charles Beebe (January 9, 1911).

"in spite of being": Beebe, "Quest in the Himalayas," 490.

contributions: Letter from William Beebe to Charles and Henrietta Beebe (June 9, 1910).

"Blair's head is swelling": Letter from William Beebe to Charles Beebe (May 25, 1910).

"I think Blair": Letter from William Beebe to Anthony Kuser (May 24, 1910) (BU 77).

"We admired the chivalry": Letter from Sara Pryor to William and Blair Beebe (May 12, 1910) (WCS, DTR General Correspondence).

HOUSE ON SEDGEWICK:

Letter from Blair Beebe to Henrietta Beebe (November 15, 1910).

Chapter 5: Reno-vation

Reno-vation: Nevada Historical Society Docent Council, *Early Reno* (Mt. Pleasant, SC: Arcadia, 2011), ch. 5; "May Lose Divorce Colony," *New York Times*, January 19, 1913, 1.

OPENING QUOTE:

Alice Tisdale Hobart, *Oil for the Lamps of China* (Indianapolis: Bobbs Merrill, 1933), 73.

IN NEW YORK:

2,400 photographs: Gould, *Remarkable Life*, 174.
car ... weekends: Gould, *Remarkable Life*, 175.

ROBIN NILES:

Gould, *Remarkable Life*, 178; "Harvard Class of 1909," *Decennial Report* (Harvard University, 1920); *Harvard Alumni Bulletin* 13:8 (November 23, 1910), 124; *Harvard Alumni Bulletin* 13:1 (October 5, 1910).

Robert Lyman Niles, *Harvard Class of 1909, Third Report, Quindicentennial Report: June 1929* (Norwood, MA: Primpton Press), 60.

Harvard Engineering Journal 11, no. 4 (1912), 254.

TRIP TO EUROPE:

Paris: William Beebe Diary (July 1912), *passim.*
England: William Beebe Diary (June 1912), *passim.*

WILLIAM BEEBE:

Columbia: Gould, *Remarkable Life*, 51; William Beebe Diaries 1886–1889.
*"his high-domed"**: Trevor Norton, *Stars beneath the Sea: The Pioneers of Diving* (New York: Carroll & Graf, 1999), 57.

RENO DIVORCES:

"who come here to find easy": Anita J. Watson, "Tarnished Silver: Popular Image and Business Reality of Divorce in Nevada: 1900–1939," Dissertation, University of Nevada, Reno, August 1989, 102.
*"Reno cruelty"**: Watson, "Tarnished Silver," 100 (quoting *Tonopah Daily*, Sunday, May 15, 1909).
*"The law allows"**: Watson, "Tarnished Silver," 102 (quoting *Reno Evening Gazette*, April 19, 1910).
"I believe that marriage": Paul Shankman, *The Trashing of Margaret Mead: Anatomy of an Anthropological Controversy* (Madison: University of Wisconsin Press, 2009), 123 (quoting Robert Staughton and Lynd)
"flexible, far-visioned": Watson, Tarnished Silver, 105–106 (quoting George A. Bartlett, *Men, Women and Conflict* [New York: Putnam, 1931], 45–46).

BEEBE DIVORCE:

"hateful to": Gould, *Remarkable Life*, 182.
Will's Gratitude to Blair (All *New York Tribune* quotes from)*: "A 50,000 Mile Trip to Study Pheasants," 60.
Will's Disparagement (All quotes from)*: "Savages and Semi-savages," *Washington Times*, November 6, 1913, 4.

BLAIR'S TESTIMONY:

In general: "Naturalist Was Cruel," *New York Times*, August 30, 1913, 1; "Mrs. M. B. Beebe Gets Divorce," *The Sun* (New York) August 30, 1913, 1; "Zookeeper Is Divorced," *Reno-Gazette Journal*, August 28, 1913, 1.
*"My husband made me a nervous"**: Carol Gould, *Remarkable Life*, 180.

*"Once he put a revolver" ... "For days at a time"**: Robert Henry Welker, *Natural Man: The Life of William Beebe* (Bloomington: Indiana University Press, 1975), 26.

typing affected sight: Gould, *Remarkable Life*, 181.

*"I have never regained" ... "he became cruel" ... "Before we went"**: "Naturalist Was Cruel," 1; "Mrs. M. B. Beebe Gets Divorce," 1.

*"He was very critical, jealous"**: "Zookeeper Is Divorced," 1.

MARRIAGE TO ROBIN:

In general: (All quotes from)*: "Mrs. Beebe Marries Again," *The Sun* (New York), September 7, 1913, 11.

"Blair's action" ... "Where Robin Niles"*: "Mrs. Beebe Wed Again in Secret," *New York Times*, September 7, 1913 (PU).

LETTER TO ROOSEVELT:

In general (All quotes from)*: Letter from William T. Hornaday to Theodore Roosevelt (September 4, 1913) (TRC).

Roosevelt's views on divorce: Watson, "Tarnished Silver," 5 (quoting Alfred Cahen, *Statistical Analysis of American Divorce* [1932], 93).

Roosevelt's Reply to Hornaday: Letter from Theodore Roosevelt to William T. Hornaday (September 5, 1913) (TRC).

BLAIR'S VIEWS ON DIVORCE:

*"A woman would rather" ... "want to be made love"**: Blair Niles, *Free* (San Diego, CA: Harcourt, Brace, 1930), 103.

DIVORCE IN VICTORIAN ERA:

"Remember that, however unsuited": Kristin Celello, *Making Marriage Work: A History of Marriage and Divorce in the Twentieth-Century United States* (Chapel Hill: University of North Carolina Press, 2009), 18.

less than .01: Infoplease, "Marriages and Divorces, 1900–2012," accessed March 15, 2020, https://www.infoplease.com/us/family-statistics/marriages-and-divorces-1900-2012

MARGARET MEAD:

Margaret Mead married three: Joyce Duncan, *Ahead of Their Time: A Biographical Dictionary of Risk-Taking Women* (Westport, CT: Greenwood, 2001), 220.

"recognize that divorce": "Dr. Mead Declares Divorce Commonplace," *Morning Call*, Paterson, NJ, December 10, 1947, 30.

"I beg your pardon": Helen Fisher, *Why Him? Why Her?: Finding Real Love by Understanding Your Personality Type* (New York: Henry Holt, 2009), 233.

MARGARET BOURKE-WHITE:

*"People seem to take it"**: Margaret Bourke-White, *Portrait of Myself* (India: Lucknow Books, reprinted 2016), chap. 2.

COVERTURE:

"By marriage": William Blackstone, *Commentaries on the Law of England* (Oxford: Oxford Press, 1932), 44.

Chapter 6: The Prison Special

OPENING QUOTE:

Stella Benson, *The Little World* (Canada: 1925), 96–97.

ELLA RIEGEL:

studied political economy: "Draw Extensive Plan for Suffrage Drive," *Evening Public Ledger*, Philadelphia, PA, March 29, 1919, 9.

Bequeathed $45,000: "College Gets Bulk of Estate," *Philadelphia Enquirer*, January 28, 1937, 3, 9.

manslaughter: "Bryn Mawr Girl Is Not Guilty of Murder," *Lancaster New Era*, Lancaster, PA, April 21, 1921, 13.

"The jury was fair": "Woman Motorist Free in Death Case," *Evening Ledger*, Philadelphia, PA, April 13, 1921, 3.

SUFFRAGE PARADE:

*"Eyes to the front"**: "Why Suffragists Will Parade on Saturday," *New York Tribune*, May 12, 1912, 1.

*"Woman suffrage has passed"**: Kimberley, *Woman's Place*, 271.

"All This Is a Natural": Johanna Neuman, *Gilded Suffragists: The New York Socialites Who Fought for Women's Right to Vote* (New York: New York University Press, 2017), 112.

*"a parade of contrasts"** ... *"There were times"* ... *One thousand men*: "Suffrage Army out on Parade," *New York Times*, May 5, 1912, 1.

"Aren't they cute?" ... *"11,863 of you"*: George Him, *How It Feels to Be the Husband of a Suffragette* (New York: Doran, 1915), 41.

ANNIE PECK:

"This was the banner": Kimberley, *Woman's Place*, 275.

*ticket agent conversation**: Kimberley, *Woman's Place*, 267.

*"The program of the woman"**: "Annie S. Peck's Views," *New York Times*, February 28, 1915, 72.

ELLEN LA MOTTE:

Hikers ... *"We want to be able"*: Cynthia Wachtell, *Ellen La Motte: The Backwash of War: An Extraordinary American Nurse in World War I* (Baltimore: Johns Hopkins University Press, 2019), 47.

"suffrage with its fangs drawn": Wachtell, *Ellen La Motte*, 50.

"women who have shaken off" ... *"heartily disapproved of suffragetting"*: Wachtell, *Ellen La Motte*, 51.

"Not a word of objection" ... *"For Bail"*: Wachtell, *Ellen La Motte*, 52.

"stepped over the line": "No Faith in Militancy," *Baltimore Sun*, August 12, 1915, 3.

rabid suffragist ... *"Outwardly I'm a good Socialist"*: Wachtell, *Ellen La Motte*, 48.

*"the rank of"**: "No Faith in Militancy," 3.

BLAIR NILES:

In general: "Suffrage in Wall St., Again," *New York Times*, July 1, 1914, 4; "Women Here Start Federal Campaign," *New York Times*, November 28, 1915, 10.

PRESIDENT WILSON:

*"I hope I shall always"**: "Vote Plea Scene Gay," *Washington Post*, December 7, 1915, 1, 3.

SUFFRAGE SPECIAL:

Contributed $1000: "Congressional Side to Be Argued," *Butte Mine*, Butte, MT, April 24, 1916, 3.

*"If you Washington ladies"** ... *"My charges"*: Christine A. Lunardini, *From Equal Suffrage to Equal Rights: Alice Paul and the National Women's Party, 1910–1928* (New York: New York University Press, 1986), 85–105 (quoting letter dated April 26, 1916).

WITHHOLDING VOTES:

"A party fears nothing": "New Castle Suffragists Name Miss Speakman Chairman; Women Predict Victory," *Evening Journal* (Wilmington, DE), March 4, 1916, 7.

"For the first time in history" ... "to punish": Doris Stevens, *Jailed for Freedom* (New York: Boni & Liveright, 1920), 41–42.

Blair's delegation: "Congressional Union Delegation to Senator O'Gorman," *The Suffragist*, April 24, 1915.

PICKETING:

"President Wilson instructed": "Bryn Mawr Pupil of President Now Suffrage Sentinel," *Oregon Daily Journal* (Portland, OR), January 24, 1917, 3.

"I certainly admire": Stevens, *Jailed for Freedom*, 68.

Supporters brought the picketers: Stevens, *Jailed for Freedom*, 70.

*"I've done sentinel"**: Stevens, *Jailed for Freedom*, 70–74.

resigned in protest: "Connecticut Suffs Split," *Daily Record* (Long Branch, NJ), September 13, 1917, 8.

*"President Wilson is deceiving"**: Stevens, *Jailed for Freedom*, 91.

*"Of course it was embarrassing"**: Stevens, *Jailed for Freedom*, 93.

Picket scenes with Alice Paul (All quotes from, except as otherwise noted)*: Stevens, *Jailed for Freedom*, 94–95.

Anne Martin: Encyclopedia Britannica, online, "Anne Henrietta Martin: American Reformer and Educator."

Doris Stevens: "Doris Stevens (1888 [1892?]–1963)," Turning Point Suffragist Memorial, accessed November 21, 2019, https://suffragistmemorial.org/doris-stevens-1888-1892-1963/.

Florence Bayard Hilles ... "What will you do for woman": Jane Bayard Curly, "My Grandmother, Florence Bayard Hilles," accessed November 21, 2019, http://www.suffragettes2020.com/leading-the-way/my-grandmother-florence-bayard-hilles.

Matilda Hall Gardner: "Is the President not": Matilda Hall Gardner, "The Suffrage Pickets," *New York Evening Post*, June 4, 1917.

Arrest and Trial (All quotes from, except as otherwise noted)*: Stevens, *Jailed for Freedom*, 102–106.

prison: Theodore Tiller, "From Picket Line to Jail and out Again," *The Sun* (New York), July 22, 1917, 39, 44; Stevens, *Jailed for Freedom*, 145–201.

*"He does not object to militancy"**: Wachtell, *Ellen La Motte*, 53.

"an odd combination" ... "I thought I would have": Neuman, *Gilded Suffragists*, chap. 8.

"I have often wondered": Elaine Weiss, *The Woman's Hour: The Great Fight to Win the Vote* (London: Penguin, 2019), 109; *Effigy*: 156–157.

Effigy Scene (All quotes from, except as otherwise noted).*: "Suffragists Burn Effigy of President," *New York Tribune*, February 10, 1919, 1.

"No picketing" ... "as unfit to hold" ..."Sparks of indignation" ... "Oh those telegrams!": Johanna Neuman, *The Women Who Won the Vote: Louisine Elder Havemeyer*, From the Square, NYU Press Blog, August 23, 1917, accessed March 15, 2020, https://www.fromthesquare.org/women-won-vote-louisine-elder-havemeyer.

PRISON SPECIAL:

*"short-haired unreasonable"**: "'Prison Special' Militant Suffragettes Do Not Represent Principle of Suffrage Movement," *Woodland Daily Democrat* (Woodland, CA), January 31, 1919, 2.

"Suffragists Who Did Time to Make Tour," *Evansville Press* (Evansville, IN), February 7, 1919, 9.

Eighty-year-old Mary Nolan: "Militants Beseech Local Women to Telegraph Wilson," *San Antonio Evening News*, February 24, 1919, 8.

FRANCES P. BOLTON:

*"I am afraid that gallantry"**: Frances P. Bolton, History, Art & Archives, U.S. House of

representatives, accessed March 15, 2020, https://history.house.gov/People/Listing/B/BOLTON,-Frances-Payne-(B000607)/.

MILDRED ADAMS:

"remarkably selfless" ... "They were working": Nancy Cott, *Theory and Methods in Women's History* (Munich, Germany: Saur, 1992), 22.

GRACE THOMPSON SETON AND IMMIGRATION:

"one of those people" ... Biblioteca Femina: "Seton, Grace Gallatin (1872—1959)," December 24, 2019, https://www.encyclopedia.com/women/encyclopedias-almanacs-transcripts-and-maps/seton-grace-gallatin-1872-1959.

"I was born" ... "One of the first matters"**: A. G. Porritt, *Connecticut Suffrage News, The Bridgeport Times,* and *Evening Farmer*, March 28, 1914, 7.

COVERTURE:

In general: Claudia Zaher, "When a Woman's Marital Status Determined Her Legal Status: A Research Guide on the Common Law of Coverture," 2002, accessed October 1, 2020, https://people.virginia.edu/~jdk3t/ZaherWMS.pdf, 459; Linda K. Kerber, *No Constitutional Right to Be Ladies* (New York: Hill and Wang, 1998), 307.

ELLA RIEGEL:

The Hague Conference on the Codification: Candice Lewis Bredbenner, *A Nationality of Her Own* (Berkeley: University of California Press, 1998), 198, 210.

Chapter 7: The Backwash of War

OPENING QUOTE:

Wachtell, *Ellen La Motte*, 19.

MINNETONKA SCENE:

In general (All quotes from except as noted): *"I feel singularly" ... ripping time ... "Paris from the standpoint"**: Wachtell, *Ellen La Motte*, 56–57.

*"I am leaving behind"**: "Miss Ellen LaMotte Leaves for Front," *Evening Sun* (Baltimore, MD), October 23, 1914, 16.

Chased by Germans (All quotes from): "Liner Races to Port Pursued by Germans," *Pittsburgh Daily Post*, August 11, 1914, 7.

Sinking of Minnetonka: Jonathan Kinghorn, *The Atlantic Transport Line, 1881–1931* (Jefferson, NC: McFarland, 2012), 13.

EXPERIENCE WITH AMERICAN AMBULANCE:

(All quotes from)*: Wachtell, *Ellen La Motte*, 170–172, 176–78.

*"The trains of wounded soldiers"**: Wachtell, *Ellen La Motte*, 26.

PARIS:

*"I believe in millionaires"**: Wachtell, *Ellen La Motte*, 63.

HÔPITAL CHIRURGICAL MOBILE NO. 1:

In general: Wachtell, *Ellen La Motte*, 44.

*En Route to Dunkirk** (All quotes from): Wachtell, *Ellen La Motte*, 200.

Sightseeing Trip (All quotes from): Wachtell, *Ellen La Motte*, 200, 204–211.
Hospital Patients (All quotes from)*: Wachtell, *Ellen La Motte*, 212–215, 118–119.

REVIEWS OF BACKWASH:

"If we were to compile": "Ellen LaMotte's Stories Gripping, Gruesome, Great," *Los Angeles Times*, January 14, 1917, 14.

*"There is a corner"** ... *"Cut out words"*: Cynthia Wachtell, "Did a Censored Female Writer Inspire Hemingway's Famous Style?" *The Conversation*, April 2, 2019, accessed March 15, 2020, https://theconversation.com/did-a-censored-female-writer-inspire-hemingways-famous-style-113722.

BLAIR NILES'S WRITING STYLE:

"unadorned truth": Janet Mabic, "Philosophy for Exploration," *Christian Science Monitor*, September 4, 1935, WM3.

"It is only in travel": Book Review, "Vignettes of the African Colony of the Caribbean," *New York Times*, May 30, 1926, BR13.

NAACP AND SWG MEMBERS:

A. Z. Penn, *Rediscovering Pearl*, 1996, excerpt online at https://www.english.upenn.edu/Projects/Buck/preface.html.

Chapter 8: Birth of a Nation

OPENING QUOTE*:

Matthew Bernstein, *Controlling Hollywood: Censorship and Regulation in the Studio Era* (London: Black, 2000), 153, fn. 10.

BLAIR'S GRANDMOTHER:

Sara Agnes Rice Pryor, *Birth of a Nation: Jamestown 1607* (New York: Macmillan, 1907).

THE CLANSMAN:

Thomas Dixon, Jr., *The Clansman: An Historical Romance of the Ku Klux Klan* (New York: Grosset &Dunlap, 1905).

remove Black people: Andrew Leiter, "Thomas Dixon, Jr.: Conflicts in History and Literature, Documenting the American South," accessed March 15, 2020, https://docsouth.unc.edu/southlit/dixon_intro.html.

D. W. Griffith:

South had suffered trauma: Melvyn Stokes, *D. W. Griffith's* The Birth of a Nation: *A History of the Most Controversial Motion Picture of All Time* (Oxford: Oxford University Press, 2008), 21.

Adelene Moffat:

Conversations on Street (All quotes from)*: "The Teaching of History by Motion Pictures," *English Leaflet, The New England Association of Teachers of English* 15, no. 128 (June 1915), 11 (statement of Adelene Moffat).

CINEMATIC TECHNIQUES:

Birth of a Nation (1915), AMC Filmsite, accessed March 15, 2020, https://www.filmsite.org/birt.html.

"When a motion picture": David Rylance, "Breech Birth: The Receptions to D. W. Griffith's 'Birth of a Nation,'" *Australasian Journal of American Studies* 24, no. 2 (December 2005), 1–20, 3.

*"It makes you laugh"**: Rylance, "Breech Birth," 4.

"coming out of a thunderstorm": Stokes, *D. W. Griffith's* The Birth of a Nation, 3–4.

ADELENE'S VIEWS OF THE KKK:

*"a fear of Negro" ... "evil band of lynchers" ... "cloaked their mental"**: "Teaching of History," 11 (statement of Adelene Moffat).

CENSORSHIP:

The Massachusetts legislature: Rylance, "Breech Birth," 1, 6; Eric Olund, "Geography Written in Lightning: Race, Sexuality, and Regulatory Aesthetics in 'The Birth of a Nation,'" *Annals of the Association of American Geographers* 103:4 (July 2013), 927; Mark R. Schneider, *Boston Confronts Jim Crow 1890–1920* (Boston: Northeastern University Press, 1997), 149.

ADELENE'S TESTIMONY:

"I can see no way": "Teaching of History," 16.

*"It is a loathsome"**: "Fighting a Vicious Film: Protest against 'The Birth of a Nation'" (Boston: Boston Branch of the NAACP, 1915), 45.

JOHNSONS AND AKELEY:

"a documentary about wilderness": Johnson, *I Married Adventure*, 176.

$250,000: Palle B. Petterson, *Cameras into the Wild: A History of Early Wildlife and Expedition Filmmaking, 1895–1928* (Jefferson, NC: McFarland, 2011), 176.

*"A year and a half of intense experiences"**: Pascal Imperato and Eleanor Imperato, *They Married Adventure: The Wandering Lives of Martin & Osa Johnson* (New Brunswick, NJ: Rutgers University Press, 1992), 109.

"nothing more than objects": Greg Mittman, *Reel Nature: America's Romance with Wildlife on Film* (Seattle: University of Washington Press, 2009), 34.

"squared with the truth" ... "than any of the deliberate" ... "It is not so amusing" ... "deliberate misrepresentations"**: Blair Niles, "Travel Books and the Travel-Reading Public," *New York Herald*, January 24, 1926, E5.

"an immeasurable difference": Blair Niles, "'We, White Men,'" *New York Herald Tribune*, July 25, 1926, F9.

*"Art itself may" ... "in which the national"**: Niles, "Human Travel Books," F20.

ZONIA BABER:

In general: Janice Monk and Marcella Schmidt di Friedberg, "Mary Arizona (Zonia) Baber, Geographers," *Biobibliographical Studies* 30 (2015), 68.

Scene with Janitor: Thabiti Asukile, "Joel Augustus Rogers' Race Vindication: A Chicago Pullman Porter & the Making of the From Superman to Man (1917)," *Western Journal of Black Studies* 35, vol. 4 (2011), 280.

*"White Race retains its childish"**: Zonia Baber, "Lost Opportunities for Teaching Geography," *Journal of Geography* 14 (April 1916), 295.

*"As a young man"**: Charles Fred Hearns, "The Birth of a Nation: The Case for a Tri-Level Analysis of Forms of Racial Vindication," Dissertation, University of South Florida, 2014, 54.

SCENE FROM SUPERMAN TO MAN:

(All quotes from): J. A. Rogers, *From Superman to Man* (Boston: Goodspeed Press, 1917), 14–17.

"the finest bit of literature": Hubert Harrison, *A Hubert Harrison Reader* (Middletown, CT: Wesleyan University Press, 2001), 302.

erase prejudice: Asukile, "Joel Augustus Rogers' Race Vindication," 290.

Chapter 9: Wanted: A Chaperone

OPENING QUOTE:

Mary Jo Binker, *If You Ask Me: Essential Advice from Eleanor Roosevelt* (New York: Atria Books, 2018), 7.

TROPICAL RESEARCH STATION:

To Study Wild Life Near the Equator: "To Study Wild Life Near the Equator," *New York Times*, January 23, 1916, 95.

"where the same area": Gould, *Remarkable Life*, 188.

*"wilderness wonderlands"**: Blair Beebe and William Beebe, *Our Search for Wilderness* (New York: Henry Holt, 1910), 17–18.

"The night" ... "Rat Race"* (All quotes from)*: Beebe and Beebe, *Our Search*, 73.

Bedtime stories: Beebe and Beebe, *Our Search*, 83–84.

*"Whole entomological" ... "Suppose it were fish"**: Beebe and Beebe, *Our Search*, 79.

"Life is delightfully": Beebe and Beebe, *Our Search*, 28–29.

Hoatzins: Letter from William Beebe to Parents (February 26, 1909) (BU Box 82).

WILSHIRE:

James Colin Campbell, Henry Gaylord Wilshire, 2016, accessed June 6, 2019, https://www.jamescolincampbell.com/henry-gaylord-wilshire/.

"She was as straight as an arrow" ... "typical American" ... "I must say that to be": Edmund R. Taylor and Alexander Moore, eds., *Selected Letters of Anna Heywood Taylor, South Carolina Artist and World Traveler* (Columbia: University of South Carolina Press, 2010), 18.

ANNA HEYWARD TAYLOR:

*"There are no soft fuzzy"**: "Suzannah Smith Miles, Artist & Adventurer," *Charleston Magazine*, January 2019, accessed May 6, 2019, https://charlestonmag.com/features/artist_adventurer (quoting Tobias).

WILLIAM MERRITT CHASE:

*"Now, for the best news" ... "I was so busy" ... "If Sargent asked me"**: Taylor and Moore, *Selected Letters*, 29 (quoting July 14, 1904, letter).

GERTRUDE MATHEWS:

*"an extremely clever"**: Letter from Anna Heyward Taylor to Nell Taylor (January 31, 1916); Taylor and Moore, *Selected Letters*, 82.

*"charming irreverence" ... "she likes to see things"**: "Likes to See Things as She Sees Them," *Evening Sun*, (Baltimore, MD), May 23, 1935, 20.

BRITISH GUIANA EXPEDITION:

*"Our party"**: Letter from Anna Heyward Taylor to Nell Taylor (January 23, 1916).

"He is used to" ... "Inness told Rachel" ... "Mr. Beebe is quite"**: Letter from Anna Heyward Taylor to Nell Taylor (January 31, 1916).

ROOSEVELT LUNCH:

*"Roosevelt is a great friend" ... "I think that he is physically" ... "I have never seen people"**: Letter from Anna Heyward Taylor to Nell Taylor (March 3, 1916).

DEMERARA SWIZZLE:

Letter from Bertha Hayes to Anna Heyward Taylor (ca. July 18, 1916) (USC Taylor).

CHAPERONE QUESTION:

"The chaperone question": Letter from Anna Heyward Taylor to Nell Taylor (March 31, 1920).

*"because otherwise"**: Letter from William Beebe to Anna Heyward Taylor (ca. July 18, 1916) (USC Taylor).

"been telling such horrid" ... *"had done everything"*: Letter from Bertha Hayes to Anna Heyward Taylor (July 8, 1916); see also letter from William Beebe to Anna Heyward Taylor (July 3, 1916).

*"I can tell"**: Letter from William Beebe to Anna Heyward Taylor (September 22, 1916); letter from Gertrude Mathews to Anna Heyward Taylor (December 11, 1916).

*"Withers talked horribly"**: Taylor and Moore, *Selected Letters*, 109.

"It struck me": Letter from Gertrude Mathews to Anna Heyward Taylor (December 11, 1916).

"As for our living together": Letter from Will to Anna Heyward Taylor (December 27, 1916).

*"make everybody just as"**: Letter from Gertrude Mathews to Anna Heyward Taylor (March 22, 1917).

"Whatever Will's opinion" ... *"at least not"*: Letter from Gertrude Mathews to Anna Heyward Taylor (January 10, 1917).

cancellation of trip: Taylor and Moore, *Selected Letters*, 116 (quoting letter from Will to Anna Heyward Taylor [March 10, 1917]).

NEED FOR CHAPERONES:

*"Men set little store"** ... *"that three times"** ... *"To be 'talked about'"*: Cecil Porter, *Not without a Chaperone: Modes and Manners from 1897 to 1914* (Los Angeles: New English Library, 1972), 85–86 (quoting Mrs. C. E. Humphry).

"had to learn" ... *"At the very top of the list"* ... *"one of the boys"*: Cas Wouters, "Etiquette Books and Emotion Management in the 20th Century: Part Two—The Integration of the Sexes," *Journal of Social History* 29, no. 2 (1995), 325.

*"Much has been said"**: Emma Robinson-Tomsett, *Women, Travel and Identity: Journeys by Rail and Sea, 1870–1940* (Manchester, England: Manchester University Press, 2013), 87 (quoting Lilias Campbell-Davidson, *Hints to Lady Travellers at Home and Abroad* [1889], 63).

*"On no account permit"**: Robinson-Tomsett, *Women, Travel and Identity*, 81 (quoting A. Leone-Moat, *No Nice Girl Swears* [1933], 124–125).

"The other passengers": Robinson-Tomsett, *Women, Travel and Identity*, 82 (quoting A. Leone-Moat, 123).

"Danger and adventure" ... *"did not admit to any feeling"*: Laura Godsoe, "Exploring Their Boundaries: Gender and Citizenship in Women's Travel Writing, 1880–1914," *Journal of the Western Society for French History* 37 (2009), accessed March 15, 2020, https://quod.lib.umich.edu/w/wsfh/0642292.0037.015/—exploring-their-boundaries-gender-and-citizenship-in-womens?rgn=main;view=fulltext.

*"safeguard their respectability"**: Cynthia Enloe, *Bananas, Beaches and Bases, Making Feminist Sense of International Politics* (Berkeley: University of California Press, 2014), 52.

"because of their sexual": Willman, "Mimic-Women," 31 (quoting Susan Roberson).

sexually promiscuous: Willman, "Mimic-Women," 37, fn. 23.

RAINBOW BOA:

Ruth Rose, "How We Caught the Beautiful Rainbow Boa," *Buffalo Times*, September 21, 1924, 13.

While they waited: "Girls Battling Jungle Dine on Kin of U.S. Rats," *Daily News*, New York, July 22, 1924, 31.

BEEBE'S SWITCH TO OCEAN EXPLORATION:

Galapagos: Gould, *Remarkable Life*, 222–223; *Sargasso*: Gould, *Remarkable Life*, 241.

Darwin: Gould, *Remarkable Life*, 242.

Chapter 10: Too Many Girl Pictures

OPENING QUOTE*:

Nancy C. Cott, *A Woman Making History: Mary Ritter Beard through Her Letters* (New Haven, CT: Yale University Press, 1991), 19.

MISSING ARCTURUS:

Beebe Ship Silent: "Beebe Ship Silent 11 Days as Radio Calls to Her in Vain," *New York Times*, April 10, 1925, 1.

*"We are childishly"** ... *"tangled mass"*: J. F., "Mysteries of Sargasso," *New York Times*, December 7, 1924, 136.

"Some Alarm Expressed": "Beebe Ship Silent 11 Days," 1.

GLORIA CHILDHOOD AND COLLEGE:

"Dear me. Goodness" ... *"The tube won't work"**: Earl Sparling, "Sight Seeing under the Ocean," *Hartford Courant*, June 15, 1933, 23.

Connecticut College: "Service League Gives Refreshments for Freshman," *Connecticut College News* 9, no. 1 (October 5, 1923), 1.

"I find that 20 minutes": Letter from William Beebe to Gloria Hollister (July 7, 1923).

*"I was setting up"**: Gloria Hollister, "Birthday in the Ocean Depth" (1958) (SWG Hollister File).

ARCTURUS:

In general: William Beebe, *Galapagos, World's End* (Mineola, NY: Dover, 2012); William Beebe, *The Arcturus Adventure* (New York: Putnam, 1926).

"intrepid girl scientists"... "And were it further necessary": "Women Plan to Chart 'Port of Missing Ships,'" *The Republic* (Columbus, IN), November 22, 1924, 2.

GEORGE AND DOROTHY PUTNAM:

*"Oh dear girl"**: Sally Putman Chapman, *Whistled Like a Bird: The Untold Story of Dorothy Putnam, George Putnam, and Amelia Earhart* (New York: Grand Central, 2009), 35.

"Can't see how" ... *"I want you to come back"**: Chapman, *Whistled Like a Bird*, 36.

"independent, self-sufficient"... "I seem to have reached": Chapman, *Whistled Like a Bird*, 37.

ON BOARD SHIP WITH WOMEN:

*"fabulously courageous"**: Letter from George Putnam to William Beebe (May 20, 1925) (PU).

*"He was a severe task master"**: Tim Berra and William Beebe, *An Annotated Bibliography* (Hamden, CT: Archon Books, 1977), 17–18.

pirate party: Gould, *Remarkable Life*, 248.

$250,000: Michael S. Reidy, Gary R. Kroll, and Erik M. Conway, *Exploration and Science: Social Impact and Interaction* (Goleta, CA: ABC-CLIO, 2007), 194.

*"The expedition is not to be all"** ... *"Both scientifically and socially"**: "Scientists Will Spend Month on Mysterious Sargasso Sea," *Brooklyn Daily Eagle*, February 15, 1925, 38.

"Fancy dress costume parties": Mark Dion, Katherine McLeod, and Madeline Thompson, *Exploratory Works: Drawings from the Department of Tropical Research Field Expeditions* (New York: Drawing Center, 2017), 54.

*"While stocks have been shooting"**: R. L. Duffus, "Chasing Angel-Fish and Groupers with William Beebe," *New York Times*, March 27, 1932, BR4.

"was the multiplication" ... *"far-off places where romance"*: "Love or Life of Adventure," *Philadelphia Inquirer*, February 21, 1926, 125.

"I expect we will all": Letter from George Putnam to William Beebe (March 17, 1925) (PU).

TOO MANY GIRL PICTURES:

*"I reckon he means the pictures"**: Letter from George Putnam to William Beebe (March 17, 1925) (PU).

*"There practically wasn't a woman"**: Letter from George Putnam to William Beebe (ca. April 1925) (PU).

"Grass": Telegram from George Putnam to William Beebe (April 17, 1925) (PU).

*"ship off alone" ... "I don't blame you"**: Letter from George Putnam to William Beebe (May 20, 1925) (PU).

"pulled [him] out of his graduate *work"*: Letter from William Beebe to Mr. Thomas (October 31, 1950) (PU) (author's emphasis).

*"In the first place"** ... *"that the women"*: Letter from William Beebe to George Putnam (May 20, 1925) (PU).

"women are not noted": Welker, *Natural Man*, 141.

"something of a gentlemanly delusion": Welker, *Natural Man*, 143.

ARCTURUS IS FOUND:

"Beebe Ship Is Safe, Says Relayed Message," *Ashbury Press*, April 11, 1925, 1; "Beebe Discovers Two New Volcanoes Erupting Magnificently in Galapagos, and Big Tide Rip Teaming with Sea Life," *New York Times*, April 17, 1925, 1.

GLORIA'S TRIP TO BRITISH GUIANA:

*"Please, Gloria Hollister"**: Letter from William Beebe to Gloria Hollister (January 5, 1926).

*"a society woman"** ... *"I jumped"**: Gloria Hollister, "I Couldn't Help It" (1933) (SWG Hollister File).

Guacharo bird: "Alumna Lectures at Conn. College on Her Jungle Exploration," *Hartford Daily Courant*, February 23, 1928, 12.

GLORIA READS ARCTURUS BOOK:

*"I am floating in mid-space"** ... *"I am twenty feet underwater"**: William Beebe, *The Arcturus Adventure* (New York: Putnam, 1926), 3, 71.

BEEBE OFFERS GLORIA JOB:

He promised to give her: Helen Welshimer, "Girl Explorer Extends Woman's World to Ocean Bottom and Jungle Depths," *Longview Daily News* (Longview, TX), July 12, 1936, 16.

"Dr. Beebe speaking" ... "Want it?": Marjorie Hessell Tiltman, *Women in Modern Adventure* (London: Harrap, 1935), 118.

"the answer to a maiden's prayer": Hollister, "Birthday in the Ocean Depth," 4.

GLORIA DIVING EXPERIENCES:

electric toy pop-gun: "Going Down!" *Miami News*, August 1, 1929, 4.

"It feels like a feather underwater": "Tells of Adventures at Bottom of Sea," *St. Louis Post-Dispatch*, March 15, 1932, 15.

Helmet malfunction: "Underwater Experiences Related by Miss Hollister," April 1935 (SWG, Hollister file).

GLORIA AND BEEBE RELATIONSHIP:

"I kissed Gloria": Gould, *Remarkable Life*, 279.

"Truth to tell": Charlotte Hubbard Prescott, "Book Chat," *Sioux City Journal*, October 12, 1927, 7.

Report of Discord: "Report of Discord in Beebe Family 'Utter Rot,' Des Moines Woman Says," *Des Moines Tribune* (August 12, 1929), 13.

FISH SKELETONS:

(All quotes from): Gloria Hollister, "Fish Magic," *Bulletin of New York Zoological Society* 33, no. 2 (1930), 72–73, 75.

BATHYSPHERE:

In general: National Broadcast Corp., "First Broadcast Transcript," 16 (PU Box 17, Folder 3); William Beebe, *Half Mile Down* (New York: Harcourt, Brace, 1934).

"It won't work.": Brad Matsen, *Descent: The Heroic Discovery of the Abyss* (New York: Vintage, 2006), 11.

"Another gadget!": Otis Barton, *The World Beneath the Sea* (New York: Crowell, 1957), 13.

Roosevelt and Bathysphere: Beebe, *Half Mile Down*, 90–91.

"ungainly ball": Barton, *World Beneath the Sea*, 27.

Bathysphere Dives:

In general: Department of Tropical Research, "Members of the B.O.E. Assisting Dives of Bathysphere," n.d. (PU Beebe Collection, Box 17, Folder 3); Department of Tropical Research, "Dives in Bathysphere," circa 1932 (PU Beebe Collection, Box 17, Folder 3).

Beebe and Barton Descent Scene Is Based on: William Beebe, *Half Mile Down* (Harcourt, Brace, 1934), chap. 6; Barton, *World Beneath the Sea*, chap. 3; "First Broadcast Transcript"; Bradford Matsen, *The Incredible Record-Setting Deep-Sea Dive of the Bathysphere* (New York: Enslow, 2003), 12; Gavin Souter, "He Went a Half Mile Down into the Sea," *Sydney Morning Herald*, May 20, 1961, 12; "Stark Drama of Oceans Abysmal Depths," *Vancouver Sun*, October 6, 1932, 7; Jon Forrest Dohlin, "Commemorating a Milestone in Ocean Exploration," *National Geographic Magazine*, August 15, 2014, accessed March 15, 2020, https://blog.nationalgeographic.org/2014/08/15/commemorating-a-milestone-in-ocean-exploration/; Bryan Cornell, "The Waters Were Boiling with Light," Library of Congress Blog, January 22, 2015, accessed March 15, 2020, https://blogs.loc.gov/now-see-hear/2015/01/the-waters-were-boiling-with-light/; "Leaks Stop Record Dive," *Indianapolis Star*, September 23, 1932, 1, 3; "1932 NBC Underwater Broadcast from Bermuda," Bernews, January 19, 2014, accessed March 15, 2020, http://bernews.com/2014/01/nbcs-underwater-broadcast-from-bermuda/; Van Couver, "Weird Lighted Fish Eye Him in Black Depths," *Des-Moines Register*, September 23, 1932, 1; William Grimes, "Crammed into a Steel Ball, Headed into the Inky Dark," *New York Times*, April 22, 2005, accessed March 15, 2020, https://www.nytimes.com/2005/04/22/books/crammed-into-a-steel-ball-headed-into-the-inky-dark.html; Dion et al., *Exploratory Works*.

Gloria in Bathysphere:

*"I had forgotten" ... "I was far too interested"**: Hollister, "Birthday in the Ocean Depth."

JOCELYN CRANE:

"From her solitary childhood": Gould, *Remarkable Life*, 295–296.

"I had to work like blazes": Edna Yost, *Women of Modern Science* (Dodd, Mead, 1964), 112; *sizable donation*: Gould, *Remarkable Life*, 295–296.

"alpha female": Matsen, *Descent*, 246.

Will's Infatuation with Jocelyn Crane: Gould, *Remarkable Life*, 316.

WOMEN ASSISTANTS:

"I am after adaptable scientific" ... "Both young women have sleek": "400 Women Sought Romance So Beebe Rejected Them," *Des Moines Register*, May 3, 1932, 16.

"Will was one of the first": Maria Louise Calavincenzo, "William Beebe: 'Softening Facts with Quiet Meditation,'" Dissertation, Princeton University, 1998, 100.

"In the interest of science": Telegram from "Gypsy Rose Lee" to Gloria Hollister (ca. 1934) reproduced in Kristen Moore, "Trail Blazing for Women Scientists: Gloria Hollister Anable's Papers," Wild Things, the Blog of the Wildlife Conservation Society Archives, September 9, 2014, accessed February 21, 2020, http://www.wcsarchivesblog.org/trail-blazing-for-women-scientists-gloria-hollister-anables-papers/.

ELSE BOSTELMANN:

In general: Edith Widder, "The Fine Art of Exploration," *Oceanography* 29, no. 4 (2016), 170.

"there was no red": Else Bostelmann. "Notes from an Undersea Studio," in Dion et al., *Exploratory Works*, 127.

"Doctor Beebe would not take me": Widder, "Fine Art of Exploration," 70, 180.

*"Possibly I did swallow" … "a fairyland"**: Bostelmann, "Notes from an Undersea Studio," 126–127.

"After I descended": Bostelmann, "Notes from an Undersea Studio," 128.

"artistic huddle" … "brain fish" … "Little by little": Widder, *Fine Art of Exploration*, 170, 175; See also: Beebe, *Half Mile Down*, 213.

"viewed marine life" … "antennae are forever protruding": Natascha Adamowsky, *The Mysterious Science of the Sea, 1775–1943* (Abington, England: Routledge, 2015), 163–164.

"Else Bostelmann gave her best": Beebe, *Half Mile Down*, 228.

ATTACKS ON BEEBE:

"What Mr. Beebe saw" … Carl L. Hubb: Richard Ellis, *Singing Whales and Flying Squid: The Discovery of Marine Life* (Guilford, CT: Rowman & Littlefield, 2006), 41.

"His description sounds a little fishy": Ab Kent, "We Were Too Cautious—Pioneer Sea Explorer," *Times Colonist* (Victoria, British Columbia), December 13, 1986, 3.

STENOGRAPHER:

Carol Bird, "Which Is More Dangerous—Shark or Boa Constrictor?" *Nebraska State Journal (Lincoln, NE)*, December 20, 1936, 42.

IMPERIALISM:

"a colonized country" … "The field stations Beebe" .. "intellectual and physical": McLeod, "Beyond the Biological," 8.

Chapter 11: Imprisoned by Whiteness

OPENING QUOTE*:

Blair Niles, *Black Haiti* (New York: Putnam, 1926).

PINK APARTMENT:

Apartment Interior: Deshin, "Adventuring with a Woman Explorer," E1, E6.

"a flash": Fitzgerald, "Women *Now* Become Geographers," 81.

DISCUSSION IN ELEVATOR:

"When I was in Haiti": Niles, *Black Haiti*, 4.

*"My Captain"**: Niles, *Black Haiti*, 5.

READING BOY:

(All quotes from, except as otherwise noted)*: Niles, *Black Haiti*, 9–11.

*"branded on her heart"**: Niles, *Black Haiti*, 14.

BLAIR'S THOUGHTS ON HAITI:

"The white face": Blair Niles, "Haiti Laughs but Knows Drab Poverty," *New York Times*, December 22, 1929, SM 1.

*"My plan"**: Letter from Gordon Rice to Franklina Bartlett (February 8, 1891).

"many standards of beauty": Blair Niles, "Setting Up an Easel in Papua," *New York Herald Tribune*, December 12, 1926, F23.

*"Race memories"**: Niles, *Black Haiti*, 182.

*Dumas story**: Niles, *Black Haiti*, 37–38.

"Haitians have little regard": Fitzgerald, "Women *Now* Become Geographers," 81.

TOUSSAINT LOUVERTURE AND THE REVOLUTION:

In general: Charles Forsdick and Christian Høgsberg, *Toussaint Louverture, A Black Jacobin in the Age of Revolutions* (London: Pluto Press, 2017), chap. 2; H. P. Davis, *Black Democracy: The Story of Haiti* (Toronto: Dial Press, 1928), 23–51.

"What is mine too": Forsdick and Høgsberg, *Toussaint Louverture*, 1.

*"gloried in the tradition"**: Niles, *Black Haiti*, 193.

BLACK HAITI REVIEWS:

"Blair Niles has not shirked" … "a member of the black": Fitzgerald, "Women *Now* Become Geographers," 81.

Mary White Ovington: Mary White Ovington, "Book Chat, 'Black Haiti,'" *New York Amsterdam News*, September 1, 1926.

Langston Hughes: Langston Hughes, "'Magic Island' of Haiti Is a Wonderful Prize for Defenders of Contest Winners," *Chicago Defender*, April 29, 1950, 6.

WILPF: Mary A. Renda, *Taking Haiti: Military Occupation and the Culture of U.S. Imperialism* (Chapel Hill: University of North Carolina Press, 2001), 66.

ZONIA BABER:

*"the second oldest" … "Marines installed a puppet president"**: Renda, *Taking Haiti*, 1.

"There was almost nothing" … "imperialist": Kristen E. Gwinn, *Emily Greene Balch: The Long Road to Internationalism* (Chicago: University of Illinois Press, 2010), 138.

"There are more ways": Gwinn, *Emily Greene Balch*, 140.

FRENCH GUIANA:

"Passengers for Eternity Board the Martinière": Blair Niles, "The Land of the 'Dry Guillotine,'" *New York Times*, July 3, 1927, SM1.

*"to know what lay"**: Blair Niles, *Condemned to Devil's Island* (New York: Grosset & Dunlap, 1928), xiii.

"Let's go to French Guiana!"… "All right!" … Henri Joseph Thaly: Deshin, "Adventuring with a Woman Explorer," E1.

Doublage: Alexander Miles, *Devil's Island: Colony of the Damned* (Berkeley, CA: Tenspeed Press, 1988), 40–41.

"startling contrast" … "the drama": Niles, *Condemned to Devil's Island*, xiii.

Chapter 12: Condemned to Devil's Island

OPENING QUOTE:

Perch Hutchinson, "Living Dead Men on Devil's Island," *New York Times*, May 13, 1928, Sec. 4, 6.

AT THE DOCK:

Martiniere: "Yarns of a Woman Explorer," *Santa Ana Register*, May 6, 1928, 25.

"flaming bars": Guy Forshey, "Devil's Island; The 'Dry Guillotine,'" *St. Louis Dispatch*, May 2, 1926, SM4.

"town's great": Miles, *Devil's Island*, 50.

Former Dutch: Miles, *Devil's Island*, 3.

*"look like fashion plates" … "the Paris mode"**: Niles, "The Land of the 'Dry Guillotine,'" SM1.

grand voyage … spelled doom: Minott Saunders, "Grand Voyage Spells Doom for Frenchmen on Way to Devil's Island," *News-Herald* (Franklin, PA), December 14, 1929, 13.

"They are entering a world": Niles, "The Land of the 'Dry Guillotine,'" SM1.

Prison Ship: Carl De Vidal Hunt, "Back to the Living Death He Once Escaped," *Courier-Journal* (Louisville, KY), May 16, 1928, SM4; Miles, *Devil's Island*, 47–48.

"bench of justice" ... "hot cell": René Belbenoît, *Prisoner No. 46635, Dry Guillotine: Fifteen Years amongst the Living Dead* (New York: Blue Ribbon Books, 1937), 44.

*"pipes from the steamer's"**: "Scalding Steam Quells Outbreak," *Oakland Tribune*, March 31, 1926, 3.

"occasionally a Spanish": Niles, "The Land of the 'Dry Guillotine,'" SM1.

forts-à-bras: Belbenoît, *Dry Guillotine*, 45–46.

"They look like gray rats"... "blinking in the strong" ... "But they know" ... "March!": Niles, "'Dry Guillotine,'" SM1.

CAMP DE LA TRANSPORTATION:

"You have arrived here": Miles, *Devil's Island*, 51.

*"the men's bodies" ... "He is no longer a man" ... "It is as though"**: Niles, *Condemned to Devil's Island*, 44.

*"one branch" ... "with apparently no thought" ... "it is as though"**: W. E. Allison-Booth, *Devil's Island: Revelations of the French Penal Settlements* (New York: Putnam, 1931), 59.

"Soon, each prisoner will understand": Niles, "The Land of the 'Dry Guillotine,'" SM2.

TYPES OF PRISONERS AND SENTENCES:

"imprisonment in French Guiana": Niles, "The Land of the 'Dry Guillotine,'" SM1.

"The question is whether": Miles, *Devil's Island*, 84 (quoting Albert Londres).

THE ISLANDS:

"lay like green leaves": Blair Niles, "On the Isle That Is World's End," *New York Times*, July 10, 1927, SM1.

In General: Frances LaGrange, *Flag on Devil's Island: The Autobiography of One of the Great Counterfeiters and Art Forgers of Modern Times* (New York: Doubleday, 1961), 144; Stephen A. Toth, *Beyond Papillon: The French Overseas Penal Colonies 1854–1952* (Lincoln: University of Nebraska Press, 2006), 12–14.

"Dans cet endroit": Belbenoît, *Dry Guillotine*, 155.

DEVIL'S ISLAND:

Niles' Boat Ride to Devil's Island (All quotes from except as noted): Niles, "On the Isle That Is World's End," SM1.

"I could think of more aesthetic": Gladys Baker, "She Dared to Visit Devil's Island," *Birmingham News*, October 23, 1932, 43.

DREYFUS AND VISIT TO CABIN:

In general: Kathryn Blaine Trittipo, "A Visual Affair: Popular Culture and L'Affaire Dreyfus," Dissertation, University of Minnesota, 2016.

"aristocrats of the condemned" ... "When Dreyfus was imprisoned" ... "It was as if he sat" ... "They remind me of Jack-in-the-Boxes": Niles, "On the Isle That Is World's End," SM1.

FICTIONAL BIOGRAPHY:

"It does not seem to me important": Niles, *Condemned to Devil's Island*, xi.

BELBENOÎT:

Escapes: Belbenoit, *Dry Guillotine*, passim.

"But there is appeal"... "In his gallant": Niles, *Condemned to Devil's Island*, xi.

"How much" ..."Whatever you" ... "Come again": Belbenoit, *Dry Guillotine*, 190.

"Ah, now that" ... "That may not be said of any soul" ... "may look into": Niles, *Condemned to Devil's Island*, xiii.

DEBUNKING OF CHARRIÈRE AS PAPILLON:

"Far from being one": John Weightman, "Moth Myth," *New York Review of Books*, October 8, 1970, accessed September 27, 2019, https://www.nybooks.com/articles/1970/10/08/moth-myth/.

"Only about 10 percent": "Small-Time Paris Thief Writes a Bestseller," *Boca Raton News*, November 5, 1970, 6A.

"Few people realize": Blair Niles, "First Woman to Set Foot on Devil's Island Returns to Tell Remarkable Story," *Winnipeg Tribune*, May 12, 1928, 29.

BLAIR'S JUNGLE TRIP:

"Try me," … "there is no nonsense" … "As among the Negroes of Haiti": Blair Niles, *Introduction*, in Morton C. Kahn, *Djuka: The Bush Negroes of Dutch Guiana* (New York: Viking Press, 1931), xi.

"Nous sommes vos ami": "The Reading Lamp," *South Bend Tribune*, February 16, 1930, 13.

"We glided along often lying" …"We took few precautions": Niles, "First Woman to Set Foot on Devil's Island."

*"The jungle is perpetually vigilant" … "There are its armies of fire-ants" … "The lush beauty"**: Blair Niles, "The Drama of Guiana, Real and Unreal" *New York Times*, August 7, 1927, SM4.

HOMOSEXUALITY:

"It is not possible to write": Peter Redfield, *Space in the Tropics: From Convicts to Rockets in French Guiana* (Berkeley: University of California Press, 2000), 96.

REVIEWS OF CONDEMNED:

"amazing. Not to be duplicated": Perch Hutchinson, "Living Dead Men on Devil's Island," *New York Times*, May 13, 1928, 4:6.

*"poignant study of the cruelty"**: Fredrick O'Brien, "Any Prison Is Hell," *Saturday Review of Books*, June 23, 1928, 983.

chicken wire: Irving Cobb, "Human Being Is Hard to Explore," *Battle Creek Enquirer*, Battle Creek, MI, June 10, 1934, 8.

BLAIR'S FAME:

"Mrs. Niles is probably" … Book Has Influence: "Book Has Influence," *News Journal* (Wilmington, DE), March 30, 1929, 7.

"powerfully realistic novel": "Previews and Reviews of Books and Bookmen," *Carion-Ledger* (Jackson, MS), February 9, 1930, 5.

"The Colossal! The Moving!": "Blair Niles Goes Traveling," *Lawrence Daily Journal World*, August 1, 1931, 4.

sunbathed: Alta May Coleman, "Erich Remarque Gets $120,000 for Next Book," *Chicago Tribune*, June 7, 1930, 12.

returned home by airplane … agitated for female Cabinet Member: Walter Trumbull, "Lights of New York," *Valley Morning Star* (Harlingen, TX), November 27, 1932, 4.

CLOSURE OF PRISON:

Washington Post: "Abolishing Devil's Island," *Washington Post*, August 22, 1955, 6.

"a land of death": Toth, *Beyond Papillon*, 151.

Chapter 13: Gay Harlem

OPENING QUOTE:

Gladys Baker, "She Dared to Visit Devil's Island," *Birmingham News*, October 23, 1932, 43.

A'LELIA WALKER'S PARTY AND CARL VAN VECHTEN:

In general: Carl Van Vechten and Bruce Kellner, *The Splendid Drunken Twenties: Selections from the Day Books 1922–1930* (Champaign: University of Illinois Press, 2003), 271, 283, 301.

"the undisputed downtown authority": Nathan Irvin Huggins, *Voices from the Harlem Renaissance* (Oxford: Oxford University Press, 1975), 100.

"Pettit frequented the homosexual": Eric Garber, "A Spectacle in Color; The Lesbian and Gay Subculture of Jazz Age Harlem," in Martin B. Duberman, Martha Vincinus, and George Chauncey, *Hidden from History: Reclaiming the Gay and Lesbian Past* (New York: Meridian, 1989), 318.

LELAND PETTIT AND COUNTEE CULLEN:

In general: Alden Reimonenq, "Countee Cullen's Uranian 'Soul Windows,'" in Alden Reimonenq and Emmanuel S. Nelson, *Critical Essays: Gay and Lesbian Writers of Color* (Minneapolis: Haworth Press, 1983); Countee Cullen, "Colors" in Gerald Early, *My Soul's High Song: The Collected Writings of Countee Cullen, Voice of the Harlem Renaissance* (New York: Doubleday, 1990).

Atheneum in Milwaukee: Patrick Vaz, "The Reverberate Hills; or The Apotheosis of the Narwhal, Poem of the Week 2016/3," accessed March 18, 2019, http://reverberatehills.blogspot.com/2016/01/poem-of-week-20163.html.

"insignificance of color": Reimonenq, "Countee Cullen's Uranian 'Soul Windows,'" 156–157.

negrotarian: Valerie Boyd, "Enter the Negrotarians," *Scholar and Feminist* 3:2 (Barnard Center for Research on Women, Winter 2005), accessed March 16, 2020, http://sfonline.barnard.edu/hurston/printvbo.htm.

"indelible conservative": Wallace Thurman, *Infants of the Spring* (Lebanon, NH: University Press of New England, 2012), 27.

"He became a white hope": Thurman, *Infants of the Spring*, 30.

DuBois Wedding: Jacqueline C. Jones, "Cullen-DuBois Wedding," in Cary D. Wintz, *Paul Finkelman, Encyclopedia of the Harlem Renaissance: A–J* (Philadelphia, PA: Taylor & Francis, 2004), 273.

Separation and Divorce: Venetria K. Patton and Maureen Honey, *Double-Take: A Revisionist Harlem Renaissance Anthology* (New Brunswick, NJ: Rutgers University Press, 2001), 554; Charles Molesworth, "Countee Cullen's Reputation: The Forms of Desire," *Transition* 107 (2012), 70; Jones, "Cullen-DuBois Wedding," 273.

*"There is a rumor in Harlem"**: Countee Cullen, *Collected Poems* (New York: Library of America, 2013), fn. 67.6 (quoting Letter from Harold Jackman to Countee Cullen [September 20, 1929]).

HARLEM:

"Everyone rushed": Martha Gever, *Entertaining Lesbians: Celebrity, Sexuality, and Self-Invention* (London: Psychology Press, 2003), 125 (quoting Mercedes de Acosta).

"I am actually stared at": Rudolph Fisher, "The Caucasian Storms Harlem," in Nathan Irvin Huggins, *Voices from the Harlem Renaissance* (Oxford: Oxford University Press, 1975), 78.

"smack of 'sexual colonialism'": Lillian Faderman, *Odd Girls and Twilight Lovers: A History of Lesbian Life in Twentieth-Century America* (New York: Columbia University Press, 2011), 68.

"Harlem nights": Langston Hughes, "The Big Sea," in Nathan Huggins, *Voices from the Harlem Renaissance*, 371.

"the epitome": Faderman, *Odd Girls and Twilight Lovers*, 68.

"stigmatized white groups": Kevin J. Mumford, "Homosex Changes," in Lucy Maddox, *Locating American Studies: The Evolution of a Discipline* (Baltimore, MD: Johns Hopkins University Press, 1999), 399.

"would have made a twenty-five":* Eric Garber, "A Spectacle in Color; The Lesbian and Gay Subculture of Jazz Age Harlem," in Duberman et al., *Hidden from History*, 318.

INTUITING GAY:

"developed a highly sophisticated": David Shneer and Caryn Aviv, *American Queer, Now and Then* (London: Routledge, 2015), Introduction.

*"How on earth"**: Blair Niles, *Strange Brother* (New York: Liveright, 1931), 199.

"undefinable something" Niles, *Strange Brother*, 220.

"Of course they had not": Duberman et al., *Hidden from History*, 327.

Queer: SWG, 1920 Annual Bulletin, 10 (SWG).

"I can be myself there": Niles, *Strange Brother*, 70.

BOOK REVIEWS OF STRANGE BROTHER:

"a panorama of abnormality": Anthony Slide, *Lost Gay Novels: A Reference Guide to Fifty Works from the First Half of the Twentieth Century* (New York: Routledge, 2013), 140.

"Blair Niles is a woman": J. T. G., "A Tragedy of Innocence," *Cincinnati Enquirer*, August 15, 1931, 7.

"It is a delicate theme" ... "Probably this book will titillate" ... "is not so much": Bruce Catton, "Book Survey," *Newark Advocate* (Newark, OH), August 15, 1931, 4.

Retailers had difficulty ... "borders between black": Kevin Mumford, "Homosex Changes: Race, Cultural Geography, and the Emergence of the Gay," *American Quarterly* 48, no. 3 (September 1996), 396.

"as a monument of good reporting": Slide, *Lost Gay Novels*, 140.

"a novel of historical": Lisa Walker, *Looking Like What You Are: Sexual Style, Race, and Lesbian Identity* (New York: New York University Press, 2001), 59.

NOTIONS ABOUT COLOR:

"dual ideologies": Patrick Brantlinger, *Dark Vanishings: Discourse on the Extinction of Primitive Races, 1800–1930* (Ithaca, NY: Cornell University Press, 2003), 1.

"The work of recording" ... "I feared": Brian Hochman, *Savage Preservation: The Ethnographic Origins of Modern Media Technology* (Minneapolis: University of Minnesota Press, 2014), 115–116.

FRANCES DENSMORE:

2,400 Indian songs: Frances Densmore (1867–1957), Smithsonian Institution Archives, 2005, accessed March 16, 2020, http://siarchives.si.edu/research/sciservwomendensmore.html.

Chapter 14: Races of Mankind

OPENING QUOTE:

Margaret Mead, "Coming of Age as a Woman in Popular Anthropology," June 1967, accessed December 14, 2019, http://www.mit.edu/~saleem/ivory/ch10.htm.

WORKING WITH RODIN:

(All quotes from): Malvina Hoffman, *Heads and Tales in Many Lands* (New York: Scribner, 1936), 15, 34–36; Didi Hoffman, *Beautiful Bodies: The Adventures of Malvina Hoffman* (Meadville, PA: Fulton Books, 2018), chap. 1.

"The first thing" ... "What a serious"**: Hoffman, *Heads and Tales in Many Lands*, 45–46.

"Sculpture is definitely": Virginia Irwin, "Heavy Worker, Refuses to Slow Down," *St. Louis Times-Dispatch*, April 14, 1948, 3C.

"To begin with": Linda Kim, "A Woman Sculptor among the Primitive Races: Gender and Sculpture in the 1930s," *Frontiers: A Journal of Women Studies* 35, no.2 (2014), 86–117 (quoting "Woman Sculptor's 12-Hour Day, Hard Work with Chisel in Workmen's Overalls, Bush House Figures," *Daily Chronicle*, July 28, 1926).

he locked the studio door: Hoffman, *Beautiful Bodies*, loc. 720.

ANATOMY CLASS:

(All quotes from, except as otherwise noted): Hoffman, *Heads and Tales in Many Lands*, 42.

Soon she was dragging: Gertrude E. Dole, *Vignettes of Some Early Members of the Society of Woman Geographers in New York* (New York: SWG, 1978), 10.

RACES OF MANKIND:

*"Have proposition to make"**: Hoffman, *Beautiful Bodies*, loc. 2033.

"Sudden vistas": Hoffman, *Heads and Tales in Many Lands*, 15.

"preserve vanishing": Tracy Teslow, *Constructing Race* (Cambridge, England: Cambridge University Press, 2014), 83.

race as hierarchical: Teslow, *Constructing Race*, 88.

"own images": Teslow, *Constructing Race*, 84.

*"race prejudice"** ... *"leave with their"* ... *"referred to the physical traits"**: Henry Field, *The Races of Man* (Chicago: Field Museum, 1933), 8.

"Armenians, Arabs": Teslow, *Constructing Race*, 100.

Malvina's First Day of Negotiation with Field (All quotes from): Hoffman, *Heads and Tales*, 16–18.

Second Day of Malvina's Negotiation with Field (All quotes from, except as otherwise noted): Hoffman, *Heads and Tales*, 16–18.

"a six-figure sum" ... *"cut out some"*: Teslow, *Constructing Race*, 124.

"It was the most ever paid": Hoffman, *Beautiful Bodies*, loc. 2085.

"Half the battle" ... *"Then .I chose the moment"* ... *"To register"*: Hoffman, *Heads and Tales*, 20.

Surfer: Hoffman, *Heads and Tales*, 13.

*"If Miss Hoffman wants"**: Linda Kim, *Race Experts: Sculpture, Anthropology, and the American Public in Malvina Hoffman's Races of Mankind* (Lincoln: University of Nebraska, 2018), loc. 971 (quoting letter from Stanley Field to Charles Simms [April 15, 1930]).

"concert pitch": Hoffman, *Heads and Tales*, 122.

"traveling around the world" ... *"peephole into reality"*: Teslow, *Constructing Race*, 122.

*"a scientific expedition"** ... *"under the guidance"*: "Sculptor to Tour World for Science," *New York Times*, September 12, 1931, 5.

"nipped at her heels": Hoffman, *Beautiful Bodies*, loc. 2065.

RACES OF MANKIND EXHIBIT:

Race classifications: Teslow, *Constructing Race*, 115, fn. 1.

"in a thick flexible rubber": Hoffman, *Heads and Tales*, 155.

Arthur Keith: Hoffman, *Beautiful Bodies*, loc. 3045.

"We are all anthropologists": Field, *Races of Man*, Introduction, 8.

*"the average man in the street"**: Kim, *Race Experts*, loc. 1128 (quoting Ralph Bunce, *A World View of Race*, 4).

"more and more fixed and crystallized": Kim, *Race Experts*, loc. 1174.

*"It was a miracle"**: Hoffman, *Heads and Tales*, 122.

"a first attempt": "Hawaiian Types to Have Place in Field Museum Hall of Living Man," *Honolulu-Star-Bulletin*, September 30, 1931, 1.

CRITICISMS OF EXHIBIT:

"a unique plan of combining": Teslow, *Constructing Race*, 132–133.

"physical traits" ... *"the total complex"*: Field, *Races of Man*, 6.

"One does not know": Helen Appleton Read, "Portraits," *Brooklyn Daily Eagle*, January 21, 1934, 30.

"Museum patrons could examine": Teslow, *Constructing Race*, 122.

an embarrassment: Kim, *Race Experts*, conclusion, loc. 4403.

*"full of consistent and glaring inaccuracies"** ... *"white pseudo-anthropology"*: Teslow, *Constructing Race*, 339.

"to promote the humanism": Marianne Kinkle, *Races of Mankind: The Sculptures of Malvina Hoffman* (Champaign: University of Illinois Press, 2011), 192.

"the primitive instinct": Hoffman, *Beautiful Bodies*, loc 3531.

"You have shown": Kim, *Race Experts*, loc. 531.

Chapter 15: Only a Passenger

OPENING QUOTE:

Jo Woolf, *The Great Horizon—50 Tales of Exploration*, (n.d.), accessed rsgsexplorers.com.

CAPTAIN RAILEY:

Scene at Settlement House (All quotes from, except as otherwise noted)*: Amelia Earhart, *The Fun of It* (Chicago: Academy Chicago Publishers, 1984), 58–59, 144.

"right sort of girl": Paul L. Briand, Jr., *Daughter of the Sky: The Story of Amelia Earhart* (New York: Duell, Sloan and Pearce, 1960), xiv.

"a pilot, well educated;": Anne Herrmann, *Queering the Moderns: Poses/Portraits/Performances* (London: Palgrave, 2000), 21.

Amelia would have to negotiate: Amelia Earhart, *20 Hrs, 40 Mins: Our Flight in the Friendship* (New York: G.P Putnam's Sons, 1928), 99.

INTERVIEWS FOR THE FRIENDSHIP FLIGHT:

"When I first met Mr. Putnam": Briand, Daughter of the Sky, xv

"sore as a wet": Chapman, Whistled Like a Bird, 99.

compensation: Earhart, *Fun of It*.

statistics: Earhart, *Fun of It*, 63.

EARLIER ATTEMPTS:

Princess Lowenstein-Wertheim: "Two More Women Plan Atlantic Flight," *Times* (Muncie, IN), September 3, 1927, 1.

"I don't believe in rushing": "Another Woman Plans Transatlantic Flight; Has Amphibian Built," *Intelligencer Journal* (Lancaster, PA), September 16, 1927, 3.

"Flying Matron": "Flying Matron Ready for Hop to Maine Today," *Daily News*, New York, October 8, 1927, 100.

"I've been dreaming": "At L. I. Field for Sea Hop; Undaunted by Tragedies," *Brooklyn Daily Eagle*, September 15, 1927, 1.

Ruth Elder's Flight: "Elder Plane Raced Death for Five Hours with Its Oil Line Broken," *Brooklyn Daily Eagle*, October 14, 1927, 1.

Frances Grayson's Flight: "Mrs. Grayson's Plane Is Forced Back 15 Minutes after Hopoff for Europe; Flight Is Postponed for Tomorrow," *Brooklyn Daily Eagle*, October 17, 1927, 1; "Outstanding News and Pictures of 1927," *Daily News*, New York, January 1, 1928, 198.

Lilli Dillenz and Elsie Mackay: "Few Women Flyers Escape Neptune's Clutches," *Star-Gazette* (Elmira, NY), January 16, 1931, 5.

Mildred Doran: "Girl Flyer, Others Not Found," *News-Palladium* (Benton Harbor, ME), August 19, 1927, 1.

AMELIA'S DECISION TO FLY:

"This is the way": Briand, *Daughter of the Sky*, xv.

NEED FOR SECRECY:

"submerged in a deluge": John Burke, *Amelia Earhart: Flying Solo* (New York: Sterling, 2007), 39.

"Even tho' I have lost": Chapman, *Whistled Like a Bird*, 99 (quoting letter from Amelia Earhart to her mother dated May 20, 1928).

DOROTHY AND AMELIA:

"What nerve, courage, intelligence": Chapman, *Whistled Like a Bird*, 93.

"How does this astonishing": Chapman, *Whistled Like a Bird*, 95.

END OF FLIGHT:

Railey and Earhart Conversation (All quotes from)*: Capt. Hilton H. Railey, "Victim of the Hero Racket," *Hartford Courant*, September 18, 1938, 59.

*"hard, calculating glance"** ... *"had a knack for showmanship"**: Mary S. Lovell, *The Sound of Wings: The Life of Amelia Earhart* (New York: St. Martin's Press, 2014), 78.

"The sky was male": Sidonie Smith, *Moving Lives: Twentieth Century Women's Travel Writing* (Minneapolis: University of Minnesota Press, 2001), 79–80.

WRITING THE BOOK:

stay with Putnams: Kristin Thiel, *Amelia Earhart: First Woman to Fly Solo across the Atlantic* (New York: Cavendish Square, 2018), 34.

book completed in two months: Sidonie Smith, *Moving Lives*, 87.

"In the routine meaning": Susan Ware, *Still Missing: Amelia Earhart and the Search for Modern Feminism* (New York: Norton, 1994), 96.

"mainly due to Putnam's brilliant": Chapman, *Whistled Like a Bird*, 92.

THE PUTNAMS' MARRIAGE:

found a love note: Chapman, *Whistled Like a Bird*, 67, 92.

insisting on intimacy: Chapman, *Whistled Like a Bird*, 107.

plane crash: Chapman, *Whistled Like a Bird*, 125–126.

"passion-scalded pig": Chapman, *Whistled Like a Bird*, 128.

Amelia announced: Chapman, *Whistled Like a Bird*, 135.

NINETY-NINES:

Air Derby: Graham Duncan, "Louise McPhetridge Thaden and the Ninety-Nines: Women in the Golden Age of Flight," *Unsweetened Magazine* (November 15, 2015), accessed March 16, 2020, https://unsweetenedmagazine.com/mag/louise-mcphetridge-thaden-2/.

"need not be a tremendously official" ... *"rather than spoiled"*: "Letter to 117 Women Pilots," Ninety-Nines, accessed March 16, 2020, https://www.ninety-nines.org/1927-invitation.htm.

"If enough of us": Dydia DeLyser, "Flying: Feminisms and Mobilities—Crusading for Aviation in the 1920s" in Peter Merriman and Tim Cresswell, ed., *Geographies of Mobilities: Practices, Spaces, Subjects* (Farnham, England: Ashgate, 2012), 92.

"good fellowship": Deborah G. Douglas, *American Women and Flight since 1940* (Lincoln: University of Nebraska Press, 2015), 17.

Potential names: Ninety-Nines, "Charter Members," accessed March 16, 2020, https://www.ninety-nines.org/charter-members.htm.

DOROTHY PUTNAM:

In July 1929, Transcontinental: Chapman, *Whistled Like a Bird*, 149.

Reno-vation: Chapman, *Whistled Like a Bird*, 157–158.

AMELIA EARHART'S PRENUPTIAL:

"You must know" ... *"In our life together"**: Chapman, *Whistled Like a Bird*, 183–184 (quoting letter from Amelia Earhart to George Putnam, ca. 1931).

SARAH HARRISON'S WEDDING:

(All quotes from, except as otherwise noted): "Papers Relating to the Administration of Governor Nicholson and the Founding of William and Mary College, Marriage of Dr. Blair and Sarah Harrison," *Virginia Magazine of History and Biography* 7:8 (January 1900), 278.

"marriage begins": "Harrison of James River," *Virginia Magazine of History and Biography* 31, no. 1 (January 1923), 84.

"There's more to life": "Amelia Earhart quotes," Quotewise, accessed March 16, 2020, http://www.quoteswise.com/amelia-earhart-quotes.html.

SOCIETY OF WOMAN GEOGRAPHERS:

"I am very much honored": Joanna Biggar, "Women Explorers' Society: Flag Bearers in a Man's World," *International Herald Tribune*, January 6, 1986, 20.

AMELIA'S SOLO TRANSATLANTIC FLIGHT:

Broken manifold and fuel leak: "Amelia E. Putnam Lands in Ireland after Solo Flight," *Corsicana Semi-Weekly Light* (Corsicana, TX), May 24, 1932, 8; "Plane Trouble Was Cause of Landing," *Corsicana Semi-Weekly Light* (Corsicana, TX), May 24, 1932, 8.

Conversation with Farmer: Kathleen Winters, *Amelia Earhart: The Turbulent Life of an American Icon* (New York: St. Martin's Press, 2010), 127.

*"I had this trouble"**: "Plane Trouble," *Corsicana Semi-Weekly Light*, 8.

EQUAL TO MEN:

proved that women were equal: Laura Edwards, "Amelia Earhart: Pilot and Feminist," July 24, 2012, *Christian Science Monitor*, accessed March 16, 2020, https://www.csmonitor.com/Technology/Tech-Culture/2012/0724/Amelia-Earhart-Pilot-and-feminist.

"What more appropriate declaration": Adolph Gillis and Roland Ketchum, *Our America* (Boston: Little Brown, 1938), 122.

"flying name": Gillis and Ketchum, *Our America*, 129.

BLIMP:

"The Society of Woman Geographers": "Mrs. Putnam to Get Medal from Blimp," *New York Times*, June 18, 1932, 6; "Washington Plans Reception," *New York Times*, June 18, 1932, 6; "National Geographic Society Honors Mrs. Putnam," *Washington Times*, June 22, 1932.

Scroll: "First Medal Awarded to the Society of Woman Geographers (to Amelia Earhart)"; SWG Box I, F 5.

"terribly afraid" ... "If Amelia Earhart": Walter Trumbull, "Lights of New York," *Valley Morning Star* (Harlingen, TX), June 18, 1932, 2.

*"Ever since I have"**: Stella Burke May, "She Feels Safer in the Jungle," *Baltimore Sun*, July 8, 1928, 112.

PRESENTATION OF GOLD MEDAL:

(All quotes from)*: SWG, 1932 Bulletin, 5.

Chapter 16: Friction

OPENING QUOTE:

Johnson, *I Married Adventure*, 274.

HARRIET CHALMERS ADAMS:

the accident: SWG, In Memory of Harriet Chalmers Adams (Society of Woman Geographers, February 1938), 16 (Tribute of Frances Carpenter Huntington).

*"The medical care was better"**: Michelle B. Slung, *Living with Cannibals and Other Women's Adventures* (Washington, DC: Adventure Publications, 2000), 208.

Battle Creek Sanitarium: Davis, "Harriet Chalmers Adams," 57.

plaster cast: Sue McNamara, "Woman Ends 27-Year World Trek Tracing Trail of Conquistadors," *Brattleboro Reformer*, November 13, 1919, 7.

"I will travel again": Elna Harwood Wharton, "A Woman Turns Geographer," *Forecast*, July 1930, 25, 56.

"Physical limitations never shut": SWG, *In Memory of Harriet Chalmers Adams*, 9 (Tribute of Marguerite Harrison).

"fierce energy and indomitable will": *In Memory of Harriet Chalmers Adams*, 9 (Tribute of Marie Peary Stafford).

"the Society would be rudderless": Letter from Harriet Chalmers Adams to Grace Barstow Murphy (November 25, 1931) (SWG Murphy file).

Barr Building: Letter from Harriet Chalmers Adams to Grace Barstow Murphy (October 26, 1931).

"interrupted several years": "The Women Triumph," *Asheville Citizen-Times*, April 4, 1929, 4.

"I am as good as new": Wharton, "Woman Turns Geographer," 56.

"After reading your letter": Letter from Harriet Chalmers Adams to Grace Barstow Murphy (February 27, 1932) (SWG Murphy file).

FRICTION AMONG GROUPS:

Various members: SWG, 1929 Annual Bulletin.

"I have always felt unworthy": Letter from Dorothy Bennett to the Society of Woman Geographers (February 1, circa 1931) (SWG Bennett file).

"Women do such wonderful things": Biggar, "Women Explorers' Society," 20.

"the future aims": Letter from Margaret Mead to Harriet Chalmers Adam (March 6, 1928).

"Who'd want to belong to a club": "Where Women Go First."

BLAIR'S THOUGHTS ON FICTION:

In general: Blair Niles, "Ninety-Five Per Cent True," *New York Herald Tribune*, January 8, 1933, H2.

"literature of escape" ... "lost its reputation" ... "are frankly"**: Niles, "Human Travel Books," E5.

$1.65: Mittman, *Reel Nature*, 31.

PEARL BUCK:

*"I grew up in a double world"**: Pearl S. Buck, "America's Medieval Women," *Harper's Magazine*, 177 (August 1938), 225.

HARRIET RESIGNATION:

Blair for president: Letter from Harriet Chalmers Adams to Grace Murphy (March 7, 1933).

We should drop all petty: Letter from Harriet Chalmers Adams to Marjorie Trumbull (February 27, 1933).

GOLD MEDAL:

"As an anthropological sculptor": Letter from Ruth Noble to Mary Vaux Walcott (November 17, 1934).

"the Society is too young" ... "unwise and a bad precedent"**: Letter from Delia Akeley to Lucille Mann (December 19, 1934) (SWG Akeley file).

Mary put the issue to a vote: Letter from Ruth Noble to Mary Vaux Walcott (November 17, 1934).

The Washington Executive Council was opposed: Letter from Lucille Mann to Ruth Noble (December 11, 1934).

FRICTION BETWEEN NEW YORK AND WASHINGTON:

"It is time others took our place": Letter from Delia Akeley to Mary Vaux Walcott (May 1, 1934).

*"deserved a special place"**: Letter from Delia Akeley to Harriet Chalmers Adams (November 25, 1927).

"thoroughbred" ... "worked like a soldier to make": Letter from Delia Akeley to Harriet Chalmers Adams (February 20, 1932).

*"Perhaps we have so many interesting things"**: Letter from Mary Vaux Walcott to Harriet Chalmers Adams (May 26, 1937).

*"to begin the friendships" ... "membership implied active work"**: Letter from Gertrude Emerson to Frances Huntington (January 12, 1931).

"differences of opinion really revolve" ... "command recognition" ... "should be the standard-bearers"... "those who are most enthusiastic"*: Letter from Ruth Noble to Mary Waux Walcott (November 25, 1933).

PEACE OFFERING:

*"Your meetings are worthwhile"**: Letter from Helen Strong to Ruth Noble (June 26, 1935).

$1,000 reserve: Letter from Helen Strong to Ruth Noble (May 28, 1935).

"The New York members" ... "looked upon her contribution"**: Letter from Helen Strong to Ruth Noble (July 17, 1935).

"The New York people seem": Letter from Mary Vaux Walcott to Lucille Mann (February 15, 1937).

*"of breeding, and background"**: Letter from Mary Vaux Walcott to Ruth Noble (ca. 1936).

Chapter 17: Networking

OPENING QUOTE:

AZquotes.com.

ADVICE, MENTORING AND COLLABORATION:

"The contacts between specialists": Rothenberg, *Presenting America's World*, 151 (quoting Harriet Chalmers Adams).

Examples of Members' Collaboration (All quotes from, except as otherwise noted): SWG, Annual Bulletins.

*"You will speak"**: Kimberley, *Woman's Place*, 199.

"Studying a country": Niles, *Colombia, Land of Miracles*, 367.

"Nine days or seven and a half hours!": "Scribes and Scriptures," *Morning Call* (Allentown, PA), September 2, 1923, 9.

*"I would get a nice sporty"**: Kimberley, *Woman's Place*, 199.

PEARL BUCK:

Malvina Hoffman rented her house: Hoffman, *Beautiful Bodies*, loc. 3066.

Officials banned: Sheila Melvin, "Pearl's Great Price," *Wilson Quarterly* (Spring 2006), accessed May 24, 2019, http://archive.wilsonquarterly.com; Pearl S Buck, *My Several Worlds: A Personal Record* (New York: John Day, 1954), 25.

"The letter—the letter!" ... "I have never left China"*: Buck, *My Several Worlds*, 30.

*"single-handedly changing"**: Buck, *My Several Worlds*, 27.

"a friendly cultural bridge": Sheila Melvin, "The Resurrection of Pearl Buck," *Wilson Quarterly Online* (Spring 2006), http://archive.wilsonquarterly.com.

"A few of them know it" *: Buck, "America's Medieval Women," 225.

*"Your home ought to be enough"**: Buck, *My Several Worlds*, 226–227.

"face the fact": Buck, *My Several Worlds*, 230.

TE ATA:

In general: Richard Green, "Crossing Paths: Te Ata and Eleanor Roosevelt in the Twenties and Thirties," *Journal of Chickasaw History*, 13 (1994).

"I hope sometime": Green, "Crossing Paths," 24.

marriage: Green, "Crossing Paths," 24.

ECLIPSE:

Dorothy Bennett: Dorothy Bennett, *Oral History* (May 19, 1995) (SWG Bennett File).

"Well, I told him": Green, "Te Ata and Eleanor Roosevelt," 186.

*"His profession"**: Blair Niles, *Peruvian Pageant: A Journey in Time* (Indianapolis: Bobbs-Merrill, 1937), 72.

HEARTACHE:

Annie Peck: SWG Bulletin (1935).

"war-like": Jane Eppinga, *They Made Their Mark*, 22.

"If I don't come back": Eppinga, *They Made Their Mark*, 74; Gertrude Emerson Sen, Oral History, 17 (SWG Sen File).

"Please know that I am quite": SWG Annual Bulletin (1937), 47 (Tribute of Marjorie Trumbull).

Last Flight (All quotes from): "Amelia Earhart Disappears," July 2, 1937, history.com, July 28, 2019, accessed September 17, 2019, https://www.history.com/this-day-in-history/amelia-earhart-disappears.

"it was our flag": SWG, Annual Bulletin (1937), 47 (Tribute of Marjorie Trumbull) (SWG).

Harriet Chalmers Adams Memorial Fund: SWG, In Memory of Harriet Chalmers Adams (1938) 27 (Tribute of Helen Strong).

"Financing expeditions": Alma Chesnut, "The Most Inquisitive Women," *Santa Ana Register*, May 26, 1928, 18.

"some expeditions" ... "to pursue her career" ... "Discouragement must never" ... "versatile enough": Catherine Filene, *Careers for Women: New Ideas, New Methods, New Opportunities—to Fit a New World* (Chicago: Riverside Press, 1934), 82.

Chapter 18: The Matilda Effect

OPENING QUOTE:

Olds, *Women of the Four Winds*, 3.

MATILDA EFFECT:

"a volcanic furnace": Susan Dominus, "Women Were Written Out of History. It's Margaret Rossiter's Lifelong Mission to Fix That," *Smithsonian Magazine* (October 2019), accessed November 19, 2019, https://www.smithsonianmag.com/science-nature/unheralded-women-scientists-finally-getting-their-due-180973082/.

"The Matilda effect": Margaret Rossiter, "The Matilda Effect in Science," *Social Studies of Science* 2 (1993), 325.

"And what about No. 2": Joyce Duncan, *Ahead of Their Time: A Biographical Dictionary of Risk-Taking Women* (Westport, CT: Greenwood, 2001), 149.

Mary Ritter Beard: Cott, *Woman Making History*, 3.

*"You say you will"**: Margaret Smith Crocco, "Forceful Yet Forgotten: Mary Ritter Beard and the Writing of History," *History Teacher* 31, no. 1 (November 1997), 8, 21.

*"We prefer to have" ... "No one knows"**: Cott, *Woman Making History*, 3.

A reviewer called: Cott, *Woman Making History*, 4.

"I would not allow": Cott, *Woman Making History*, 3–4.

*"characterized women's"**: Crocco, "Forceful yet Forgotten," 25.

"to reconstruct history to include women": Alice Alvarado, "Left Out: Women's Role in Historiography and the Contribution of Mary Ritter Beard," *Saber and Scroll* 1, no. 2 (2012), 94.

reluctant to book: Enright, *Osa and Martin*, 199.

WOMEN WHO WORKED WITH BEEBE:

pittance: Gould, *Remarkable Life*, 317.

"Yes, salaries at the Zoological": Calavincenzo, "William Beebe," 108.

"No wage money": Letter From William Beebe to Anna Heyward Taylor (November 30, 1920).

*"I have spells of getting up in the air"**: Letter from Anna Heyward Taylor to Nell Taylor (September 9, 1920).

"I wanted to make one brief": Harvey Breit, "Talk with William Beebe," *New York Times*, June 5, 1949, 119.

editing of Will's work: Letter from William Beebe to Charles Beebe (August 17, 1902) (BU 78).

"I am to do a whole" ... "I know I'm getting a rotten": Jeffrey Meyers, *Conrad: A Biography* (New York: Cooper Square Press, 2001), 197 (quoting correspondence between Kitty Crawford and Jane Anderson).

MARGARET MEAD:

"seemed to have a special place": Shankman, *Trashing of Margaret Mead*, 16.

*"all hell broke loose" ... "matchless deed"**: Shankman, *Trashing of Margaret Mead*, 8.

"falling body": Shankman, *Trashing of Margaret Mead*, 17.

"their whispered confidences": Society of Woman Geographers, *All True! The Record of Actual Adventures That Have Happened to Ten Women of Today* (New York: Brewer, Warren and Putnam, 1931), 94–118.

*"That a Polynesian prank"**: Shankman, *Trashing of Margaret Mead*, 9–10 (quoting from Freeman, *The Fateful Hoaxing of Margaret Mead* [Basic Books, 1999], 68).

Freeman attacked: Shankman, *Trashing of Margaret Mead*, 16.

Margaret considered an affair: Shankman, *Trashing of Margaret Mead*, 202 (quoting letter from Margaret Mead to Eda Lou Walton).

"although Mead's personality": Shankman, *Trashing of Margaret Mead*, 19.

*"one academic shade short" ... "Mead's conclusions"**: Ellen Goodman, "Who Portrayed the Real Samoa?" *Reno Gazette-Journal*, June 1, 1983, 15.

"not simply to revise": Shankman, *"Fateful Hoaxing" of Margaret Mead*, 51, 62.

*"It now appears that Mead was bamboozling"**: "Charlatan," *Wall Street Journal*, July 24, 1983, 27.

*"foremost woman anthropologist" ... "It seems Mead accepted"**: Shankman, *Trashing of Margaret Mead*, 14 (quoting *Time* magazine).

"the worst nonfiction" ... In 2009: Benjamin Wiker: Shankman, *Trashing of Margaret Mead*, 27.

NEW YORK TIMES:

Overlooked: Amisha Padnani and Jessica Bennett, "Overlooked," *New York Times*, March 8, 2018, accessed September 7, 2019, https://www.nytimes.com/interactive/2018/obituaries/overlooked.html.

Collaborated with Wife: "Charles A. Beard, Historian, Is Dead," *New York Times*, September 2, 1948, 23.

ROGER ATKINSON PRYOR:

In general: Sara Agnes Pryor, *My Day, Reminiscences of a Long Life* (New York: Macmillan, 1909); Robert S. Holzman, *Adapt or Perish: The Life of General Roger A. Pryor, C.S.A.* (Hamden, CT: Archon Books, 1976).

"match that exploded": "Gen. Roger A. Pryor Dies in 91st Year," *New York Times*, March 15, 1919, 15.

Pryor's speech was telegraphed: Holzman, *Adapt or Perish*, 56.

Beauregard designated Roger ... "all orders transmitted": Holzman, *Adapt or Perish*, 56–57.

"You are the only man" ... "I would not"*: Holzman, *Adapt or Perish*, 58–59 (also quoting Edmund Ruffin's journal for April 12, 1861, in which Ruffin claims that he was ordered to fire the first gun and that he was honored to do so).

he did not order: Blair Niles, Letter to the Editor, "The First Gun at Sumter: Pryor Had Authority to Order the Battery to Open Fire," *New York Times*, July 6, 1935, 12.

Atonement: Blair Niles, *East by Day* (Toronto: Farrar & Rinehart, 1941).

AWARDS:

Constance Lindsey Skinner Award: WNBA Award, accessed March 16, 2020, https://wnba-books.org/wnba-award/ (award is now the Women's National Book Award).

one of twenty books ... gold medal ... best book in English ... Department of Navy: SWG, Annual Bulletin (1944).

MARY RITTER BEARD:

"without documents; no history": Trigg, *Feminism as Life's Work*, 168.

Chapter 19: Seeing with Both Eyes

OPENING QUOTE:

Mary Austin, *The Young Woman Citizen* (New York: Womans Press, 1918), 19.

FIFTY PERCENT OF THE WORLD:

"Why Were Women Written Out of History? An Interview with Bettany Hughes," English Heritage, February 29, 2016, accessed October 15, 2019, http://blog.english-heritage.org.uk/women-written-history-interview-bettany-hughes/.

"almost wholly written from a masculine point of view": Charles Beard and Mary Ritter Beard, *American Citizenship* (New York: Macmillan, 1917), vi.

"less than half": Beard and Beard, *American Citizenship*, vii.

"men still count most" ... "what is feminine is hysterical"*: Trigg, *Feminism as Life's Work*, 22.

*"folly of pretending"**: Trigg, *Feminism as Life's Work*, 42.

MARY AUSTIN:

"Civilization as we now": Austin, *Young Woman Citizen*, 17.

*"for so many centuries"**: Austin, *Young Woman Citizen*, 6.

"know their own prophets": Glenda Riley, *Women and Nature: Saving the "Wild" West* (Lincoln: University of Nebraska Press, 1999), 79.

*"wall of men"**: Melody Graulich, "Creating Great Women" in Denise Knight, *Charlotte Perkins Gilman in the Company of Friends* (Tuscaloosa: University of Alabama Press, 2004), 153, fn. 6 (quoting No. 26 Jayne Street 6).

"man had the power": Josephine Conger Kaneko, *Woman's Voice: An Anthology* (Boston: Stratford, 1916), 49.

MARY RITTER BEARD:

*"to bring a feminine"**: Sarah D. Bair, "Citizenship for the Common Good: The Contributions of Mary Ritter Beard (1876–1958)," *International Journal of Social Education* 21, no. 2 (Fall/Winter 2006), 4.

*"the most encouraging fact of the twentieth century"**: Mary Ritter Beard, *Women's Work in Municipalities* (New York: Appleton, 1917), 97.

MICHELLE WESTMORLAND/CAROLINE MYTINGER:

"Headhunt Revisited": Sherry Stripling, "Photographers Recreate Adventurers' Journey," *Chicago Tribune*, May 11, 2005, 8:7.

"evolving traditions": "Headhunt Revisited," *PNG Air Magazine* 9 (September 2017), 9, 10–12, accessed October 19, 2019, https://headhuntrevisited.org/press/png-air-mag-09-headhunt-revisited/.

MALVINA HOFFMAN:

"an exhibition that goes out of its way": Edward Rothstein, "'Looking at Ourselves: Rethinking the Sculptures of Malvina Hoffman' Review," *Wall Street Journal*, March 22, 2016, accessed March 11, 2020, https://www.wsj.com/articles/looking-at-ourselves-rethinking-the-sculptures-of-malvina-hoffman-review-1458683771.

"overall thrust": Jennifer Schuessler, "'Races of Mankind' Sculptures, Long Exiled, Return to Display at

Chicago's Field Museum," *New York Times*, January 20, 2016, accessed March 11, 2020, https://www.nytimes.com/2016/01/21/arts/design/races-of-mankind-sculptures-long-exiled-return-to-display-at-chicagos-field-museum.html.

"You can forgive" ... "But the Social Darwinists" ... "the scientific racism"*: Steve Johnson, "Corrected Vision," *Chicago Tribune*, January 17, 2016, Sec. 4:1, 4:6.

ELSE BOSTELMANN:

In general: Edith Widder, "The Fine Art of Exploration," *Oceanography* 29:4 (2016), 170.

OMISSION OF WOMEN FROM HISTORY:

"If women have": Crocco, "Forceful yet Forgotten," 8, 21.

SYLVIA EARLE:

Sylvia Sails Away: Susan Hall Melton, "Oceanographer and Pioneer Sylvia Earle Has Earned the Title, 'Your Deepness,'" *Coastal Living*, September 7, 2017, accessed March 15, 2020, https://www.coastalliving.com/lifestyle/the-environment/sylvia-earle-first-woman-chief-scientist-noaa.

Tektite Project (All quotes from, except as otherwise noted): Mick Brown, "Meet 'Her Deepness'—the 82-Year-Old Deep Sea Diver Who Spent Two Weeks Living under Water," *Telegraph*, November 18, 2017, accessed March 15, 2020, https://www.telegraph.co.uk/women/life/meet-deepness-82-year-old-deep-sea-diver-spent-two-weeks-living/.

*"After Tektite, we were called"**: Carl Edmonds, Christopher Lowry, and John Pennefather, *Diving and Subaquatic Medicine* (Oxford, England: Butterworth-Heinemann, 1992), 62.

Her Deepness: Melton, "Oceanographer and Pioneer."

KATHRYN SULLIVAN:

"The notion that women might menstruate": "Kathryn Sullivan, First Woman to Walk in Space," in *Firsts: Women Who Are Changing the World* (New York: Liberty Street, 2018).

Military pilot prerequisite ... "It is just a fact" ... makeup in space*: Erin Blakemore, "When Sally Ride Took Her First Space Flight, Sexism Was the Norm," History, March 16, 2019, accessed March 15, 2020, https://www.history.com/news/sally-ride-first-astronaut-sexism.

space suit: Meredith Newman and Antonia Jaramillo, "The Real Reason NASA's All-Female Spacewalk Is Not Happening. Hint: It's Not Discrimination," *Florida Today*, March 27, 2019; accessed September 28, 2019, https://www.floridatoday.com/story/tech/science/space/2019/03/27/its-not-discrimination-why-nasa-cancelled-all-female-spacewalk/3290926002/.

"I'm still not over": Jennifer Sangalang, "All-Female Spacewalk Canceled Due to Lack of Medium-Sized Spacesuits. Twitter Reacts," *Florida Today*, March 26, 2019, accessed September 28, 2019, https://www.floridatoday.com/story/news/2019/03/26/female-spacewalk-canceled-spacesuits/3275536002/.

Reaction of IFC Dover (All quotes from): "'Leaders must make tough calls,' NASA, Spokane Astronaut Explain Cancellation of All-Female Spacewalk," KHQ, March 27, 2019, accessed March 27, 2019, https://www.khq.com/news/leaders-must-make-tough-calls-nasa-spokane-astronaut-explain-cancellation-of-all-femalespacewalk/article_05ed8704-5096-11e9-a05d-7b8c70a5c95d.html; Loren Grush, "This Company Says It Has a Lunar Space Suit That Will Be Ready for NASA's 2024 Moon Mission," *The Verge*, July 29, 2019, accessed September 28, 2019, https://www.theverge.com/2019/7/29/8910216/nasa-artemis-space-suit-moon-mission-collins-aerospace-ilc-dover-next-generation.

BEN BARRES:

math problem: Ben Barres, *The Autobiography of a Transgender Scientist* (Cambridge, MA: MIT Press, 2018), ix.

"Even when it was implied": Barres, *Autobiography of a Transgender Scientist*, 108.

"Ben Barres gave a great" ... "people who don't know" ... 2.5 times more productive*: Ben Barres, "Does

Gender Matter?" *Nature*, July 12, 2006, accessed October 10, 2019, https://www.nature.com/articles/442133a.

JANE GOODALL:

*"Jane's credentials were"**: Karen Karbo and Jane Goodall, "How a Woman Redefined Mankind," *National Geographic Magazine*, January 18, 2019, accessed March 15, 2020, https://www.nationalgeographic.com/culture/2019/01/jane-goodall-book-excerpt-praise-difficult-women/.

"It is precisely" ... *"Today there is no argument"* ... *"is seen as an illegitimate"*: Moshe Gilad, "Jane Goodall on Trump's Dominance Ritual and Other Monkey Business," Haaretz, March 19, 2017, accessed March 15, 2020, https://www.haaretz.com/us-news/.premium.MAGAZINE-jane-goodall-on-donald-trump-and-other-chimpanzees-1.5450452.

Epilogue: The Loss Will Be Ours

OPENING QUOTE:

Michael C. Thomsett and Jean Freestone Thomsett, *A Worldwide Dictionary of Pronouncements from Military Leaders, Politicians, Philosophers, Writers and Others* (Jefferson, NC: McFarland, 2015), 90 (quoting Pearl S. Buck, *What America Means to Me* [1943]).

KATHRYN SULLIVAN:

invitation: "Where Women Go First."

EXPLORERS CLUB:

Carl Sagan (all quotes from)*: Letter from Carl Sagan to Fellow Members of the Explorers Club (ca. 1981), reprinted in Letters of Note (March 9, 2011), accessed March 15, 2020, http://www.lettersofnote.com/2011/03/if-membership-is-restricted-to-men-loss.html.

"You have no idea": Rick Hampson, "Explorers Club Takes Final Dare; Votes to Admit Women Members," *Paducah Sun* (Paducah, KY), April 13, 1981, 3; Wendy Altschuler, "Spotlight on LGBTQ Adventurers and the Explorers Club Community," *Forbes*, October 20, 2020, https://www.forbes.com/sites/wendyaltschuler/2020/10/20/spotlight-on-lgbtq-adventurers-and-the-explorers-club-community/?sh=46eeda76e313.

"even a single female": Rick Hampson, "The Fair Sex in Explorers' Future?" *Poughkeepsie Journal*, April 12, 1981, 6A.

THE ADVENTURERS' CLUB:

In general: Emma Starer Gross, "Ladies' Night at the Adventurers' Club," accessed March 15, 2020, https://thelandmag.com/ladies-night-adventurers-club-lincoln-heights/; "Adventure Club of LA Votes to Bar Women from Joining," *Times Leader* (Wilkes-Barre, PA), November 8, 2014, 6.

PRESS REACTION:

"The Explorers Club Discovers Women": Judy Watson, "All-Male Bastions Slowly, Finally Admitting Women," *Indianapolis Star*, November 2, 1980, 119.

"The walls of another male bastion" ... *"We don't know where"*: Editorial, "A New Adventure," *Daily News*, New York, April 15, 1981, 196.

KATHRYN SULLIVAN:

*"Maybe I'll go"**: "Where Women Go First."

ACKNOWLEDGMENTS

Many people have supported and helped me as a solitary writer, and my thanks goes out to them. Thanks to:

My husband of forty years, Steve Wohlrab, who read early drafts and made incisive comments, always leading me in the right direction. He stepped up and took over household chores while I was busy writing or traveling. I am fortunate to have married a true feminist.

My mother, Barbara Zanglein, for believing in me and teaching me "stick-to-it-tive-ness."

My son, Colin Wohlrab, for long conversations about writing.

My son, Spencer Wohlrab, for sharing my love of travel.

Kadie Otto, whose advice on writing style and reminders that the woman geographers were "overlooked but not forgotten" helped me to focus.

Beth Jones, my travel buddy, for visiting Devil's Island with me. How I wish we could return to see our guides Nelson Wens (Suriname) and Nathalie Prudent (French Guiana).

Barbara Jo White, for listening to the story of the woman geographers, again and again.

Hannah Kimberley, author of *A Woman's Place is at the Top*, for a lovely phone conversation and her generous advice about getting an agent.

Ann Gerster, who actually read a book by Blair Niles: what a treat to talk to someone who knew of Blair!

Constance Carter, the amazing woman who worked in Trinidad with Gloria Hollister, Jocelyn Crane, and Will Beebe, for her wonderful reminiscences and assistance at the Library of Congress.

All those who helped me refine my ideas when I applied for (but did not receive) a biography fellowship, most especially Robert Pleasure (I remember those long car rides and talks with affection), Les Standiford (who teaches a great class on book structure), and my colleagues Mimi Fenton, Pan Riggs, Andrea Moshier, and Martha Diede.

John Mahaffie, for delightful conversations about his grandmother, Isabel Cooper, and for the loan of her diaries.

Leftwich Kimbrough, for his impressions of Robin Niles.

The Cullowhee Writer's Group, consisting of Lisa Bloom and Rus Binkley, whose gentle and supportive advice—repeated many times—finally sunk in. I could not have had better writing companions on this journey. Please read their books when they are published!

Heather Newton, of the Flatiron Writers Room, for hosting such wonderful workshops, for connecting me with Lisa Bloom, and for talking to me on the plane!

Robert Estep, for promising to read the book.

Western Carolina University, College of Business, who provided travel grants for archival research.

Western Carolina University, Hunter Library, for research assistance, especially interlibrary loans. Oh, how I love ILL!

Nanjing University for holding up construction of Pearl S. Buck's house so that I could visit it, and Nanjing Normal University for arranging the visit.

Mary van Balgooy, of the Society of Woman Geographers, for her assistance in archival research and quick responses to email questions.

Maddie Thompson and Sana Massod of the Wildlife Conservation Society for assisting me with the Department of Tropical Research Archives and photographs.

Jane Parr, for her assistance with the Elswyth Thane Collection at the Howard Gotlieb Archival Research Center, and for the joy of having the first baby born among our group during this project.

Mike Berry, at the South Caroliniana Library, for assistance with the Anna Heyward Taylor Collection.

Conrad Froehlich, director of The Martin and Osa Johnson Safari Museum for being so pleasant and easy to work with!

AnnaLee Pauls at Princeton's Firestone Library, Rare Books and Special Collections for assistance with the William Beebe Collection. I hope the construction is finally complete!

Elizabeth Garber at the Harry Ransom Center, University of Texas, who made my first trip to an archive unintimidating!

My agent, Amy Bishop of Dystel, Goderich & Bourret, LLC, who did an incredible job finding a publisher.

My editors, Anna Michels (mother of the second baby born during the project) and Shana Drehs for their excellent guidance, and to Sourcebooks, the largest woman-owned publisher in the United States.

ABOUT THE AUTHOR

Jayne Zanglein is passionate about publicizing the accomplishments of women ignored by history and chronicling the challenges that women face today. Like the founding members of the Society of Woman Geographers, she believes that marginalized groups become visible through empathic reporting, law, and democracy. Before the coronavirus curtailed her travels, she visited fifty-eight countries; ten for this book. She is a lawyer by profession, and this is her first non-law book. Jayne lives in the mountains of North Carolina with her husband, Steve Wohlrab, who serenades her with beautiful guitar music from afar while she writes. You can visit her website at thegirlexplorers.com.